Christianity, Empire and the Spirit

Theology and Mission
in World Christianity

VOLUME 11

The titles published in this series are listed at *brill.com/tmwc*

Christianity, Empire and the Spirit

(Re)Configuring Faith and the Cultural

By

Néstor Medina

BRILL

LEIDEN | BOSTON

Cover illustration: Design Center, www.dcenter.com.gt.

The Library of Congress Cataloging-in-Publication Data is available online at http://catalog.loc.gov
LC record available at http://lccn.loc.gov/2018023624

Typeface for the Latin, Greek, and Cyrillic scripts: "Brill." See and download: brill.com/brill-typeface.

ISSN 2452-2953
ISBN 978-90-04-35736-5 (paperback)
ISBN 978-90-04-36309-0 (e-book)

I dedicate this volume to my dad, Pedro Feliciano Medina, my brother, Luis Humberto Medina Bermejo, and the millions of people who everyday die prematurely!

∴

Contents

Acknowledgements

There are many factors that made it possible for me to complete this book. Moving between different cultural contexts has made me more attentive to some of the richly complex dynamics and negotiations that take place within the processes of culturalization. I was born in Guatemala, a very small country yet one which is incredibly diverse ethnoculturally. My country of birth gave me an insight into the dangers of cultural intolerance as well as the possibilities for intercultural coexistence. I have lived more than half my life in Canada where the utopic myth of a benevolent nation is offset by the historic reality of the despoliation of Indigenous lands and peoples and where the current realities of racism and inequity intermingle with the hope of a flourishing interculturality. I have worked in the increasingly polarized and militarized U.S.A., have travelled to many different contexts in the world, and have taught in Cuba for the last eleven years. In my travels, I have also seen how different denominational traditions find expressions in a variety of social, cultural, and religious contexts. In many ways, I can say that my life-journey has been and continues to be an experiment with the relationship between faith experiences and the cultural dimension. There is no doubt that these experiences have shaped my thinking, sometimes provoking me and challenging me, and at other times allowing me to see glimpses of what is possible.

I am deeply grateful to those Latina/o colleagues, theologians and scholars of religion who nourish my thinking and inspire me to reflect more intentionally on the cultural. There are a number of people that I wish to thank for their support of my research and work. I am grateful to Amos Yong, who supported this project early on as my Dean. I thank Mark Toulouse, the Principal at Emmanuel College, for welcoming me as a Visiting Scholar at the Center for Research in Religion which allowed me to have library access to complete my research. I also wish to acknowledge grant support from the Louisville institute, which made it possible for me to carry out my research without major financial concerns. I am indebted to Neomi DeAnda, Orlando Espín, Lee Cormie, and Reinerio Arce-Valentín for their willingness to read a version of this monograph and for giving me their incredibly rich feedback. I am sure this volume is much better because of their keen eyes. I am particularly grateful to Becca Whitla for her editorial work and dedication, always challenging me to be clear with my ideas. And finally, my deep thanks to my spouse Samia Saad; your work and struggle for justice inspires me. Thank you for your support and accompaniment as I worked through the issues I discuss in this volume.

Introduction

Understanding the phenomena of cultures and "culture" as a category for cataloguing aspects of the human experience is part of the modern project and a relatively recent endeavour. But for humans, the actual codification of life, the basic construction of cultures, what I call the complex processes of culturalization which encompass the concrete and complex phenomena of cultures, can be traced back as far as the emergence of the *homo sapien* as a distinct species. This book is a historial-cultural-theological retrieval of the role of the cultural in Christian faith. It is an attempt at thinking theologically about the phenomena of the cultural and cultural processes in their multiple concrete expressions without following inherited theological frames that draw a wedge between human material existence and the reality of the divine.

The complex reconfiguration of the world's geopolitical structures; the expansion of neoliberal globalizing forms of capitalism accompanied by decidedly cultural underpinnings; the present global immigrant crisis by which millions of human beings are on the move across political borders due to war, poverty, hunger, environmental catastrophes, and local political upheaval; the accelerated growth of multicultural urban centres around the world; the present global climate of cultural and religious clashes; and the dynamic international exchanges of capital, technology, goods and people have created the conditions for entire societies to be exposed to diverse and at times divergent cultural symbols, practices, and traditions. These multiple shifts on different fronts have also turned the cultural into one of the central concerns for the twenty-first century. As a result, many disciplines are extensively engaging cultural concerns. However, theology lags behind in its monumental failure to properly account for the impact of the cultural in religious traditions, especially given these complex social issues and in its incapacity to account for the theological cultural voices from the Global South. Together, this set of global geopolitical shifts and changes signal the complexification of human existence and have brought questions of "culture" and cultural diversity to the forefront of social, political, and religious debates

The Problem with "Culture"

The notion that the singular term "culture" can be used to appropriately describe and speak about the complex processes of culturalization and of all the richly diverse cultures of the world has been debunked for some time now.

© KONINKLIJKE BRILL NV, LEIDEN, 2018 | DOI 10.1163/9789004363090_002

Its use is chiefly problematic because of its inherent modernist Eurocentric baggage, establishing European cultures as the normative highest expressions of human "development" in a hierarchy of cultures. "Culture" as a category and idea is ambiguous and polysemic, and as such it needs to be deconstructed and interrogated. Stephen Long helps us see the category *culture* heuristically as a metaphor. He is correct in pointing out that the meaning of the term is difficult to discern because it bears different levels of significance in different disciplines.[1] In the practical sense, he considers that "culture" should be viewed not as explaining anything definitively but as an invitation to conversation about why humans engage in the (cultural) activities they do. He adds that when the use of the notion forecloses conversation, it ceases to function as a metaphor.[2]

As Long points out, scholars have dealt with, written about, and defined "culture" and cultural processes in many ways. "Culture" is conceived to be a set of practices, customs and traditions. One of the most common aberrations has been to equate culture with the notion of civilization, most often assuming a coherent and finished system that reflects the "advanced" nature of technology and level of "development" and "progress" of a given racialized group. In many contexts *civilization* conveys ideas about "modernization" and "advancement," all of which are often fraught with Western European and Euro North Atlantic ethnocentric colonizing underpinnings.[3] The term civilization assumes an inevitable "upward," hierarchical, quasi–evolutionary social shift by which "civilized" groups have surpassed an earlier stage of human (cultural) (under)development.

More often than not, those that claim to be "civilized" perceive themselves as more scientifically, culturally, militarily, industrially, technologically sophisticated and biologically superior compared to those perceived to exist in a "less advanced" (cultural) human stage. The assumption here is that all peoples invariably must follow the same evolutionary cultural path toward "advancement" or "maturity." It comes as no surprise that civilization was one of the terms used to justify the colonial and imperial projects of the last five hundred years. The goal of civilizing explained and justified the misplaced "good-intention"

---

1   Stephen Long, *Theology and Culture: A Guide to the Discussion* (Eugene, OR: Cascade Books, 2008), 8–9.

2   Ibid., 22.

3   In Latin America, a good example is the work of Domingo Sarmiento at the turn of the twentieth century in Argentina, in which he juxtaposes the European "civilized" and the "indigenous barbarians." See Domingo Faustino Sarmiento, *Facundo* (Buenos Aires, Argentina: Grupo Editor Altamira, 2001).

of the colonizers to respond to their "divine calling" to share (read forcefully impose) their "culture" and knowledge on those they encountered.

The colonizing character at the heart of the idea of civilization is not merely a matter of the past. Today, civilization is still the prevalent term to describe the technocratic orientation toward profit making, with "progress" and "modernity" expressing the process more concretely in globalizing neo-liberal economic structures. In its inability to value the enormous diversity of ethnocultures in the world, this hegemonic approach threatens cultural diversity and reduces local cultures to exotic products for mass consumption and as means for the promotion of capitalism and profit making.[4] It is for this reason that decolonial scholar Walter Mignolo notes the oppositional relation between "culture" and "civilization." He considers that "civilization" stands opposite to culture and seeks to tame it: "Culture is ... linked to passion whereas civilization is portrayed in terms of reason ..."[5]

Culture has also been understood as the guidelines that groups collectively assume for elite interpersonal protocol and social interaction. In this case, the "cultured" person is assumed to display specific characteristics and social etiquette that draw their inspiration from elite social groups. Culture here refers narrowly to a specific taste in music, the arts, culinary practices, as well as dress code, specific levels and kind of institutional education, and specific behaviors in social contexts. The inevitable outcome of such notions of culture is the hierarchical reorganization of societies that ensure the protection of elite cultural values and their dissemination at the expense of more "popular" cultural expressions. Even when there may be a recognition that popular cultural expressions are vital for those communities, the "cultured" person does not see them as equal in value and social standing.

The concept "culture" has also been used to describe the larger philosophical, intellectual, and religious complex behind the emergence of secularism. For example, the growing disenchantment with religion in North America and Europe, fueled by the scientific approach and an insistence that education and civil policy should be conducted without the influence of religious beliefs, has meant that secularism has become yet another descriptor for specific cultural orientations. In the context from which the notion emerged, it is worth noting that "secularism" often does not refer to the absence or lack of religion, but

---

4   P. Mario L. Peresson, "Inculturación del Evangelio en un mundo pluricultural," *Omnis Terra* 328, año XXXV (Marzo 2003): 104–17, Http://www.sedos.org/spanish/peresson_2.htm (accessed October 19, 2006).

5   Walter Mignolo, *Local Histories / Global Designs: Coloniality, Subaltern Knowledges, and Border Thinking* (Princeton, NJ: Princeton University Press, 2000), 38.

more to a move away from Christianity. Harvey Cox reminds us that it is within Christian Protestantism itself that one finds the very attitudes that later contributed to the secularization of society.[6] In societies were Christianity was the dominant religion, the move away from Christianity can be easily perceived as a move away from religion. However, the increasing clash of religious traditions in many of these countries, including those where Christianity enjoyed supremacy, demonstrates that religion is not being abandoned. Because of multiple factors such as immigration, communications technology, and ease of transportation across political borders, large metropolises are becoming increasingly religious and more religiously plural.

Another misuse of the concept *culture* involves its use by cultural subgroups within a society as a way to imagine themselves as cultural traditions disconnected from the larger sociocultural context. For instance, youth cultural expressions or cultural trends are perceived as freestanding cultures rather than as subsets of the larger cultural fabric. In many ways this idea is similar to so-called notions of a "Christian culture." Specific cultural expressions from cultural subgroups, like youth and Christians, are born and take place within inherited frames as part of their larger cultural milieu from which they borrow key elements. The discussion in chapters two through six are good examples of this kind of approach, an approach which does not clearly delineate the relationship between Christianity and its immediate cultural context.

In other contexts, cultures are perceived as foreign elements. For example, in many of the growing multicultural urban centres, members of a dominant racialized ethnocultural group often do not see themselves as belonging to a particular cultural tradition, even though they may actually be part of a context and culture which features great cultural diversity. In many of these contexts, particularly in countries in the Global North, culture is something perceived as possessed only by "ethnics," foreigners, migrants, or ancient peoples.[7]

As we can see, the category "culture" has many uses. This multiplicity of meanings adds to the difficulty in appropriately using "culture" to speak about the complex processes of culturalization. As I show in this book, some scholars are beginning to resist facile definitions of the complex, intersecting, and at

---

6   Harvey Cox, *The Secular City: Secularization and Urbanization in Theological Perspective* (New York, NY: Macmillan, 1965).

7   One good example is how Canadians perceive that "those with culture are primarily "ethnics"—in other words, ethnic and racial minorities, non-English-speaking people and immigrants who identify with their country of origin and maintain the language and traditions of that country while living in Canada" (Carl E. James, *Seeing Ourselves: Exploring Race, Ethnicity and Culture* [Toronto, ON: Thompson Educational Publishing Inc., 1995], 10).

times contradictory elements one encounters when thinking about the concept of culture. In particular, the term is becoming increasingly unsustainable because of its narrow "modernist" inheritance. The term carries a specific set of assumptions about the phenomena of the cultural, cultural contexts, and cultural traditions as manageable closed systems with air tight self-contained frames that can be studied scientifically as objects of analysis. It is assumed that the researcher does not have to be immersed in those cultural traditions s/he studies or engage the members of the given cultural group.[8] The term culture operates as a clearly definable category, with abstractions drawn by the anthropologists out of the concrete "facts" of socially significant behaviors,[9] but leaves behind the basic understanding that to speak of culture and cultures means necessarily to speak about human beings within their proper (cultural) ecosystem. This type of analysis of culture belies the fact that it is not cultures that enter into contact with each other but persons and communities each from within their cultural fields.[10] The difficulties one encounters with the narrow use of the term "culture" also correspond to the arbitrary lumping together of the wide gamut of cultural elements, traditions, customs, and artifacts, which are in fact irreducible to a single category or definition.

The Cultural

Because of these problems with "culture," in this book I adopt the notion of *the cultural*. There are four main reasons for this shift in language. First, I believe the cultural appropriately lends itself to the task of speaking about the ubiquitous phenomena that define, shape, condition, and impact the ways humans engage life, and interact with their immediate environment, each other and the divine. The "cultural" also helps us identify the necessary interpretive

---

8   Clifford Geertz was correct in asserting that the analysis of "culture" is an interpretive endeavour. But as will become evident, I intend to go beyond semiotic frames because of their inherent assumptions of "culture" as a closed "system," an approach which when applied to other cultural traditions can guide us to "understand" such culture's most basic ideas and intellectual structures without needing to immerse oneself within it. See Clifford Geertz, *The Interpretation of Cultures; Selected Essays* (New York, NY: Basic, 1973).

9   Kathryn Tanner, *Theories of Culture: A New Agenda for Theology*, Guides to Theological Inquiry Series (Minneapolis, MN: Fortress Press, 1997), 31.

10 Bastide as cited in Jacques Audinet, *The Human Face of Globalization: From Multicultural to Mestizaje*, trans. Francest Dal Chele (New York, NY: Rowman & Littlefield Publishing, Inc, 2004), 52.

"tools" (know-how) for (de)codifying human existence, the interconnected web of codes utilized for understanding and making sense of our world, as a result of human cultural activity. Second, the cultural permits the recognition and celebration of the fact that all human collectives and individuals engage in cultural activities and the construction/creation of cultural elements and traditions. In this sense, the cultural carries a "democratizing" affirming-effect on the value of all ethnocultural communities and their cultural traditions without resorting to the colonizing tendencies of cataloguing them hierarchically as "cultures." Third, the cultural is useful for speaking about the broad range of rich, complex, changeable, unfinished/open-ended, dynamic, contested, fluid, and interconnected processes of culturalization that are part of the human experience in its greatly diverse multiplicity of concrete cultural traditions, to which I will refer using the plural "cultures." As I will show, the term "culture" in the singular suggests clearly delineated systems easily identifiable and demarcated, whereas with the notion of the cultural, as I intend it here, points to the actual (plural) human activity of cultural construction in which every human being/collective engages within their own historical, geographic, and contextual specificity and beyond it as well. And fourth, the cultural makes room for considering the complex processes of culturalization in their intimate relation to experiences and expressions of (religious) faith and religious traditions. This fourth rationality for "the cultural" is the central thread of this book. Focusing specifically on the Christian tradition, I argue that the cultural has a profound impact and is intimately connected to the ways in which people conceive, engage, and think about the divine it its multiply diverse concrete contexts and expressions.

My intention is to demonstrate the interwoven character of the cultural and the religious (and consequently the theological). To that end, I revisit key moments in the history of Christianity along with key authors and theologians to shed light on the interconnected character of their approaches. As I will show, current articulations of the relationship between the cultural and the "gospel," "Christ," and "the Christian faith" fall short because they preserve the radical distinction between the two. Instead I argue that these must be understood as working together. Each of the chapters contributes to demonstrating the complex nature of processes of culturalization, and how these find themselves intertwined with religious underpinnings, concerns, and interests. More often than not my research shows remarkable deficiencies in Christian understanding of the cultural. The unmasking of lapses in Christian approaches to the cultural lead me to a theological articulation of the cultural in the last chapter. Stated differently, this book is my attempt to retrieve the role of the cultural in understandings of human existence, especially its pivotal role in the historical development of Christianity, and including the theological articulation of the relationship between Christianity and the cultural.

Without digressing, I want to point out that in the context of Latin America, questions of "lo cultural" (the cultural) are subsumed to the larger discussion on "lo popular" (the popular). Lo popular here refers specifically to those complex, richly diverse, culturally fluid and concrete expressions of the faith of the people, which resist facile interpretations as syncretism. Latin American scholars show how the faith expressions of the people put on display a unique blend of local cultural elements and faith traditions.[11] Similar discussions can be found in the work of Latina/o theologians. Discussing the profound impact of the cultural in the way people express their faith and conceive the divine, they have gone to great length to emphasize the intersection of the cultural with the popular.[12]

The Chapters

Chapter 1 delineates the breadth of the notion of the cultural. Instead of a definition, the chapter discusses the broad range of aspects that are included in human cultural activity and complex processes of culturalization. In no way is this broad description understood as a comprehensive definition. Rather, it provides general guidelines for the rich character of cultural processes. This broad description serves as the frame against which other notions of "culture" and civilization that appear in the book are contrasted, and serves as the

11 For a small sample of resources, see Diego Irarrázaval, *Cultura y fe latinoamericanas* (Santiago de Chile: Ediciones Rehue Ltda.; Instituto de Estudios Aymaras, 1994); Diego Irarrázaval, "Catolicismo popular en la teología de la liberación," in *Teología y liberación: Religión, cultura y ética: Ensayos en torno a la obra de Gustavo Gutiérrez* (Lima, Perú: Instituto Bartolomé de Las Casas-Rimac; Centro de Estudios y Publicaciones, 1991), 71–105; Milagros Palma, ed., *Simbólica de la Feminidad: La Mujer en el Imaginario Mítico Religioso de las Sociedades Indias y Mestizas*, Symposio del 40 Congreso Internacional de Americanistas, Amsterdam 1988, Colección 500 Años (Quito, Ecuador: Abya Yala, 1993).

12 For a small sample, see Orlando O. Espín, *The Faith of the People: Theological Reflections on Popular Catholicism*, foreword by Roberto S. Goizueta (Maryknoll, NY: Orbis Books, 1997); Alejandro García-Rivera, *St. Martín de Porres: The "Little Stories" and the Semiotics of Culture*, foreword by Virgilio Elizondo, introd. by Robert J. Schreiter (Maryknoll, NY: Orbis Books, 1995); Ada María Isasi-Díaz, "'Apuntes' for a Hispanic Women's Theology of Liberation," *Apuntes: Reflexiones Teológicas Desde el Márgen Hispano* 6, no. 3 (1986): 61–71; Allan Figueroa Deck, "Latino Theology: The Year of the 'Boom'," *Journal of Hispanic / Latino Theology* 1, no. 2 (1994): 51–63.

blueprint for my theological articulation on the cultural in the final chapter of the book.

I divide chapter 2 into two sections. In the first section, I revisit the biblical text exploring the ways in which processes of culturalization are found in the narratives. My claim is that the stories in the Hebrew Bible and New Testament demonstrate the profound impact of cultural traditions in the articulation of religious faith. Engaging specific pericopes helps me highlight the internal multilevel, fluid, uneven, and conflicted processes in the formation of Israelite cultural, ethnic, and religious identity. It also helps me in articulating the role of the cultural in the formation of Christian identity amidst a context of dynamic cultural exchange and contestation. In the second section of this chapter, I focus my attention on how cultural forces contributed to the profound cultural shift in Christianity and its ecclesial structures from being the persecuted church to becoming the persecuting church. As I argue, the Christian faith was coopted by Roman imperial culture. For Christianity to become the religion of the Empire, a wide range of complex, contested, dynamic processes of cultural negotiation with the dominant Roman context of the day had to take place. As a result of this shift, Christianity was profoundly changed and reconfigured becoming almost inseparable from Roman imperial culture.

This marriage between the imperial cultural ethos and Christianity becomes the platform for analyzing the Western European and Euro North American imperial projects I discuss in chapter 3. I show how cultural notions of empire and the self-understanding of Western Europeans as civilized and superior were always interconnected with their self-perception as Christians. As a result, when Europeans left Europe to invade the world, they engaged in sophisticated processes of "othering," through ideological (mis)identification, (mis)recognition and (mis)representation of the other peoples of the world. I show how European authors and thinkers "represented" these peoples as everything the Europeans were not: inferior, barbarians / uncivilized / savages, and pagans. In other words, I argue that the cultural and religious blinders of the Europeans (and subsequent Euro North Americans) conditioned them to *not* see the cultures, religious traditions, and humanity of the others of the world who they encountered in their imperial path. Discussing the processes of culturalization and the role of the cultural helps illuminate how imperial projects must be understood as essentially cultural projects.

I continue this discussion in chapter 4 to demonstrate how the interwoven character of Christianity and imperial ethos inspired the ideas that European cultures were/are essentially Christian and the Christian mission of evangelization was essentially a European (and subsequently Euro North American) culturalization mission. In the first section of the chapter, I show how Catholic and Protestant missionaries and scholars conflated the Christian mission of evangelization with assimilation into Western European culture(s). And in the second section, I show how concerns about the cultural in its relation to the Christian faith gained prominence. I argue that as Western European and Euro North American Protestant theologians were confronted with the intellectual, cultural, and religious crisis in Europe (as a result of two world-wars and numerous geopolitical changes) at the turn of the twentieth century, they sought to rethink questions of the relationship between Christianity, Christ, the gospel and the cultural.

In chapter 5 I analyze the work of more recent Protestant scholars from the last quarter of the twentieth century and beginning of the twenty-first century. My goal is to provide a brief sampling of how scholars are rethinking the role of the cultural in Christian faith as a result of being confronted with the global (and local) reality of ethnic and cultural plurality. In the first portion of the chapter, I discuss in broad strokes how the World Council of Churches has shifted more attention towards issues of the cultural by acknowledging the contextual nature of Christian faith experiences. In the second portion, I briefly exhibit how scholars remain trapped in Richard Niebuhr's paradigm of the relationship between Christianity, Christ, the gospel and "culture" (read the cultural), while attempting to reformulate it. My concern in this chapter is to show how a new generation of scholars—with all their limitations and con-tradictions—are beginning to consider the cultural as playing a central role in the way people live and express their faith.

The Catholic Church has been undergoing its own processes of rethinking the relationship between Christian faith and the cultural. Chapter 6 traces some of the important changes the Catholic Church has been undergoing since the middle of the twentieth century. Focusing on the Second Vatican Council as starting point, this chapter analyzes some of the most important official papal documents with respect to the role of the cultural in relation to the Christian faith/the gospel including some recent documents written by Pope Francis. Here I demonstrate that while the notion of inculturation has become the key term for identifying the Catholic official stance on the cultural, Pope Francis recent writings invite us to deeper considerations of the role of the cultural in its impact on faith experiences and expressions.

As I will show by engaging each of the authors I mention—with notable exceptions, a dualism can be detected; the cultural seems to be conceived as incompatible and at times simply irreconcilable with Christ. I argue that to go beyond inherited approaches, there is need to think more critically about how the most basic aspects of the cultural operate in shaping the way people understand and approach the gospel and the divine, and how the divine can be imagined as active within the cultural sphere. It is this theological imagining that occupies my reflections in the final chapter. In chapter 7 I propose an alternative interpretation that reclaims the intimate relationship between (religious/Christian) faith and the cultural. I reject ideas that the divine is incompatible with the cultural and instead propose the cultural as divine gift constitutive of our humanity and of our divine imaging. Overall, my goal is to show that the Christian faith is incomplete without an appreciation of the role of the cultural; the cultural is a fundamental ingredient for approaching the divine and understanding the divine self-disclosure.

To clarify, let me point out that all of the scholars I engage—in chapters 4 to 6—subsume discussions of the cultural, the processes of culturalization and their diverse concrete expressions under the category "culture." Although I think the scholars I engage are really speaking about processes of culturalization, what I term *the cultural*, they invariably write using the singular "culture." In part I suspect this is the case because they are so entrenched in the Western European cultural and intellectual tradition which does not allow them to think about the cultural in the plural sense. I also think their use of "culture" reveals their "modernist" assumptions of a fixed reality that can be catalogued, categorized, studied and managed. With that in mind, and in order to avoid confusion, in my discussion I preserve their use of the singular *culture* because to do otherwise would carry the potential of changing the content of their assertions. That said, in the introduction and conclusion of each of the chapters I will be reverting back to the use of *the cultural* as my preferred category in order to account for the complexity of the debates, the complex processes of culturalization, and the enormous diversity of cultural traditions as concrete expressions of such complex processes. Moreover, I also preserve the singular *culture* when quoting directly, as well as when it is modified by an adjective, for example Latina/o culture, Japanese culture, etc.

In many ways, one could say that I am drawing on the notion of the cultural as a form of a metanarrative or as a theoretical superstructure. However, my choice of *the cultural* is merely heuristic, pointing to the rich complexity of interconnected issues and processes that coincide and stem from human (cultural) activity. In other words, I believe that all people engage in cultural activities and I also believe that all cultural communities do it differently. There is no single pattern or way by which people groups and cultural communities engage the complex processes of the creation of cultures and processes of culturalization. The adoption of the cultural then creates the opportunity for appreciating the multiple concrete ways and expressions in which human cultural activity shapes, frames, and impacts human existence, activities, intellectual and religious traditions, and theological affirmations.

It will become evident that I draw on multiple disciplinary fields. I draw on history, theology, cultural theory, to name a few. Anticolonial perspectives as they emerge in the middle of the twentieth century in Africa and Asia inspire many of my reflections. I draw on postcolonial and cultural studies, and although I mention other scholars, I particularly engage the works of Stuart Hall and Edward Said. The more recent work of Latin American Decolonial thinkers also influences my perspectives in terms of identifying the coloniality in Western European Euro North American cultures.

I also engage with and draw on multiple theological currents. They reflect a wide gamut of cultural theological traditions: Catholic, mainline Protestant, Evangelical and Pentecostal, Western European, First Nations, Native Americans, Japanese, etc. That said, liberation theologies are key sources for the articulation of my understanding of the connection between the cultural and religious/Christian faith. I particularly draw from Pentecostalism in its appreciation and celebration of the activity of the Spirit in this world. Although my reinterpretation of Pentecost is not directly connected to the Pentecostal tradition, it was the Pentecostal theological ethos of discerning the work of the Spirit that inspired my rereading of the event. Even more strongly, I draw on Latina/o theologians in their insistence on the centrality of the cultural in theology and their insight that the cultural is a *locus* of theological reflection. Among the multiple Latina/o scholars who inspire me, the work of Orlando Espín and Justo González helped me enormously in organizing my ideas and articulating my reflections. Admittedly, Latina/o scholars also work with the "modernist" notion of "culture," so in a sense this work is an invitation to continue the conversation. That said, I would venture to say that in this book I follow Latina/o theology to its next logical step.

Overall, it will become evident that I engage many theological voices often absent from mainstream theological and academic circles. My intention is to provide a sample of the wide range of scholars from other cultural traditions that can and are enriching and reconfiguring mainstream theological debates on the cultural. This book is a sampling of those multiple voices that can no longer remain silenced or on the sidelines of theological reflections: Christianity has travelled and is growing in the Global South; the present shift of power in the church will have to account for the cultural traditions that have adopted Christianity. It will also have to account for the theologies of these communities as they express and reflect upon their experience of faith in God from their own cultural vantage point. These cultural communities show us that Christianity is irreducible to a single cultural tradition. In addition, because of more recent migratory waves, many of these people from the Global South now make up large portions of the population in the Global North. These multiple cultural communities offer us great insights that advance mainstream theological reflections on the cultural.

CHAPTER 1

Toward a Broad Description of the Cultural

In the kitchen one afternoon with her mother, Sarah asked her why she always cut the bone off of the ham. "I don't know," she replied, "that's the way my mother did it." Later, Sarah's mother asked her mother why she always cut the bone off the ham before she cooked it. "That's the way my mother did it." Sarah's grandmother replied. Later, Sarah's grandmother asked her mother why she always cut off the bone on the ham, Sarah's great grandmother said, "I cut the bone off so it would fit in the pot."

Introduction

The cultural is not some finished product that is added to a "finished" human being; rather, it is part of the very essence of humanity.[1] As I understand it here, at least in terms of a "working definition," the cultural refers to the complex dynamic network of socially and historically inherited codes and segments of codes that allow and make possible inter-human interaction in a given society, that provide the interpretive frame and lenses for reality; and that constitute the set of guiding principles by which humans and societies interact with their surrounding environment and the divine. The cultural corresponds with the complex and constantly changing processes of culturalization inherited from generation to generation which regulate human behavior and include all aspects of life including language, epistemology, rationality, interpretation of emotions, imagination, and the socialized ways in which people think and reflect about life. I must emphasize that I do not intend this working definition to be comprehensive. I approach debates on the cultural from the position that no single definition can comprehensively explain the broad range of elements and aspects of the human experience encompassed in the cultural. This plurivocal approach is consistent with the ethos I hope to establish for this book. My goal is, first, to briefly sketch some of the factors and dynamics that coincide in the phenomena of the cultural and the processes

---

1 Clifford Geertz engages anthropologists in this discussion noting that culture is not a phenomenon that emerged suddenly. In fact, its development has taken millennia. See his *The Interpretation of Cultures*, Chapter 2.

© KONINKLIJKE BRILL NV, LEIDEN, 2018 | DOI 10.1163/9789004363090_003

of culturalization. Second, I explore the interconnected relationship between cultural expressions and issues of religious and faith traditions, practices, and expressions. It is this "broad description" of the cultural that will serve as the platform and frame for understanding subsequent chapters.

Social Dimension of the Cultural

Max Weber via Geertz states: "man is an animal suspended in webs of significance he himself [*sic*] has spun." Geertz takes the cultural to be those webs, the analysis of which must be "an interpretive one in the search of meaning."[2] In light of these two statements, I want to offer further qualifying comments: I argue that the complex processes of human cultural construction—or what I call processes of culturalization—are contextually located and historically grounded.

Now, to speak of the cultural means to speak of human beings;[3] that is, of our being human. As Jacques Audinet puts it, "To acknowledge a person in their specific culture is to accept them as human beings."[4] Stated differently, we cannot conceive human beings and human activity without the accompanying phenomena of cultures,[5] just as we cannot conceive human beings outside the context of relationships to other humans, animals and the environment. The cultural is constitutive of being human, just as people are relational! Socialization is part of specific cultural collectives including all activities, skills and tools which encompass what people learn as human behavior.[6]

At heart, the cultural identifies the human communal construction that includes a broad spectrum of social activities. Without setting aside the connections of the cultural dimension to the environment, we could say that

---

2 Geertz, *The Interpretation of Cultures*, 5.

3 Justo L. González, *Culto, cultura y cultivo: Apuntes teológicos en torno a las culturas* (Lima, Perú: Centro de Investigaciones y Publicaciones; Ediciones Puma, 2008), 9.

4 Jacques Audinet, *The Human Face of Globalization*, 15.

5 According to Geertz, the development of human beings and culture are so intertwined that it is impossible to conceive humans without culture. For him, humans without culture would be "unworkable monstrosities with very few useful instincts, fewer recognizable sentiments, and no intellect: mental basket cases" (Geertz, *The Interpretation of Cultures*, 49).

6 Oliver Sacks states it clearly: "our capacity for language, for thought, for communication, and culture—do not develop automatically in us, are not just biological functions, but are, equally, social and historical in origin ... they are a *gift*—the most wonderful of gifts—from one generation to another. We see that Culture is as crucial as Nature" (Cited in M. Nourbese Philip, *Frontiers: Essays and Writing on Racism and Culture* [Stratford, ON: Mercury Press, 1992]), 14.

cultures are what "human beings and human communities have created to make the earth a habitat for communities of human beings."[7] At the most basic level, cultural traditions help us identify the relational and gregarious nature of human beings; to be human is to relate to other humans at the level of the everyday. According to Justo González, all cultures have an internal aspect, a series of signs and symbols that allow human groups to communicate among themselves.[8] Human beings have the inherent capacity to relate to each other; when they relate with other people, it is their particular cultural tradition that provides the know-how, the grammar for the success of such interactions. When people relate with each other, they do so following specific general rules of conduct to which all members of the social cluster (willingly or unwillingly, tacitly or explicitly) ascribe, accept, and conform. This relating is deployed and (re)configured in their everyday lives.

At this inter-human level, the idea of the cultural (the processes of cultur-alization) and cultures (the diverse local specific expressions) is used to refer to the sum total of these rules with which people groups create customs, tra-ditions, and beliefs about themselves, other cultural communities, nature, and reality. For example, when people from similar cultural contexts interact with each other they greet each other using specific culturally determined gestures such as a hug, kiss, hand shake, hand wave, bow, assent with head, etc. In their particular contexts, each gesture functions to acknowledge the presence of the other person and, in some cases, represents a crucial expression of respect. Yet, no single approach is applicable to all groups. In fact, each group has their own unique set of internal interpersonal rules. To state the obvious, different groups create different mechanisms and methods for daily activity and interaction.

The cultural does not only refer to the interpersonal relational aspect of humanity, of course. It also unveils sophisticated processes of social organi-zation which come to us in an irreducible variety. They include the particular ways in which people choose to live as a group, ways of living that impact their customs, values, and the way they organize themselves. These are the charac-teristics that are often used to distinguish groups and to separate them under the rubric of ethnic identity.

Cultural traditions understood as frameworks that include the diverse facets of community living comprise many (cultural) subcategories. These include elements of housing such as architecture, the production of food and culinary

---

7   Mercy Amba Oduyoye, "Gospel and Culture in Africa: Through Women's Eyes," in *Women's Perspectives: Articulating the Liberating Power of the Gospel* (Geneva: World Council of Churches Publications, 1996), 36.

8   González, *Culto, cultura y cultivo*, 39.

practices, and various levels of technological proficiency, diverse methods of communication and of understanding and recording history (e.g. cyclical or linear). They also include: social organizational structures that could be defined as tribal, monarchy, constitutional society; the understanding of familial ties (e.g., nuclear, extended, communal) and familial dynamics (e.g., monogamy, polygamy, polyandry); physical signs of being part of a group as well as the rites of passage associated with physical-body signs (e.g., circumcision, body piercing and/or painting, quinceañera);[9] traditions and personal allegiances (family, friends, spouse); understandings of health or sickness (e.g., form of punishment by the spirits, imbalance in one's Chi or inner energy, physical deterioration); religious traditions (e.g., Christianity; Islam, Voodoo, Lukumí); and religiously charged devotions and rites (ancestor worship, respect for the elderly).

The plurality of cultural traditions also points to a plurality of intellectual sources and epistemologies, the ways in which entire cultural communities construct knowledge. Debates on the connection of the cultural and human thought have a long-standing history.[10] Although the proposals are diverse, all seem to agree on the important connection between cultures and the human cognitive capacity. I highlight the multiply diverse ways people construct knowledge but I also reject the general tendency to organize them hierarchically. Often the hierarchical organization of knowledge serves the interests of the powerful and wealthy sectors of society. People conceive, conceptualize, and articulate ideas differently according to their cultural traditions. It is impossible to separate what we do or think from the cultural tradition of which we are part.[11] In other words, even a hierarchical structuring of systems of knowledge *is* culturally bound. Members of a specific cultural community receive the intellectual tools developed by their communities; how to know, what to know, how to produce knowledge, and what is considered knowledge worth learning. For example, many groups in the world do not privilege reason-rationality or the scientific method as sole arbiters for determining knowledge. Intuition, dreams, spirituality, customs, traditions and experience, among other things, are also thought to be essential means to get at specific forms of

---

9   Among many Latina/o and Latin American communities the celebration of the 15th birthday of a teenage girl culturally marks the transition from being a girl to being a woman. This is called quinceañera.

10   Michael Cole and Sylvia Scribner, *Culture and Thought: A Psychological Introduction* (Toronto, ON: John Wiley & Sons Inc., 1974).

11   González, *Culto, cultura y cultivo*, 49.

knowledge inaccessible by way of reason alone.[12] Entire communities look to wisdom, sages, myths, legends, and the collective memory of their people as valuable sources of knowledge.

Language is the quintessential cultural distinctive of a people insofar as it symbolizes entirely diverse worlds in the way cultural groups process information, tell their own stories, produce and value knowledge, and articulate that knowledge among themselves and in relation to other groups. We think and know of the world through language.[13] González affirms language as reflecting and molding the cultures that express it; that is, the attitudes towards things, people, relationships, and reality.[14] I want to emphasize, that by language, I do not only mean the specific systems of linguistic communication more or less articulated following a specific grammar. In language and the capacity of peoples to articulate and communicate their thoughts and ideas I also include the nonverbal side. I propose that the production of knowledge by the majority of the world's population incorporates embodied elements expressed in the forms of mannerisms, bodily gestures, noises, and non-verbal elements. Orality is another aspect of language by which peoples build, share, and exchange knowledge. These culturally learned and conditioned elements also constitute forms of knowledge and communication that cannot be separated from the linguistic specificity of a people. Learning a language involves far more than mastering its vocabulary and grammatical structure. A language also includes a host of aspects that are part of an entire cultural ethos and imagined universe of assumed, not always verbally articulated forms of communication. Language understood broadly in this way serves as lining for interhuman interaction, and which cannot be learned unless one immerses oneself into and interacts with members of that linguistic-cultural community.

Physical context and topography play an important role in how cultures are constructed as well. The geographical setting in which groups exist impacts their development as cultural communities; cultural expressions reveal how people interact with the world. Cultural expressions make visible the complex processes of codification that allow people to coexist and interact with each

---

12 We are reminded that the "Classic meaning of culture insisted on the superiority of reason over the obscure forces of dream and myth." We are seeing a shift now by which the human sciences seem to be reinstating "what science had for a time definitely discarded: customs, rites, beliefs specific to any given group of people" (Audinet, *The Human Face of Globalization*, 16).

13 Rebecca S. Chopp, *The Praxis of Suffering: An Interpretation of Liberation and Political Theologies* (Maryknoll, NY: Orbis Books, 1986), 124.

14 González, *Culto, cultura y cultivo*, 41.

other as part of the human pattern of life in response to the immediate environment.[15] Cultures mark the ways in which we humans orient ourselves, make sense of and interact with reality in all its dimensions. They constitute the created and developed elements with which human beings facilitate their interaction with the environment, animals, and other human collectives. Using the paradigm of "culture" as both cultivation and cult, González notes that culture as cultivation is one of the oldest expressions in human communities in the form of agriculture and hunting for food. He adds, as humans begin to change work in order to maximize how nature works to their advantage, they become aware of their control over their environment and animals.[16]

However, like all aspects of the cultural, the attitudes one finds among cultural groups concerning nature and their immediate surroundings differ greatly. While there is no doubt that humans have impacted and continue to impact and change their world, not all cultural collectives relate to the environment in the same way. I want to foreground the many Indigenous and aboriginal communities in the world that try to live in harmony with nature and reality, and maintain an attitude of respect for the rest of creation.[17] These Indigenous and originary groups see humans as sharing-coexisting in a fine balance with the rest of creation. Such cultural approaches stand in opposition to pervasive modernist, technocratic, and capitalist modes that depart from the human being as point of reference. By seeking to exploit and commodify natural resources, these approaches change the environment in fundamental ways without any consideration of the depletion of non-renewable resources,

---

15   For example, response to the physical environment was one of the salient features in the working definition of the Pan African Christian leadership assembly in 1976. See Bruce J. Nicholls, *Contextualization: A Theology of Gospel and Culture* (Downers Grove, IL: InterVarsity Press, 1975), 11. At the other end of the spectrum, Sherry Ortner has spoken of culture as the product of human consciousness, a system of thought and technology by which humanity asserts control over nature. Cited in Kwok Pui-lan, *Postcolonial Imagination and Feminist Theology* (Louisville, KY: Westminster John Knox Press, 2005), 217.

16   González, *Culto, cultura y cultivo*, 38. Here I want to point out that the Latin *colere* is the root of the words "*culture*" and *cult*, but it is also the root word of *colonize*. The interconnection between notions of civilization (culture), worship/religion/Christianity (cult), and colonization—issues that permeate this entire volume—are found even at the etymological level.

17   See F. Suazo, "Cultura occidental y culturas indígenas," in *Inculturación y teología indígena*, ed. Jesús Espeja (Salamanca, Spain: Editorial San Esteban, 1993), 136–51; Rodolfo Kusch, *El pensamiento indígena americano*, Biblioteca Cajica de Cultura Universal (Puebla, México: Editorial José M. Cajica, Jr., S.A., 1970).

the destruction of delicate ecosystems, and the dislocation of entire cultural communities from their ancestral lands. I do not wish to engage in a full-fledged environmental discussion here. My intention is simply to highlight the fundamental importance of cultural traditions in discussions of issues like the environmental destruction and the related problem of rapacious un-checked global capitalism. The very fact that these issues are of great concern in the present time shows their deeply cultural condition. The same invasive colonial capitalist factors that led to the marginalization and eradication of the cultural in many contexts are the very factors that are driving these forces today.

Contested Nature of Cultural Traditions

Cultural values, beliefs, norms, practices, etc., are part of a larger dynamic—and messy—process of contestation. No cultural tradition is a monolithic bloc nor is there such a thing as a naïve or simple development of a single tradition that grew without conflict or contradiction since "every culture bears witness to an internal history of conflict and struggle for the determination and control of its values, meanings, logic, and overall contour."[18] Cultural traditions develop through long processes of communal collective exchange and interaction; "a person alone does not have culture."[19] What we know today is very much the legacy of our ancestors, things we have learned that have been passed down from generation to generation,[20] with the exception of instances where that legacy has been erased. In some other instances, however, the cultural legacy remains despite systemic or intentional attempts at erasing or obscuring. All this to say that our cultures, their "values and symbols, belong not to any one individual, but to a tradition and to a community that span generations ..."[21] On one hand, as each generation engages their received cultural material, they adapt it according to their changing context. A complex process of negotiation ensues by which the inherited cultural practices are changed and reconfigured. On the other hand, intergenerational expectations fill these processes with complications as well. When members of a cultural group do not live according to the cultural expectations and conventions, they provoke tensions

---

18 Orlando O. Espín, *Grace and Humanness: Theological Reflections Because of Culture* (Maryknoll, NY: Orbis Books, 2007), 24.

19 Daniel Migliore, *Called to Freedom: Liberation Theology and the Future of Christian Doctrine* (Philadelphia, PA: The Westminster Press, 1980), 74.

20 González, *Culto, cultura y cultivo*, 47.

21 Chopp, *The Praxis of Suffering*, 124.

and crises that put pressure on the cultural traditions to change, whether by opening up to make room for new perspectives or by closing down and rejecting unwelcome influences.[22] We can identify a dialogical relationship: the "culture" of a group functions in ways that impact, influence, and regulate the activities and behaviours of the members of the group. As part of that process, members of the group also change and mould their culture.

The tensions between generations are further complicated by tensions between members of different social sectors within a cultural group especially in relation to multifaceted power plays in which those with power try to control others by exerting cultural pressures. How societies determine their values, practices, traditions, and customs is part of this larger complex web of power relations. Antonio Gramsci's notion of hegemony helps us identify the internal tug-of-war in which the most powerful sectors make use of well-manufactured ideologies to persuade the rest of society.[23] Often, "culture" is wrongly identified with a group of intellectuals, who see themselves as the guardians of the national cultural tradition and defenders of national values[24] at the expense of the discrimination and marginalization of the majority of the population.

The connection between power and the cultural is also made evident in Foucault's insistence that knowledge is often produced with the goals of controlling the population. According to him, behind the establishment of "normalcy" there are underlying epistemological assumptions designed to control the populace.[25] Because cultural traditions are also located, deployed, and reproduced by social institutions and structures, they are often used to help maintain the power differential in a cultural collective. More concretely, notions of race, ethnic identity, gender, and class, as cultural registers among others, put on display the internal multiple levels of struggle among different sectors of a society. The presence of poor, marginalized and discriminated-against people exposes a society's own power fissures as well. Cultures bear

22   Kathryn Tanner, *Theories of Culture*, 52.
23   See Luciano Gruppi, *El concepto de hegemonía en Gramsci* (Mexico, D.F.: Ediciones de Cultura Popular, 1978).
24   Rafael Polo Bonilla, *Los intelectuales y la narrativa mestiza en el Ecuador* (Quito, Ecuador: Universidad andina Simón Bolívar, Ediciones Abya Yala, Corporación editora nacional, 2002), 67.
25   Michel Foucault, *Madness and Civilization: A History of Insanity in the Age of Reason*, trans. Richard Howard, reprint, 1965 (New York, NY: New York American Library, Mentor, 1967); Michel Foucault, *Discipline and Punish: The Birth of the Prison*, trans. Alan Sheridan (New York, NY: Vintage Books, 1979); Michel Foucault, *An Introduction*, vol. 1 of *The History of Sexuality*, trans. Robert Hurley (New York, NY: Random House, Vintage, 1978).

within them the struggle between competing strands of traditions; "Every cultural universe carries the tension between oppression and liberation."[26] As ethicist Marilyn Legge correctly states:

> the assumption that people's cultural behaviour defines and expresses their whole lives must be qualified by greater attention to the realities of power. Any society has differences in power which cause significant inequalities in people's participation in symbolic-expressive cultural processes. Without attention to such inequalities, cultural power will continue to reside unproblematically in the "dominant ethos."[27]

The power differential among sectors of a given cultural collective is also found in the ways in which the elite present themselves as the gatekeepers of the cultural tradition of the group. The cultural practices, customs and traditions of the working classes are generally denied. They are reduced to "popular" expressions, or marginalized as exotic or folkloric and thus stigmatized as emptied of serious social and cultural significance.[28] Thus, in order to understand the idea of "collectively" shared cultural symbols in a society, the particular tensions within a cultural tradition must be recognized.

The remarks I make here concerning the messy and contested nature of the cultural finds resonance in the work of Gramsci. In particular, his articulation of the cultural notion of hegemony provides rich insights in terms of understanding the function of ideology in social, political and cultural spaces of contestation. Though Gramsci felt intellectually indebted to Marx and Lenin, he did not understand hegemony as something that could be reduced to the economic (Marx) or the political (Lenin).[29] Briefly put, Marx understood economic relations and the formation of social classes as the defining character,

---

26 Cited in Orlando O. Espín, "Toward the Construction of an Intercultural Theology of Tradition," *Journal of Hispanic/Latino Theology* 9, no. 3 (February 2002): 52, note 62. Jorge Klor de Alva notices how the tensions in a culture change the ways in which it is perceived. He notes that culture is viewed as a tool of domination if used to conceal reality but is considered liberative if used to unmask the oppressor. See his "Aztlán, Borinquen and Hispanic Nationalism in the United States," in *Aztlán: Essays on the Chicano Homeland*, Rodolfo A. Anaya and Francisco A. Lomelí (Alburquerque, NM: Academia / El Norte Publications, 1989), 138.

27 Marilyn J. Legge, *The Grace of Difference: A Canadian Feminist Theological Ethic*, American Academy of Religion Series, Vol. 80 (Atlanta, GA.: Scholar's Press, 1992), 120.

28 Klor de Alva, "Aztlán, Borinquen and Hispanic Nationalism in the United States," 142.

29 Hughes Portelli, *Gramsci y el Bloque Histórico*, 4a. edición, trans. María Braun (Mexico, D.F.: Siglo Veintiuno Editores, SA, 1977), 66–70.

driving force, and orientation of history. On the contrary, Lenin's notion of the "hegemony of the proletariat" strongly emphasized the State apparatus; hegemony for him had deeply political overtones.[30] But Gramsci understood hegemony instead in cultural and moral terms. His use of hegemony was referring to the ideological construct deployed by the dominant class as a mechanism designed to manipulate (read lead) the masses in terms of how to perceive reality. As Luciano Gruppi confirms, for Gramsci, hegemony encompassed all aspects of social life including the way people think, their theoretical orientations, even their mode of knowing; hegemony includes a conception of the world.[31]

For Gramsci, hegemony, that is, the ideological power to "lead" the masses by the dominant class, functions at two levels: in civil and political realms. These two levels, civil society and political society form what he labeled the social and ideological superstructure.[32] The function of hegemony in civil society is to spread the ideology of the dominant class by persuading (convincing) the masses of the rightness of the ideology of the dominant classes so that dominant class ideology becomes common sense. Meanwhile, political society refers to the ideological direction of society by way of direct dominion and functions as the enforcer of hegemony through the state, military and police apparatus which are all designed to preserve "order." Gramsci succinctly puts it as follows: "The State = political society + civil society, that is to say, hegemony dressed with coercion."[33] Political society, then, ensures that the hegemonic powers remain undisturbed.[34] The persuasive power of hegemony in the civil society is complemented with the coercive power in the political society.[35]

In the Gramscian schema, the hegemonic objective of the dominant class is ideological coherence and homogeneity, that is, the uniform dissemination

---

30   Ibid., 66–70.

31   See Gruppi, *El concepto de hegemonía en Gramsci*, Chapter I.

32   For a fuller discussion of the inter- relation between superstructure, historical bloc and hegemony see Portelli, *Gramsci y el Bloque Histórico*, Chapters II and III.

33   Cited in Portelli, *Gramsci y el Bloque Histórico*, 55.

34   Portelli, *Gramsci y el Bloque Histórico*, 28.

35   The intimate correspondence between persuasion and coercion is clearly described by Gramsci as he writes: "A system where only consensus" is needed is "pure utopia, because it is based on the presupposition that all [people] are really equal, and, therefore, equally reasonable and moral, that is willing to accept the law spontaneously, freely and not by coercion ..." (Cited in Portelli, *Gramsci y el Bloque Histórico*, 30). Portelli adds, as to the question of domination based exclusively upon force, "it cannot be but provisory, and expresses the crisis of the historical bloc when the dominant class, when it no longer has the ideological direction, maintains it artificially by force" (Ibid., 30).

of the ideas of the dominant class about the world to all levels of society in order to create "common sense."[36] When the ideas of the dominant class are widespread as common sense among the people, uniting society, a historical bloc is formed.[37] Stated differently, the historical bloc is the particular historical situation when the civil society and the political society complement each other.[38]

A Gramscian discussion of the dynamic and contested character of the cultural, as I outlined it here, is a worthwhile endeavor. The discussion could shed light on understanding the role of ideology in theopolitical maneuverings (chapter 2) on shaping historiographical approaches (chapters 2–3) and most particularly on understanding its function in theological debates in different Christian traditions (chapters 4–7). Moreover, the discussion of Gramsci would also expand our understanding of the role religion plays in establishing, disseminating, and perpetuating hegemony.[39]

The rich capacity of the Gramscian paradigm to help us understand the function of ideology in the cultural dimension notwithstanding, it is not without its limitations. Gramsci's understanding of the cultural dimension is described in dualistic oppositional relation; there is always the dominant group and the dominated/subaltern.[40] In the same way, he preserves traditional social and class hierarchies; it is only the dominant group which determines the direction and content of the cultural. Also, he focuses primarily

---

36   Of course, not all segments of society, not all classes display the same level of ideological homogeneity and coherence. The ideology among the dominant group is far more elaborate when compared to the fragments of ideology one finds among the populace. Thus we can speak about degrees of hegemony: at the "highest" levels it is a sophisticated philosophical articulation, among the "lowest" levels it is manifest in the form of folklore, and in the largest group, which stands in between the two extremes hegemony manifests in the form of common sense and religion. See Portelli, *Gramsci y el Bloque Histórico*, 20.

37   It is for this reason that Gramsci insisted on the inseparable character of history and philosophy. For him, the history of a period really was the history of the philosophy of that period, or, the history of the ways in which the dominant class managed to persuade the masses and to determine reality. See Portelli, *Gramsci y el Bloque Histórico*, 20–22.

38   Portelli, *Gramsci y el Bloque Histórico*, 82.

39   Here Otto Maduro's insight, however dualistic, is valuable. For him, "the religion of the majority of the members of the dominant classes becomes the dominant religion. It is the most efficient vehicle of a worldview capable of procuring the consent of the subordinate classes to the dominance exercised by the dominators." (Otto Maduro, *Religion and Social Conflicts*, introd. by Augusta Neal [Maryknoll, NY: Orbis Books, 1982], 131).

40   Portelli, *Gramsci y el Bloque Histórico*, 86.

on the rational-intellectual dimension of these cultural debates. The battle
between social classes takes place among intellectuals who represent each
class and the intellectual dimension is the space where the war between
social groups takes place.[41] Thus for Gramsci, subaltern groups really play
no significant role in the formation of the cultural content of a society,
except to reflect (or mimic) what they have received from the leading classes
through cultural organizations such as the school system, the media, and the
church.[42] But such a perspective leaves out the majority of social movements
from the "subaltern" groups for their crucial critical role in transforming society and cultures. It also leaves out expressions of embodied knowledge and
modes of knowing often dismissed by Western European and Euro North
American rationalism. In the end, not even Gramsci can escape the hegemonic power of the Enlightenment and coloniality of the Western European
intellectual tradition.

For our purposes, Gramsci's paradigm is too neat! Adopting such a perspective would prevent us from conceiving the fluid and unfixed character
of power relations. It would also undermine the fluid character of human
cultural agency which occupies different spaces at different times within
the broad network of sociocultural dynamics and identities. A dualist
oppressed/oppressor paradigm does not allow for movement back and
forth between the two categories or for the possibility that one person can
be both oppressor and oppressed simultaneously, something that becomes
ubiquitous as soon as the complexity of identities is acknowledged (e.g.,
race, class, gender, ability, etc.).

Because of these limitations, engaging in such an analysis at length
would ultimately take us in a different critical cultural direction. While
I value Gramsci's cultural-ideological-political orientation, my focus is more
cultural-historico-theological; I seek to primarily trace the ways in which
the relationship between the cultural and Christianity has been articulated
theologically over the years. My priority it to tease out how the processes
of culturalization take place and allow for the irruption of the Spirit within
them, that is, how we can understand divine activity within the phenomena
of the cultural.

---

41   I also consider Gramsci to be strongly elitist in his organization of ideas. He focuses
      primarily on the rational-intellectual dimension of these cultural debates, making the
      intellectual dimension the space where the war between social groups takes place. See
      Portelli, *Gramsci y el Bloque Histórico*, Chapter IV.
42   Portelli, *Gramsci y el Bloque Histórico*, 24.

The Dynamic between Cultures

There is an external aspect to cultural tensions as well. Interaction between different cultural groups adds more fuel to the fire of cultural processes of negotiation and contestation. In fact, people are only really made aware of their cultural tradition when it is contrasted with that of another cultural group. The dynamic web of multiple interconnections in cultures becomes evident as people come to see and understand themselves in relation to other cultural groups through the patterns provided by their cultural tradition. Cultures are the "historically and ecologically possible means and ways through which a people construct and unveil themselves" to themselves and (though secondarily) to others as meaningfully human.[43] In the same dynamic, cultural traditions also point to and provide the stuff with which a people organizes its life and living in contradistinction to any other people,[44] as well as create the conditions within which the identity of a people is formed.

As cultural traditions interact with each other tensions and problems arise.[45] A brief look at human history will show that for millennia humanity has been characterized by a plurality of cultures. It will also show that there have been serious clashes between groups. As groups clash, peoples' cultures and identities are formed and transformed. In the same way, ethnocultural ideas, stereotypes and prejudices are gestated. Human history is rife with culturally related tensions and disputes of this nature. History teaches us that ethnic strife, acts of genocide, and more specifically, the modern European colonial project of imperialism-colonialism were in fact culturally motivated. I do not mean to suggest that there are no economic or political factors that can be identified, but political maneuverings and economic interests are also part of larger pervasive cultural complexes like capitalism. In the case of European imperialism, the unfortunate historical

---

43 Orlando O. Espín, "Migration and Human Condition: Theological Considerations on Religious Identities and Unexpected Inter-Religious Dialogue," in *Migration und Interkultiralität: Theologische und Philosophische Herausforderungen*, ed. Raúl Fornet-Betancourt (Aachen, Germany: Wissenschaftsverlag Mainz, 2004), 178.

44 Philip, *Frontiers*, 13 See also Carl E. James, *Seeing Ourselves*, 2; Oscar García-Johnson, *The Mestizo/a Community of the Spirit: A Postmodern Latino/a Ecclesiology* (Eugene, OR: PickWick Publications, 2009), 49.

45 As González puts it, "Las culturas se nos presentan siempre en una irreducible variedad, y frecuentemente esa variedad resulta conflictiva" (González, *Culto, cultura y cultivo*, 34).

legacy reveals that the encounter between different cultural groups was
not an encounter in which they saw others as equals, resulting in violent
exchanges of enormous proportions. Ideologies of superiority,[46] advancement, progress, and development, blinded members of the powerful cultural
groups and prevented them from interacting with or, even learning from the
cultural groups they invaded, oppressed, and exploited. In chapters 3 and 4
I will show how these fallacious notions served to ensconce ethnocentric
sentiments of superiority within the colonizing-imperialist project, and how
the social sciences and other pseudo sciences, the humanities, and religion
were complicit in the process.

These same tensions between cultural groups continue today and, in many
ways, have been intensified as the most powerful nations continue the imperialistic legacy of their ancestors. In addition, the clash between cultural groups
has been exacerbated and is harder to untangle in multicultural societies. As
diverse cultural groups are thrown together and share the same geographical
area, historical notions of superiority and entitlement perpetuate societal
divisions between a dominant-majority group for whom social structures are
designed to perpetuate privilege, and numerous minoritized groups who deal
with enormous social disadvantages. Orlando Espín notes that in a context of
cultural plurality, cultural groups create themselves and their memories, along
with alternative versions of what they understand the cultural tradition of a
society. He contends minoritized cultures are sometimes identified as folkloric,
ignorant or subversive by the dominant culture, and at other times are considered to be meaningless, outdated, irrelevant, superstitious, or dangerous.[47]
According to Robert Schreiter, the confrontation between different groups
is the birth place of ethnicity. By ethnogenesis, he means the ways in which
minoritized groups rally around specific identity markers which enable them
to face a common threat and hostility, even though those markers did not originally function in such ways.[48] Analyzing these cultural tensions from a critical
cultural perspective is crucial to understanding the multiple intersections of

---

46   I am aware that where many would write "racial superiority" I am using the term "cultural
     superiority." I will return to this discussion later in the book. Here, I simply note that when
     the concept of race was discredited at the turn of the twentieth century, culture quickly
     replaced it. Today it is the category most often used to speak of features that were previ-
     ously connected to notions of race. It seems race has been culturalized and culture has
     been racialized.

47   Espín, "Migration and Human Condition," 177–79.

48   Robert J. Schreiter, *The New Catholicity: Theology Between the Local and the Global*
     (Maryknoll, NY: Orbis Books, 2000), 94.

specific social, political, and economic interests (of members of specific sectors) and influence of these interests in the structuring of entire societies, in ways that preserve an uneven power differential between cultural collectives and among members of a specific cultural group.

This discussion points to the fact that the cultural tradition of a people is crucial to understanding the internal dynamics of a society and how it relates to other cultural groups. Along with Kathryn Tanner, I affirm that no people has more culture than any other and that no single cultural tradition is more "mature" than any other, and is therefore a model to which other cultural groups can aspire.[49] Rather, says Geertz, "understanding people's cultures exposes their normalness without reducing their specificity."[50] The notion of "culture" is therefore not a criterion by which groups can be evaluated or organized hierarchically with some cultures being assessed as "bad" and others as "good," and some cultural expressions as "high" vis-á-vis those that are "low."[51]

---

49   I am working with the understanding that all cultural groups have in themselves the resources to advance and reach sophisticated expressions. As such, any levels of cultural "maturity" are not and cannot be determined by one cultural or social group that sees itself as the epitome of human advance, the highest expression of "civilization," "development," and "evolution." Each culture or cultural group can reach its own level of maturity independently, without following or imitating processes that other groups implement. Moreover, I agree with Rodolfo Kusch who argues that however we perceive "maturity," be it technological, cultural, or otherwise, different cultural groups arrive to it differently. More specifically, each cultural group has its own concerns, goals, and challenges to which they respond which means that each culture determines what they mean by advance or maturity. Culture is therefore not something that can be easily imported to resolve the problems of another society. See Rodolfo Kusch, *América profunda*, Enfoques Latinoamericanos (Buenos Aires, Argentina: Editorial BONUM, 1975). Rodolfo Kusch also argues that the originary peoples of Latin America display radical differences from the Western European perspective in their approximation to the world, reality and immediate environment. For him, "La cultura y mentalidad indígena tiene su propia estructura y coherencia interna, que debe entenderse paralela a la occidental y no menos o inferior que ella" (Kusch, *El pensamiento indígena americano*, 58).

50   Geertz, *The Interpretation of Cultures*, 14.

51   Tanner, *Theories of Culture*, 36. There is often a value ascribed to the dichotomy between the high and low cultures. Leopoldo Zea claims that, in many cultural contexts, what is considered important is imposed as the "fine arts" while what is considered the "low" culture of the people is viewed as execration. See his "Convergencia y especifidad de los valores culturales en América Latina y el Caribe," in *Latinoamérica encrucijada de culturas*, vol. 1, ed. Leopoldo Zea and Magallón Mario, Latinoamérica fin de milenio (México, DF: Instituto Panamericano de Geografía e Historia, Fondo de Cultura Económica, S.A. de C.V., 1999), 12.

Here I reject the false modern anthropological claims that foster the "disinterested suspension of judgment in the interest of fair description."[52] There are several implications that flow from this affirmation, the first of which is that no researcher of cultures or of another cultural group can escape the cultural fabric of which they are part and within which they function. They cannot bracket it out (suspend it) in the course of engaging (read studying) other cultural groups. The cultural background of the researcher is the lenses-filter with which they interpret another cultural tradition. Wolfgang Iser accurately describes the dynamics of interaction between cultural groups: "a foreign culture is not simply subsumed under one's own frame of reference; instead, the very frame is subjected to alterations in order to accommodate what does not fit."[53] The power relations between cultural groups, including those of the researcher and the subjects (objects) of the research cannot be ignored. The fallacy that "all cultures are equal and just different" fails to see the power dynamics at play from those cultures that are more dominant.[54] Most importantly, cultures do not remain the same when they meet; people weave their cultures together as they encounter other people. The point where cultures meet becomes the place where clashes and exchanges are possible and do take place. Antonio Sousa Ribeiro notes incisively that "every cultural act takes place, essentially, on the borders;"[55] in the zones of contact, at the intersectionalities, where peoples, relationships, and cultures collide. At the border between cultures the dynamic vortex of power relations and struggle is put on display.

The Dynamic Character of Cultures

In order for new possibilities for understanding the phenomenon of the cultural to emerge, cultures need to be understood as unfinished products. Such a change of premise moves away from notions of cultures as finished

---

52   Tanner, *Theories of Culture*, 37.

53   Cited in António Sousa Ribeiro, "The Reason of the Borders or a Border Reason? Translation as a Metaphor for Our Times," *Eurozine* 8 (2004), Http://www.eurozine.com/articles/2004-01-08-ribeiro-en.html (accessed January 28, 2008).

54   Tanner, *Theories of Culture*, 55. Tanner further elaborates: "However well-intentioned, the separate-but-equal view of self-contained cultures expresses tolerance by ignoring the political realities of inequality" (Ibid).

55   Sousa Ribeiro, "The Reason of the Borders or a Border Reason?"

products, impermeable, air-tight, and clearly defined.[56] To repeat, cultures are not monolithic. They must be understood as being in constant state of fluctuation and alteration, shifting according to the social processes within a cultural group and in relation to external factors, both human and environmental. While people cannot function without adopting the cultural elements inherent in their society or human collective, they enter into the equally inherent, complex, uneven, and contested spaces of cultural reconfiguration that contribute to constant changes as well. In the words of Sousa Ribeiro, if we share the assumption that "every culture is necessarily incomplete in itself and that there is no such thing as a self-contained, homogeneous culture, then the very definition of a given culture has to include what I would call intertranslatability."[57]

Translation is a central descriptor of what happens as cultures meet. Cultures are not partial views of the world. Rather, they embody totalizing views of the universe.[58] Each cultural group represents a universal view of reality: universal understanding, interpretation, and interaction with the world and fellow humans.[59] Yet, no one cultural group alone can claim all the elements of knowledge, beliefs, and expectations for the future of all humanity. Since no cultural view applies to all groups universally, translation is a necessary process for inter-cultural interaction and communication.

---

56   Tanner points out that the problem with notions of culture as art is that they presume that they are finished products instead of being in the process of formation. See Tanner, *Theories of Culture*, 42.

57   Sousa Ribeiro, "The Reason of the Borders or a Border Reason?"

58   I need to qualify here that I do not think that all aspects of culture can be translated into other cultural traditions. I agree with Sousa when he argues that in encountering different cultural traditions, there are elements of one culture that remain untranslatable into another culture. See Sousa Ribeiro, "The Reason of the Borders or a Border Reason?" 20. See also Lal Vinay, "Unhitching the Disciplines: History and the Social Sciences in the New Millennium," *Futures* 34 (2002): 13.

59   See Raúl Fornet-Betancourt, *Filosofía Intercultural* (Mexico, DF: Universidad Pontífica de México A.C., 1994). María Pilar Aquino speaks of "parcels of reason" to describe how each cultural group constructs modes of arriving to knowledge and in the process creates *"conceptual frameworks for grounding visions of the world with valid claims to universality"* (italics original) (María Pilar Aquino, "Theological Method in US Latino/a Theology: Toward an Intercultural Theology for the Third Millennium," in *From the Heart of Our People: Latino/a Explorations in Catholic Systematic Theology*, ed. Orlando O. Espín and Miguel H. Díaz, [Maryknoll, NY: Orbis Books, 1999], 10).

Cultures are porous living "systems." When people from different cultural traditions meet and interact, they acquire elements from each other's cultural groups and traditions. There is a pragmatic aspect to the ways in which cultural groups relate to others by making use of foreign cultural elements and adapting them for their own cultural inventory. One of the clearest examples of this dynamic is the incorporation of language elements, by which words, terms, and categories are imported from other cultural groups to convey ideas previously not present in the host culture. Of course, these dynamics of cultural borrowing and exchange must also be interrogated for the power dynamics that regulate such exchanges. Nevertheless, it follows that the limits of cultures are imprecise and fluid, and cannot be delimited scientifically.[60] We cannot know objectively where a person's or a group's culture ends and another begins.

For these reasons, the cultural is slippery and it escapes facile definitions. It is not something that can be easily captured conceptually using essentialist terms. In many ways, the phenomenon of the cultural goes beyond our understanding and resists being reduced or characterized by the use of stereotypes, binaries or generalizations. By the same token, our understanding and description of cultures are always preliminary, incomplete, and provisional. I echo Tanner's viewpoint that in dealing with the question of the cultural, it is important to preserve the elements of indefiniteness and inconsistence.[61]

The Breadth of the Cultural

By identifying the complex interconnected elements as part of this discussion of the cultural, one ought not to avoid appreciating its large encompassing character as well. Many disciplines have identified and attempted to engage the cultural from their unique vantage points. For example, discussing cultural identity in his Ecuadorian context, Manuel Espinosa Apolo identifies at least six theoretical approaches to the cultural (he uses culture): semiotic, technological, sociological, ideological, anthropological, and as an artificial production of goods and values,[62] each of which have bearing on discussions on cultural processes and identity.

Among these approaches, semiotics has been adopted by key scholars. The semiotic perspectives define the cultural as a special type of language with a

---

60   González, *Culto, cultura y cultivo*, 73.

61   Tanner, *Theories of Culture*, 171.

62   Manuel Espinosa Apolo, *Los mestizos ecuatorianos y las señas de identidad cultural* (Quito, Ecuador: Centro de estudios Felipe Guamán Poma de Ayala, 1995), 23–25.

set of codes and symbols, signifiers and signifieds proper to a specific human group and which are decipherable by those that are part of such group.[63] Geertz' own semiotic approach bears the identifying feature of cultures as a "web of signs and symbols" that need to be interpreted.[64] Schreiter draws on the semiotic perspective to articulate his own three-fold view on the cultural. For him, culture(s) is first

> ideational—it provides systems or frameworks of meaning which serve both to interpret the world and to provide guidance for living in the world. Culture in this dimension embodies beliefs, values, attitudes, and rules for behavior. Second, culture is performance—rituals that bind a culture's members together to provide them with a participatory way of embodying and enacting their stories and values. Performance also encompasses embodied behaviors. Third, culture is material—the arte-facts and symbolizations that become a source for identity: language, food, clothing, music, and the organization of space.[65]

Schreiter's perspective in outlining the interpretive meaning-making function of the cultural is quite helpful. Semiotic approaches appropriately empha-size the complex network of relations of symbols and elements designed to give meaning to our reality along with the complex processes of codifica-tion that create the condition for people to coexist-interact with each other, with nature, and with the cosmos. It is at this level of meaning-making that González's twofold view of the cultural as cultivo and culto meet: the cultural as cultivo encompasses the environment and the cultural as culto interprets it and gives it meaning.[66] However, emphasizing the meaning-making function

---

63   Espinosa Apolo, *Los mestizos ecuatorianos y las señas de identidad cultural*, 25. One key author in the study of semiotics is the philosopher Ferdinand de Saussure and his study of (linguistic as well as non-linguistic) signs and symbols and the complex process of meaning making. See Ferdinand de Saussure, *Course on General Linguistics*, ed. Charles Bally, Albert Sechehaye, and Albert Riedlinger, trans. Roy Harris (La Salle, Ill: Open Court, 1959).

64   Geertz, *The Interpretation of Cultures*, 5.

65   Robert J. Schreiter, *The New Catholicity*, 29.

66   González, *Culto, cultura y cultivo*, 13. Cultivo is the word traditionally used to describe the act of cultivation of the land, or what González describes as the way in which cul-ture confronts the environment and provides human beings with the skills to confront it. Meanwhile culto is the word used to speak of religious worship. According to González, culture as culto refers specifically to the interpretive frame of the world; in other words, culture provides the necessary meaning to make sense of the world. See Ibid.

of the cultural leaves out the role of human agency, the impact of cultures on human relations, the internal processes of contestation inherent in all groups as they struggle to create some kind of "consensus," and finally, how these culturalization processes find expression in social structures. Critiquing the semiotic and modernist approaches to the cultural, Tanner accurately argues that the concept "culture" is an abstraction from the "concrete facts of socially significant behaviors." She affirms that semiotic approaches introduce the cultural as "the meaning dimension of social life" but as operating independently from social behaviors.[67]

We have gone full circle in our description: having started with the social dimension of the cultural, I have moved through discussing its contested nature and dynamic character, and now I return once again to its social dimension. By way of reiteration, the social dimension of life is the context, the soil within which the cultural is germinated. The social dimension cannot be excised from the understanding of the cultural proposed here because it is only in the social dimension that human activity begins and ends, along with the cultural, the result of human social phenomena.[68]

Because the social dimension is unstable, cultures are also in a state of perennial alteration. Again, cultures are porous, open-ended, unfinished, and fluid. That does not take away from their totalizing function providing members of a group with a sense of overall coherence. By coherence I do not mean that all aspects of any given cultural tradition fit neatly together or that there are no internal contradictions in any given cultural "system." Rather, cultures provide members with a sense of totality, a sense of coherence, a meta-frame that explains—albeit limitedly—all aspects of life and reality. Cultures encompass the entire gamut of social phenomena in human collectives.[69]

It is important to hold in tension the cultures' sense of coherence with the dynamic sense of fluctuation and constant change. It is also worth emphasizing that the coherence[70] of a cultural tradition is not determined by outside observers. Historically, comparative cultural approaches have evaluated cultural groups by creating hierarchies among them exposing expressions

---

67   Tanner, *Theories of Culture*, 31.

68   Sergio Arce Martínez, "Fe y cultura," *Caminos* (n.d.): 47.

69   Ibid.

70   I agree with Geertz who notes that coherence cannot be a test of validity for a cultural description. Geertz, *The Interpretation of Cultures*, 17. In my view, the determination of the coherence of a culture can only be done by the members of that cultural tradition.

of ethnocentric and colonizing human hubris, which ought to be rejected. Similarly, the cultural is not "located" or primarily "expressed" through the technological, scientific, philosophical, or literary achievements of a sector of a cultural group. Rather, the cultural more accurately refers to the "whole social practices of meaningful action, and more specifically to the meaning dimension of such action—the beliefs, values, and orienting symbols that suffuse a whole way of life."[71]

In attempting to account for this aspect of coherence in cultural traditions, scholars have used different categories. One such approach that characterizes the quality of coherence in cultures was articulated by the German ethnologist Leo Frobenius. He wrote that *culture* (read the cultural) must be understood in terms of *paideuma*, by which he meant something like a *gestalt*, an organizing structure and principle which incorporates all cultural aspects into a functional whole.[72] But he meant more than a *gestalt*; for him *culture* was an absolute entity with a life of its own. In other words, it is organic in and of itself, not created by humans but living through them.[73] It is unclear how Frobenius understood the origins of the cultural. But it is evident that he saw it as independent from yet in close relation to humans.

It is in reaction to these kinds of perspectives that semiotic approaches, like that of Geetz emerged.[74] Notions of cultures as organisms, along the lines of Frobenius, rule out the possibility of human activity in the construction of cultures. They operate with the understanding of the existence of some thing we call "culture" (in the case of Frobenius *paideuma*, for instance), which can be conceived abstractly, connected to human collectives causing multiple concrete expressions, but may ultimately be applied universally. Frobenius *paideuma* is a kind of cultural version of Hegel's Geist, a force that moves humanity in the direction of a specific, idealized orientation, but which is also, we now know, coterminous with the Western European, Euro North American civilizing project.

---

71 Tanner, *Theories of Culture*, 70.

72 Leo Frobenius, *La cultura como ser viviente: Contornos de una doctrina cultural psicológica*, 4th. ed., Máximo José Kahn (Madrid, España: Espasa-Calpe, S.A., 1934).

73 Ibid., 95.

74 Jeff Todd Titon, "Textual Analysis or Thick Description," in *The Cultural Study of Music: A Critical Introduction*, ed. Martin Clayton, Trevor Herbert, and Richard Middleton (New York, NY: Routledge, 2012), 78.

Other scholars have used the language of worldview to describe this sense of coherence in the cultural. For example, S. M. Michael argues that cultures are embedded in worldviews which give cultural traditions that sense of comprehensive coherence.[75] Somewhat differently, Augie Fleras also views cultures as systems that encompass a complex range of beliefs and values.[76] Meanwhile, G. Lynwood Barney focuses on the intellectual side of the cultural insisting that it is the composite of a series of layers, the deepest of which are ideology, cosmology and worldview. In its functional integrative capacity, cultures, he claims, constitute a group's "shared cognitive orientation."[77]

In the midst of these multiple perspectives, it is important to recognize a general comprehensive sense of totality of the world (worldviews) and degree of coherence ("systems"). However, the adoption of the notion of worldview either as a totalizing interpretive frame or as ready-made systems under which all aspects of the cultural can be subsumed prematurely forecloses any discussion on the cultural. Along this line, Geertz observes that the use of an all-encompassing worldview or "a priori *Weltanschauungen* is to pretend a science that does not exist and a reality that cannot be found."[78]

Cultures also exhibit cosmogonies, or the interpretive material for explaining the existence of the universe, both in present day cultural groups as well as in ancient human collectives. Therefore, it is important to identify the functional integrative capacity of cultures not merely as visions or views of the world, but as visions of the cosmos, as cosmovisions that are formed, shaped, reshaped and reconfigured as people live life. I am reminded here of Raimon

---

75   S. M. Michael, "Christianity and Culture Authentic in Dialogue: Beyond Relativism and Ethnocentrism," paper presented at the seminar Prophetic Dialogue: Challenges and Prospects in India (Ishvani Kendra, Pune, 2003), Http://www.sedos.org/english/michael_2.htm (accessed October 19, 2006).

76   Augie Fleras and Jean Elliot, *Multiculturalism in Canada: The Challenge of Diversity* (Scarborough, Ontario: Nelson Canada, 1992), 137. For Fleras, notions of culture as system are useful in the context of interaction and tensions in multicultural societies. She writes, "Employed comprehensively, culture is defined as a shared system of meanings and symbols that account for patterned behaviours between individuals and among groups ... Culture in the anthropological sense encompasses a complex range of beliefs and values that (a) define and generate behaviour, (b) contribute to the security, identity, and survival of community members, and (c) impart meaning and continuity during periods of social change. It represents a living and lived-in reality for ethnoracial minority members" (Ibid.).

77   Cited in Nicholls, *Contextualization*, 11.

78   Geertz, *The Interpretation of Cultures*, 20.

Panikkar's notion of the cosmotheandric as an integrated vision,[79] although I suggest it is not as seamless as he proposes. Instead, I see this integrated vision of cultures as constitutively incorporating inherent contradictions and multiple levels of internal contestation.

My hesitation in identifying cultures in definitive, totalizing terms relates directly to the instability and changeability of culturalization processes. I suggest that the fluid, contradictory and indefinite character of cultures stems from the fact that they are constructed as people live life, in the everyday interaction with reality, other people, and the world. I contend that cultures are best understood in relation to the particular ways in which cultural communities understand and choose to live life in all its diverse expressions. Cultures encompass all those aspects that people receive as being part of a social and human collective. Initially, they simply imitate this information. But with time, it gains significance as principles, values, and identity markers when people conceive and imagine themselves within and oriented toward life. The following quote from Juan Carlos Scannone brings my point across:

> Cultures: ... I do not understand this term in the sense of "enlightened culture[s]," in a way that only the person who knows science, art, philosophy, etc., can be called "cultured." I take "culture[s]" in the sense of the cultural *ethos* of a people ..., that is to say, [their] peculiar mode of inhabiting the world, [their] relationship with nature, with other human beings, and with God. Therefore, it is about ... life style[s] that [imply] an specific sense of life and death as its cultural ethical nucleus, a nucleus of a sapiential sense that gains concreteness in historical experiences and cultural objectifications (economic, political, artistic, religious, etc.).... In a way, a people may not have a high degree of civilization and technology, and still be considered "cultured" because it knows the sense of life and death.[80]

Not surprisingly other scholars from the majority world resonate with this perspective on life and the cultural as needing to be outside scientific approaches which reduce the cultural to an object of scientific investigation. Tinoco Guerra,

---

79   See Raimon Panikkar, "Is History the Measure of Man? Three Kairological Moments of Human Consciousness," in *Invisible Harmony: Essays on Contemplation and Responsibility*, by Raimon Panikkar (Minneapolis, MN: Fortress Press, 1995), 135–44; Raimon Panikkar, *The Cosmotheandric Experience: Emerging Religious Consciousness* (Maryknoll, NY: Orbis Books, 1998).

80   Juan Carlos Scannone, *Nuevo punto de partida de la filosofía latinoamericana* (Buenos Aires, Argentina: Editorial Guadalupe, 1990), 173.

for example, privileges life to the degree that he considers the cultural as
a politics of life and strategy for the here and now.[81] And Samuel Silva Gotay
states: "Culture is life; it is the way of life." Taking the agricultural metaphor of
cultivation, he expands: "Culture cultivates those who possess it. Since infancy
it teaches us to see, feel, speak, understand, love, and to discriminate. From then
on, we incorporate criteria, methods and information with greater complexity
that we convert into practices of personal or social life."[82] Concurring with Silva
Gotay, Geertz writes: "Our ideas, our values, our acts, even our emotions, are, like
our nervous system itself, cultural products."[83] In other words, how we understand the very elements of our being humans and how we interpret their function are culturally informed, conditioned and therefore constructed. Thus, the
cultural functions as the context within which things are described intelligibly.

A paradigmatic shift becomes evident. From this perspective on life mediated
necessarily through cultures, it follows that cultures can be seen as a crucial aspect
without which we cannot live out our humanity. The cultural must be understood
in light of the everyday: "the meaning of everyday things and happenings, the personal side of things, activities performed, persons, and relationships; culture is
lived in all of this."[84] In the same way, I must affirm there is no aspect of human life
that is not constructed, understood, defined, filtered through, or interpreted without accessing the complex web of cultural symbols, codes and segments of code
that are socially translated, appropriated, and reconfigured by historical communities in the everyday. The cultural pervades all aspects of life; it is so pervasive
precisely because it is the ubiquitous aspect of our lives and existence. Without
the cultural we cannot function, interact with other people and the environment,
or make sense of reality. Notions of gender, economy, politics, class, ethnoracial
identity, intellectual traditions and currents, history, ideology, political borders,
nationality, citizenship, etc., are culturally constructed, contextually conditioned,
and related to historical developments proper to specific cultural traditions. Here
I am adopting a quasi-metatheoretical perspective on the cultural. The cultural
points to the pervasive processes of culturalization and formation of cultures, the
ubiquitous human constructs that we find in all human collectives. Yet, as I have

---

81   Tinoco Guerra, *Latinoamérica profunda: Aproximación a una filosofía de la cultura*, Colección:
      Ideas y Pensamientos (Maracaibo, Venezuela: Fondo Editorial Esther María Osses, 1996), 46.
82   Samuel Silva Gotay, "Impacto cultural del protestantismo en Puerto Rico: 1898–1998,"
      in *Impacto cultural de cien años de protestantismo misionero en Puerto Rico*, ed. Z. Miriam
      and Angel L. Gutiérrez (Puerto Rico: Editorial Chari, 2000), 36.
83   Geertz, *The Interpretation of Cultures*, 50.
84   Diego Irarrázaval, *Inculturation: New Dawn of the Church in Latin America* (Maryknoll,
      NY: Orbis Books, 2000), 37.

also been arguing, such notions need to be balanced with a second affirmation: all groups articulate, conceive, express and engage the cultural differently.

Religion (Christianity) as a Cultural Element

Of course, this multi-pronged descriptive approach to the cultural and cultural traditions is incomplete without a discussion of the relation between religion/ religious expressions and the cultural. These concerns are central to this book which is dedicated to an exploratory analysis of the intersections between cultural concerns and religious traditions and faith; how they have played out over-time at different historical points; and how they can be articulated theologically.

The discussion on the intersection of religion and the cultural is part of a larger debate. On one hand, it is important to emphasize the need to decon-struct the notion of "religion" as a modern concept which is foreign to the ancient world and to the present-day majority world. Religion was/is not understood as something that is separate or can be separated from the rest of life. On the other hand, it is crucial to resituate religious traditions and expe-riences within specific cultural traditions and dynamics. Religious traditions draw on available cultural resources; religious experiences are conditioned and shaped by specific cultural worlds; and religious expressions take place within and draw from the cultural fabric of specific ethnocultural communities.

Religion: Another Modern Notion

E. B. Tylor's *Primitive Cultures* is often seen as foundational to the study of "religion." In the book, Tylor made the connection between African people's religious traditions and their cultural traditions. I wish to argue, however, that the very idea of religion has its own roots in the Western European colonial projects which read "other" religious expressions through an imperial (mis)understanding of Christianity beginning at the turn of the sixteenth century.[85] It is a modern

---

85   As I will show in chapter three and fourth, material written by Christian missionaries served as the initial sources upon which anthropological studies of other cultures and peoples were based. In the words of John Beattie (1964), "it was the reports of eighteenth- and nineteenth-century missionaries and travelers in Africa, North America, the Pacific and elsewhere that provided the raw material upon which the first anthropological works, written in the second half of the last century, were based" (Robert Segal, "Religion and Culture," in *The Routledge Companion to the Study of Religion*, ed. John R. Hinnells [New York, NY: Routledge, 2005], 4). Sharpe adds that many of these reports came from Jesuit missionaries. See Eric Sharpe, "The Study of Religion in Historical Perspective," in *The Routledge Companion to the Study of Religion*, ed. John R. Hinnells (New York, NY: Routledge, 2005), 25.

concept that has brought about enormous misunderstandings of the human experience in many ethnocultural communities.[86] Eric Sharpe is correct stating that the portrayals of the "religious" non-European worlds were often wildly inaccurate, reminiscent of *Indiana Jones and the Temple of Doom*.[87] There was an operative understanding of other peoples informed by their (mis)reading of the biblical text and (mis)understanding of the Christian religious experience. Sharpe continues, "in those days the heathen were expected to perform bizarre rituals and carry out abominable sacrifices in the name of their idols – the Bible said so! What else there might be behind the rituals, very few in the West knew."[88] In earlier and even some contemporary studies of non-Christian ancient and contemporary religious traditions we find something akin to the dynamics described by Edward Said's *Orientalism*. In the Americas, we see a type of *indianization/indigenization* in which we learn more about the culture and religious traditions of the scholar and specific inherited stereotyped ideas of other religious traditions than about the actual traditions being studied.

At least four key issues stem from this debate. I follow the work of Brent Nongbri here in articulating these issues. First, the particular concept of religion did not exist in the ancient world. Nongbri demonstrates that none of the terms (Greek *threkeía*, Latin *religio*, Arabic *dîn*, Sanskrit *dharma*, and Chinese *dao*) in the ancient world that have been translated as "religion" by Western religion scholars correspond directly with the Western notion of religion. Such translations are misleading. As he explains, they *should* not be confused with modern religious systems.[89] Each of these terms covers a wide range of meanings referring to law, customs, social order, ethnicity, worship, rite, washings, reverence, and rule, among other things, which fall outside modern concepts of religion.[90]

---

86   According to Nongbri, in the Americas, there were no words equivalents to "religion." In fact, the native terms for "religion" that one finds in Spanish dictionaries of the sixteenth and eighteenth centuries "were in reality constructed by the Spanish ethnographer-missionaries in order to promote evangelization and the conversion of the indigenous people" (Brent Nongbri, *Before Religion: A History of a Modern Concept* [New Haven, CT: Yale, 2013], 26).

87   Sharpe, "The Study of Religion in Historical Perspective," 27.

88   Sharpe, "The Study of Religion in Historical Perspective," 27. In a similar vein, Robert Segal criticizes the works on religion by David Hume, Adam Smith, Ferguson, and Montesquieu, Condorcet and others, as writing without evidence. While they made brilliant speculations, in fact they "deductively argued from principles which were for the most part implicit in their cultures. They were really philosophers and historians of Europe, not anthropologists" (Segal, "Religion and Culture," 49). Sharpe adds, "Most of the Enlightenment's information about China came directly from the reports of Jesuit missionaries" (Sharpe, "The Study of Religion in Historical Perspective," 25).

89   See Nongbri, *Before Religion*.

90   See Nongbri, *Before Religion*, 28–45.

The same criticism can be applied to the use of labels such as Hinduism and Buddhism, which emerged as a result of the clash between colonial powers with other cultures and peoples in the world. Labeling was often the result of misunderstandings of particular communities and their practices by the colonial outsiders.[91] Nongbri adds that even the term *Ioudaismos* was part of a larger field of Greek vocabulary about ethnicity pointing to the "defense of Judean ethnic customs and civic life ..."[92] Of course it does not mean that ancient peoples were not religious, claims Nongbri. Rather, the *particular* concept of religion as it emerged in modern European thinking is "absent in the ancient world."[93]

Second, the category religion has undergone its own developments over time and it has meant different things at different times. During the late Roman republic, the term *religiones* was used to describe various monastic orders and the term *religio* was used to describe different types of Christians under vows such as Anchorite, the nun, the prioress, the abbess.[94] Christianity was not understood as a distinct religious tradition in the way it is today. Nongbri is helpful in this regard by noting that Eusebious of Caesaría saw Hebrew people as Christians. For him, non-Christians could "be seen as a deviation of a pure, ancient Christian past."[95] Nongbri also mentions how in the Middle Ages John of Damascus thought of Muhammad followers not as a separate religion but as Christian heretics.[96] Contrary to how modern scholars of religion speak of these groups as distinct religions, these examples show that there was a different operative way of conceptualizing "religions" with distinctions between groups being nebulous. Sometimes, people did not differentiate themselves from one another at all.[97]

Third, contemporary notions of religion do not easily correspond with "religious" practices in the ancient world and in many places in the world today. The

---

91   The labels "Hinduism" and "Buddhism" emerged in 1787 and 1801 respectively. Referring to Hinduism, for example, Nongbri points out that there is no such word in the ancient Indian language that approximates Hinduism. See Nongbri, *Before Religion*, 110.

92   Nongbri, *Before Religion*, 50. Discussing 2 Maccabees, Nongbri notes that the passage condemns taking on Greek customs using the term *Hellenismos*. The alternative in the passage is *Ioudaismos*. The introduction of Judaism in relation to Hellenism was coined in the midst of a dispute among some Judeans over how much "foreign" practice ought to be adopted. "In that context *Ioudaismos*, or "Judaizing," was an aggressive promotion of a Judean way of life formed in dialogue with the actions of some Judeans who were perceived as engaging in *hellenismos* or *allophulismos*, or practicing foreign customs" (Ibid 49–50).

93   Nongbri, *Before Religion*, 4.

94   Ibid., 21, 32.

95   Ibid., 57.

96   Ibid., 66.

97   Ibid.

idea that *religion* is a natural and universal phenomenon, a fact of life always present throughout human history in all human groups is simply incorrect![98] Contemporary notions of religion have a history in European colonialism and the development of European Enlightenment ideas. I agree with Nongbri that the idea of religion as private and self-contained does not register with what we know of the ancient world or the present majority world experiences. The idea of religion as a self-contained and coherent system with exclusive focus on belief in a supernatural being, encompassing privately held beliefs, adhered to by voluntary association, and as part of an individual's private spiritual journey, separate from the economic and political spheres is "born out of a mix of Christian disputes about truth, European colonial exploits, and the formation of [European] nation states"[99] from the sixteenth and seventeenth centuries. As European colonial forces interacted with other cultures and traditions, their projected views of Christianity as the only "true" religion had the effect of categorizing other religious expressions as "new" individual religions.[100] At the same time, the reformation established the idea of religion as an "internal, private," depoliticized entity separate from other aspects of life.[101]

---

98   Nongbri argues that scholars of religion have assumed that religion is a universal phenomenon, part of the human experience which is essentially the same across cultures and throughout history. In light of his study, however, one cannot make such an affirmation. See Nongbri, *Before Religion*, 1–2. Similarly, Mark Hulsether argues that religion "is not an independent matter just sitting there for all to see, but a term that its user chooses to associate with certain kinds of phenomena" (Mark Hulsether, "Religion and Culture," in *The Routledge Companion to the Study of Religion*, ed. John R. Hinnells [New York, NY: Routledge, 2005], 502).

99   Nongbri, *Before Religion*, 154. He adds, the "new" peoples whom Europeans "discovered" became ammunition for intra-Christian sectarian disputes. European Christians arguing about which form of Christianity was true drew comparisons between rival Christian sects and the worship of practices of the new "savage" peoples in Africa and the Americas. See Ibid., 6.

100 Nongbri claims that, "*Religion* is not a native category to ancient cultures. The idea of religion as a sphere of life separate from politics, economics, and science is a recent development in European history, one that has been projected outward in space and backwards in time with the result that religion appears to be a natural and necessary part of the world" (Nongbri, *Before Religion*, 7). Elsewhere he notes that in terms of the peoples of the Americas, Africa and India, those new peoples "were clearly not Christians, but neither were their ways of life wholly foreign and unintelligible. There were perceived similarities. The inhabitants of these distant lands venerated invisible beings similar to saints or demons; they had stories not completely unlike Christian scriptures; they had people who somewhat resembled clergy; they had buildings that were sort of like temples; and even though the native peoples did not group these items together, Europeans did do so for comparative purposes. Such comparative acts resulted in the generation of new religions" (Ibid., 10).

101 Nongbri, *Before Religion*, Chapter 5.

The fourth point is an extension of the previous one; "being religious" requires the accompanying notion to be "not-religious," a dichotomy that was absent from the ancient world. The division between the "religious" and "secular" spheres is foreign to ancient cultures and the majority world. According to Nongbri, the religious/secular dualism played out differently in late Medieval Latin. Just as *religious* described members of different monastic orders, *secularis* described Christian clergy not in a monastic order.[102] It is for this reason that he argues that, there needs to be a "distinction between ancient worlds (in which the notion of religion and being religious did not exist) and "modern" worlds (in which ideas of religion produced from the sixteenth to the nineteenth century have come to structure everyday life in many parts of the world)."[103]

The glaring implication from these four points is that the idea of "religion" as self-contained and independent from other aspects of life distorts our understanding of reality. Ancient peoples did not divide aspects of life between the religious and the non-religious; the gods were understood to be involved in all aspects of life. In the same way, in the majority world today "religious" customs, practices, and rituals are woven into the quotidian aspects of life and constituted within the cultural fabric of entire communities. For instance, Joseph Epes Brown argues that for many Native Americans *religion* is not "a separate category of activity or experience that is divorced from culture and society. Rather, religion is pervasively present and is in complex interrelationships with all aspects of the people's life ways."[104] He adds, "No one term can translate 'religion.'"[105] The "religious" is, then, not something that is carried out as a separate private sphere but as part of the cultural activities of people.

Religion as a Cultural Activity

I am not merely intending to say that religion plays a fundamentally cultural role like the role of the church in my discussion of Gramsci's work above.[106] I want to affirm that the cultural cannot be separated from the religious dimension of

102   Ibid., 5.
103   Ibid., 154.
104   Joseph Epes Brown, *The Spiritual Legacy of the American Indian* (New York, NY: Crossroads, 1982), x.
105   Ibid., 2.
106   Along those lines, Maduro reminds us that the structures of dominance of "any class society establishes—in a specific manner linked to the differentiation of classes within it and the asymmetric relationships of power among these classes—the limits within which any religion can function in it, and the *tendencies* that will permeate / and orientate the activity of this religion in this society." (Maduro, *Religion and Social Conflicts*, 50–51).

life because the cultural constitutes all aspects of human existence, including religion.[107] Here I disagree with Adam Cohen, Michael Shengtao Wu and Jacob Miller who argue that religious traditions can be thought of as "cultures."[108] Instead, I agree with Hulsether that "religious culture" should be understood as subset of "culture at large."[109] No religious tradition constitutes its own cultural universe but shares the values, vision of the world, and norms for interpersonal relations with the larger cultural world of society, even while those within a religious tradition may also be critical of it.

In fact, religion and the cultural are so intimately related precisely because all aspects of any religious traditions can only be expressed and understood culturally.[110] There is interdependence between religion/religious traditions and the cultural.[111] Religion and religious expressions and experiences cannot be conceived outside the space of the cultural and the cultural cannot be conceived without the religious (or religious-like) elements and dimension of life in any specific cultural group. If indeed religion and faith experiences are so intimately connected to the cultural, then we need to enquire about the role of the cultural in both. I posit that both religious traditions and faith experiences are conditioned by and cannot take place outside the sphere of the cultural. Moreover, since the cultural maybe understood as that which informs, conditions, shapes and is present in all that we do, then the cultural must shape and condition religious traditions and faith experiences as well. The cultural provides us with the tools and the material know-how to conceptualize, understand, and approach the reality of the divine. In sum, religious expressions are also intrinsically cultural expressions. In other words, although not everything we do—in terms of cultural practices—is religious in nature, certainly all religious traditions, expressions and rituals are culturally conditioned.

---

107 Irarrázaval, *Inculturation*, 37.

108 Adam B. Cohen, Michael Shengtao Wu, and Jacob Milleer, "Religion and Culture: Individualism and Collectivism in the East and West," *Journal of Cross-Cultural Psychology* 47, no. 9 (2016): 1236–49.

109 Hulsether, "Religion and Culture," 500.

110 Not to mention that religious traditions are historically situated. In the words of Maduro, "every religion … is a situated reality—situated in a specific human context, a concrete determined geographical space, historical moment, and social milieu. Every religion is, in each concrete case, always the religion of these or those determinate human beings." (Maduro, *Religion and Social Conflicts*, 41).

111 I use here religion and religious traditions to speak of complex religious "systems." For example, Christianity, Islam, and ancestral religions. I use religious expressions to speak of specific rituals, symbols, rites, or ceremonies that are celebrated as part of a given religious tradition.

I note briefly here that "religion" as a category is fraught with negative associations because of modernist positivist prejudices and colonizing impetuses
which elevated "scientific" approaches above all else. As I hinted earlier and will
show in chapters 3 and 4, these attitudes were wedded to a Western European
ethnocentrism that influenced how the religious practices and cultures of the
world outside of Western Europe were understood as inferior. The denigration
of other religious expressions and faith traditions can be traced to the period
of European imperial expansion and accompanying cultural attitudes as well
as practices of cultural genocide that began in the fifteenth century.[112] Despite
potential semiotic pitfalls, the category of religion is still useful for pointing to
those multiform faith practices, rituals, activities, and expressions that assume
the existence of and interaction with (a) divine being(s). It is important to keep
in mind, however, that in many contexts "religious" sentiments and practices
are interwoven with aspects more directly related to ethnic and cultural identity and the customs and practices of a people, which fall outside the scope of
modern notions of "religion." In those instances, the interwoven nature of the
cultural and the religious is quite evident.[113]

Aside from affirming the interconnection and interrelation between the
religious and the cultural, I also want to affirm the religious as pivotal in the
cultural development of ethical and moral values and principles. The way in
which the relation between the cultural and the religious gets negotiated is
a complex matter in lived reality; it cannot be reduced to facile categories.
For example, in her celebration of the oral tradition among Latinas/os in the
U.S.A., Ana María Pineda maintains that cultural traditions are the accumula-
tion of well-established patterns of human relation that limit and regulate the

---

112 Luis Cardoza y Aragón, "Los indios de Guatemala," in *1492–1992: La interminable con-*
     quista, ed. Heinz Dietrich Steffan (México, DF: Grupo Editorial Planera, 1990), 13–22;
     Luis N. Rivera-Pagán, "Bartolomé de Las Casas y la esclavitud africana," in *Sentido*
     Histórico del V Centenario (1492–1992): 16th Simposio de CEHILA (1989: Santo Domingo,
     Dominican Republic), ed. Guillermo Meléndez (San José, Costa Rica: DEI, 1992), 63–84;
     Enrique Dussel, *The Underside of Modernity: Apel, Ricoeur, Rorty, Taylor, and the Philosophy*
     of Liberation, ed. and trans. Eduardo Mendieta (Atlantic Highlands, NJ: Humanities
     Press, 1996).

113 In their comparative study on Western and Eastern religious tendencies of individ-
     ualism and collectivism, Cohen, Wu and Miller lament that many Western Scholars
     think of "belief in supernatural agents" as the aspect on which definitions of religion
     rise or fall. For them, this issue is crucial particularly because Easter religions such as
     Daoism, Confucianism, and Buddhism "have many of the hallmarks of religion, such
     as community structures, rituals, and moral codes," but which do not explicitly have a
     belief in a "supernatural" being (Cohen, Wu, and Miller, "Religion and Culture," 1242).

manner in which a given group behaves. But for her, the importance of this dynamic relation is that it provides people with cultural values and morality as part of the same movement.[114]

The interconnection between the cultural and religious traditions can be seen in how the cultural ethos of a people encompasses their dreams and aspirations, as well as their spirituality and orientation to a divine reality. In many cultural communities, the religious is explicitly understood as woven into the cultural and social fabric. In fact, some descriptions of the cultural from the majority world include religion and spirituality.[115] For instance, Mercy Amba Oduyoye notes that African groups have inherently religious cultures: their whole ways of life emerge from and revolves around religious beliefs.[116] Muslim societies and Indigenous originary communities are also good examples of the interwoven nature of the cultural and religious traditions. There are other societies that claim to be "secular" or strive to maintain the distance between church (religion) and state (society), but implicitly deploy religious practices and symbols from specific religious traditions. For example, in European and Anglo North American countries where Christianity was historically the dominant religion, Christian religious symbols, rituals, and practices, continue to surface as part of the larger social dynamics and imaginary.[117]

Communities express the relationship between the cultural and the religious differently. It is possible that some may find my comments as being broadly applicable in the context of other religious traditions; I would not be surprised if other scholars from other traditions are already invested in similar projects. For the sake of this discussion however, I locate myself within the Christian tradition; my exploration of the relation between the cultural and religious faith will centre exclusively in Christian contexts. Given these limits, let me assert that the relation between the cultural and religious faith in Christianity must be contextually, historically, and geographically understood. Tanner

---

114   Ana María Pineda, "The Oral Tradition of a People: Forjadora de Rostro y Corazón," in *Hispanic / Latino Theology: Challenge and Promise*, ed. Ada María Isasi-Díaz and Segovia Fernando (Minneapolis, MN: Fortress Press, 1996), 106.

115   Nicholls, *Contextualization*, 11.

116   Oduyoye, "Gospel and Culture in Africa," 36. See also Agbonkhianmeghe E. Orobator, *Theology Brewed in an African Pot* (Maryknoll, NY: Orbis Books, 2008).

117   Here, I am not only referring to the celebration of key holidays that are fraught with Christian overtones such as Christmas, Thanksgiving, Easter, and Remembrance Day celebrations. I also include uses of terms by political leaders like God Bless the USA or God Bless Canada along with such things as the production of films portraying some apocalyptic end times that resemble the book of revelations, for example.

affirms the complex and partial nature of such a study: "Ideas about God and Christ are admittedly only part of the life orientations of cultures influenced by Christianity."[118] The operating assumption here is that knowledge and belief in Christianity relate to specific historical and contextual events and multiple interconnected social, political, economic, and ideological factors, just as all aspects of the study of the cultural are contextual and complex.

The religious is both part of the larger complex of cultural traditions to which it actively contributes, shaping and changing a given culture, just as it is shaped and changed in the process. The interaction between cultural traditions and religious traditions is so powerful that it often, if not always, results in the actual transformation of the religious tradition. Referring to the Christian tradition specifically, religious practices differ greatly not only because of the internal diversity of traditions in Christianity—which themselves are culturally shaped, of course—but because of the multiple cultural traditions that have adopted it, many by way of imposition. Overtime expressions of Christianity have been transformed, reshaped, and reconfigured. One can confidently say that, Christianity as a religious "system" and "tradition," in its multiply diverse expressions, is deeply shaped and conditioned by local cultures. More to the point, there is no such thing as an *a*-cultural religion, just as there is no such thing as an a-cultural expression of Christianity.[119]

In the following chapters, I seek to explore how the relation between Christianity and the cultural has been understood, developed, and articulated. My intention is to demonstrate that discourses and concerns related to the intersection of the cultural and faith in Christianity have always been at the forefront since its inception (chapter 2). I will show how in the development of the Christian tradition questions of the cultural and faith have been front and centre over the years. Furthermore, they were an intrinsic part of Western European imperialism and the intellectual tradition that accompanied it (chapters 3 and 4). Important in this conversation is a consideration of the ways in which Christian scholars (theologians) have attempted to think about the intersection between the cultural and Christianity (the gospel). With this in mind, I will enter into conversation with contemporary scholars by exploring their proposals and offering alternative perspectives as to how to understand the dynamic of faith and the cultural in theological terms (chapters 5, 6 and 7).

---

118 Tanner, *Theories of Culture*, 65.

119 Orlando O. Espín, "An Exploration Into the Theology of Grace and Sin," in *From the Heart of Our People: Latino/a Explorations in Catholic Systematic Theology*, ed. Orlando O. Espín and Miguel H. Díaz (Maryknoll, NY: Orbis Books, 1999), 123.

The Cultural and Theology

The types of reflections I engage require that I connect the theological task with debates on the phenomena of the cultural. Just as religious traditions, rituals, and expressions are intimately connected to and conditioned by cultures, so also theology. Theological discourses, ideas and categories are also human constructions; they are attempts to understand and articulate the experience of faith in the divine. I note that many of the characteristics one finds in studies of the cultural are also displayed in the discipline of theology. At the risk of being repetitive, I choose to briefly articulate some of the connections between theology and the cultural.

Theological articulations and reflections do not emerge solely from abstract conceptions disconnected from the reality of the people, *ex nihilo*. They are situated within and born from specific cultural traditions, and emerge from particular historical, political, social, economic, and religious contexts. A theology done from (and for) one social, political, economic, and cultural context cannot be easily imported and does not necessarily respond well to the challenges and questions of a different context. What I am rejecting here is the pretension that anyone theological discourse has universal relevance and, therefore, can be applicable in all places and all times. This challenge to the universality of Christian theological discourses is one of the greatest theological shifts of the last 70 years. As the peoples of the majority world have realized they can (and must) think theologically for and with their communities, they have rejected the pretension that Western Enlightenment inspired theology serves all cultures and peoples. The fundamental shift is the recognition that Western European and Euro North American intellectual traditions are also constitutively contextual and cultural theologies. These theologies have historically claimed universal relevance, but are unable to respond to human and theological concerns and challenges for all times and for all historical and cultural contexts.

By asserting the role of context in theology, I also affirm that it is not possible to think theologically separated from one's own historical circumstances and personal social location. This move is methodologically intentional. There is an unavoidable correspondence between theological reflections and the immediate cultural context of a person. Theology's purpose is to seek to be a coherent articulation of the fundamental elements of our faith in God. Theology does not examine the reality of God *per se*, but reflects on our experiences of faith in God, what they say about what we believe about God, and how we can articulate them in connection to a wide range of religious practices. It is an interpretive circle that comes out of the reality of faith communities as it responds to the questions and challenges of those communities.

To pretend to think about God in the abstract without any connection to reality, to the communities of faith that nurture one's soul, is to pretend one can bypass or stand outside of the reality of contextually grounded human experiences.[120] It is presumptuous to say that one can theologize outside of the context of the cultural or pretend—or even argue—that one's cultural tradition has nothing to contribute to such theological considerations. The cultural is a *conditio sine qua non* for theological considerations. That is to say, there is no understanding of God, life, faith, Christ, etc., that is not explicitly bound to and profoundly influenced by our own cultural context and background. All theological discourse is conditioned by the cultural context from which it emerged. To be able to stand outside of the cultural would mean that human beings can be removed from their historical existence and placed in the space of floating ideas, which is an impossibility.

The historically grounded and culturally conditioned character of human existence is also marked by divine disclosure. Through incarnation God entered the historical and cultural human spaces and allowed God-self to be impacted by it. Seen this way, the divine self-disclosure gains cultural significance. The understanding of the divine disclosure we experience is not only mediated through specific cultural traditions, but it can only be interpreted through those traditions. I will discuss this more fully in the last chapter.

Even more important is the fact that no theological discourse is innocent, neutral, disinterested, or objective. All theological articulation emerges from, and has the potential to reproduce, and preserve the structures of power and "normativity" crystallized in a given social collective. Accordingly, we must approach all theological discourses with a measure of suspicion for what they may uphold and maintain. Here a hermeneutics of suspicion becomes a useful tool in interrogating what is presupposed by a given theological articulation, even when it does not express it explicitly. It becomes necessary to examine

---

120 Discussing the historical and cultural boundedness of theology, c.s. Song concluded that "No matter what branch of theology is your main concern and no matter what you do to become competent in it, your effort must lead you to a theological understanding of the life and history of your own country, and you must be able to relate that understanding to your faith derived from the Christian Bible. Our theology must have enough room for the histories of Asian countries as well as the history of Israel and the history of the Christian church" (Choan-seng Song, *Theology from the Womb of Asia* [Maryknoll, NY: Orbis Books, 1993], 23). He goes further affirming that for him, a crucial task of theology is to identify signs of Emmanuel in "Asian history and culture, and wrestle with them in the life and history of the 'silent millions'." For him, this is "Immanuel theology, God-with-us-theology" (Ibid., 26).

the epistemological edifice and structures of knowing and knowledge that are presented as "normative." A hermeneutics of absence is essential as well, in order to reclaim and recover elements that have been excluded from or that are absent in dominant hermeneutics or discourses, and to create spaces for these other voices to be heard.[121]

Reality is a necessary third element that must be added to our considerations on the cultural and theology. Whether we speak of it as our context, or as a collection of elements that we confront in our daily life, our reality is an indefinable aspect of life which is irreducible to categories of analysis. The cultural helps us to interact intelligibly with reality, and gives us a cosmovision, but our ideas, categories, or cosmovisions remain connected-bound to our particular context. Other human groups in other contexts perceive, understand, and interact with reality in different ways. Our theological task is always contingent; it is based upon the slippery sociocultural reality in which we live. Yet, it is from within this reality that we conceive, encounter and interact with the divine.

In sum and to repeat, every aspect of human activity is understood and interpreted through the prism of the cultural. Since the cultural is in a constant process of change, and since our theological articulations are informed and conditioned by our cultural background, our theology is also intrinsically provisional and unfinished. Any kind of dogmatism becomes unsustainable.

When it comes to our interpretations of the Bible text, for instance, and even though our sacred book informs our theological reflections, still even these are always also limited. They stand to be enriched by the vision of God of other cultural groups. In other words, our understanding of God can be and is impoverished when we do not engage in conversation with other versions/ visions of God from other cultural groups, denominations, and religions. I am arguing that there is no human ethnocultural group that has a monopoly on the revelation of God or a greater ability to reflect the truth revealed by God in Christ. I contend that it is only when we enter into conversation with the other peoples of the world that our visions of God, Christ, life, salvation, grace, etc., become fuller in a kind of tapestry construction made up of the voices and views of God from the various cultural horizons of the world. This is a risky, painful, and unsettling process of *Intercultural kenotic divine disclosure*: it is this kind of interactive, intercultural intersection between peoples in which the divine is disclosed more fully.

---

121   Néstor Medina, "Orality and Context in a Hermeneutical Key: Toward a Latina/o Canadian Pentecostal Life-Narrative Hermeneutics," *PentecosStudies* 14, no. 1 (2015): 97–123.

In closing, let me reiterate the contextuality, preliminary character, and changing nature of theology. Like Tanner, I question notions of tradition which are claimed to be unchanging and relevant for all peoples of all times.[122] Like Espín I insist on keeping my eyes on the phenomena of cultures. As he avers, cultures do change, grow and even die. "But in the very long history of cultures, individuals and communities never explain or view themselves except through the tools of understanding granted them by culture."[123] Because of this, he adds, it would be malarkey to assume that changes in the cultural tradition of members of the church do not also change the way in which the church understands the divine-human relationship and the gospel.[124]

Concluding Comments

The intention of this chapter has been to sketch the multiple interconnected issues, factors, elements that must be taken into account in debates on the cultural. As I have been emphasizing throughout this chapter, cultures are not monolithic. The phenomena of cultures must be understood as a series of dynamic, open-ended, interminable processes. It is these series of dynamic processes of culturalization that operate as people engage in the construction of cultures and draw on cultures to understand reality, live life, construct societies, interact with their immediate environment and each other, make sense of the world around them, and engage the divine. For these reasons, I suggest that in Christianity the relationship between faith and the cultural must be understood in more intimate interconnected ways, and that the cultural must not be viewed as another phenomenon that can be easily distinguished or separated from the gospel message.

---

122 Tanner challenges notions such of a fixed tradition including the three following points. 1. Tradition does not change overtime such that Christians always and everywhere believe the same thing. 2. Tradition only changes with little increments. The Bible and Jesus are applied to new issues but the Bible remains timeless. 3. Tradition and culture are the collection of ideas, texts, and works of art which have a timeless universality. She also critiques notions of tradition which argue for the collection of a normalizing cannon that ought to be preserved and protected by specific structures of authority and magisterium. See Tanner, *Theories of Culture*, 129–31. See also Orlando O. Espín, "Traditioning: Culture, Daily Life and Popular Religion, and Their Impact on Christian Tradition," in *Futuring Our Past: Explorations in the Theology of Tradition*, ed. Orlando O. Espín and Gary Macy (Maryknoll, NY: Orbis Books, 2006), 1–22.

123 Espín, "An Exploration Into the Theology of Grace and Sin," 122.

124 Ibid., 123.

These multiple interconnections and issues will continue to emerge throughout the book. I wish to insist here that, exploring these large and complex debates foregrounds the centrality of cultural processes and the importance of reinterpreting them in theological terms. In the next chapter, my goal will be to provide concrete examples of how the Bible and early Christianity engaged and negotiated the intersection between cultural concerns and religious traditions. The intention is simply to illustrate briefly how the dynamic processes of culturalization are woven together with religious traditions (as cultural expressions) in ways that cultural phenomena unavoidably shape religious practices and concerns, at the same time that religious traditions also shape cultural traditions.

CHAPTER 2

Culture in Early Christianity

"... We must abandon any older views that try to drive a wedge between what we call 'religion' and what we call 'culture' or 'politics' or anything else ... we require for a proper understanding is far more all-embracing vision, a worldview in which all human life is woven together into a (potentially) coherent whole."[1]

N.T. WRIGHT

•••

For almost three hundred years, the church had lived under the constant threat of persecution. All Christians were aware of the possibility that some day they would be taken before Roman authorities, and there placed before the awesome choice between death and apostasy. During the prolonged periods of quiet in the second and third centuries, there were those who forgot this; and when persecution did arrive, they proved too weak to withstand the trial. This in turn convinced others that security and comfortable living were the greatest enemies of the church, and that these enemies proved stronger during periods of relative peace. Now, when the peace of the church seemed assured, many of these people saw that very assurance as snare of Satán.[2]

JUSTO GONZÁLEZ

Introduction

Until very recently when biblical scholars discussed the intersection between the cultural and the biblical they limited themselves to three main foci: First, the most prevalent approach has been to discuss the cultural traditions of the ethnic groups mentioned in the Bible. Second and more recently, biblical scholars from outside mainstream biblical scholarship have challenged the

---

1 N. T. Wright, *Paul and the Faithfulness of God Part I* (Minneapolis, MN: Fortress Press, 2013), 315.
2 Justo L. González, *The Story of Christianity: The Early Church to the Dawn of the Reformation* (New York, NY: Harper San Francisco, 1984), 136.

inherited "Eurocentric" character of traditional hermeneutics to emphasize the importance of contextualization and the role of empire in the bible text, in traditional biblical interpretation, and in theology.[3] Third, and almost simultaneously, other scholars have emphasized the role of the individual reader and his/her response to the text from their social vantage point.[4] These discussions, however, have left out critical analyses on the impact of the cultural in the Bible: how the cultural contributed to the Bible's formation;[5] how ethnicity and cultural identity became key contributing factors in the way Israel conceived and distinguished itself from the rest of the groups of the Levant, and how Israelites (and the Christian subset) developed a sense of peoplehood.

With that in mind, my goal in this chapter is to demonstrate that culturalization processes are central for understanding the biblical text and the subsequent development of Christianity. The cultural conditioning of Christianity is twofold. First, the very sources of the Christian faith, the Bible writings and inherited traditions were themselves heavily shaped, impacted, and conditioned by the cultural traditions and sociocultural milieus within which those writings and traditions were first articulated. And second, many societies in the majority world

---

3   Myriad are the scholars who have engaged in the task of uncovering empire in the biblical text, and voluminous are their contributions to biblical scholarship. Here are a few examples among a vast body of work: Silvia Regina De Lima, "Rereading the Bible as a Latin American Black Woman," in *Women's Perspectives: Articulating the Liberating Power of the Gospel* (Geneva: World Council of Churches Publications, 1996), 23–27; Sharon H. Ringe, "Places at the Table: Feminist and Postcolonial Biblical Interpretation," in *The Postcolonial Bible*, ed. R. S. Sugirtharajah (London, UK: Sheffield Academic Press, 1998), 136–51; Musa W. Dube, *Postcolonial Feminist Interpretation of the Bible* (St. Louis, MO: Chalice Press, 2002); Jean-Pierre Ruiz, *Reading from the Edges: The Bible and People on the Move* (Maryknoll, NY: Orbis Books, 2011).

4   One important example is the collection of articles exploring a wide range of modes of interpretation in George Aichele, et al., *The Postmodern Bible*, ed. Elizabeth A. Castelli, et al. (New Heaven, CT: Yale University Press, 1995).

5   In terms of the formation of the Bible, I also note that many scholars focus primarily on the following themes: retracing how the Bible was transmitted and changed over time, paying attention to the translation of the Bible in multiple languages, its distribution around the world beginning with the creation of the printing press; and discussing how the Bible was received and functioned as part of European Cristianity (in all its diversity) running from the early church through to the Middle Ages, the Reformation, and contemporary times. Little attention is given to discussing the sociocultural, political, and historical issues of the time that contributed to those changes. Similarly, while scholars discuss the internal cultural diversity of the Bible and highlight its potentially liberative character, they give no attention to how the Bible is a cultural document which embodies the cultural memory of Israel in the Hebrew Bible and the memory of the early Church in relation to the cultures of the time.

today are religious cultures. How these societies receive and practice Christianity and read the Bible is heavily conditioned by their own cultural traditions.

The biblical narrative tells the story of religious societies. The clashes between groups narrated from one end to the other of the Bible carried cultural and religious underpinnings. These underpinnings are easily found throughout the history of Israel in the Hebrew scripture: the survival of Israel in Egypt and its liberation from it; the taking of the land of Canaan; the interaction with neighbouring ethnic groups; the experience of exile and return; and so on. In each case, the religious-cultural context provides the interpretive framing. Likewise, in the New Testament, events like the interaction of the Jews with Rome, the narrative of Jesus' life and ministry, The Council of Jerusalem; Paul's imprisonment and journey to Rome, etc., have embedded in them the religious-cultural dimension which provides the interpretive structure. These events also mark the historical clash of different cultural traditions.

In the first section of this chapter, I show how the writers of the biblical text deployed and utilized their immediate cultural world and interpretive tools to describe the creation event, frame the divine interaction with all of creation, understand the human interaction with the divine and nature, and articulate their collective sense of identity. In the second section, I show how cultural processes were central in informing and shaping the development of Christianity in the ancient Roman world and subsequently. My intention is to illustrate the dynamic processes of culturalization in all their complex power negotiations, historical shifts, social reconfigurations, and in their transformation of religious practices and beliefs.

My discussion is but a bird's eye view of much more complex issues and factors at play, which warrant a much deeper analysis than I can provide. Here I am only able to briefly sketch how issues pertaining to the process of culturalization are found in the biblical text and early Christianity. This sketch will bolster my claim that the cultural—understood as the complex dynamic network of socially and historically inherited codes and segments of codes that allow and make possible inter-human interaction in a given society, that provide the interpretive frame and lenses for reality; and that constitute the set of guiding principles by which humans and societies interact with their surrounding environment and the divine—has an essential role in mediating religious experience and expressions. In fact, I would argue that religious experiences and expressions in the Bible, in early Christianity and elsewhere cannot really be understood outside of the cultural. My hope is that this chapter will also begin to hint at new ways in which the cultural and the processes of culturalization can be understood and reflected upon in theological terms; it is my contention that theology also is always culturally mediated.

The Bible as Cultural Document

As often as not, Christians think of the Bible as the "Word of God." It is for many the written instrument containing the divine record of God's self-disclosure in history through the story of the formation of the people of Israel, their subsequent exile, and the renewed spiritual hope brought by the person of Jesus. The message of good news, God's intention to enter into relationship with humanity is the epithet used to speak of the Bible. But the Bible is much more than a spiritualized record of "salvation history." It can also be considered the religious memory of the people of Israel documented in the Hebrew Scripture and the religious accounts of the newly-born Christianity in Ancient Near East in the New Testament.

I propose that the Hebrew scripture can also be appropriately understood as the cultural memory of the people of Israel, a cultural memory which cannot be separated from religious memory.[6] The various literary genres and the content of the narrative are cultural elements used as tools for the religio-cultural reproduction and expression of the faith of the people in YHWH. As for the New Testament, the accounts recording the Jesus event and the communication of the (*Evangelion*) good news draw on the cultural and religious reservoir of Judaism. The images, language, theological terms and concepts bear the cultural and historical heritage of the religious culture of the people of Israel along with cultural influences of the day, principally Hellenistic and Roman.

The Processes of Ethnocultural Construction of Israel in the Hebrew Scripture

As is commonly known, the stories narrated in the Hebrew scripture find resonance in the cultural world of the ancient Near East. Scholars have demonstrated the multiple points of cultural intersection, exchange, borrowing and mutual crossfertilization among the cultural groups that inhabited the region at the time. The narratives demonstrate that Israel emerged in an exceedingly complex set of socioeconomic, cultural, and political changes; their newly born religious tradition shared much in terms of existing cultural elements, notions of agriculture, and religious practices with

---

6 In the words of N.T. Wright, when considering the impact of Roman culture on Paul's theology: "We must abandon any older views that try to drive a wedge between what we call 'religion' and what we call 'culture' or 'politics' or anything else ... [what] we require for a proper understanding is far more all-embracing vision, a worldview in which all human life is woven together into a (potentially) coherent whole" (N.T. Wright, *Paul and the Faithfulness of God*, 315).

the surrounding cultural groups.[7] Israel did not exist in a cultural or religious vacuum but in a world of cultural exchange. In fact, it is not difficult to see that the formation of Israel's cultural-religious self-perception and historical imaginary borrowed extensively from and also clashed with the neighboring ethnocultural groups.

According to Lucien Legrand, though Israel differentiated itself from the neighboring nations and expressed its identity in terms of opposition to the Canaanites, "they did it from within a common stock of shared cultural environment."[8] The names of people, of places, and the way in which stories are told, all bear the mark of the culturally mixed context including the plural religious traditions of the ancient Mediterranean and Mesopotamian world. Some examples of cultural and religious sources of crossfertilization are *The Epic of Atrahasis*, *The Enuma Elish,* and *The Epic of Gilgamesh.* These documents written before their biblical counterpart show the religious topography, cultural activities, events, beliefs, and perceptions of the peoples of the regions. They show compelling similarity with the Hebrew scripture accounts of creation, the garden of Eden, and the flood. Other examples of cultural mixing included the resonance between Israel's Torah (the Law) and the Babylonian Hammurabi's Code;[9] the adaptation of an old Canaanite hymn to the storm god Baal in Psalm 29; and the striking parallels between Israelite covenants and ancient Near Eastern treaties.[10]

---

7   Lucien Legrand, *The Bible on Culture: Belonging or Dissenting?* (Maryknoll, NY: Orbis Books, 2000), 4.

8   Legrand, *The Bible on Culture*, 6. According to Legrand, Hebrews and Canaanites had a common stock of language and world vision. The cultural commonalities between these groups is astounding. Archaeology shows that there is structural similarity between the Jerusalem temple and those temples found in Meggido, Lachish, Beth-Shan and Arad. Apart from the "absence of idols, the *cult* performed in the Yahwist temple(s) had much in common with the Canaanite ritual" (Ibid., 12). All this to say, Legrand claims, that Israel and Canaan shared an extensive common cultural and religious background, and that in terms of religious tradition, "Israel shared in the fundamental experience of the Semitic world. Israel did not invent a new God" (Ibid., 14).

9   Of course, there is a great deal of originality of the Hebrew law-code. Legrand reminds us that the development of Hebrew Law did not involve borrowing from the Canaanites because they did not have a law-code. The Hebrew law-code therefore had the specific stamp of its faith vision as "Israel took part of the noble quest for justice, which characterized the culture of Western Asia" (Legrand, *The Bible on Culture*, 11). We may conclude, however, that the similarities between ancient laws and the Hebrew codes of the Pentateuch correspond with similar concerns for the same problems often treated in identical ways in other law codes.

10   René López, "Israelite Covenants in the Light of Ancient Near Eastern Covenants (Part 2 of 2)," *CTS* 10 (Spring 2004): 72–106.

Noting the similarities and cultural crossfertilization allow us to see how the Levant region was a place of rich intercultural exchange. It also makes more evident the cultural rupture that Israel underwent in the process of self-formation as a people. As Israel emerged, ethnic and cultural identity played a fundamental role in the process of distinguishing Israelites from the surrounding groups. As Legrand points out, Canaan stood for what Israel rejected in the Semitic cultural background from which it originated. The antagonism was not only religious in nature,

> it "covered all aspects of human life," from family life to social and political organization, from structures of ownership to faith and rituals. It extended even to culinary matters in the case of food taboos, which are also important forms of cultural assertion. It was the confrontation of two cultures, or rather the encounter between a counterculture and an established culture.[11]

Not surprisingly, the Hebrew scripture narratives show a dynamic process of exchange and cross-fertilization and one that was deeply conflicted. In the way Israel related to the neighboring nations, we encounter "the puzzling tangle of intercultural dependence and counterculture, of osmosis and protests, of a shared common stock carrying an inborn conflict, of a community of life permeated with the acute tension of ongoing confrontation."[12] Ezekiel's 16:3 serves as a reminder that Israel's ancestry and birth "were in the land of the Canaanites; your father was an Amorite and your mother a Hittite." It elucidates the context of strong tensions and sometimes war within which Israel's ethnocultural identity was formed. The stories demonstrate the shifting and unstable nature of the process of culturalization as radical changes, internal reconfigurations, and profound rethinking ensued, forcing the cultural imagination of Israel to change, at times radically.[13]

---

11   Legrand, *The Bible on Culture*, 15.

12   Ibid., 16.

13   According to Legrand, Israel was in constant tension with the neighboring nations, at times elevated to holy wars, as can be found in the books of Deuteronomy, Joshua and Judges. He notes that those books express Israel's realization of the profound incompatibility with the religious perspectives of the other nations. The religious vision was not based on abstract theological notions, he claims. At the same time, he insists that the "opposition of Israel to Canaan was not mere 'war of religion.'" The complexity of the issues is based on the fact that these was not just one religion facing another. Rather, "the conflict was cultural; it implied all the economic, social, political and religious dimension of [their cultural tradition]" (Legrand, *The Bible on Culture*, 7). It was a clash of civilizations!

I mention these few well-known instances as reminders of the dynamic processes of cultural exchange and inter-mixture that took place among these cultural groups. My intention is simply to chart in broad strokes how cultural elements were deployed even though religious issues were the expressed primary concern of the authors. One must keep in mind that these Hebrew scripture passages are also part of larger complex oral and literary traditions; that there are many multilevel debates concerning their inter-pretation, their formation, the different oral and textual traditions reflected in the text, the processes of transmission, and many other factors. These factors are also part of the complex process of culturalization. In order to further explore the intersection between the cultural, religious/faith tra-ditions, and theological reflections, let us look at some specific examples in which the authors of these passages drew on their cultural resources to make sense of human existence, justify particular social structures, and articulate their faith in YHWH.

In the particular moments I discuss we can see how cultural processes play a crucial role in the naming of animals and plants and finding a mate in the first and second creation accounts (Gen 1–3); the inclusion of the biolog-ical dimension of the cultural in the establishment of the covenant between God and Abraham starting in Genesis 12; the linguistic side to cultural and clan conflict in Judges 12; the problem of intermarriage in Ezra (9–10) and Nehemiah (13); and demands of internal marital cultural conventions in Israel in Ruth. As these examples will show, the intersection between the cultural and the religious crosses multiple dimensions of life. They demon-strate that questions of the cultural mark the biological aspects of human existence, help define the boundaries of groups' identities, and shape the conflict between groups impacting even their linguistic and marital areas of life.

The Cultural in the Creation Accounts

Let us begin with the book of Genesis and consider two examples that relate to the relation between humans and the divine, the naming of the animals and the creation of a mate. The narrative in chapter 2 describes God's creative act of making all animals, "the beasts in the field and all the birds of the air" (2: 19).[14] The theologian imagines the man as collaborator with God in the creative act, which results in a twofold cultural and creative activity: one, the naming of all living animals, and two, finding a mate for the man. Behind the narrative

---

14   Unless otherwise indicated all quotes from the Bible are from the New International
       Version.

is the author's theological understanding that part of the divine creative act is in turn to engage human creative activity, concretely expressed in the creative act of naming and finding a mate for the man; both of which are culturally informed and culturally bound activities.[15]

We know already that Genesis 1:27 (and 5:2) describes humanity as including both the male and female. The degree to which sexuality is socially and culturally constructed is a matter of debate today, but for the author of the first Genesis account, humanity encompasses both sexes.[16] I note that the pericope does not explicitly assign "gendered" differences or roles until after the "fall." The cultural mandate to "Be fruitful and increase in number; fill the earth and subdue it. Rule[17] over the fish of the sea and the birds of the air and over every living creature that moves on the ground" (1:28) is but a matter-of-fact description of what is necessary for the continuation of the human species.[18]

While chapter 1 of Genesis shows how the author used cultural descriptors to describe how he imagined the divine creative act, the author of the second creation account starting in Genesis two reveals more explicitly the impact of cultural notions and, along with them, complex processes of gendering. Chapter 2 and three serve explicitly to create the cultural groundwork for the

---

15   Gianfranco Ravasi reminds us that for the author of the Genesis account, at creation there is an alliance between God and the man, in the same way that Israel would be God's allied in Sinai desert. As far as Ravasi is concerned, the narrative also interwoven with yet another cultural activity, namely, work. Inspired by the narrative he writes: "es preciso celebrar una especie de liturgia del trabajo, dirigida por el Señor del cosmos." (Gianfranco Ravasi, *Guía espiritual del Antiguo Testamento: El libro de Génesis* [*1–11*] [Ciudad Nueva, Madrid: Editorial Herder, 1992], 75).

16   Donald M. Joy, "Toward a Symbolic Revival: Creation Revisited," *Religious Education* 80, no. 3 (Summer 1985): 399–412. According to Claus Westermann, "This is what human existence means and what human institutions and structures show. Every theoretical and institutional separation of man and woman, every deliberate detachment of male from female, can endanger the very existence of humanity as determined by creation" (Claus Westermann, *Genesis 1–11: A Commentary*, trans. John J. Scullion [Minneapolis, MN: Augsburg Publishing House, 1984], 160).

17   I have no intention to revisit or endorse here disputed notions of "dominion" and the enormous cost such (mis)interpretation has meant for creation. I only mean to show that the authors of these passages are already conditioned by their middle eastern cultural tradition.

18   I concur with Westermann who notes that the blessing is effective for all living creatures: "This blessing does not give humans any advantage over the animals; it is the power of fertility that makes the continuance of the species possible, as the words of blessing say unequivocally" (Westermann, *Genesis 1.11*, 160).

division of humanity into genders, roles and differences which are located in God's handiwork. The Genesis theologian seems to imply that the gender roles (male: till the land; female: bear children) emanate from God and not necessarily as a result of their act of "disobedience." However, after the fall in Genesis 3, the collaborative and creative role of humanity is redefined; male and female identities are tied to specific sociocultural roles. There is a sense in which the author is validating gendered divisions and protecting gender social structures by ascribing them to God. The theology of this second creation account serves to enforce the cultural patriarchal structures and male privilege that one encounters in the rest of the Genesis (and the rest of the Bible) story.

Despite the "disobedience" described in chapter 3, the care of God for humanity is still affirmed though it is significantly redefined. The Genesis theologian wants us to think that as the father of creation God enters into cultural activities on behalf of Adam and Eve. After the "transgression," both become aware of their nakedness. In passing, I note that awareness and shame are culturally learned. To resolve the situation, we are told that God clothed them with animal skin (3:21). By implication the author provokes the readers to trace the origins of clothing back to God.[19] He makes God the one who fabricates something out of available material, an action humans mimic as they engage the activity of work.[20] The passage is interesting because it places "manual labor" as part of the divine creative act. The narrative also points to a theology of divine caring; God's protective care accompanies Adam and Eve even as it puts distance between humanity and God.[21] The expression of divine care and protection is concretized in the production of a cultural item, clothing. In these instances—the naming of animals, the setting of gendered structures, and the making of clothes—one sees the interconnectedness between the creation theology of the author and the culturally shaped perceptions of the time. These aspects are certainly part of the complex processes of cultural formation. The narrative opens up the liminal space between ideas about the divine (however incipient in the story), processes of cultural formation, theological and cultural ideas for the organization of societies, the creation of

---

19   Ravasi, *Guía espiritual del Antiguo Testamento*, 115.

20   According to Westermann, this part of the story must be a later insertion of another tradition. Nevertheless, he claims, "The statement retains its meaning in the context; the last action of the creator toward his creature before expelling him from the garden is an action of care and concern" (Westermann, *Genesis 1.11*, 269).

21   Westermann, *Genesis 1.11*, 269.

cultural artifacts, and the deployment of cultural elements to communicate-narrate the human-divine relationship.

The Cultural Content in the Covenant with Abraham

Another example replete with multiple meanings is the establishment of a covenant between Abraham and God. The story takes as point of departure the divine promise of prosperity and the formation of a great nation by Abraham's offspring (Gen 12). Soon after, the promise is amended to also include land as well as an amplification of the earlier idea of Israel as a "great nation" for the progeny to many nations (13:14–18).[22] The covenant eventually received concrete expression through God's act of name-changing of Abram and Sarai to Abraham and Sarah and in the practice of circumcision. Circumcision is crucial here for a number of reasons. One, it materially signifies the establishment of the covenant between Abraham's seed and God. Two, it preserves the covenant's male centred character because its symbol and seal is carried by men in their bodies just as the fulfillment and preservation of the promise in women is enacted through their ability to carry male children.[23] And three, circumcision eventually becomes an essential aspect of the people of Israel's ethnocultural identity. Here identity goes beyond the merely sanguineous, since children who are not direct descendants of Abraham, but identify with Israel are required to also carry the sign of the covenant (17:12). Circumcision as ritual takes on a double dynamic of inclusion into the covenant with God and into ethnic Israel. In the rest of the Hebrew scripture, circumcision gains added meanings (e.g., (un)circumcision of the heart marks people's devotion or lack of devotion/obedience to God) but this double entendre—distinguishing the "people of Israel" from all other ethnocultural groups and in identifying their covenant with God as "God's people"—remains constant.

For our purposes, the practice of circumcision is compelling because it marks the biological aspect of culturalization. Circumcision is a religious act fraught with ethnocultural signifiers, not the least of which is the physiological dimension. The example of circumcision demonstrates the interwoven character of culturalization; when biologized it has a profound impact shaping the very way bodies and the bodily are understood, perceived, and constructed. Moreover, circumcision as

---

22   According to the story, when God enters into a covenant with Abraham God reiterates the promise of land and multitude of offspring.

23   There are many issues related to gender in these passages. For an exploration of them in terms of translation in the Genesis account in chapters 1–4 see Helen Kraus, *Gender Issues in Ancient and Reformation Translation of Genesis 1–4* (Oxford, UK: Oxford University Press, 2011).

a cultural-religious act serves to enforce the culturally patriarchal and androcen-
tric character of this covenant. Once again, the biblical narrative enforces the idea
of the interconnectedness between the religious and the cultural in such a way
that one conditions the outcomes of the other and vice-versa.

The Linguistic Side to the Cultural

As I stated in chapter 1, processes of cultural formation are fluid and carry internal contestation and conflict. The complex processes of Israel's cultural formation
are revealed by a crucial aspect of Jephthah's story in the book of Judges chapter
twelve which provides a good case in point. The account tells us of the multiple
clan differences internal strife and discriminatory acts between different groups
from among the people of Israel (13). Jephthah, the "champion" and defender of
the people of Israel is threatened by his cousins and he struggles to hold power.[24]
The narrative describes an internal division and puts forth questions of identity.
On one hand, the people of Gilead are described as "renegades from Ephraim and
Manasseh" (12:4).[25] The phrase questions the status of the Gileadites and suggests an identity as outsiders or refugees, not "original" to the area.[26] As a result,
they decide to exact revenge on the people of Ephraim by entering into battle
with them (12: 3.5). On the other hand, Gileadites devise a clever, culturally identifiable strategy to distinguish them from the Ephraimites. Here the regional dia-
lect differences stand out, since the Gileadites would not have been able to tell the
differences between them and the Ephraimites by ways of physical features. They
opt for obvious linguistic differences instead and focus on the (mis)pronunciation
of the *Sh* in Shibboleth, which identifies the Ephraimites as foreigners.[27]

Today "shibboleth" is used to point to specific customs, principles, or beliefs
that distinguish a particular class or group of people, but in the narrative, it

---

24   Susan Niditch, *Judges: A Commentary* (Louisville, KY: Westminster, John Knox, 2008), 137.
25   In his examination of the same pericope in Judges, Victor Matthews notes that Jephthah
      was already identified as a foreigner by his half-brothers because he was the son of a
      prostitute. They were unwilling to share their inheritance with him because he was born
      outside of the normal inheritance pattern. It is very likely that tension between Jephthah
      and the Ephraimites had to do with Jephthah's unwillingness to share part of the spoils
      after defeating the Ammonites. See Victor H. Matthews, *Judges and Ruth* (Cambridge,
      UK: Cambridge University Press, 2004), 117–18.
26   Niditch, *Judges*, 137.
27   According to Susan Niditch, the issue with foreign language occurs in other places in the
      Old Testament. In passages such as Ezekiel 3:5 foreigners are described as people with
      obscure speech and difficult language. In Jeremiah 5:15 they are described as people who
      have a language they do not know. More to the point, those that cannot be trusted are also
      those who speak an alien tongue in Isaiah 28:11. See her *Judges*, 139.

refers more directly to the linguistic nuances, accents, and regional inflections by which people come to be distinguished, and through which questions of identity get negotiated. In the case of the Ephraimites, it was this distinct culturally identifiable mark, this "simple" test word which forty-two thousand Ephraimites were unable to pronounce resulting in their death.[28] From the perspective of culturalization, it is clear that notions of identity and insider/outsider are fluid and in constant change. The multilevel boundaries that are always actively negotiated and in tension are at times momentarily "resolved" by way of clashes and sometimes bloody encounters. This particular incident shows an aspect of the internal negotiations that take place between insiders, and how the boundaries insider-outsider were constituted as Israel's cultural identity developed.

The Cultural in Marriage Customs

In the following two examples, I show how cultural issues regulate family relations in the context of inter-ethnic encounters. The first example can be interpreted as potentially ambiguously positive-liberative in the story of Ruth. The second example can be misconstrued as having more xenophobic implications in the book of Ezra. Here I want to warn against anachronistic misinterpretations of Ezra while, at the same time, remind modern readers of the perils of national/identity formation as a potentially exclusionary act. The fact that these two threads are in the Bible also point to the complex process of culturalization.

The book of Ruth expands our understanding of the processes of culturalization of Israel. It reveals some of the multiple levels of complexity as the people of Israel engaged other groups. The entire book provides a wealth of material for exploring the permeability of the boundaries of cultures. For the purpose of my discussion here, I want to focus on the intersection of the religious activity of "redemption" and how such a notion gets culturalized in the process of establishing responsibilities both between people of the same genealogical tree, and in the cultural opening-up through the welcoming of a foreigner.[29] The story revolves around the Moabite "faceless" woman named Ruth,[30] who has decided to accompany her Israelite ex-mother-in-law Naomi

---

28   Ryan Roger, *Judges*, A New Bible Commentary (Sheffield, UK: Sheffield Phoenix Press, 2007), 94.

29   For a brief discussion of the role of the redeemer or goel in the Old Testament see Vanthanh Nguyen, "Dismantling Cultural Boundaries: Missiological Implications of Acts 10:1–11:18," *Missiology: An International Review* XI, no. 4 (October 2012): 455–66.

30   Much has been written about the fact that Ruth remains faceless in the account. Her physical features are not mentioned in the narrative, as was commonly done concerning women. For instance, Sarah, Rebeka and Rachel were described as beautiful, while

back to the land of her ancestors. As the narrative unfolds, Ruth is said to make the heart-wrenching decision to leave behind the world she knew and accompany Naomi to Bethlehem. As a widow who does not have many resources, Naomi finds out that she still has distant relatives. Two themes emerge in the story although not explicitly stated: One, the good treatment to foreigners as mandated by God in the Law (Ex. 22:21; Lev. 19:33; Deut. 10:19) is certainly at play here; and two, the people of Israel were also instructed not to exploit the poor (Lev. 25:35; 27:19). In fact, the poor, the widow, and the foreigner are included together when instructions against injustice are given in the Law (Deut 27: 19). Ruth and Naomi together represent these three groups as widows, poor women, and in the case of Ruth, a foreigner. So the nature of the narrative is such that it touches on very important divine (cultural) mandates set up to regulate the people of Israel at the time, leaving the reader expecting to see how this entire saga will unfold.

Let us briefly consider the well-known dilemma: Boaz is willing to step up to the plate and marry Ruth and provide offspring in memory of Elimelech and his Sons (Deut. 25:5), but he is also aware that he is not the next in line (Ruth 3:12). Although he is obviously interested in Ruth, he wants to follow the proper cultural-religiously established protocol. The tension between what is divinely mandated duty and the observance of the culturally required public formalization becomes evident. The nearest kinsman-redeemer is willing to buy the piece of property from Naomi and by extension from Ruth (4:4). But when he is told by Boaz that the land comes attached with responsibility to Ruth and because of the prescribed religious and cultural duty to provide offspring to Elimelech and preserve his name (4:5), the kinsman-redeemer backs out. It is unclear whether the perceived risk by the nearer kinsman-redeemer to his own state was related to the fact that Ruth was a foreigner. What is clear is that a public ceremony exposing his unwillingness for not "building up his brother's house" is carried out which traditionally included the cultural gestures of removing his sandals—and henceforth being known as "the house of

---

Leah was described as having weak eyes (Gen. 29:17). In the case of Ruth nothing is said of her. For many feminists, this lack of physical description has been a source of celebration insofar as they interpret Ruth as establishing her sense of womanhood on the basis of other characteristics and not the conventional aesthetic requirements of beauty. For example, Michael Maswari and Rachel Havrelock write: "Ruth rescues women from patriarchal scrutiny as much as she saves Naomi from anguish. Her facelessness allows a break from tradition which equated women's value with their beauty" (Mishael Maswari and Rachel S Havrelock, *Women in the Biblical Road: Ruth, Naomi, and the Female Journey* [Lanham, MD: University Press of America, 1996], 169). See also pages 155–190 in Ibid.

the unsandalled one"—and having Ruth spit in his face to shame and humil-
iate him (Deut. 25:5–10).[31] Although the spitting is not recorded, we are told
that the relative did remove his sandal (4:8). Boaz then marries Ruth, preserving the name of the lineage of Elimelech, and fulfilling his divine duty to his
relatives (4:9–13).

The intersection between the cultural and religious dimensions cannot be
overstated in the story of Ruth. The story also reveals the dynamic and changing character of culturalization in general and the porous nature of identity
formation. By the end of the story, Ruth and Boaz are included in the ancestral
line of David (4:22). By the time one gets to the New Testament, Ruth is celebrated as ancestress in the distinguished lineage of Jesus along with Rahab, her
identity fully transformed (Matt. 1:5).

The last example I offer from the Hebrew scripture is the question-crisis of
mixed marriages in the books of Ezra (9–10) and Nehemiah (13:23). As generally known, the books record the painstaking process of rebuilding the city of
Jerusalem as remnants of Israel. There are enormous commonalities between
both accounts: both books include a narrative that deals with the question of
mixed marriages, both mention radical measures toward endogamy at the end
of each book, and both make the matter with mixed marriages part of the larger
concern for the idolatry of other nations and the Israelite sin of unfaithfulness
through marriage to foreign women. But there are some crucial differences
as well. Mixed marriages in Ezra relate not necessarily to our contemporary
notions of "racialized prejudices." Rather, they relate to the complex process
of asserting differences in order to exert control over the region and establish/
maintain/construct the lines of ethnic boundaries.[32] Racialized differences are
being created and religion plays a central role in this negotiation. In Ezra, marriage with other peoples is perceived not so much as a biological-racialized
threat but as potentially irreconcilable cultural (and religious) differences.
Since the racialized cultural and the religious are so intertwined, intermar-
riages could potentially signify the eventual undermining of the people's own
ethnocultural traditions and religious imaginary. Attitudes of cultural and

---

31   Many scholars have explored the possible connections between the removal of the san-
      dal and humiliation of the kinsman-redeemer. For a thorough study on the topic and
      good explanation of the connections between the removal of the sandal and the humil-
      iation/punishment of the kinsman-redeemer see Calum M. Carmichael, "A Ceremonial
      Crux: Removing a Man's Sandal as a Female Gesture of Contempt," *JBL* 96, no. 3
      (1977): 321–36.

32   Katherine E. Southwood, *Ethnicity and the Mixed Marriage Crisis in Ezra 9–10: An
      Anthropological Approach* (Oxfor, UK: Oxford University Press, 2012), 125.

racialized xenophobia expressed in the books expose the nexus between the desire to reclaim Israel's sense of identity as people along with their cultural traditions. The concern about miscegenation with neighboring groups relates to the perceived long-standing differences as well as the reminder of the emotional trauma/memory of historical exile embodied in those who returned and those who stayed.

Meanwhile, in Nehemiah it is unclear what will happen with people who marry foreign women, but the taboo against it is made clear.[33] The prior rejection of intermarriage with cousins who are Ammonites and Moabites (Gen 19–37ff) is connected to their centuries-old unwelcoming attitude "because they had not met the Israelites with food and water but had hired Balaam to call a curse down on them" (13:2). As to the women from Ashdod, they may have been considered descendants of the earlier enemies of the Israelites, the Philistines.[34] The responsibility for purity falls upon the Levites who are instructed to purify themselves "of everything foreign" (13:30). Yet, the book comes to an abrupt ending leaving the reader wondering about what happened. Curiously, Nehemiah centres on the intersection between the "holy" character of the people of Israel as being "set apart," over and against implicit "other" cultural elements that threaten it. The narrative tells us that Nehemiah was enraged when he discovered that half of the children of the men of Judah "spoke the language of Ashdod or the language of one of the other peoples, and did not know how to speak the language of Judah" (13:24). What becomes clear is that there is an intimate connection between religious affiliations, devotion, and cultural elements. The Ezra-Nehemiah account of the conflict between Israel and other groups helped crystallize the ethnocultural identity of the returnees.[35] In this case, the linguistic-cultural element makes concrete the expression of both religious faith as well as extreme religious zeal.

---

33   There is much debate as to whether these stories are two different accounts or part of a single tradition and that is being reproduced differently by Ezra and Nehemiah. According to R. J. Coggins, "it seems more likely that one tradition concerning the putting-away of foreign women has been told in varying forms" (R. J. Coggins, *The Books of Ezra and Nehemiah: A Commentary* [Cambridge, UK: Cambridge University Press, 1976], 143).

34   Coggins, *The Books of Ezra and Nehemiah*, 143.

35   Jonathan Dyck engages in a comparative study of the various ethnocultural and religious identity dynamics at work as the people of Israel confronted diaspora. According to him, Ezra-Nehemiah displays a "vertical" construction of identity while Chronicles offers a levelling "horizontal" view of Israelite identity. As he sees it, problems of identity were front-and-center as those in the diaspora wrestled between assimilation into or separation from the neigbouring ethnocultural groups. See Jonathan E. Dyck, "The Ideology of Identity in Chronicles," in *Etnicity and the Bible*, ed. Mark Brett (Leiden, NL: Brill, 1996), 89–116.

Intrinsic to the decision of the priestly class to separate themselves from their foreign wives was the conscious awareness of their own identity as "holy people." Nāsili Vaka'uta reminds us that there are several ways in which notions of uncleanness and impurity operate in this passage. His discussion raises at least three ways in which these can be interpreted; the people of the land as untouchables, ceremonial impurity, and sexual, ritual, and geographical uncleanness. According to him, these three meanings have been loaded by the "chiefs" "on to the phrase 'peoples of the land,' providing ... a strong basis for their objection to inter-marriage" between the men among the returned exiles and the women of the peoples of the land.[36] The historical connection to Solomon in Nehemiah 13:26 adds a level of meaning concerning idolatry. But as Katherine Southwood explains, the language of the "elected" status of Israel operates front and centre as the "motivation for avoiding intermarriage (Deut. 7:3–4), or any alliances with other nations ..."[37] Moreover, by turning away and serving "other gods" of the other nations, "Israel would compromise its 'holy' status (Deut. 7:4–5)."[38] Thus, she claims that, Ezra seems to have conflated these notions of holiness and applied them to all of Israel to the extent that they ought to regulate their personal lives in the fashion that is required from the priests. In the Ezra story, resonating with Nehemiah, "holiness" bears multiple levels of applicability, including to the ethnocultural boundaries of Israel. As Israel wrestled with what it meant to be an Israelite, part of "the holy people," the construction of ethnic and cultural boundaries became necessary in order to navigate and negotiate such complex and contested process in such a culturally diverse context. Stated another way, the deeply religious meaning of "the holy people" of Israel received its concrete expression in the creation of cultural boundaries as markers to distinguish them from other groups.

The Ezra-Nehemiah passage has been a source of great debate in contemporary cultural, identity, and race theories. However, I agree with Vaka'uta in that we must make a distinction between the contextualization of the biblical text and the contextualization of biblical interpretation.[39] In other words, it would be a mistake to take the claims for "separateness" and insistence on endogamy in Ezra and Nehemiah, as ancient examples of outright xenophobic prejudices which focus on racial purity as understood today. For example, there

---

36   Nâsili Vaka'uta, *Reading Ezra 9–10 Tu'a-Wise: Thinking Biblical Interpretation in Oceania* (Atlanta, GA: Society of Biblical Literature, 2011), 126.

37   Southwood, *Ethnicity and the Mixed Marriage Crisis in Ezrah 9–10*, 126.

38   Ibid.

39   See Vaka'uta, *Reading Ezra 9–10 Tu'a-Wise*.

are biblical passages in which the Israelites welcome those who voluntarily are prepared to adopt their religious and cultural traditions (Ezra 6:21).[40] Katherine Southwood has convincingly argued that this debate is far more complicated and nuanced and cannot be reduced to contemporary racialized concerns.[41] That said, it is possible that the Israelites in the story might have had sentiments toward racialized purity embedded in the cultural boundaries they established which rejected other peoples. However, we cannot directly infer it from this passage. For our purposes, the illustration of culturalization in biblical narratives, the Ezra-Nehemiah crisis of intermarriage displays yet another example of the protracted process of the construction of the ethnic and cultural identities of Israel as they came into contact, clashed, and interacted with other groups of the region. The intention here it is not to either condemn or condone the events described in the narrative, it is rather to elucidate how the intimate interconnectedness between the religious and the cultural play out. Here the complex negotiations along with contested notions of faith in YHWH, ethnicity, cultural processes and symbols, as well as how to express one's devotion toward God are made manifest.

These incidents of mixed marriages could yield much more material for analysis about social constructions, the arbitrary nature of ethnic and cultural boundaries, and the power differentials in the process of negotiating such boundaries. However, I cannot address those issues here, without digressing significantly. In addition, the passages could also be examined from the point of view of gender analysis. In fact, others have engaged in such detailed analyses of gender concerns.[42] I do wish to note, however, that the issue of gender here relates to the process of culturalization I have been describing. It is women who are made responsible for the straying of Israelite men away from their religious and cultural tradition and toward "idolatry." The passages suggest that cultural concerns, like Israelite identity, are also at stake. From a gendered perspective, the importance of women in the passing down of religious traditions stands out; women are the responsible bearers and communicators of the culture of their ethnic group for the coming generations. The contrast between the children who do not speak the language of their Jewish fathers but that of their "foreign" mothers (13:24) highlights this very point. In the end, the abandoning of their wives and children by Israelite men, as instructed

---

40   Coggins, *The Books of Ezra and Nehemiah*, 56.

41   Southwood, *Ethnicity and the Mixed Marriage Crisis in Ezrah 9–10*.

42   For a gendered reading of foreign women in Ezra-Nehemiah see Harold C. Washington, "Israel's Holy Seed and the Foreign Women of Ezra-Nehemiah: A Kristevan Reading," *Biblical Interpretation* 11, no. 3/4 (2003): 427–37.

by Ezra, raises many questions about the patriarchal nature of the sociocultural structures as this "remnant" of Israel was being reconstituted.

The mixed-marriages concern and the extreme measures in the favor of endogamy as described in Ezra-Nehemiah contrast with the story of Ruth's concern and care for widows and foreigners. These two themes are at odds with each other, but they appropriately exemplify how the culturalization process conveys enormous internal tensions and contradictions.

The Hebrew scripture is certainly the record of a centuries-long set of historical events, and of the social, political, economic, religious, and human factors and conditions that contributed to those events. As I have been insisting, the Hebrew scripture also functions as the cultural memory of the people of Israel. As such, it shows how, over time, the people's understandings of God became culturalized in the very fabric of Judaism and the identity of the Hebrew people. The biblical text, when studied from the perspective of the complex and dynamic process of culturalization, yields multiple instances in which we can discern the complexity behind the contested and changing nature, the instability and the porous character in the formation of cultures and subsequently religious practices as cultural phenomena, in this case, the cultural and religious tradition of the people of Israel.

Religious Cultures and Cultural Intersections in the New Testament

Over the years, the religious culture of Israel changed and modified in each new historical circumstance. New movements were born, including Christianity which was one of the movements that emerged from within Judaism and contributed to profound cultural and religious (re)configurations. As the Christian movement developed, ethnic and cultural identity played a central role. The affirmation of Jesus Jewish identity in the gospels sheds lights on how Judaism took seriously the notion of ethnicity, "and the messianic movement associated with Jesus of Nazareth was not exception to this rule."[43]

Christianity brought about an opening-up to Gentiles, which was accompanied with profound transformations to the Judaic religious cultural tradition of the first Christians and the religious landscape of the time. In the context of a region which was culturally plural at the time of Jesus, the New Testament is a retelling of how Christianity—as a sect of Judaism—moved away from the monocultural impetus of its religious parent.

---

43   David Sim, "Christianity and Ethnicity in the Gospel of Matthew," in *Ethnicity and the Bible*, ed. Mark Brett (Leiden, NL: Brill, 1996), 171.

In this section, my goal is not merely to emphasize the intersection of multiple cultural traditions in the context of first century Palestine. Others have already documented that in great detail.[44] I also do not intend to engage in a comprehensive analysis of each of the passages I mention. Rather, I use them as concrete examples of the complexities of cultural exchanges as part of the processes of culturalization. In broad strokes, I bring attention to the ways in which the text itself unveils the confluence, intersection, and tensions among the multiple ethnocultural traditions that inhabited the region. In other words, I enquire how these exchanges and clashes at the everyday level got woven into the larger story of the people of Israel, the Jesus story, and the emergence of Christianity.

The writings of the New Testament emerge at the very juncture which marks the emergence of a new Jewish "faction" and its transformation into Christianity. As part of the complexity of this new context, and precisely because the New Testament includes "Christian" documents, it is important to acknowledge that the images, language, theological terms and concepts in the narrative still bear the cultural and historical heritage of the religious culture of the people of Israel. At the same time, and due to the constant interchange and clash of ethnocultural groups in the region, the reader also encounters numerous instances in which ideas, notions, and images from Greek, Roman, and other cultural traditions appear. These dynamic cultural crossfertilizations which occurred in the ancient Near East find expression in the New Testament as well. One key example of these cultural exchanges is the fact that—as a result of the Hellenization that took place—the books and epistles in the New Testament were written in Greek, not in Hebrew or Aramaic. Greek philosophical and mythological ideas gained currency and were deployed in the process of articulating and thinking theologically about the meaning of the gospel message (e.g., John 1:1 notion of Logos, Rev. 1:18, 6:8 the notion of Hades; 2 Pet. 2:4 the notion of Tartarus). Their differences are marked in the text: "Jews demand signs and Greeks desire wisdom, but we proclaim Christ crucified ..." (1 Cor 1:22). Moreover, living under a state of occupation by the Roman empire the New Testament authors and narratives make use of Roman cultural imagery and ideas (e.g., centurion in Mat. 8:5, 8,13, Mark 15:44–45, Acts 10:1, 22; soldier in Phi. 2:25, 2Ti. 2:3–4; Armor in Rom. 13:12, Eph. 6:11; legion in Mark 5:9, 15; denarius in Mat. 20:2, 9–10, etc.), and work out theology in conversation with those cultural elements.

---

44   Richard A. Horsley, *Galilee: History, Politics, People* (Valley Forge, PA: Trinity Press International, 1995); Virgilio Elizondo, *Galilean Journey: The Mexican-American Promise* (Maryknoll, NY: Orbis Books, 1983).

In the New Testament, however, one finds much more than simple expressions of Greek or Roman ideas. The New Testament records show that first century Palestine had become the crossroads of multiple cultural and religious traditions, and as such was a culturally volatile context. Of course, the texts also illustrated some cultural conflicts that were centuries-old as they found new expressions in these culturally mixed contexts. But they also reflected new resulting clashes between ethnocultural and social groups, based on different ethnic, cultural, religious, and socially informed prejudices and discriminatory attitudes among the groups themselves (e.g., from Jews toward Samaritans and Greeks, and from Romans toward Jews). The ethnocultural and regional markers in the New Testament narrative are unavoidable: Greek (John 7:28, 12: 20), Syrophenician (Mark 7:26), Gadara (Mat. 8:28), Jerusalem, Judea, and the ends of the world (Acts 1:8). The complexity of the cultural milieus and differences among social groups trickle into the writings. Though differences of ethnic and cultural tradition, class and gender are not challenged or even dismissed in passages like Galatians 3:28 "There is no longer Jew nor Greek," for example, elsewhere cultural mixing and conflict are abundantly evident. In what follows, I illustrate the kind of multilevel cultural, ethnic, social, and religious clashes that are part of the complex processes of culturalization drawing on the following examples: the conversation of Jesus with the Samaritan woman in John 4; Jesus's exchange with the Syrophoenician woman in Mark 7:25–30 / Mat. 15:21–38; and Peter's "conversion" experience and interaction with Cornelius and his family in Acts 10.

The Cultural in Jesus and the Samaritan Woman

The conversation between the Samaritan woman and Jesus brings to mind the crisis of mixed marriages in Ezra-Nehemiah discussed earlier, and the problem of mixed children that were born from those unions. 2Kings 17 records the historical circumstances that brought about the ethnic, cultural, and religious tensions between the Jews and the Samaritans.[45] The old internal tensions and differences between religious "factions" seem to remain unresolved in the John passage, this time with added complexities. Jesus' unplanned visit through Samaria signals a cultural and religious shift and challenge to prevailing Jewish ideas about the Samaritans.

---

45   The mutual hatred of Jews and Samaritans intensified during the postexilic period as narrated by Ezra-Nehemiah, particularly when Zerubabel did not allow the Samaritans to help rebuild the Temple (Ezra 4). "So around 300 BCE the Samaritans built their own shrine on Mount Gerizim as a rival to the Temple in Jerusalem" (Teresa Okure, "Jesus and the Samaritan Woman [Jn 4:1–42] in Africa," *Theological Studies* 70 [2009]: 407).

The passage can be understood as an encounter between members of two colonized peoples[46] and a careful analysis shows that questions of ethnicity, gender, and cultural and religious tradition haunt their interaction.[47] At bottom, Teresa Okure claims, "the fulcrum ... of the entire episode between Jesus and the Samaritan woman is her discovery of who Jesus is."[48] Their conversation revolves around redrawing the shifting lines of the existing ethnocultural boundaries in a way that Jesus' identity is presented as ambiguous, moving from being explicitly Jewish to being incorporated among the Samaritans.[49] While Jesus can be said to represent the colonizer Jews, writes Sung Uk Lim, the woman's act of anti-colonial mimicry of mixing Jewish and Samaritan identity blurs the lines of distinction between them in a way that "the colonial authority of Jesus as the colonizer from the perspective of the Samaritans as the colonized is damaged."[50] There is tension in the act of mimicry in the story (4:40–42). The woman represents the Samaritans "who are Jews but not completely."[51] The Samaritans also claim to worship YHWH but are not part of mainstream Judaism. She too becomes the "missionary" to her own people, like Jesus, "but not completely."[52] In the process, Jesus' identity as the colonizer gets complexified through the invitation to stay with them (4:42). By the urge of the villagers, Jesus gets "Samaritanized;"[53] his unwillingness to exercise his social privileges gains him acceptance into the woman's ethnic group. As

---

46   Sung Uk Lim, "*Speak My Name*: Anti-Colonial Mimicry and the Samaritan Woman in John
       4:1–42," *Union Seminary Quarterly Review* 62, no. 3–4 (2010): 35–51.

47   Okure reminds us that Jesus' Galilean background suggests he had experience with
       being discriminated against and rejected. At the same time, she notes, Rabbis used to
       think of Samaritan women as perpetually unclean, a permanent source of uncleanness
       to their communities. See her "Jesus and the Samaritan Woman," 406–7. The "study of
       Jesus' encounter with the Samaritan woman, then, has surfaced their shared experiences
       of prejudice, racism, and sexism flowing from the social norms of their societies" (Ibid.,
       416). Indeed, argues Musa Dube, Jesus' act of entering the land reinscribes colonial rela-
       tions: the Samaritan woman and the Samaritan people must be entered, won and domes-
       ticated. See Musa Dube, "Reading for Decolonization (John 4.1–42)," in *Voices from the
       Margins*, R. S. Sugirtharajah (Maryknoll, NY: Orbis Books, 2006), 309.

48   Okure, "Jesus and the Samaritan Woman," 409.

49   Lim, "*Speak My Name*," 46.

50   Ibid., 47.

51   Ibid., 37.

52   There is a sense in which the woman reproduces colonizing relations by mimicking Jesus'
       missionary act. Dube is correct to note that when these passages are read as only promoting
       the missionary enterprise, they "hardly propose relations of liberating interdependence
       between races, cultures and genders" (Musa Dube, "Reading for Decolonization," 314).

53   Lim, "*Speak My Name*," 46.

Lim puts it, in this move the colonizer is assimilated into the colonized; Jesus embodies the colonizer and the colonized at the same time.[54]

Curiously enough, Jesus' identity is later challenged in relation to the Samaritans in John 8, where he is accused of being a Samaritan, an accusation which he does not refute. And in the other gospels, Jesus takes the Samaritans, the very people who are looked down upon by the Jews as object lessons of piety and devotion. The story of the good Samaritan in Luke 10:30–36 is a good example.

These postcolonial readings of Jesus' conversation with the Samaritan woman notwithstanding,[55] the story also demonstrates the intersection of cultural and ethnic identity and how these change, shift, and move in the everyday context. Moreover, it also shows that power cannot be removed from interethnic and cultural relations. For John's mainly Jewish audience, the jarring effect of the story is that the ethnocultural "outsiders" are elevated in dignity. The Samaritans are not required to relinquish or change their ethnocultural identity; they (the Jews) are required to change their perceptions of the Samaritans. Most importantly, the passage concretely shows the dynamic contested and porous character of cultures and ethnic identities as they get configured and reconfigured as part of the larger processes of culturalization.

The exchange between Jesus and the Syrophoenician woman (Mark 7:25–30) is even starker in its portrayal of the differences between the people of Israel and other groups. Many scholars have found great insights in this pericope, but they seem to agree that the exchange between Jesus and the woman reenacts the type of challenges concerning questions of ethnicity that faced the early church.[56] Jesus' crude remark "'First let the children eat all they want,' he told her, 'for it is not right to take the children's bread and toss it to their dogs'" (7:27) is certainly unsettling. Jesus' response makes clear that the Jews are placed in priority and the Gentiles are of lesser importance. Julien

---

54   Ibid., 50.

55   Postcolonial critical studies are a branch of cultural studies that help identify the power dynamics that impact social relations in a context of empire. In this pericope, the postcolonial vantage point enables us to see the social privilege ascribed to Jesus and how these are subverted in his interaction with the Samaritan woman and people.

56   For greater in-depth analysis of the pericope from different cultural and disciplinary perspectives see Alan H. Cadwallader, "When a Woman is a Dog: Ancient and Modern Ethology Meet the Syrophoenician Women," *The Bible and Critical Theory* 1, no. 4 (2005): 35.1–35.17; Surekha Nelavala, "Smart Syrophoenician Woman: A Dalit Feminist Reading of Mark 7:24–31," *Expository Times* 118, no. 2 (2006): 64–69; Julien C. H Smith, "The Construction of Identity in Mark 7:24–30: The Syrophoenician Woman and the Problem of Ethnicity," *Biblical Interpretation* 20 (2012): 458–81.

Smith correctly states that given the context of the pericope the readers expect the miracle to take place.[57] The simultaneous dynamic back-and-forth play of insider/outsider and the multiple ways in which people move in and out of ethnic and cultural boundaries becomes evident. On one hand, Jesus has crossed cultural, geographical and ethnic boundaries, and in doing so has become a foreigner himself; geographically the woman is the insider of her own story.[58] On the other hand, Jesus' slurs unmask his Jewish ethnocentric patriarchal gaze making it clear that the woman is a "triple outsider" because of gender, cultural-religious affiliation, and ethnicity.[59]

The woman's riposte is no less complex. On the face of it, she seems simple enough; she corrects Jesus by replying "'Yes, Lord' ... 'but even the dogs under the table eat the children's crumbs'" (7:28). According to Smith, however, there is a twofold dynamic at play in the text; while Jesus' slurs challenge the woman's expectations, the author also challenges the readers notions of ethnic identity.[60] Jesus' remarks are a riddle that the woman resolves with her reply, argues Smith, but the author also uses the story to suggest to "the reader that Jesus has now abolished *all* social and ethnic boundaries."[61] The woman "corrects" Jesus by turning his dismissal on its head and using it to her advantage.[62]

---

57 Smith, "The Construction of Identity in Mark 7:24–30," 465.

58 Many are the issues that stem from this encounter between Jesus and the Syrophoenician woman. As Nelavala Surekha asks, "What was Jesus' mission in the Gentile territory? Was it to break the boundaries between the Jews and the Gentiles? Is it a religious colonialism? Should he be blamed for religious invasion? Or, does Jesus' crossing the border represent his magnanimity to include Gentiles into salvation history?" (Nelavala, "Smart Syrophoenician Woman," 68). These and other questions highlight the complexity of this passage.

59 Elisabeth Schüssler Fiorenza, *But She Said: Feminist Practices of Biblical Interpretation* (Boston: Beacon Press, 1992), 12. Smith notes that the passage reveals common ethnic slurs used by Jews to speak of Gentiles. But the apparent unwillingness of Jesus to break the boundaries by administering healing to those outside the ethnic boundaries of Israel must be interpreted in light of his (Jesus) own crossing "from the region of Galilee into the region of Tyre [which] represents a crossing of the boundary between the familiar and the strange. Jesus' crossing of social and geographical boundaries to come to Tyre signals that he is making 'an onslaught upon boundaries, because he sees holiness as a reality which spreads cleanness'" (Smith, "The Construction of Identity in Mark 7:24–30," 468).

60 Smith, "The Construction of Identity in Mark 7:24–30," 476.

61 Ibid., 477.

62 The shift of attention from Jesus to the woman is crucial here. There is a play on words undetected in the translation; Jesus (the logos of God) is not identified as speaking logos. Rather, it is the woman, with her reply, who is identified as speaking "logos." See Cadwallader, "When a Woman is a Dog."

Instead of entertaining Jesus' insult, she plays smart and teaches him a lesson from the experience of the disenfranchised: "the excluded are able to eat
even from the leftovers." Surekha is correct in insisting that liberation does not
occur unless the oppressor is reconciled. Jesus' reaction and response show his
moment of conversion to the cause of the woman and her daughter. "The evangelizer was evangelized."[63] The woman speaks from the spaces of exclusion;
she challenges the cultural, religious and ideological cannon within which
they are perpetuated and prevail. As a result, her daughter is freed from the
destructive spirit.[64] Seen from the perspective of the implied Christian readers, claims Smith, people do not have to abandon their ethnic identity in order
to adopt the Gospel; "there is no room for thinking that the gospel is to be
circumscribed within a community of a particular ethnic identity."[65] Similarly,
the passage provides an example for subaltern groups, cultures and ethnicities
to interrogate the assumed, often unquestioned, claims to entitlement in any
given cultural context. They also show that Christianity changes overtime and
according to the cultural contexts that adopt it; here the Son of God himself
changes radically.

The Cultural and Notions of Alterity

Similar dynamics of ethnocetrism and discrimination toward other ethnocultural groups by the Jews appear in the interaction between Peter and Cornelius
the centurion in Acts 10. It is important to note that, the notion of ethnic privilege never led the Jews to prevent Gentiles from converting to Judaism.[66] Yet,
David Sims points out that while most Jews of the period were content to live
among larger populations of Gentiles, "they took steps to restrict their contact with Gentiles in order to preserve their social and ethnic identity."[67] One
crucial activity in this regard was the unwillingness to share meals with their
Gentile neighbors. Thus, consistent with those practices, the story in Acts is
framed around questions of (im)purity and (un)cleanness, reflecting how the

---

63   Nelavala, "Smart Syrophoenician Woman," 69.

64   Fiorenza, *But She Said*, 12.

65   Smith, "The Construction of Identity in Mark 7:24–30," 479.

66   Sim, "Christianity and Ethnicity," 174.

67   Sim, "Christianity and Ethnicity," 173. According to David Esler, for Jewish people, eating
      was "fraught with the possibility of breaching the purity code, one of the most crucial
      aspects of the Mosaic Law for the maintenance of the separate identity of the Jewish
      ethnos" (Philip F. Esler, "Group Boundaries and Intergroup Conflict in Galatians: A
      New Reading of Gal. 5: 13–6:10," in *Etnicity and the Bible*, ed. Mark Brett [Leiden,
      NL: Brill, 1996], 225).

Israelites viewed themselves in relation to all other neigbouring ethnocultural groups (11:2–3). It also reflects the culturally contested and difficult challenges that the early Christian movement had to face as it emerged.

A crucial point of debate in the passage is the question of food, notes Chris Miller.[68] Much like in the previous passage with the Syrophoenician woman, this text highlights the playful intersection between the cultural and ethnic differences and in the resulting tension, in this case centred on issues of eating.[69] The issues that emerge in the text revolve around "the sociocultural dynamics of food, meals, and table fellowship."[70] In this case, Peter's (and the Christian Jews') inherited understanding of cleanness is put into question.[71] As part of the experience with Cornelius' entire household, his (Peter's) and his Jewish companions' particular ethnic, cultural, and religious claims to exclusivity collapse, and his sense of divine "chosenness" must be profoundly rethought. The theological implications are enormous: "God has now granted the Gentiles not only repentance unto life, but also the fullness of the Holy Spirit and full acceptance into His household as first-class citizens."[72] Stated differently, by having Peter enter the house of Cornelius Luke no longer regards "Gentile homes as

---

68 Chris A. Miller, "Did Peter's Vision in Acts 10 Pertain to Men or the Menu?" *Bibliotheca Sacra* 159 (July-September 2002): 302–17.

69 Miller insists that the accusation against Peter that he was "eating with Gentiles" in Acts 11:3 most likely "had everything to do with *Gentiles* and nothing to do with what they were *eating*" (Miller, "Peter's Vision in Acts 10," 316). By contrast, acknowledging the complexities and limitations set in place by Jews around eating, Philip Esler correctly points out that the issue in the episode was not about the gospel being "preached to Gentiles, but the far more particular fact, of great ethnic and social significance, that Peter has lived and eaten with them" (cited in Nguyen, "Dismantling Cultural Boundaries," 461). For this reason, I agree with Sanders Willson who reminds us that the Acts 10 passage may be used to counter and unmask present day racist, sexist, and discriminatory attitudes among Christians. For him, the passage is a reminder and a call to Christians to struggle against rules and regulations that enforce those types of discriminatory attitudes from one sector of the Church to another. See his " 'God Does not Show Favoritism': Acts 10," *Presbyterion* 29, no. 1 (Spring 2003): 1–8.

70 Nguyen, "Dismantling Cultural Boundaries," 460. Nguyen appropriately notes that questions of eating encompass multiple social issues. As he puts it, in Acts 10, "meals/food serve as social boundary markers distinguishing what one eats, where one eats, when one eats, how one eats and with whom one eats" (Ibid., 461).

71 Nguyen avers that "the Jewish antipathy toward dining with Gentiles was affecting the mission of the early church," so much so that Jewish-Gentile table fellowship had become a matter of intense controversy and debate as recorded in Luke-Acts. See Nguyen, "Dismantling Cultural Boundaries," 461.

72 Miller, "Peter's Vision in Acts 10," 316.

unclean and off limits for Jewish Christians."[73] Viewed from the perspective of culturalization, the encounter between Peter and Cornelius serves as an object lesson of the deep changes that all cultural traditions often need to undergo—because of ethnic and cultural clashes/tensions, internal cultural changes, or historical, social, political and cultural circumstances—as they begin to make room for "others," for "outsiders."

The encounter between Peter and Cornelius is also important because the Spirit is said to be poured on all those present in the house of Cornelius, despite the fact that there is no record that he or those present ever adopted Judaism. Peter himself in Acts 11:17 testifies that the occurrence at the house of Cornelius made him realize that he and the other followers of Jesus needed to rethink the distinctions and separations they had inherited. The book of Acts in particular provides us with crucial insights as to how the transformation of the Jewish ethnocultural and religious perceptions of Gentiles were being transformed as Christianity was being born.

Though we know that the incident at Cornelius' house provoked controversy, the ensuing debates did not resolve the ethnocultural challenges that early Christians faced. Interethnic and intercultural tensions remained in the early Church as is evident in Paul's writings (e.g., Galatians 2: 1–14), which demonstrates how these tensions persisted in other church communities. The Jewish contingent was not easily dissuaded from giving up cultural practices. For example, the Jerusalem Council allowed Gentiles not to adopt Judaism but did insist in the observance of laws akin to Levitical rules governing foreigners in the land of Israel.[74] Still, Sim is correct is saying that the entrance of Gentiles into Christianity without requiring them "to convert in the normal Jewish manner is ... the single most important event in the entire history of the Christian church."[75] In my view, this series of incidents show how ethnic and cultural identity are woven together with peoples religious traditions.

Of course, there is much more that can be gleaned from these passages; biblical scholars remind us of the complexities of issues behind these apparently simple narratives. Yet, even in this brief analysis, we can see that the passages reflect the historical contexts which include multiple multilayer exchanges, tensions, and clashes among the ethnocultural groups that inhabited the region. The record of these clashes in the New Testament indicate that, the cultural universes of the "other" groups are beginning to leak into and

---

73   Nguyen, "Dismantling Cultural Boundaries," 458.

74   Sim, "Christianity and Ethnicity," 181.

75   Ibid., 179.

contribute to the profound process of reconfiguration that eventually came to be identified as Christianity. Beneath the narrative presented mainly in "religious" terms, the complex dynamic of cultural reproduction and exchange is manifest, demonstrating that the New Testament must also be understood as a cultural document and a cultural product.

The Early Christians and the Cultural

In this section I wish to show that from the days of the inception of Christianity among Jewish Christians, to its transition into the gentile cultural world, to the establishment of Christianity as the religion of the empire, cultural concerns were a central feature in the growth and expansion of Christianity. In its inception, Christianity was connected with Mesopotamian cultures and traditions. By the time of its encounter with Constantinianism, processes of culturalization resulted in its cooptation by the culture of the Roman Empire. One major event that I wish to focus here is the Arius-Athanasius disputes as a concrete example of the cultural dynamics that figured prominently during this controversy.

Cultural Negotiations in the Early Church

As the Church began to grow and to find its identity, cultural issues needed to be renegotiated. More often than not, early Christians have been understood as a "countercultural" force who stood in radical opposition to the dominant Roman religious culture. They also had to learn to navigate their relationship with the Jewish religious tradition. We know that the Jerusalem council had grappled with these kinds of tensions between cultural groups because their decision that believers were not required to convert to/adopt Judaic religious practices but they were expected to stay away from Roman religious practices and activities are recorded in Acts 15:6–29. The presence of believers from cultural groups other than Hebrews brought new tensions as well (Acts 7). Still, the event of Pentecost, along with the subsequent Jerusalem council created the space for the new arrivals to celebrate their Christian faith in God from their own cultural vantage point. Ironically, though the Jerusalem council prevented the assimilation of gentiles into some form of Judaism, it may have also contributed to the emergence of some incipient supersessionist attitudes. Eventually, Judaism and Christianity came to be seen as incompatible.

As they began to form a new religious movement, early Christians had to negotiate the cultural tensions of distancing themselves from Judaism and

avoiding participation in Roman socioreligious activities despite the fact that
they inhabited Roman contexts. Many early Christian writers engaged in this
balancing act. For example, Ignatius (CE 35–98) in his letter to the *Magnesians*
admonishes the Judaizers: "It is absurd to profess Christ Jesus, and to Judaize.
For Christianity did not embrace Judaism, but Judaism Christianity, that
so every tongue which believes might be gathered together to God."[76] Also,
Clement of Rome's (d. 99 or 101) first letter chides the Corinthians for their
loss of humility and draws on the history of the people of Israel to exemplify
the potential outcome of "bad behavior."[77] The author also shows the influence
of Roman culture as he draws on Roman military images to promote order
and obedience for "the preservation of the whole body."[78] Meanwhile, Clement
of Alexandria (150–215) goes to great lengths to debunk and critique Greek
mythology and Roman culture by comparing it to the Christian message.[79]
Here already we begin to see a separation between Christianity and the larger
social context.

The intersection of different cultural traditions in early Christianity must
be underlined. At this early stage diversity was not subsumed under the impetus for unity. In his *first Apology*, Justin Martyr (CE 100–165) exhibits his own
critical stance against Rome. He claims he presents "this address and petition
on behalf of those of all nations who are unjustly hated and wantonly abused,

---

76   Ignatius, "The Epistle of Ignatius to the Magnesians," in *The Apostolic Fathers, Justin
      Martyr, Irenaeus*, vol. I, trans. and ed. Alexander Roberts and James Donaldson, Revised
      and chronologically arranged, with brief prefaces and occasional notes, by Alexander
      Cleveland Coxe, Ante-Nicene Fathers (Grand Rapids, MI: William B. Eerdmans Publishing
      Company, 1885), Chapter 10, Http://www.ccel.org/ccel/schaff/anf01.pdf (accessed,
      November 12, 2014).

77   Clement of Rome, "The First Epistle of Clement to the Corinthians," in *The Apostolic
      Fathers, Justin Martyr, Irenaeus*, vol. I, trans. and ed. Alexander Roberts and James
      Donaldson, Revised and chronologically arranged, with brief prefaces and occasional
      notes, by Alexander Cleveland Coxe, Ante-Nicene Fathers (Grand Rapids, MI: William
      B. Eerdmans Publishing Company, 1885), 10–70, Http://www.ccel.org/ccel/schaff/anf01
      .pdf (accessed, November 12, 2014).

78   Ibid., Chapter 37.

79   Clement of Alexandria, "Exhortation to the Heathen," in *Fathers of the Second
      Century: Hermas, Tatian, Athenagoras, Theophilus, and Clement of Alexandria (Entire)*,
      vol. II, trans. and ed. Alexander Roberts and James Donaldson, Revised and chronolog-
      ically arranged, with brief prefaces and occasional notes, by Alexander Cleveland Coxe,
      Ante-Nicene Fathers (Grand Rapids, MI: William B. Eerdmans Publishing Company,
      1885), Chapter 2, Http://www.ccel.org/ccel/schaff/anf02.pdf (accessed, November
      12, 2014).

myself being one of them."[80] His defense against the charge of atheism points to the fact that Christians are accused according to the Roman pantheon but not according to the God of the Christian faith.[81] A crucial point in his defense is that Christian believers now come from every nation. In fact, among "... all races of men there are some who look for Him who was crucified ..."[82] There is no move to subsume the rich diversity of the church here. Justin Martyr's polemic against Rome can also be seen in his short treatise on divine government, where he juxtaposes Christian monotheism and the vain pretensions of false Roman gods.[83]

Similarly, Iranaeus (120–202) displayed a unique "global" idealism and impetus for catholicity in his *Against Heresies* which he connects to the creeds of the church and the drive for both unity and right doctrine.[84] He writes: "The Church, though dispersed throughout the whole world, even to the ends of the earth, has received from the apostles and their disciples this faith ..."[85] He adds "As I have already observed, the Church, having received this preaching and this faith, although scattered throughout the whole world, yet, as if occupying but one house, carefully preserves it."[86] In a text bent on warning and defending Christians from Gnosticism, the importance of

---

80   Justin Martyr, "The First Apology of Justin," trans. G. Reith, in *The Apostolic Fathers with Justin Martyr and Irenaeus*, vol. I, ed. Alexander Roberts and James Donaldson, Revised and chronologically arranged, with brief prefaces and occasional notes, by Alexander Cleveland Coxe, Ante-Nicene Fathers (Grand Rapids, MI: William B. Eerdmans Publishing Company, 1885), Chapter 1, Http://www.ccel.org/ccel/schaff/anfo1.pdf (accessed November 2, 2014).

81   Ibid., Chapter 6.

82   Ibid., Chapter 32.

83   Justin Martyr, "On the Sole Government of God," trans. G. Reith, in *The Apostolic Fathers with Justin Martyr and Irenaeus*, vol. I, ed. Alexander Roberts and James Donaldson, Revised and chronologically arranged, with brief prefaces and occasional notes, by Alexander Cleveland Coxe, Ante-Nicene Fathers (Grand Rapids, MI: William B. Eerdmans Publishing Company, 1885), 776–90, Http://www.ccel.org/ccel/schaff/anfo1.pdf (accessed November 2, 2014).

84   The emphasis on unity and catholicity eventually contributed to the rejection of diversity in the Church.

85   Iraneus, "Against Heresies," trans. Alexander Roberts, in *The Apostolic Fathers, Justin Martyr, Irenaeus*, vol. I, ed. Alexander Roberts and James Donaldson, Revised and chronologically arranged, with brief prefaces and occasional notes, by Alexander Cleveland Coxe, Ante-Nicene Fathers (Grand Rapids, MI: William B. Eerdmans Publishing Company, 1885), 10:1, Http://www.ccel.org/ccel/schaff/anfo1.pdf (accessed, November 12, 2014).

86   Ibid., Chapter 10:2.

unity amid the empire stands out. For him, the Church more than the empire can speak about catholicity even while celebrating its breadth throughout the earth.

The conflictual relationship between the early church and Rome can also be seen in Tertullian's (160–225) *Apologia*, which exudes an air of rhetoric and a culturally fluid relationship with Rome.[87] Tertullian uses Roman culture and history to articulate his own polemic. His apology was a "forensic defense" of the legitimacy of Christianity, a legal argument modelled after the Roman legislative tradition.[88] Minucius, a contemporary of Tertullian more sharply disparages Roman culture and religion: "All that the Romans hold, occupy and possess is the spoil of outrage; their temples are all of loot, drawn from the ruin of cities, the plunder of gods and the slaughter of priests. It is an insult and mockery to serve vanquished religions, first to enslave and then worship the vanquished"[89] For him, the contrast between the power of God and the power of Rome is clear. The power of Rome is empty power: All empires fall under God's dispensation; before Rome, God was.[90] The important connection worth making at this point is that the critique of Rome is made at the level of

---

87   Mark Burrows, "Christianity in the Roman Forum: Tertullian and the Apologetic of History," *Vigiliae Christianae* 42 (1988): 209.

88   Burrows, "Christianity in the Roman Forum," 210. Tertullian's appeal is to Roman law: "If you, the magistrates of the Roman Empire,—you, who, in the light of day, set on high, at the very head of the state, preside to do justice,—if you are not allowed openly to investigate, face to face to examine, the Christian issue, to learn what it is in truth;—if, in this phase of life, and this alone, your authority either dreads or blushes to inquire in public, with all the care that Justice demands;—if finally (as recently befell) persecution of this school is so busy in the domestic tribunal as to block the way of defence;—then let truth be allowed to reach your ears at least by the hidden path of silent literature" (Tertullian, "Apology," trans. S. Thelwall, in *Latin Christianity: Its Founder, Tertullian*, vol. III, ed. Allan Menzies, Ante-Nicene Fathers [Grand Rapids, MI: William B. Eerdmans Publishing Company, 1885], Chapter 1:1, Http://www.ccel.org/ccel/schaff/anf03.pdf [accessed November 30, 2014]).

89   Minucius Felix, "The Octavius of Minucius Felix," trans. Robert Ernest. Wallis, in *Fathers of the Third Century: Tertullian, Part Fourth; Minucius Felix; Commodian; Origen, Parts First and Second*, vol. IV, ed. Phillip Schaff, chronologically arranged, with brief notes and prefaces by Cleveland A. Coxe, Ante-Nicene Fathers (Grand Rapids, MI: William B. Eerdmans Publishing Company, 1977), Chapter 25:5–6, Http://www.ccel.org/ccel/schaff/anf04 .html (accessed November 14, 2014).

90   "And after all, under God's dispensation, before Romans existed, Assyrians, Medes, Persians, Greeks too and Egyptians ruled great empires, although they had no Pontiffs, no Arval Brothers, no Salii Vestals or Augurs, no cooped chickens to rule the destinies of state by their appetite or distaste for food" (Minucius Felix, "The Octavius of Minucius Felix,"

cultural values and morality. The distancing from Rome that these Christians leaders seek relates directly to Rome's culturally religious fabric that counters the principles of the gospel message.

The Montanist[91] period of Tertullian's life was not seen by him as a departure from the Christian faith. Rather, he saw it as even more faithful.[92] Given that Montanism was an anti-Roman Christian renewal subgroup, Tertullian's move should be understood more like a disenfranchisement with the establishment he himself helped to create. In his earlier writings such as *On Penitence* he admonishes and encourages catechumens into baptism and church order. But later when he wrote *On Modesty* (also known as *On Purity*, Latin *De Pudicitia*), Tertullian sternly condemns a bishop (usually thought to be the pope) for allowing remarrying and forgiveness of those who commit adultery and fornication.[93] As a Montanist, he quickly condemned the moral decline of the

---

Chapter 25:12). See also Origen's scathing discussion of the Roman cult and idolatry composed at the outbreak of Maximian's persecution, and in which his friends Protectus and Ambrose were imprisoned. Origen, "Exhortation to Martyrdom," in *Origen: Prayer, Exhortation to Martyrdom*, trans. John J. O'Meara (New York, NY: Paulist Press, 1954), 141–94.

91   The New Prophecy, also known as Montanism, was a religious movement that came into being in the region of Prygia during the second century. It sought to revive the church from spiritual deadness, and was lead by Montanus and two women prophetesses: Maximilla and Priscilla (also Prisca). The New Prophecy was said to be radical because of its distinctive beliefs that the Holy Spirit and spiritual manifestations were for the present time; Montanists held that there was a continuance of the miraculous gifts of the apostolic church, especially the continuance of prophecy. For a fuller discussion see Ronald E. Heine, *The Montanist Oracles and Testimonia*, vol. 14, Patristic Monograph Series (Machon, GA: Mercer University Press, 1989).

92   The New Prophecy did not take away from the authority of scriptures but were believed to simply "illuminate and support them … The original Montanists-and Tertullian himself-saw themselves here as even more faithful to the sacred texts of the Apostles than the Catholics" (David Rankin, *Tertullian and the Church* [Cambridge, UK: Cambridge University Press, 1995], 48).

93   Tertullian writes: "In opposition to this (modesty)," could I not have acted the dissembler? I hear that there has even been an edict set forth, and a peremptory one too. The *Pontifex Maximus* 707—that is, the bishop of bishops—issues an edict: "I remit, to such as have discharged (the requirements of) repentance, the sins both of adultery and of fornication" (Tertullian, "On Modesty," trans. S. Thelwall, in *Fathers of the Third Century: Tertullian, Part Fourth; Minucius Felix; Commodian; Origen, Parts First and Second*, vol. IV, ed. Phillip Schaff, Chronologically arranged, with brief notes and prefaces by Alexander Cleveland Coxe, Ante-Nicene Fathers [Grand Rapids, MI: William B. Eerdmans Publishing Company, 1885], Chapter 1, Http://www.ccel.org/ccel/schaff/anf04.html [accessed November 14, 2014]).

church. Could it be said that the church lost touch with the Gospel because
of the moral corruption in the Roman world?[94] As a result, one can infer
that Tertullian joined the "New Prophecy" group in Carthage because of the
church's moral decline.[95] Montanism represented a renewal of Christianity,
a charismatic renewal at that, and a radical cultural shift that, among other
things, gave women substantive power inside the church. More to the point,
Tertullian's shift can also be seen as a reaction against the church's becoming

---

94   Cyprian of Cathage (200–258), a contemporary of Tertullian, gives us a glimpse of the
      corruption of which the Montanist and others accused the Roman Forum Church. In
      To Donatus he wrote: "Then turn your gaze in that direction: there you will discover
      things more odious than ever, so that thence you will be more desirous of turning away
      your eyes, although the laws are carved on twelve tables, and the statutes are publicly
      prescribed on brazen tablets. Yet wrong is done in the midst of the laws themselves;
      wickedness is committed in the very face of the statutes; innocence is not preserved
      even in the place where it is defended. By turns the rancour of disputants rages; and
      when peace is broken among the togas, the Forum echoes with the madness of strife.
      There close at hand is the spear and the sword, and the executioner also; there is the
      claw that tears, the rack that stretches, the fire that burns up—more tortures for one
      poor human body than it has limbs. And in such cases who is there to help? One's
      patron? He makes a feint, and deceives. The judge? But he sells his sentence. He who
      sits to avenge crimes commits them, and the judge becomes the culprit, in order that
      the accused may perish innocently. Crimes are everywhere common; and everywhere
      in the multiform character of sin, the pernicious poison acts by means of degraded
      minds. One man forges a will, another by a capital fraud makes a false deposition; on
      the one hand, children are cheated of their inheritances, on the other, strangers are
      endowed with their estates. The opponent makes his charge, the false accuser attacks,
      the witness defames, on all sides the venal impudence of hired voices sets about the
      falsification of charges, while in the meantime the guilty do not even perish with the
      innocent. There is no fear about the laws; no concern for either inquisitor or judge;
      when the sentence can be bought off for money, it is not cared for. It is a crime now
      among the guilty to be innocent; whoever does not imitate the wicked is an offense to
      them" (Cyprian of Carthage, "To Donatus," trans. Robert Ernest Wallis, in *Fathers of the
      Third Century: Hippolytus, Cyprian, Caius, Novatian, Appendix.*, vol. V, ed. Alexander
      Roberts and James Donaldson, Revised and chronologically arranged, with brief pref-
      aces and occasional notes, by Alexander Cleveland Coxe, Ante-Nicene Fathers [Grand
      Rapids, MI: William B. Eerdmans Publishing Company, 1885], Chapter 1:10, Http://
      www.ccel.org/ccel/schaff/anf05.pdf [accessed November 10, 2014]).

95   Tertullian's affiliation with Montanism can also be seen as answer to the Christian ques-
      tion of how to live a Christian life in a pagan society. See Timothy Barnes, *Tertullian*
      (Oxford, UK: Clarendon Press, 1971), 88, 93, 94. Tertullian himself shows this concern in
      his own writings on "The Chaplet" and "On Spectacles."

too Roman; accommodating Roman culture, which, for him, run counter the Christian faith.

Prior to Constantine, Christians were often accused of disrupting the social, cultural, economic, and religious fabric of Rome. Politics, power, religion, traditions, the arts and social life all depended on each other and were part of the cultural ethos of Imperial cult. Origen mentions Celsus, one who accused Christians of entering "secret associations with each other contrary to law ..." He added that while some of their "associations ... are public, and that these are in accordance with the laws; others, again, secret, and maintained in violation of the laws."[96]

These kinds of accusations triggered many Christians to write multiple letters to defend their faith. For example, Cyprian of Carthage's (200–258) letter *To Demetrianus* is precisely a response to the accusation that Christianity was responsible for all the misfortunes with which the world was distressed because they did not worship the Roman gods.[97] According to Demetrianus, wars, famines, and all sorts of calamities that befell the known world were the responsibility of the Christians;[98] they disrupted the *pax deorum* and Roman religious rights and cultural fabric in general. In contrast, Cyprian was convinced that whatever calamity materialized, it was due to Roman unrighteousness and not grounds for the persecution of Christians; God would vindicate them.[99] He argued that Christians were part of a whole

---

96   Origen, "Origen Against Celsus," trans. Frederick Crombie, in *Fathers of the Third Century: Tertullian, Part Fourth; Minucius Felix; Commodian; Origen, Parts First and Second*, vol. IV, ed. Phillip Schaff, chronologically arranged, with brief notes and prefaces by Alexander Cleveland Coxe, Ante-Nicene Fathers (Grand Rapids, MI: William B. Eerdmans Publishing Company, 1885), Book 1, Chapter I, Http://www.ccel.org/ccel/schaff/anf04.html (accessed November 14, 2014).

97   Cyprian of Carthage, "An Address to Demetrianus," trans. Robert Ernest Wallis, in *Fathers of the Third Century: Hyppolytus, Cyrpian, Caius, Novation, Appendix by Phillip Schaff*, vol. V, ed. Alexander Roberts and James Donaldson, Revised and chronologically arranged, with brief prefaces and occasional notes, by Alexander Cleveland Coxe, Ante-Nicene Fathers (Grand Rapids, MI: William B. Eerdmans Publishing Company, 1885), 1061–75, Http://www.ccel.org/ccel/schaff/anf05.pdf (accessed November 13, 2014).

98   Ibid., Chapter 3–4.

99   As he writes, "You should not suppose then that under such a putative agreement you could call into court against us those events that have taken place ... the anger of God would come upon the unrighteous, that the persecutions that injure our human condition would in the future vanish" (Cyprian of Carthage, "An Address to Demetrianus," Chapter 21).

other kind of humanity that should not be judged by the Roman legal system. He preserved this radical distinction of Christians up to his execution as martyr.[100] The tensions between Christianity and Rome cannot be ascribed to the purely religious. Rather, one must take into account that ancient Rome was a religious culture. The refusal by Christians to pay homage to the imperial cult and embrace its ethical and moral practices initially drove a wedge between their communities and Rome, creating the conditions for martyrdom and violence of Rome against them.[101]

Persecutions in the early period increased or waned depending upon the current emperor and the need for political scapegoats or even simple amusement, though the negotiations, one way or another, played out in the cultural arena and were measured by how culturally and religiously obedient Christians were to their Roman context.[102] Sometimes how emperors dealt with persecution was part of a larger thirst for power. According to Maureen Tilley, sometimes religious groups served as "game pieces in the contest for ultimate power. There was peace when emperors were distracted, but repression returned when opportune for an imperial party of another."[103] Eusebius records some of those Christians who "were honored with divine martyrdom by becoming

---

100   Allen Brent describes this tension embodied in Cryprian: "Behaving like a Roman patrician to the last, he gave twenty-five gold coins (*aurei*) to his executioner. Behaving like a bishop, he handed his dalmatic to a presbyter and to a subdeacon" (Allen Brent, "Introduction," in *On the Church: Selected Treatises: St. Cyprian of Carthage*, translation with introduction and commentary by Allen Brent [Crestwood, NY: St. Vladimir's Seminary Press, 2006], 17).

101   Christians who were martyred were reduced to a status of mere existence so that they could be eradicated without legal accountability. Using Giorgio Agamben's analysis, they became the *homo sacer*; those who had no rights or place for legal purposes in Roman political life and culture. See his Giorgio Agamben, *Homo Sacer: Sovereign Power and Bare Life*, trans. Daniel Hellen-Roazen (Stanford, CA: Stanford University Press, 1995).

102   At the beginning of the second century Pliny the Younger describes his approach toward Christians in his Epistle X96 with an air of cynicism: "This is the course I have taken with those who are accused before me as Christians. I asked them whether they were Christians, and if they confessed, I asked them a second and third time with threats of punishment. If they kept to it, I ordered them for execution; for I held no question that whatever it was that they admitted, in any case obstinacy and unbending perversity deserves to be punished" (Pliny, "The Christians in Bythinia: Pliny's Dilemma, c. 112: Pliny," in *A New Eusebius: Documents Illustrating the History of the Church to AD 337*, ed. J Stevenson, rev. W.H.C. Frend [Grand Rapids, Mi: Baker Publishing Group, 1957], 13–14).

103   Maureen A Tilley, "Introduction," in *Donatist Martyr Stories: The Church in Conflict in Roman North Africa*, translated with notes and introduction by Maureen A Tilley (Liverpool, London: Liverpool University Press, 1996), XIII.

food of wild beasts."[104] He even tells the story of how Leonides, the father of Origen died under the persecution by Septimus Severus (lasting from 193 to 211) and how the "kindled flame of persecution blazed forth mightily, and many thousands were crowned with martyrdom."[105] The last and worst persecution experienced by Christians (The Great Diocletian Persecution which began on February 23, 303) had rescinded their legal rights making it possible for them to have property confiscated, to be imprisoned, or executed without a legal trial unless they observed the rituals and practices of the traditional Roman religious culture. Although there were minor persecutions throughout the empire, especially the eastern section, before and after, Galerius' *Edict of Toleration* on April 30, 311 did generally ameliorate the social conditions for most Christians. This edict deeply changed the mainly polarized relation between Christianity and Rome.

> XXXIV: Among our other regulations to promote the lasting good of the community we hitherto endeavored to restore a universal conformity to the ancient institutions and public order of the Romans; and in particular it has been our aim to bring back to a right disposition the Christians who had abandoned the religion of their fathers. ... In return for this indulgence of ours it will be the duty of Christians to pray to God for our recovery, for the public weal and for their own; that the state may be preserved from danger on every side, and that they themselves may dwell safely in their homes.[106]

The changes in Roman attitude toward Christians signal the path toward incorporating Christianity into the larger Roman cultural imperial apparatus. It signaled an opening up in the Roman body politics for Christians while at the same time co-opting Christianity and its ethnocultural diversity by empire. Although it might not have been perceived that way at first, the Edict strategically turned Christianity into yet another religious avenue for the betterment

---

104   Eusebius of Caesarea, "The Church History of Eusebius," translated with prolegomena and notes by Arthur Cushman McGiffert, in *Eusebius Pamphilius: Church History, Life of Constantine, Oration in Praise of Constantine*, vol. 1, ed. Philip Schaff, trans. Arthur Cushman McGiffert, Nice and Post-Nicene Fathers Series II (Grand Rapids, MI: William B. Eerdmans Publishing Company, 1890), Book VII, Chapter 12, Http://www.ccel.org/ccel/schaff/npnf201.pdf (accessed November 18, 2014).

105   Ibid., Book VI, Chapter 2:3.

106   Galerius, "Edict of Toleration (311)," in *Documents of the Christian Church*, fourth ed., ed. Henry Bettenson and Chris Maunder (London, UK: Oxford University Press, 2011), 16.

of the Empire and potentially, by a kind of coercion to Roman cultural structures, of equal status to the significance of pagan imperial religious thought
and practice. The Edict of Toleration of 311 offered Christians a "right to exist"
only if they did not "offend against public order."[107] The "freedom" that was proclaimed operated as a mechanism to fit Christianity into the Imperial cultural
mold. For the sake of the prosperity of the republic, public order, and "universal conformity to the ancient institutions," and as correspondence to the
"indulgence" of the Empire Christians are to now pray for the divine protection
of the Empire. The 313 third Edict of Milan, signed by Constantine (272–337)
and Licinius (263–325), went even further. The freedom proclaimed is not
only for Christians, it is also proclaimed for all other religions:

> XLVIII: When we, Constantine and Licinius, met at Milan ... we decided
> that of the things that are of profit to all mankind, the worship of God
> ought rightly to be our first and chiefest care, and that it was right that
> Christians and all others should have freedom to follow the kind of
> religion they favoured; so that the God who dwells in heaven might be
> propitious to us an all under our rule. We therefore announce that, not-
> withstanding any provisions concerning the Christians in our former
> instructions, all who choose that religion are to be permitted to continue
> therein, without any let or hinderance, and are not to be in any way trou-
> bled or molested. Note that at the same time all others are to be allowed
> the free and unrestricted practice of their religions; for it accords with the
> good order of the realm ...[108]

At this time, Christians were not yet the favorite choice of the Empire.
Constantine was more concerned with bringing social, cultural and political stability than bringing justice or care for the Christians. This Edict was
another critical sociocultural and political maneuvering in creating an alliance with the Christian God and with Christians in order to protect Rome.
Constantine was bidding for the protection of the Roman Empire from the
wrath of the Christian God whom he considered the strongest Deity. Thus,
the Edict of Milan reveals the Roman culture's obsession with seeking the
intervention of the gods more than the religious beliefs of Constantine or
Licinius.

---

107   Ibid.
108   Constantine and Licinius, "Edict of Milan (313)," in *Documents of the Christian Church*,
       fourth ed., ed. Henry Bettenson and Chris Maunder (London, UK: Oxford University Press,
       2011), 17.

Because of Constantine's experience in battle and his vision of the cross, Christianity came to be seen as a potential vehicle for the success of the Empire. Christianity could become the glue that provided cultural unification for the survival and stability of the Empire. At the same time, cultural acceptance of Christians and their practices improved with the proclamation of freedom for Christians in the *Edict of Toleration*, and the returning of their social humanity in the *Edict of Milan*. The cultural impact of these shifts on the way Christians saw themselves was enormous. But Roman culture was significantly reconfigured as well by making social space for Christianity. The *Edict of Milan* opened up a new world for Christianity, a new world steeped in the imperial matrix of power/technology of power in fourth century Roman culture. The two edicts mark the end of persecution, but they also reveal the slow process which paved the way for the eventual turning of Christianity into the chosen religion of the Empire.

In the process of the culturalization of Christianity into a dominant cultural religion, there were many who disagreed with the blending between it and Roman imperial religious culture. Two prime examples of early Christianity's cultural critique and protest against Rome were embodied in the traditions of the monastics and the desert fathers and mothers. Although its origins are difficult to trace, and it is evident that monasticism was not exclusively born as a reaction to the emergence of the imperial church, there is evidence that many opted for monastic lives in response to the marriage of the Church to Roman religious culture. While many like Eusebius of Caesarea welcomed the ascendancy of Christianity to the highest levels of recognition by Roman culture, others, in contrast, lamented what they considered the corrupt and coopted levels to which Christianity had descended.[109] In the words of Justo González, "Bishops competed with each other after prestigious positions. The rich and powerful [came] to dominate the life of the church."[110]

As with some in the monastic tradition, the desert fathers also expressed their strong rejection to Christianity coming together with the dominant Roman religious, cultural, and social fabric. They chose to stand outside the political, social, and cultural life of the Empire as a form of protest. Choosing to live at the periphery of the Empire they pursued what they thought was true Christian life and abhorred the corruption of Christianity when it functioned under imperial protection and endorsement. The desert fathers held different views of God and Christian life, building a different way of life with different values that contravened the emerging type of Christianity under the

109   González, *The Story of Christianity*, 136.
110   Ibid.

patronage of Rome-Constantine. In a short timespan of about 50 years, the cultural change was very dramatic; instead of persecution and a death sentence, Bishops were rewarded with increased power and social, political and cultural authority.

The particular theocultural conflicts and resolutions that were being played out in the larger scene were also being played out in the theocultural conflicts between particular people. The Arius-Athanasius controversy can be interpreted as representing the multiple cultural and religious-theological issues and tensions that were taking place. The unity of empire sought by Constantine since his endorsement of Christianity was at risk because the controversy had the potential to rend the Empire into pieces over incessant theo-cultural bickering between Christian factions. According to González, "Constantine's ecclesiastical policy consisted in turning the church into 'the cement of the Empire.'"[111] On one hand, Arianism represented the Roman sponsored church while Athanasius (296–373) was more in touch with the counter (Roman) cultural Christianity of the desert fathers. While Eusebius (260–339/40), a staunch Arianist, chronicled Constantine and Christianity through the eyes of empire,[112] Athanasius (296–373) ignored the emperors and focused on the life of the desert fathers, particularly St. Anthony.[113] In fact, in his *The Church History*, Eusebius hardly mentions the Desert Fathers. Inexplicably, he does not record Constantine's interaction with St. Anthony, an exchange which unveiled the different attitude of the monastics toward the Empire.[114] Yet, he covered

---

111   Justo L. González, *A History of Christian Thought: From the Beginnings to the Council of Chalcedon* (Nashville, TN: Abingdon Press, 1970), 273.

112   See Eusebius of Caesarea, "The Life of Constantine," translated with prolegomena and notes by Arthur Cushman McGiffert, in *Eusebius Pamphilius: Church History, Life of Constantine, Oration in Praise of Constantine*, vol. 1, ed. Philip Schaff, trans. Arthur Cushman McGiffert, Nice and Post-Nicene Fathers Series II (Grand Rapids, MI: William B. Eerdmans Publishing Company, 1890), 1152–1433, Http://www.ccel.org/ccel/schaff/npnf201.pdf (accessed November 18, 2014); Eusebius of Caesarea, "The Church History of Eusebius."

113   Athanasius, "Vita S. Antoni (Written Between 356–362)," in *Athanasius: Select Works and Letters*, vol. IV, ed. Philip Schaff, et al., Nicene and Post-Nicene Fathers of the Christian Church Series II (Grand Rapids, MI: William B. Eerdmans Publishing Company, 1953), 570–640, Http://www.ccel.org/ccel/schaff/npnf204.pdf (accessed November 20, 2014).

114   Constantine is said to have summoned Anthony: "One day Abba Anthony received" a letter from the Emperor Constantius, asking him to come to Constantinople, and he was wondering if he ought to go. So he said to Abba Paul, his disciple, "Ought I to go?" He replied, "If you go, you will be called Anthony, but if you stay here, you will be called Abba Anthony" (Anthony, "Sayings of Anthony in Egypt," Http://www.fatherpius.littleway .ca/desert02.html [accessed November 24, 2014]). Concerning the same exchange, Athanasius also narrates Anthony's reaction to Constantine's letters: "and [Anthony] said,

much of the development and fall out from Arianism (to be expected because he was a contemporary and himself an Arianist) even going so far as to seek the reconciliation between Alexander the Bishop of Alexandria (d. 326/328) and Arius (250/256–336).[115] At the same time, his description of Constantine in *The Life of the Blessed Emperor Constantine*, serves a rhetorical function over a historical account and, while it presents much of the religious reforms, shifts and struggles of Christianity becoming a valid religion in the Empire, it elevates Constantine's significance for Christianity. Constantine is compared to Moses frequently seen as a kind of Exodus figure who brough freedom for the Christians in a hostile pagan system. Eusebius writes: "Constantine, who was shortly to become their destroyer, but at that time of tender age, and blooming with the down of early youth, dwelt, as God's servant Moses had done, in the very home of the tyrants."[116] It is not surprising to notice that Constantine is considered a saint by the Orthodox Church.

At no moment did the cultural impact and power of Rome—now Constantinople—over Christian affairs become as evident as in the Arian controversy. Constantine had given the bishops of the church much respect and honor in the public scene. And he gave enormous resources toward building sacred edifices and embellishing the august sanctuaries of the Church.[117] Constantine dressed the church with a new royal garb and ostentation. The concerns for unity (by now it means Catholicity) and the power of the Roman Emperor converged for Arius; Constantine was the only one capable of healing divisions. He "appeared to be the only one on earth capable of being [God's] minister for this good end."[118] The connections are also found in Arius letter to Constantine:

> According as your piety, beloved of God, commanded, O sovereign emperor, we here furnish a written statement of our own faith, and we

---

'Do not be astonished if an emperor writes to us, for he is a man; but rather wonder that God wrote the Law for men and has spoken to us through His own Son' … he was unwilling to receive the letters, saying that he did not know how to write an answer to such things. But being urged by the monks because the emperors were Christians, and lest they should take offence on the ground that they had been spurned, he consented that they should be read, and wrote an answer approving them because they worshipped Christ, and giving them counsel on things pertaining to salvation …" (Athanasius, "Vita S. Antoni [Written Between 356–362]," 628).

115   Eusebius of Caesarea, "The Life of Constantine," Book II, Chapter LXIX.
116   Ibid., Book I, chapter XII.
117   Ibid., Book I, Chapter XLII.
118   Ibid., Book III, Chapter V.

protest before God that we, and all those who are with us, believe what is here set forth .... Wherefore we appeal to your piety, O our emperor most beloved of God, that, as we are enrolled among the members of the clergy, and as we hold the faith and thought of the Church and of the sacred Scriptures, we may be openly reconciled to our mother, the Church, through your peacemaking and pious piety; so that useless questions and disputes may be cast aside, and that we and the Church may dwell together in peace, and we all in common may offer the customary prayer for your peaceful and pious empire and for your entire family.[119]

The letter shows the subservient character of Christianity to the power of the "pious" Empire. Arius's epistle also reveals the rift that had taken place at Nicea.[120] As a result of his letter to Constantine, Arius was acknowledged by Constantine as following the teachings of the *Catholic* church and welcomed-called back into communion by some bishops.[121] In his *Ecclesiastical History*, Sozomen explains how Constantine actually switched allegiances and sent

---

119 Salaminius Hermias Sozomen, "The Ecclesiastical Story of Sozomen, Comprising a History of the Church from A.D. 323 to A.D. 425," rev. Chester D. Hartranft, in *Sopcrates and Sozomenus Ecclesiastical Histories*, vol. 2, ed. and trans. Philip Schaff and Henry Wave, Nicene and Post-Nicene Fathers Series II (Grand Rapids, MI: William B Eerdmans, 1980), Book II, Chapter XXVII.

120 Constantine's address to the council at Nicea sums up his intentions: "... thanks to God the universal King, because, in addition to all his other benefits, he has granted me a blessing ... to see you not only all assembled together, but all united in a common harmony of sentiment ... [I]n my judgment, intestine strife within the Church of God, is far more evil and dangerous than any kind of war ... Accordingly, when, by the will and with the co-operation of God, I had been victorious over my enemies, I thought that nothing more remained but to render thanks to him, [but] as soon as I heard ... of your dissension, I judged it to be of no secondary importance, but with the earnest desire that a remedy for this evil also might be found through my means, I immediately sent to require your presence. And now I rejoice in beholding your assembly; but I feel that my desires will be most completely fulfilled when I can see you all united in one judgment, and that common spirit of peace and concord prevailing amongst you all, which it becomes you, as consecrated to the service of God ..." (Eusebius of Caesarea, "The Life of Constantine," Book III, Chapter XII). As can be seen, Constantine's speech describes his mandate to those attending the council to resolve all differences; divisions and differences are not good for the empire.

121 González notes that Arius adopted a seemingly reconciliatory position that persuaded Constantine that "it was the anti-Arians that were stubborn and rebellious" (González, *A History of Christian Thought*, 273).

Athanasius into exile on account of the machinations of the Arians.[122] Not too long after the Council at Nicea, Athanasius became an outlaw of the imperial police; the same Christian/Roman system of which he was part.[123] He found refuge among the desert fathers. Athanasius did not accept Constantine's decision passively. Of note are his report of Anthony's strident rejection of Arianism[124] and his defense letter to Constantine, in which he described that nearly ninety Bishops had been under persecution, "and that their Churches were given up to the professors of Arianism; that sixteen had been banished, and of the rest, some had fled, and others were constrained to dissemble" because "they refused to subscribe to my condemnation."[125] These actions by Athanasius demonstrate the complex dynamics of power play and struggle as the church was being culturally reconfigured and theological tensions were being negotiated.

There is little doubt that these two strong forces resisted each other, making for political maneuvering, intermixing social and political interests, and contributing to profound cultural and religious changes. In many ways though, it looked as if Christianity had come of age, eschewing its status as second-class citizens and embracing the power of empire.

122 Sozomen, "The Ecclesiastical Story of Sozomen," Book II, Chapter XXVIII. According to González, Athanasius had defended himself from accusation by the Arians in 331, but when a synod gathered in Tyre under the direction of Eusebius of Nicomedia condemned and deposed him, and Constantine had him banished. See González, *A History of Christian Thought*, 276.

123 William Harmless, *Desert Christians* (New York, NY: Oxford University Press, 2004), 94.

124 As he describes, "And once also the Arians having loyingly asserted that Anthony's opinions were the same as theirs, he was displeased and wroth against them. Then being summoned by the bishops and all the brethren, he descended from the mountain, and having entered Alexandria, he denounced the Arians, saying that their heresy was the last of all and a forerunner of Antichrist. And he taught the people that the Son of God was not a created being, neither had He come into being from non-existence, but that He was the Eternal Word and Wisdom of the Essence of the Father. And therefore, it was impious to say, 'there was a time when He was not,' for the Word was always co-existent with the Father" (Athanasius, "Vita S. Antoni [Written Between 356–362]," 621).

125 Athanasius, "Defence Before Constantius," in *Athanasius: Select Works and Letters*, vol. IV, ed. Philip Schaff, et al., Nicene and Post-Nicene Fathers of the Christian Church Series II (Grand Rapids, MI: William B. Eerdmans Publishing Company, 1953), Page 697, Section 27, Http://www.ccel.org/ccel/schaff/npnf204.pdf (accessed November 20, 2014). Consistent with Arius defense letter, instead of attacking the Nicene formula because it was Constantine's beloved achievement, the Arians organized against the individuals who were the main supporters of the Nicene formula. See González, *A History of Christian Thought*, 274.

This climactic shift into becoming the cultural religion of the empire would wait sixty-seven more years to be formalized. On February 27, 380 the Edict of Thessalonica issued by Gratian, Valentinian II and Theodosius declared Nicene Trinitarian Christianity to be the only legitimate religion of the empire and the only one entitled to be called Catholic.

> It is our desire that all the various nations which are subject to our Clemency and Moderation, should continue to profess that religion which was delivered to the Romans by the divine Apostle Peter, as it has been preserved by faithful tradition, and which is now professed by the Pontiff Damasus and by Peter, Bishop of Alexandria, a man of apostolic holiness. According to the apostolic teaching and the doctrine of the Gospel, let us believe in the one deity of the Father, the Son and the Holy Spirit, in equal majesty and in a holy Trinity. We authorize the followers of this law to assume the title of Catholic Christians; but as for the others, since, in our judgment they are foolish madmen, we decree that they shall be branded with the ignominious name of heretics, and shall not presume to give to their conventicles the name of churches. They will suffer in the first place the chastisement of the divine condemnation and in the second the punishment of our authority which in accordance with the will of Heaven we shall decide to inflict.[126]

The tectonic shifts had reached unprecedented heights. Constantine's perceptive eye had realized the important role Christianity would play in preserving the Empire as united. This was one of the motivations that led him to convene the Council at Nicea (325). As the religion of the Empire, Christianity provided the material for crystallizing the unity of the Roman Empire.[127] The system that once martyred Christians now openly protected them, inviting them into the dominant culture of the Empire, and disseminating a specific version of the Christian faith clothed with political and cultural power. In the words of González

---

126   Theodosius I, Gratian, and Valentinian II, "Edict of Thessalonica," *Wikipedia*, Http://en.wikipedia.org/wiki/Edict_of_Thessalonica (accessed November 17, 2014).

127   As Harvey Cox notes, the connection between the word religion and the strategic drive toward uniting the kingdom is important to note here: "the main purpose of religions (the word literary means 'bonds') was to hold a people together. Religion provided social cement, and as the older religions declined, Constantine-always a realist-saw the need for something to take their place. He knew little about Christianity, but he knew—or thought he knew-what he, and his empire needed" (Harvey Cox, *The Future of the Faith* [New York, NY: HarperCollins, 2009], 100).

... the same protection, which gave Christians the possibility of developing their theology to an extent that was previously impossible, also implied the possibility of imperial condemnation or favor to one theological position or another. And this in turn gave theological controversies a political dimension that they had not previously had. This is what happened in the Arian controversy.[128]

Meanwhile, the mixture of exclusiveness and zeal displayed by Christians with imperial power transformed Christianity into a "persecuting force without parallel ..., which would attack both those who claimed to be Christians and outsiders such as Jews and pagans."[129]

The shift of Constantine's affection from paganism to Christianity served as the catalyst for Christianity to envision itself as part of the constituting power of the empire. It also created the conditions for the entrance of the Roman aristocracy into the ranks of the clergy, thereby retaining and exerting "their power within the community of faith."[130] Men with great financial and cultural means but with little knowledge and experience of the faith increasingly filled the ranks of the church. By the time Christianity had been adopted as the religion of the Empire, the shift was complete. Christianity was no longer the religion of the socially marginalized cultural communities; it had effectively become the religion of the highest echelons of the society of the time.[131]

---

128 González, *A History of Christian Thought*, 262.

129 Streeter, "Introduction: De Ste. Croix on Persecution," in *Christian Persecution, Martyrdom, & Orthodoxy: G.E.M. de Ste. Croix*, ed. Michael Whitby and Joseph Streeter (Oxford, UK: Oxford University Press, 2006), 5. Tilley writes about instances of Christians persecuting other Christians pre-Constantine. Illustrating the tensions between Roman Catholic Christians and the Donatists, she narrates an event in Carthage (304) where "there was a riot outside the entrance to the prison. Christians coming in from the countryside to visit their friends and relatives in prison were pushed, shoved, whipped ... The noteworthy fact was that these Christian rustics were beaten not by the local Roman authorities, but by troops employed by Mensurius, the Christian bishop of the city, and by Caecilian, his deacon" (Tilley, "Introduction," xi). Moreover, Tilley shows how those Christians outside Constantine's favor were persecuted and repressed. During 317–321 and 346–348 there were periods of severe repression and stories of martyred Donatists. According to her, Constantine backed the bishop of Carthage and repressed those who refused to recognize his authority. At one point, she writes, the whole congregation was martyred within their Donatist church. See Ibid., xv–xvi.

130 González, *A History of Christian Thought*, 262.

131 The work of Michelle Renee Salzman is an excellent source for exploring of the cultural significance of the aristocracy in terms of political power and religious influence in Christianity. She notes: "If religious conversion was the sole concern, Christian emperors

The historical shift by which Christianity was co-opted into becoming the chosen religion of the Empire is marked by the moment when the formerly persecuted Church became involved in the imperial apparatus of persecution against other Christians. We see the blending of imperial and Christian cultural, religious, and class interests. Christian Catholicity began to also shift in meaning, rejecting any critique of the teachings and the leadership of the Church as divisive. Christianity in its elite expressions became corrupt. And the liturgical celebration shifted from more or less secret meetings to the all-out Roman expressions in the basilica with all its many imperial trappings (stoles, processions, formalization, etc.). As theological argumentations failed, and sometimes even before making use of them, "one could always make use of the resources of politics and have one's [theological] enemies banished."[132] The shift of power turned horrific for the sake of "peace" and "unity" after Constantine's Edict of Milan when Christians with power turned against Christians who disagreed with them. Those were the practical conditions under which the Donatist controversy was fought. Consider the following excerpt:

> "Therefore, when one discovers wolves hiding in sheep's clothing, either those who were deceived by ignorance ... Therefore, may the sweet mother Church proclaim the enduring faith of her children. May the den of the most cruel thieves call to mind the fruit of their work ... and the Devil appeared as counselor for all of them. Their practices were rooted in the old Serpent."[133]

These remarks were not directed at pagan emperors or pagan society but towards those within the established "Catholic" Church system supported by the Empire. Christians who protested against the Imperial version of Christianity faced punishment, persecution, and in some cases, martyrdom.

---

would have appointed only Christians. They did not; even by the end of the fourth century, when there was a larger pool of Christians to choose from, Christianizing emperors like Gratian and Theodosius continued to appoint pagan aristocrats to office. By and large, the Christian emperors did not want to alienate pagan aristocrats" (Michelle Renee Salzman, *The Making of a Christian Aristocracy: Social and Religious Change in the Western Roman Empire* [Cambridge, MA: Harvard University Press, 2004], 193).

132   González, *A History of Christian Thought*, 273.

133   Maureen A Tilley, "A Sermon on the Passion of Saint Donatus and Advocatus Given on the 4th Day Before the Ides of March," in *Donatist Martyr Stories: The Church in Conflict in Roman North Africa*, translated with notes and introduction by Maureen A Tilley (Liverpool, London: Liverpool University Press, 1996), 53.

Even Augustine reasoned that some measure of violence was justifiable if that meant the "correction" of those that have "gone astray."[134] Augustine was convinced that there was sufficient scriptural warrant to impose punishment on the Donatists. He took pride in describing how former Donatist church communities, after being coerced, thanked God for their deliverance.[135] Behind Augustine's reasoning, As Michael Gaddis points out, is the justification of the use of violence as disciplinary discourse.

> They "employed calibrated violence not to destroy its targets but to chastise, reform, and even educate them. This was the violence of the center, the establishment-the emperor and his functionaries, or ecclesiastical authorities who enjoyed the recognition and support of the state and had recourse to its means of enforcement. Its motives, in theory, were not anger or vengeance but rather paternalistic compassion. But as mildly as this approach may have sought to present itself, ultimately it depended upon coercive power backed up by the very real possibility of violence."[136]

What we see, then, is the Church's adoption of the cultural model of the Imperial *pater familia* who disciplined and controlled his children and the members of his household; in an ecclesial context, this cultural model was justified as insisting on the "truth" for the sake of an orderly home/church/empire.

Beyond the Early Church

As I have shown, attention to the Bible from a cultural perspective reveals the dynamic and complex processes of culturalization. The stories in the Hebrew Bible, I insisted, demonstrate the profound impact of cultural traditions and illustrate the internal multilevel, fluid, uneven, and conflicted processes in the formation of Israelite cultural and ethnic identity. Moreover, I pointed out that although the Hebrew Bible is appropriately considered a religious document, its religious concerns are never separated from cultural interests and dynamics, and for this reason can be also considered to be a cultural document.

---

134 Augustine of Hippo, "Letter xciii (a.d. 408): To Vincentius," trans. J. G Cunningham, in *The Confessions and Letters of St. Augustin, with a Sketch of His Life and Work*, vol. 1, ed. Philip Schaff, Nicene and Post-Nicene Fathers Series I (Grand Rapids, MI: William B Eerdmans, 1886), 851–85.

135 Ibid., Chapter II, Sections 5–7 and Chapter V, Section 16.

136 Michael Gaddis, *There is No Crime for Those Who Have Christ: Religious Violence in Christian Empire* (Berkeley and Los Angeles, CA: University of California Press, 2005), 133.

These processes are not unique to the people of Israel. Reflecting on the New Testament, I showed that the multiple dynamics of cultural exchange, contestation, and development are also found in the exchanges among different cultural groups. Christianity was deeply influenced by the diverse cultural groups that inhabited the region. The Jewish religious apparatus, practices, and organizational frame particularly operated as the early Christians' point of reference to think about the reality of God and Christian life. But the church was also heavily influenced by Greek and Roman cultures. Early Christians read the Hebrew Scriptures, drew from the images and metaphors of Roman military culture and Roman imperial cult, and engaged Greek philosophers and mythological themes. The hermeneutics of the early church were a cultural hermeneutic.

The processes of culturalization, as I have been explaining, can also be identified in the shift of Christianity and its ecclesial structures from being the persecuted church to becoming the persecuting church. As I showed, for Christianity to become the religion of the Empire, a wide range of complex, contested, dynamic processes of cultural negotiation with the dominant Roman context of the day had to take place. Similarly, by the time Christianity was proclaimed the religion of the Empire, it was well on its way to becoming a religion governed by aristocrats. As a result, Christianity was profoundly changed and reconfigured in the process of becoming almost inseparable from Roman imperial culture.

As the Arius-Athanasius controversy demonstrates, religious councils also served social, economic and political interests. These interests were part of the larger fabric of cultural imperial power plays. The debates, controversies, and efforts to define the main tenets of the Christian faith continued. The councils kept negotiating the theological fine points of "orthodoxy," "heterodoxy" and "catholicity," but the meanings ascribed to such terms remained determined by the larger cultural influence of the context of Empire. Concerns about the relation between the larger cultural contexts in which Christianity found itself and its Romanized expression remained alive.

The cultural continued to play a key role in Christianity as it spread throughout the regions of the Middle East, Asia Minor and Western Europe. Many different expressions of Christianity emerged adapting to their new contexts and by adopting the local cultural practices and symbols to communicate and express the Christian faith. In Western Europe, Christianity also continued to grow; it changed, diversified and multiplied to include numerous religious monastic orders, and numerous religious practices and rituals. As Christians expressed their faith in their immediate cultures Christianity also changed; the multiply diverse expressions in Western Europe today attest to these processes of culturalization.

However, Christianity was deeply impacted by the fact that it became the dominant religion through Constantinianism as Christendom came into being. Notions of Empire and images of God as "Grand Emperor" and Christ as "King" (Christus Rex) were popularized, and theology reflected those changes. Through to the middle-ages and beyond, (Roman) imperial cultural ideas were still shaping theology. The liturgical celebration displayed the degree to which Roman imperial and cultural artifacts and traditions became standardized. For example, Anselm's now classic *Cur Deus homo* illustrates the influence of the Empire in portraying the event of the cross of Jesus as taking place within a divine royal court.[137] Other cultural influences like Hellenism also continued to shape the content of theological articulations. For example, Augustine's blending of Platonism and Christianity demonstrates this fruitful cross-fertilization. Centuries later Hellenistic influence was still evident in the Aristotelian influence on works like Aquinas' *Summa Theologica*.

We encounter the processes of culturalization as the intricate interwoven connections between Christianity and "Western European" cultures were solidified over the ensuing centuries. As Christianity developed it became common to identify Western Europeans as Christians and vice-versa; wherever Europeans went so also did Christianity. Amidst the climate of competing imperial powers and cultural traditions, the Christian church amassed political, social and economic power with the interests of European monarchies and aristocracies often intertwined.

---

137   For an analysis of the deep impact of the imperial cultural ethos in Christian theology see
       Joerg Rieger, *Christ & Empire: From Paul to Postcolonial Times* (Minneapolis, MN: Fortress
       Press, 2007).

CHAPTER 3

The Cultural on the Other Side
of the Imperial Mirror

Every idea thrown into the mind of the Negro is caught up and realized with the whole energy of his will; but this realization involves a
wholesale destruction ... it is manifest that want of self-control distin-
guishes the character of the Negroes. This condition is capable of no
development or Culture, and as we see them at this day, such they have
always been. The only essential connection between the Negroes and
the Europeans is slavery ... we may conclude slavery to have been the
occasion of the increase in human feeling among the Negroes.[1]

GEORG WILHELM FRIEDRICH HEGEL

•••

La grandeza de España es inmensa cuando esta es comparada con
la bajeza y degradación de los pueblos nativos: Compara [las dotes
españolas de] prudencia, ingenio, magnanimidad, templanza,
humanidad y religión, con las de esos hombrecillos en los que ape-
nas se pueden encontrar restos de humanidad, que no sólo carecen
de cultura, sino que ni siquiera usan o conocen las letras ni conser-
van monumentos de su historia, sino cierta oscura y vaga memoria
de algunos hechos consignada en ciertas pinturas, carecen de leyes
escritas y tienen instituciones y costumbres bárbaras.[2]

JUAN GINÉS DE SEPÚLVEDA

•••

Le mécanisme de cette mort de la culture et des civilisations sous
le régime colonial commence à être bien connu. Toute culture pour

---

1 Cited in Paul Gilroy, *The Black Atlantic: Modernity and Double Consciousness* (Cambridge,
MA: Harvard University Press, 1993), 41.
2 Juan Ginés de Sepúlveda, *Demócrates Segundo: De las justas causas de la guerra contra los
Indios*, ed. and trans. Angel Losada (Madrid, España: Consejo Superior de Investigaciones
Científicas: Instituto Francisco de Vitoria, 1951), 35.

s'épanouir a besoin d'un cadre, d'une structure. Or il est certain que les éléments qui structurent la vie culturelle du peuple colonisé, disparaissent ou 'abâtardissent du' fait du régime colonial.[3]

AIMÉ CÉSAIRE

• • •

History teaches us that, in certain circumstances, it is quite easy for a stranger to impose his rule on a people. But history equally teaches us that, whatever the material aspects of that rule, it cannot be sustained except by the permanent and organized repression of the cultural life of the people in question.[4]

AMILCAR CABRAL

Introduction

As I showed in chapter 2, Constantinianism marked both the unique blending of Christianity with an imperial cultural ethos and the historical moment at which Christians ceased to be considered a minority. According to John Howard Yoder, prior to Constantinianism the church was conceived in terms of a theology of the invisible church-*ecclesia invisibilis*; before Constantine, "one knew as a fact of everyday experience that there was a believing Christian community but one had to 'take it on faith' that God was governing history."[5] But with the age of Constantinianism, this perception of the church changed; people knew that (the Christian) God was in control of history. The church and the empire were inseparable, and the emperor was perceived as God's regent on earth.

I allude here (too) briefly to these complex debates in order to highlight the radical shift Constantinianism signified for the theological articulation of the church. For our purposes, it is important to note these shifts contributed overtime to Western European imperial projects in all of their multiple and at times contradictory expressions. The self-perception of Europeans as Christians was interwoven with cultural concerns hidden behind notions of civilization. From the late Middle Ages onward, as Europeans went out of their political boundaries to "explore" the

---

3   Aimé Césaire, "Culture et colonisation," *Liberté* 5, no. 1 (25) (January-February 1963): 20, Http://id.erudit.org/iderudit/30187ac (accessed January 25, 2015).

4   Amilcar Cabral, "National Liberation and Culture," *Transition* 45 (1974): 12.

5   John Howard Yoder, *The Priestly Kingdom: Social Ethics as Gospel* (Notre Dame, IN: University of Notre Dame Press, 1984), 137.

world, they invested enormous resources in the complex process of constructing their sense of identity as Christian, civilized, and superior, in other words as entirely different from the rest of the world.[6] Simultaneously, as they encountered other regions and peoples, they engaged in a concerted strategic process of "othering," in the negative ideological construction of other groups as the binary opposite of the Europeans; those groups were deemed inferior, barbarian / uncivilized / savage, and pagan. In other words, European cultural blinders conditioned them *not* to see the cultures, religious traditions, and humanity of the others of the world they encountered in their imperial path.

In this chapter, I propose that the entire European colonial project—starting with the Spanish and Portuguese conquests at the end of the fifteenth century and extending up to today—was and is fundamentally cultural in nature. I intend to show that in order to assert themselves as superior, civilized and Christian, those belonging to the family of Western European cultures entered into orchestrated processes of systematizing, categorizing and organizing hierarchically the cultural knowledges of the other peoples of the world. The result was a dynamic and violent process of (mis)identification and (mis)recognition which demonstrated the "inferiority," "barbarity" ("uncivilized state"), and "paganism" of the "other" and justified their imperial and colonial projects.

In multiple ways Christianity played a constitutive role in the expansion of European culture, its imperial and colonial projects, and the construction of the idea of "savage" inferior others. In this and the following chapter, I elucidate the ways in which Christianity was complicit with the imperial cultural projects in their various expressions.

The Emergence of "Western Europe"

In considering the emergence of what British cultural critic Stuart Hall calls the "idea of the West,"[7] many choose 1492 as historical marker for the radical shifts by which Europe was placed at the centre of world affairs.[8] Felipe Fernández

6 For a brief analysis of some of the reasons why Europeans had remained within their geographical borders see Stuart Hall, "The West and the Rest: Discourse and Power," in *Modernity: An Introduction to Modern Societies*, ed. Stuart Hall, et al. (Oxford, UK: Blackwell Publishers Ltd., 2000), 184–227.

7 Hall, "The West and the Rest."

8 See Enrique Dussel, "World-Systems and 'Trans-Modernity,'" trans. Alessandro Fornazzari, *Nepantla: Views from the South* 3, no. 2 (2002): 221–44, Http://muse.jhu.edu/journals/nepantla/v003/3.2dussel.htm (accessed January 15, 2006).

Armesto reminds us, however, that for most peoples in the world the year was fraught with historical events, which had great global significance and which at the time overshadowed the importance of Christopher Columbus' "stumbling" on what later came to be known as the Americas.[9] By tracing the multiple other historical events around the world occurring at the same period, he unmasks the process by which "Europe" gained ideological supremacy with the year 1492 as the pivotal point in which such an ideology gained worldwide prominence. Fernández Armesto's challenge coincides with decolonial scholar Enrique Dussel's proposal that up to the fifteenth century Europe occupied the periphery of what he calls the "sistema interregional" (inter-regional system).[10] As Dussel explains, the centre of this system was India, and the other economic power of the time, China, had no interest in Europe because it had its eyes set on India.[11] Spain (and the rest of Western Europe was to follow suit) had but one opportunity to be the centre, and that was by turning to the West. These multiple issues—which deserve a fuller treatment than I can give them—intersect with the emergence of "the West" as the operative concept behind the ascendency of Europe; the "West" described European cultures, identified non-Europeans cultures, and justified the European imperial and colonizing impetus.

Hall helps us parse out the complexity of the concept of "the West." According to him, there are four crucial interwoven functions inherent in the concept. First, it functions as a mechanism of classification of societies and peoples into oppositional categories. Second, it is an image connected to a larger set of images that are condensed into "a composite picture of what different societies, cultures, peoples, and places are like."[12] As Hall insists, it is a "system of representation" because it does not stand on its own but in conjunction with other images and ideas with which it forms a set: Western—urban—developed in relation to its opposite counterpart non-western—rural—non-industrial—agricultural—underdeveloped.[13] Third, it provides a standard model of comparison; "it allows us to compare to what extent different societies resemble, or differ from, one

9   Felipe Fernández Armesto, *1492: The Year Our World Began* (New York, NY: Bloomsbury, 2009).

10   Enrique Dussel, *Ética de la liberación en la edad de la globalización y de la exclusión* (Valladolid, España: Editorial Trotta, 1998), 55.

11   Dussel, *Ética de la liberación*, 54. See also Enrique Dussel, "Más allá del eurocentrismo: El sistema-mundo y los límites de la modernidad," Oscar Guardiola-Rivera, in *Pensar (en) los intersticios: Teoría y práctica de la crítica poscolonial*, ed. Santiago Castro-Gómez, Oscar Guardiola-Rivera, and Carmen Millán de Benavides (Santa Fe de Bogotá: CEJA: Instituto Pensar, 1999), 150.

12   Hall, "The West and the Rest," 186.

13   Ibid.

another. Non-western societies can accordingly be said to be "close to" or "far away from" or "catching up with" the West."[14] And fourth, the idea of "the West" provides the criteria of evaluation against which other societies are ranked and around which powerful positive and negative feelings cluster. As he explains, the "West" is desirable, good, and developed, while the "non-West" is undesirable, bad, and underdeveloped.[15] It is because of these complex sets of mutually supporting ideas that, Hall insists, the West is a historical construct and not a geographical one; "the West" functions as an ideology.[16]

Hall's ideological schema helps to identify the multiple and interconnected parts in the concept of the West. It is important to note that, for him, in this particular configuration of ideas the West is synonymous with "modernity."[17] However, ideas of "development" and "industrialization" which he includes, in the second point above, came some time later during the eighteenth century. In other words, the range of images that initiated this process of the emergence of "the West" at the end of the fifteenth century revolved more around the interwoven ideas of "culture" as civilization, racialized superiority, and Christianity. Furthermore, the

---

14   Ibid.

15   Ibid.

16   Ibid.

17   Hall, "The West and the Rest," 186. There are many debates concerning the historical birth point of "modernity." One of the usual explanations for the emergence of modernity rests on the uncritical affirmation that "modernity" was the innocent result of the intellectual brilliance of Europe. One good example of this perspective is evident in Hannah Arendt's work. She traces European "advance" and "development," and the birth of modernity back to the internal qualities of Europe, with no attention given to the rest of the world. As far as she is concerned, Columbus stumbling on the Americas, the invention of the telescope and the Reformation preceded modernity. See Hannah Arendt, *The Human Condition*, Second ed., introd. by Margaret Canovan (Chicago, IL: University of Chicago Press, 1958), 248, 312–13. According to Hall, even the Enlightenment was considered a very European affair. "European society, it assumed, was the most advanced type of society on earth, European man (*sic*) the pinnacle of human achievement. It treated the West as the result of forces largely *internal* to Europe's history and formation" (Hall, "The West and the Rest," 187). Meanwhile, Dussel argues that the myth of "modernity" must be interrogated by its underside, by those outside of "modernity." Modernity must be measured by the violence exacted against the Indigenous peoples and the African slaves. It must also be measured by the subsequent exploitation orchestrated by such a "world-system" (*sistema-mundo*) when it was imposed upon the rest of the world. He concludes that, all these elements are constitutive both of Europe today and of the myth of Modernity, which begins in 1492 because of the conquest of the Americas and not in the Enlightenment. See Enrique Dussel, *The Underside of Modernity*.

"standard of comparison," as discussed in the third point, played a central role in articulating the justifications for the imperial and colonizing projects form the fifteenth century onwards.

Of no less importance is the connection between Christianity or the idea of Christendom and the idea of "the West," "Western civilization," and European imperial/colonial projects. During the Middle Ages Christendom had become synonymous with Europe; in fact, Europe was called "Christendom" more often than "Europe."[18] Even as the notion of Christendom was eventually de-emphasized—it was gradually replaced by the discourse[19] of "Europe and Western civilization," those in power continued to draw from elements of the earlier discourse of "Christendom."[20] Still today one finds embedded in the discourses of "Europe" and the "West" traces of the past discourses of Christendom.[21] Thus, Christianity was part and parcel of the European imperial cultural project of expansion, conquest, colonization, and eventual enculturation of the peoples of the "New Worlds."[22]

18   Hall, "The West and the Rest," 197.

19   Here, I am using Foucault's notion of discourse by which he means a series of "discontinuous segments whose tactical function is neither uniform nor stable. To be more precise, we must not imagine a world of discourse divided between accepted discourse and excluded discourse, or between the dominant discourse and the dominated one; but as a multiplicity of discursive elements that can come into play in various strategies" Michel Foucault, An Introduction, vol. 1 of The History of Sexuality, trans. Robert Hurley (New York, NY: Random House, Vintage, 1978), 100. In discovering the function of a discourse, we must engage in an examination of what is said and what is hidden. Thus, it would be a mistake to think in terms of discourse of power and its opposite, a discourse that runs against it. Rather, "discourses are tactical elements or blocks in the field of force relations; there can exist different and even contradictory discourses within the same strategy" Foucault, An Introduction, 101–2. In other words, I want to bring to light the power play and dynamics at work in the creation of discourses such as "Europe," "Western Civilization," and "the West." This family of discourses functions as technologies in the affirmation of the Western European self-perception vis-á-vis the rest of the world.

20   The discourse functioned as a rallying banner under which the internal differences of the countries of Western Europe were gradually de-emphasized and "began to conceive" themselves as part of a single family or civilization—"'the West'" (Hall, "The West and the Rest," 197). According to Hall, the challenge of Islam was an important factor in solidifying Western Europe as a concept and the idea of "the West."

21   Hall, "The West and the Rest," 202.

22   The term "New World" is often reserved to speak about the Americas after the Spanish and Portuguese conquests and invasions. Here, I am using the plural "New Worlds" to refer to the multiple cultures, human collectives and Indigenous and originary groups all over the world, who entered European consciousness and imaginary as "others" as a result of European imperial expansion and colonialism.

All of these multiple aspects contributed to the formation of the idea of "Western civilization," which became: the banner of European superiority; the interpretive lenses for understanding the peoples of the "New Worlds;" and the religious motivation and referent for imposing a self-perceived superior European *culture* based on this blend of Christianity with European cultural elements.

Constructing Knowledge Systems about the Rest of the World

Looking into the Mirror of "Western Civilization": Sources

In his book *Orientalism*, Edward Said analyses the various discourses, intellectual structures and institutions which constructed and produced "the *Orient*" as an object of learning, discovery, and practice;[23]—as the object of knowledge construction. According to him, Orientalist discourses made sense because they depended "more on the West than on the Orient."[24] But since the Orient was virtually unknown and was perceived as hostile territory, it (the Orient)

> needed first to be known, then invaded and processed, then re-created by scholars, soldiers, and judges who disinterred forgotten languages, histories, races, and cultures in order to posit—beyond the modern Oriental's ken—as the true classical Orient that could be used to judge and rule the modern Orient.[25]

As the Orientalists "learned" (read produced knowledge) about the Orient, they (mis)represented it. What mattered *was not* "the actual Orient, but what the Oriental [said] about the Orient."[26] As Said explains, the Orient that is present through Orientalism is based on a system of representation framed by a

---

23   Edward W. Said, *Orientalism* (New York, NY: Random House, Vintage, 1979), 73.

24   Said, *Orientalism*, 22. According to Foucault, the knowledge which a discourse produces constitutes a kind of power, exercised over those who are "known." When that knowledge is exercised in practice, those who are "known" in a particular way will be "subject (i.e., subjected) to it" (Cited in Hall, "The West and the Rest," 204–5). Thus, the discourse operates within an established power-relation.... "Those who produce the discourse also have the power to *make it true*—i.e. to enforce its validity, its scientific status" (Ibid., 205).

25   Said, *Orientalism*, 82.

26   Said, *Orientalism*, 21. The Orientalist acknowledged that there was something properly called the Orient, but they also operated under the assumption that it only gained intelligibility through interaction with the British; it was not intelligible on its own. See Ibid., 40.

whole set of forces that brought the Orient into the scope of "Western learning, Western consciousness, and later, Western empire."[27] The ultimate result was the development of the *Orientalist gaze* that viewed the Orient as a "locale requiring Western attention, reconstruction, even redemption."[28]

What Said describes in terms of the invention of Orientalist discourses, intersects in significant ways with how "The West" related to and interacted with "the Rest" of the world; "the West's" creation of multiple, at times contradictory discourses did not only target the Orient and the Orientals, it also targeted the entire range of "New Worlds" that were encountered post 1492. As with the Orientalist project though with significant differences in approach and practice in relation to each of these peoples of the "New Worlds"[29]— Western Europeans resorted to the creation/production of knowledge about all people groups they knew nothing about. The "New Worlds" entered into Western European consciousness and came under Europe's imperial gaze.

Drawing on Said, Hall reminds us that central to the project of knowing these *other* peoples was the creation of a library or archive that would serve as repository of information/knowledge "about" the natives.[30] As already mentioned, the development of the discourses of the "West," "Europe," and "Western civilization" formed in relation to the other peoples of the world. In order to assert their own self-perception as "superior," "advanced," "civilized" and Christian, Western Europeans amassed "evidence" that the rest of the world was "inferior," "uncivilized," "savage/barbarian," and "heathen."[31] This massive domination of the world by Europe was accomplished through a

---

27 Said, *Orientalism*, 203. Orientalism, claims Said, "is a school of interpretation whose material happens to be the Orient, it civilizations, peoples, and localities" (Ibid.).

28 Said, *Orientalism*, 206. According to Said writes, every one of the authors and Orientalists "kept intact this separateness of the Orient, its eccentricity, its backwardness, its silent indifference, it's feminine penetrability, its supine malleability; this is why every writer on the Orient, from Renan to Marx (ideologically speaking), or from the most rigorous scholars (Lane and Sacy), to the most powerful imaginations (Flaubert and Nerval)," saw the Orient needing Western intervention and attention. (Ibid.).

29 I wish to make clear that Said did not concern himself with 1492 or the earlier conquest of the Americas. Unfortunately, his analysis of orientalism does not connect the European (mis)representation of the oriental with the larger European imperial project more fully which included the Americas.

30 Hall, "The West and the Rest," 206.

31 According to Said, the essence of Orientalism was the "ineradicable distinction between Western superiority and oriental inferiority" (Said, *Orientalism*, 42). In other words, the distinctions made in orientalist discourses were neither innocent nor neutral, and were only deepened and hardened over time. See Ibid.

systematic, concerted, production of knowledge of the other peoples of the world in the form of written material, maps, legends, stories, and even theological treatises. Eventually, they also produced pseudoscientific studies, as well as anthropological, historical, geographical, ethnographical, biological/phenotypical[32] and missionary reports with the intention of "knowing" the various aspects of the peoples of the "New Worlds." It is this information, like the ones Said documents, which served as the justification for the conquests of these peoples, and which, during the highest phase of Western European imperialism served to justify later imperial colonizing projects and expansionism.

This written material constituted a family of ideas and unifying set of values "proven" in various ways to be "true" which functioned as interpretive points of reference in the encounter with the inhabitants of the "New Worlds." According to Stuart Hall, there were four sources that undergirded this information / knowledge about the peoples of the "New Worlds." They were: 1. *Dependence on mythological stories*—the Spaniards, for example, arrived to South America and were looking for legendary places; 2. *Tales of travelers* from those who had ostensibly been there; 3. *Classical Knowledge,* from ancient Greek philosophers such as Plato and Aristotle; and 4. *Religious/Christian and biblical sources* which became the lenses through which many of the events were understood.[33] These sources appear again and again in various ways in the voluminous production of knowledge collected over the centuries concerning not only the "New Worlds," but more generally "non-Europeans." Let us utilize Hall's fourfold division as a heuristic devise to further examine and illustrate the set of interrelated Western European concerns, interests, values, and ideas that intersected in the complex processes of the construction of knowledge about the "New Worlds" and the concurrent developments of the idea of "Western Europe."

---

32   Although one could say that race was a cornerstone for this complex system, it was not until later on in the eighteenth century that "race" as category of differentiation between Europeans and the rest of the world was deployed. Admittedly, racialization was already at work in Latin America's *mestizaje,* for example, as "purity of blood" was an operating category of social organization. Thus, while it is true that a "pigmentocracy" was at play in the ways in which people were "organized" in colonial societies, the debates on racial superiority and inferiority came much later. It is for this reason that I am not mentioning it at this juncture. See Alejandro Lipschutz, 2nd. ed. in *El problema racial en la conquista de América y el mestizaje* (Santiago, Chile: Editorial Andres Bello, 1967); Arthur de Gobineau, *The Inequality of Human Races,* trans. Adrian Collins, introd. by Oscar Levy (London, UK: William Heinemann, 1915).

33   Hall, "The West and the Rest," 206–7.

Mythological Stories

Mythological stories served several functions. Often, they functioned to put on display the "superior" humanity of the Spanish (and other Western Europeans), which gave them the right to invade Indigenous communities and plunder their riches. They also promoted Spanish virility and superior courage in contrast to the inferior fearsome natives who needed to be "civilized." As the Europeans encountered the "New Worlds" they projected many ideas about mythological places that were part of the European imaginary. For example, it was Francisco de Orellana who—during the first quarter of the sixteenth century—sailed the length of the great river in the American continent and gave it the name *Amazon*, due to the attacks on him by women warriors.[34]

One of the greatest mythological stories was about the long-searched-for city of *El Dorado*. According to Claire Taylor, the myth that *El Dorado*—that place of extreme abundance of precious stones and gold—could be located in the "New Worlds" was inspired around 1534, out of a Chibcha ceremony where the high priest covered in powdered gold, threw gold and other precious objects into the bottom of the lake.[35] As narrated by W. H. Brett, *El Dorado* was thought to have been established by a branch of the "royal race of the Incas," and had riches that exceeded those of Peru.[36] Those in search of the city of Manoa—the location of *El Dorado*—among whom there were Spaniards, Portuguese, German, French, and English adventurers, believed that the houses were "covered with plates of that precious metal; and not only were all the vessels in the royal palace made of the same, but gold-dust was so abundant that the natives sprinkled it over their bodies, which they first anointed with a glutinous substance, that it might stick to them."[37] Special interest was given to the Prince of the city, who according to Gonzalo Fernández de Oviedo y Valdés was adorned

---

34   Claire Taylor, "The Spanish and Portuguese Empires," in *The Routledge Companion to Postcolonial Studies*, ed. John McLeod (New York, NY: Routledge: Taylor & Francis Group, 2007), 50.

35   Ibid., 51.

36   William Henry Brett, *The Indian Tribes of Guiana; Their Condition and Habits, with Researches Into Their Past History, Superstitions, Legends, Antiquities, Languages, Etc.* (London, UK: R. Clay, son, and Taylor, 1868), 37.

37   Brett, *The Indian Tribes of Guiana*, 37–38. The Spaniards believed that *El Dorado* was located in the Northern parts of todays South America. After repeatedly failing to find it, they concluded that it was probably in the Orinoco. As Brett writes, "About the end of the sixteenth century, the search for El Dorado was chiefly carried on in another direction. Having been vainly sought elsewhere, it was thought that it must be in the eastern part of Guiana (as yet unexplored), and somewhere near the Caroni" (Ibid., 41). Narrating his own expedition of 1595, Walter Raleigh confirms the search for *El Dorado* in Guiana. He recalls the

in gold daily by his chamberlains. In the evening, he washed himself off the gold only to be "gilded anew in the morning," which proved "that the empire of El Dorado is infinitely rich in mines." All this was believed and became the object of many expeditions on the part of the early Spanish conquistadors.[38] The most detailed account of how the legend/myth of *El Dorado* was created is found in Walter Raleigh's own 1595 expedition into Guiana.[39] Of course, many explorers perished in the pointless search for the legendary city and once stricken with the fever for *El Dorado*, many explorers and adventurers sold everything they had including their lands to finance their voyages. I note that among these there were many priests.[40]

Other legends emerged as the Spaniards encountered the natives of the "New Worlds." Amerigo Vespucci recounted the legendary might of the Spaniards, stating that sixteen of them fought and defeated two thousand of the natives and stole their houses.[41] In another letter he wrote that the natives lived a long time, and that he met a man who had lived one hundred and thirty-two years.[42]

---

first European encounter with the city of Manoa: "the first that ever saw Manoa was Juan Martínez, master of the munition to Ordaz. At a port called Morequito, in Guiana, there lieth at this day a great anchor of Ordaz's ship and this port is some three hundred miles within the land, upon the great River Orinoco." (Walter Raleigh, *The Discovery of Guiana, and the Journal of the Second Voyage Thereto* [London, UK: Cassell & Company, Limited, 1887], 28).

38   Cited in Brett, *The Indian Tribes of Guiana*, 38.

39   Raleigh, *The Discovery of Guiana*, 28–32. Raleigh wrote that "I have been assured by such of the Spaniards as have seen Manoa, the imperial city of Guiana, which the Spaniards call El Dorado, that for the greatness, for the riches, and for the excellent seat, it far excee-deth any of the-world, at least of so much of the world as is known to the Spanish nation; it is founded upon a lake of salt water of two hundred leagues long, like unto *mare caspiũ*" (Ibid., 24).

40   Brett tells us that as late as the 1775–1776 one expedition lost one hundred people search-ing for the majestic city. In other case, large expeditions were also prepared: "Berrio, the Spanish Governor of Trinidad, sent an agent to prepare in Europe an expedition of two thousand men; and adventurers, selling their lands, embarked on a small crusade in that expedition; to which a number of priests and monks were attached" (Brett, *The Indian Tribes of Guiana*, 41).

41   Américo Vespucio, "Carta del 18 de julio de 1500, dirigida desde Sevilla a Lorenzo Pier Francesco de Medici, en Florencia," in *El Nuevo Mundo: Viajes y documentos completos*, trans. Ana María R. de Aznar, notes by Fernández Navarrete, et al. (Madrid, España: Ediciones Akal, S.A., 1985), 11–27.

42   Américo Vespucio, "Carta de 1502: Enviada desde Lisboa a Lorenzo Pier Francesco de Medici, en Florencia," in *El Nuevo Mundo: Viajes y documentos completos*, trans. Ana María R. de Aznar, notes by Fernández Navarrete, et al. (Madrid, España: Ediciones Akal, S.A., 1985), 39–45.

Christopher Columbus added his own set of legends and myths. Near the end of 1492, he spoke of the natives of the Americas as "timorous" and "cowardly and fearful" in contrast to the mighty Spaniards who fought like biblical legendary soldiers. Columbus recounted that ten Spaniards could put ten thousand of the natives to flight.[43] Another contemporary of Columbus, Francisco López de Gómara also contributed to this mythology about the courage of the Spaniards; he narrated the struggle between the forces of Hernán Cortés and the natives of Mexico and registered only 50 Spaniards lost in the battle while 100,000 natives died, without counting those who died of hunger and sickness.[44] These stories re-enforced Spanish (and European) self-perceived superiority over the natives.

Tales of Travelers

No less fantastical were the stories and tales by travelers concerning the natives of the "New World" of the Americas and other places. These stories of deformed or half-human beings supported Spanish doubts about the humanity of the natives. As Lewis Hanke noted, "The literature presented portraits of the natives of distant regions as giants, pygmies, dragons, griffins, children with white hair, women with beards, human beings adorned with tails, acephalous creatures with eyes in their stomachs or in their chests, and other fabulous beings."[45]

There are many examples of how the Spanish were certain they would find mythical creatures who were half human and half beast. Diego Velázquez told Hernán Cortés to seek among the Nahua people with flat ears and the faces of dogs.[46] The stories and tales abound: Amerigo Vespucci related yet another incident in which some Spaniards had told him they had encountered giants. The information he received described them as being so tall that on their

---

43   Christopher Columbus, *The Journal of Christopher Columbus*, trans. Cecil Jane, with an appendix by R.A. Skelton (New York, NY: Bramhall House, 1970), November 27.

44   Francisco López de Gómara, *Cortés: The Life of the Conqueror by His Secretary Francisco López de Gomara*, ed. and trans. Leslie Byrd Simpson (Berkeley; Los Angeles, CA: University of California Press, 1964), 131–44.

45   Lewis Hanke, *El prejuicio racial en el Nuevo Mundo: Aristóteles y los Indios de Hispanoamérica*, trans. Marina Orellana (Santiago de Chile: Editorial Universitaria, S.A., 1958), 19. As early as the fifth century evidence of this kind of mythological fancy is evident in Augustine who had dedicated a chapter of his *City of God* to reflecting on whether "the descendants of Adam and the children of Noah had produced human monsters" (cited in Ibid.).

46   Hanke, *El prejuicio racial en el Nuevo Mundo*, 20.

knees they were still taller than a Spaniard standing.[47] Tales of giants in the land of today's Mexico appeared later-on in the writings of Fernando de Alva Ixtlilxochitl. In his *Relaciones* he wrote that

> In New Spain there were giants; besides the evidence of bones found in many parts, the old Tultec historials, called *Quinametzín*, got to know them and had many wars and tensions with them.... They said that in these lands where the ancient Chichimeca empire was, there are provinces with men who are as tall as thirty palmos [20 feet]; it is not surprising that even the Spaniards who have not gone further inland have found men measuring eleven and twelve palms [7 feet] in the coast ... and there are news about others who are taller.[48]

Inspired by and at times contrasted with Greek and Roman mythologies, tales of natives with animal heads and human bodies or vice-versa were not uncommon.[49] Hall quotes one of those instances in relation to Northern Africa and India:

47   Vespucio, "Carta del 18 de julio de 1500." He describes them as follows: "que cada uno de ellos era de rodillas más alto que yo de pie. En conclusión eran de estatura de gigantes ..." (Ibid.).

48   Don Fernando de Alva Ixtlilxochitl, *Obras Históricas de Don Fernando de Alva Ixhilxochilt*, vol. I: Relaciones, ed and annotated by Alfredo Chavero (México, DF: Oficina Tipografía de la Secretaria de Fomento, 1891), 17. "En esta Nueva España hubo gigantes, de más de la demostración de sus huesos que se hallan en muchas partes, dicen los antiguos historiadores Tultecas que se llamaban *Quinametzín*, y que alcanzaron a conocer y tuvieron muchas guerras y disensiones con ellos.... Y dicen que en estas tierras ... en donde estaba el antiguo imperio de los Chichimecas, hay provincias donde viven hombres que tienen más de treinta palmos de altura; y no es de espantarse, que aun nuestros españoles, con ser aún no han entrado en la tierra dentro, sino por estas costas ... han hallado hombres ... de once y doce palmos, y noticias de haber otros más altos."

49   For example, Gonzalo Fernández de Oviedo compared Greek mythological figures with the experiences of the Spaniards in the "New World." Those heroes, he wrote "no son comparación bastanta á vuestros españoles, en las cosas en estas nuevas tierras han experimentado, las fabulosas novelas de Jason y Medea con su vellocino dorado. Callen los pregoneros de Theseo aquel laberinto y su Minotauro, pues sabida la verdad, esas metáforas reducidas á historia cierta. son burlas y niñerías, si se cotejan y traen á comparación de lo que en estas Indias nuestras se ha visto y se ve cada día ... y lo han visto mis ojos." (Gonzalo Fernández de Oviedo y Valdés, *Historia general y natural de las Indias, islas y tierra-firme del már océano*, vol. II, Cotejada con el códice original, enriquecida con las enmiendas y adiciones del autor, é ilustrada con la vida y el juicio de las obras del mismo por José D. Amador de los Rios [Madrid, España: Imprenta de "la Real Academia de la Historia," 1852], 2). In the end, according to Fernández de Oviedo, the Spaniards were living mythological figures.

In the land of the Indian there are men with dogs' heads who talk by barking [and] ... feed by catching birds.... Others again have only one eye in the forehead.... In Libya many are born without heads and have a mouth and eyes. Many are of both sexes ... Close to Paradise on the River Ganges live men who eat nothing. For they absorb liquid nourishment through a straw [and] live on the juice of flowers.... Many have such large underlips that they can cover their whole faces with them.... In the land of Ethiopia many people walk bent down like cattle, and many live four hundred years. Many have horns, long noses and goats' feet. ... In Ethiopia towards the west many have four eyes ... [and] in Eripia there live beautiful people with the necks and bills of cranes.[50]

One of the better-known writers of legends leading up to the "discovery" of the Americas was John Mandeville. He deeply influenced the Western European imagination concerning peoples outside the boundaries of Western Europe in his writing about the many places and peoples he had reputedly met in his many voyages. A pseudonymm for Jean de Bourgoigne, or à la Barbe, a physician from Lüttich, Mandeville told many tales of his travels that lasted 30 years: 1332–1356. It is important to note, however, that while he lived in Egypt for some time, he never actually visited any other foreign country; he never visited the places he mentioned in his writings, nor did he know the people about whom he wrote.[51] Giving

---

50   Cited in Hall, "The West and the Rest," 207.

51   According to Otto Hartig, the primary sources for Mandeville's accounts were missionary stories, which sometimes paraphrased though often he copied them word for word. Hartig writes:

> His chief sources are the accounts of the travels of the first missionaries of the Dominican and Franciscan orders (see *Geography and the Church*), who were the first to venture into the interior of Asia. He describes Constantinople and Palestine almost entirely according to the "Itinerarius" of the Dominican William of Boldensele written in 1336; he made use moreover of the "Tractatus de distantiis locorum terræ sanctæ" of Eugesippus, the "Descriptio terræ sanctæ" of John of Würzburg (c. 1165), and the "Libellus de locis sanctis" of Theodoricus (c.1172). He was able out of his own experiences to give particulars about Egypt. What he has to say about the Mohammedan is taken from the work "De statu Saracenarum" (1273) of the Dominican William of Tripolis. His account of the Armenians, Persians, Turks, etc., is borrowed from the "Historia orientalis" of Hayton, the former Prince of Armenia and later Abbot of Poitiers. For the country of the Tatars and China he made use almost word for word of the "Deseriptio orientalium" of the Franciscan Odoric of Pordenone, and in parts of the "Historia Mongolorum" of the Franciscan John of Plano Carpini. Apart from

free rein to his imagination, he described peoples with heads of animals, without heads, with one eye and other strange features. Below I include an extended excerpt from Mandeville's account to illustrate the kind of Western European imaginary about peoples from distant lands that was already being constructed, and which eventually was projected on to the peoples of the "New Worlds":

> In one of these isles be folk of great stature, as giants. And they be hideous for to look upon. And they have but one eye, and that is in the middle of the front. And they eat nothing but raw flesh and raw fish. And in another isle toward the south dwell folk of foul stature and of cursed kind that have no heads. And their eyes be in their shoulders.
>
> And in another isle be folk that have the face all flat, all plain, without nose and without mouth. But they have two small holes, all round, instead of their eyes, and their mouth is flat also without lips.
>
> And in another isle be folk of foul fashion and shape that have the lip above the mouth so great, that when they sleep in the sun they cover all the face with that lip.
>
> And in another isle there be little folk, as dwarfs. And they be two so much as the pigmies. And they have no mouth; but instead of their mouth they have a little round hole, and when they shall eat or drink, they take through a pipe or a pen or such a thing, and suck it in, for they have no tongue; and therefore they speak not, but they make a manner of hissing as an adder doth, and they make signs one to another as monks do, by the which every of them understandeth other.
>
> And in another isle be folk that have great ears and long, that hang down to their knees. And in another isle be folk that have horses' feet. And they be strong and mighty, and swift runners; for they take wild beasts with running, and eat them.
>
> And in another isle be folk that go upon their hands and their feet as beasts. And they be all skinned and feathered, and they will leap as lightly into trees, and from tree to tree, as it were squirrels or apes.

---

books of travels he plagiarised from works of a general nature, the old authors Pliny, Solinus, Josephus Flavius, and the comprehensive "Speculum Historiale" of Vincent of Beauvais (Otto Hartig, "Jean de Mandeville," in *The Catholic Encyclopedia*, vol. IX [New York, NY: Robert Appleton Company], Http://www.newadvent.org/cathen/09587b.htm [accessed January 21, 2015]).

And in another isle be folk that be both man and woman, and they have kind of that one and of that other. And they have but one pap on the one side, and on that other none. And they have members of generation of man and woman, and they use both when they list, once that one, and another time that other. And they get children, when they use the member of man; and they bear children, when they use the member of woman.

And in another isle be folk that go always upon their knees full marvellously. And at every pace that they go, it seemeth that they would fall. And they have in every foot eight toes.[52]

Not surprisingly one finds allusions to similar creatures in the writings of some of the earliest European travelers. Columbus himself—usually thought to be influenced by Mandeville—also related that in his "communications" (by sign language) with the natives he understood that there were people with one eye and others with dog noses who ate people.[53]

At the turn of the sixteenth century large numbers of travelers inspired by the events of 1492 went out to *explore* the—until then *unknown* by Europeans—rest of the world. One of the better known authors of the time was Fernández de Oviedo y Valdés, known for his multivolume *Historia general y natural de las Indias*, in which he catalogued animals, plants, and many of the customs of the peoples he encountered.[54] Adolph Francis Bandelier's bibliography on the Central American zone shows the surge of researchers interested in the region.[55] Similarly, Donald Brand lists hundreds of researchers in the

---

52   Sir John Mandeville, *The Travels of Sir John Mandeville*, ed. A.W. Pollard (London, UK: MacMillan and Co, Limited, 1915), 133–34.

53   Columbus, *The Journal of Christopher Columbus*, November 4.

54   Gonzalo Fernández de Oviedo y Valdés, *Historia general y natural de las Indias, islas y tierra-firme del már océano*, vol. I–III, Cotejada con el códice original, enriquecida con las enmiendas y adiciones del autor, é ilustrada con la vida y el juicio de las obras del mismo por José D. Amador de los Rios (Madrid, España: Imprenta de la Real Academia de la Historia, 1851–1853). Among some of the better-known writers are the multivolume works of Alvar Nuñez Cabeza de Vaca's *Naufragios*; Antonio Herrera's *Historia general de las Indias*; Francisco López de Gomara's *Historia general de las Indias;* and Pietro Martire d'Anghiera's *Decades of the New World or West India*.

55   Adolph Francis Bandelier, *Notes on the Bibliography of Yucatan and Central America; Comprising Yucatan, Chiapas, Guatemala (the Ruins of Palenque, Ocosingo, and Copan). and Oaxaca (Ruins of Mitla)* (Worcester, UK: Press of Chas. Hamilton, 1881).

region of Brazil alone.[56] He mentions scholars from all disciplines: historians, geographers, linguists, naturists, botanists, and anthropologists, among others who swept and surveyed the land, the inhabitants, and their customs.[57] Their writings are left to us as incontrovertible testimony of the great surge of interest sparked by the arrival of the "New Worlds" into the Western European imaginary. Many of these authors were instrumental in the complex processes of cataloguing the topography, geography, and plant and animal lives of newly "discovered" regions. As part of this information gathering, they "organized" and catalogued the natives' life styles, (lack of) cultures, customs, practices, and religious traditions. Once again, the church was involved not only because of the work of evangelism, but because of the extensive participation of priests in the cataloguing/creating of this material/knowledge.[58]

The Classics

As Western Europeans sought to make sense of the "New Worlds," the ancient "Old World" provided them with frames of reference for critical comparison. The "classics" functioned as the standard to determine the level of civilization of the natives. According to Diego Durán, some writers made parallels between the Nahua and the Romans, claiming both to be "inspired by the same Spirit."[59] For instance, he compared Moctezuma who received revelations through the priests with the Romans of the past.[60] He noted that just as Rome adopted its name from its founder Romulos, so also the Nahua came to call themselves after Mecitin (which means Mexicans) on account of the priest that led them named Meci.[61] Similarly, Garcilaso de la Vega argued that the great centre of the Incan Empire, the city of Cuzco was another Rome.[62] Furthermore, while he acknowledged the idolatrous practices of the Incas, he admitted that it was

56   Donald Brand, "A Brief History of Anthropology in Brazil: Part I," *New Mexico Anthropologist* 5, no. 4 (October-December 1941): 99–150.

57   Ibid.

58   Among the works written by priests in the sixteenth century are: Diego Durán's *Historia de las Indias*; Bernardino de Sahagún's *Historia general de las cosas de Nueva España*; Bartolomé de las Casas' *Historia de las Indias;* José de Acosta's *Historia Natural y Moral de las Indias.*

59   Diego Durán, *Historia de las Indias de Nueva España y Islas de tierra firme*, vol. I, ed with notes and illustrations by José F. Ramírez (México, DF: Imprenta del J. M. Andrade y F. Escalante, 1867), XIII.

60   Ibid., 522.

61   Ibid., 19.

62   Inca Garcilaso de la Vega, *Comentarios Reales de los Incas*, vol. I, ed. Ángel Rosenblat (Buenos Aires, Argentina: Emecé Editores, S.A., 1943), 8.

not because they lacked instruction, because even "the Romans and the Greeks had thirty thousand gods."[63] Phelipe Guamán Poma de Ayala also made connections with Roman culture (though in relation to the conquistadors) when he spent time discussing what he claimed were Roman genealogies, from which he claimed to be able to trace the ancestry of Francisco Pizarro and Diego de Almagro the Conquistadors of Peru.[64]

In addition to comparisons with Greek and Roman cultural practices and structures, many authors drew on Greek philosophers to makes sense of the new reality with which they were being confronted. For instance, López de Gómara at the beginning of his *Historia General de las Indias* engaged in what can only be called a philosophical-theological treatise in which he drew on ideas of multiple worlds proposed by ancient Greek philosophers, physicists, and thinkers such as Democritus, Epicurus, Anaximander, Heraclitus, Plutarch, Pythagoras, and Leucippus.[65] Classical Greek philosophers and Christian theologians provided the platform on which to debate the status of the Indigenous peoples in the "New World" of the Americas. In the same first pages of his *Historia General*, López de Gómara alludes to the works of Augustine, Origen, Clement, Jerome, and Bernard de Clairvoux[66]

In no other place does the interconnection between the Greek philosophers and Christian theologians became so central as it is in the discussion on the humanity of the natives of the "New World" of the Americas, which I will discuss more fully later on. For now, suffice it to say that the discussion was based on Aristotle's theory of slavery as natural (as found in his *Politics* and *Nicomachean Ethics*) and in conversation with Augustine and Thomas Aquinas. By drawing on these sources, Juan Ginés de Sepúlveda justified the invasion of the Americas along with the spoliation and enslaving of the native inhabitants.[67] Not surprisingly, it was also in conversation with Aristotle, Aquinas, Augustine and Don Scotus that Francisco de Vitoria sought to

---

63   de la Vega, *Comentarios Reales de los Incas*, I.ix. "los romanos y los griegos tenían treinta mil dioses."

64   Phelipe Guamán Poma de Ayala, *La obra de Phelipe Guamán Poma de Ayala*, editado y compilado por Arthur Posnansky (La Paz, Bolivia: Editorial del Instituto "Tihuanacu" de Antropología, Etnografía y Prehistoria, 1944), Folio 32.

65   Francisco López de Gámara, *Historia general de las Indias*, vol. I (Madrid, España: Calpe, 1922), 8–11.

66   Ibid., 9–10.

67   Ginés de Sepúlveda, *Demócrates Segundo*. See also Hanke, *El prejuicio racial en el Nuevo Mundo*.

articulate a defense for the full humanity of the natives.[68] Other theologians participated, and all drew from the same intellectual and theological reservoir. In this way, the uncivilized state of the natives was demonstrated and the need for European civilization was confirmed

The Christian Story as Source

As has become evident by now, the Christianity to which Western Europeans ascribed (beginning with the Portuguese and Spanish) was a unique blend of Western European cultural mores, economic-political interests, perception of the world, and religious concerns. In fact, Christianity was understood more or less synonymous with European culture. As far as they were concerned, there was no perceivable difference or separation between European culture and the Christian religion. The Christian story provided a sense of coherent framing for the multiple sources mentioned above. The lack of Christianity among the natives contributed to the interpreting of conquest, invasion and colonization as necessary concomitants of evangelization.[69] As I noted earlier, the amalgam of Christianity with imperial cultural garb during the Constantinian era governed the frame for viewing the world. Christianity, and more specifically the desire to (re)build Christendom, fueled the European imaginary and was a strong catalyst for European expansion and colonialism. Stuart Hall articulates the identification between Europe and Christianity when he writes:

> For centuries, the concepts "Europe" and "Christendom" were virtually identical. Europe's cultural identity—what made its civilization distinct and unique—was, in the first instance, essentially religious and Christian.... The encounter with the new worlds—with

---

68   Francisco de Vitoria, *Relecciones teológicas*, trans. D. Jaime Torrubiano Ripoll (Madrid, España: Librería Religiosa Hernández, 1917), 1–87.

69   As Marcello Azevedo asseverates that if the discovery of the non-European peoples and their colonization was done from the European cultural vantage point, and which had the cost of "repression and the destruction of the autochthonous culures, or, at least, a considerable indifference or relation of domination," it was not any different in the case of evangelization. In fact, he adds, "the Christian faith spread in its european cultural garment and more concretely, Spanish, Portuguese, French, English, German, Italian, Belgian, Dutch," and others (Marcello de Carvalho Azevedo, "Comunidades eclesiales de base en Brasil: ¿posible mediación para la inculturación de la fe?" trans. Silvia Sinoott and Eduardo Sinnott, in *Identidad cultural y modernización*, vol. ii, ed. Carlos Galli and Luis Scherz, América Latina y la doctrina social de la iglesia: Diálogo latinoamericano-alemán [Buenos Aires, Argentina: Ediciones Paulinas, 1991], 234–35).

difference—actually reinforced this new identity. It promoted that "growing sense of superiority" ... an "Eurocentric" "view of the world."[70]

One key indication of the strong interpretive role Christianity played is the
fact that as the Spaniards and Portuguese and eventually Western Europeans
encountered the "New Worlds," they baptized the islands, regions, and places
with Christian-inspired names. Places like El Salvador, La Navidad (settlement in
today's Haiti), Santo Domingo, Dominica, Guadalupe, St. Croix (San Francisco,
Los Angeles in the United States of America, Saint John's, Newfoundland, Saint
Catherines, Ontario, Canada) attest to how profoundly Christianity influenced
their perception of the "New World" of the Americas. Christianity functioned
as the point of reference for the Western European historical, cultural, and religious imagination, which had taken centuries to crystallize.

A few further examples will bolster my point. Already Mandeville had
insisted that the name "Gran Khan" (the emperor of China) related directly
to Ham (he called him Cham), the son of Noah.[71] Columbus likewise drew on
biblical illusion and divine intervention to justify his voyages. He relates that as
he prepared to set sail in his first voyage he confronted mutiny when the sailors
wanted to go back to Spain. A sudden wind came which he interpreted to be
a miracle from God comparable to the biblical event of the parting of the Red
Sea: "So that high sea was very necessary for me, because such a thing had not
been seen save in the time of the Jews, when [those] of Egypt came out against
Moses who was leading them out of captivity."[72] Even Amerigo Vespucci being
amazed at the many species of animals in the "New World" of the Americas
wondered whether so many of them did fit in Noah's Ark.[73] Like Columbus
and many others, he thought that the "New World" was the biblical paradise.[74]

---

70   Hall, "The West and the Rest," 201.
71   Sir John Mandeville, *The Travels of Sir John Mandeville*, 145. Contrary to others who saw
     Africans as the "cursed" children of Ham, Mandeville insisted that Ham (he called him
     Cham) took Asia, Shem took Africa from whom come the Saracens, and Japheth (he calls
     him Japhet) took Europe, from whom come the people of Israel. Cham, he wrote, was the
     greatest and mightiest and it is because of him that the king is called Gran Khan. See Ibid.
72   Columbus, *The Journal of Christopher Columbus*, September 23.
73   Vespucio, "Carta de 1502."
74   When Vespucci arrived to the region he thought "haber llegado al paraíso terrenal de lo
     hermoso que era" (Vespucio, "Carta de 1502"). Columbus thought that the Orinoco river
     in today's Venezuela "flowed out of the Garden of Eden" (Hall, "The West and the Rest,"
     207). Adam Nicolson also tells us that the translators of the King James version had in
     mind the forests and landscape of the Caribbean as they wrote the first verses of the
     Genesis accounts. As he claims, John Layfied wrote "And out of the ground made the Lord

According to Lewis Hanke, even the Biblical places of Gog and Magog were thought to exist somewhere in the "New Worlds."[75]

To these examples one can add the multiple allusions to the Christian faith that seemed to "regulate" the activities and decisions of the Spanish and Portuguese crowns and subsequent Western European soldiers, adventurers, and explorers. Christianity had a huge influence on the ground, in terms of imperial attitudes toward those outside of Europe. Of course, the Spanish Crown interpreted the increase in the size of their empire through the acquisition of new lands as divine providence, as a reward for Christian faithfulness.[76] For example, as early as 1456 Pope Callixtus III issued the papal bull *Inter Caetera* (not to be confused with the 1493 *Inter Caetera* by Alexander VI) in which he recognized Portugal's right to the lands they had "discovered" in the West African coasts, along with the enslavement of the infidels and heathens they captured there.[77] King Manuel of Portugal wrote to the monarchs of Spain, Ferdinand and Isabella that, the principal motives for the enterprise (by which he meant the Portuguese imperial project) had been "the service

God to grow euery tree that is pleasant to the sight, and good for food: the tree of life also in the midst of the garden, and the tree of knowledge of good and euill. And a riuer went out of Eden to water the garden." As he did so

"he would have had in mind those incomparable forests of Dominica, where 'the trees doe continually maintaine themselves in a greene-good liking'—extraordinary phrase partly of many fine Rivers, which to requite the shadow and coolenesse they receive from the Trees, give them backe againe, a continuall refreshing of 'very sweete and tastie water.'" Nicolson concludes, "The seventeenth-century English idea of Paradise, a vision of enveloping lushness, was formed by the seduction of an almost untouched Caribbean." Adam Nicolson, *God's Secretaries: The Making of the King James Bible* (New York, NY: Harper Collins Publishers, 2003), 104.

75   Hanke, *El prejuicio racial en el Nuevo Mundo*, 21.

76   Jose D. Amador de los Ríos expresses this sentiments as follows: "La Providencia que asi premiaba los nobles desvelos de la Reina Católica, quiso también coronar la purísima fé de sus creencias,poniendo á sus plantas el vasto imperio de un Nuevo Mundo" (José D. Amador de los Ríos, "Vida y escritos de Gonzalo Fenández de Oviedo," in *Historia general y natural de las Indias, islas y tierra-firme del már océano*, vol. Primero de la Segunda Parte, Segundo de la Obra, Cotejada con el códice original, enriquecida con las enmiendas y adiciones del autor, é ilustrada con la vida y el juicio de las obras del mismo por José D. Amador de los Ríos [Madrid, España: Imprenta de la Real Academia de la Historia, 1852], x).

77   See "Pope Callixtus III" in *Wikipedia,* http://en.wikipedia.org/wiki/Pope_Callixtus_III (accessed February 04, 2015).

of our God our Lord and our own advantage."[78] Columbus himself, in the first words of his diary, showed the same double motivation of finding gold and wealth so that he could fund his own crusade to Jerusalem for the expansion of the Christian faith.[79] These Christian justifications for greed and violence, notwithstanding, there were also waves of missionaries that arrived from every corner of Western Europe to do the work of "evangelism."

The intertwined character of European culture with Christianity is particularly evident in European accounts of encounters with the natives. In them one finds a range of contradictory and at times judgmental perspectives about the natives which really teach us more about the Western Europeans and their imaginary than they do about the lives of the natives.[80] Scholars like Franz Fanon,[81] Edward Said,[82] and Homi Bhabha[83] have highlighted these tensions in the European imaginary in different ways: in terms of attraction and repulsion (Fanon), admiration and disparagement (Said), and assimilation but not fully (Bhabha). Allow me to enumerate several other examples of these contradictory perspectives: the lack of morality of the natives contrasted with European descriptions of the beautiful bodies of the women;[84] European repulsion and shock about the natives' "open" sexuality and yet seeming admiration and

---

78   Cited in Hall, "The West and the Rest," 204.

79   Columbus, *The Journal of Christopher Columbus*, 4.

80   Columbus was so amazed by what he saw that he exclaimed that the beauty of the place is such that the "best lands in Castile for beauty and fertility could not be compared with these" (Columbus, *The Journal of Christopher Columbus*, December 13).

81   Frantz Fanon, *Black Skins White Masks*, trans. Charles Lam Markmann (New York, NY: Grove Press, 1967).

82   Said, *Orientalism*.

83   Homi K. Bhabha, *The Location of Culture* (New York, NY: Routledge, 1994).

84   For example, Columbus stated: "they are all naked, men and women, as their mothers bore them. It is true that the women wear only a piece of cotton, large enough to cover their privy parts and no more, and they are of very good appearance, and are not very black, less so than those of the Canaries" (Columbus, *The Journal of Christopher Columbus*, November 6). There was also an operative racialization and aesthetic at work. For example, in one instance where the natives were of fairer skin he wrote: "This king and all others went naked as their mothers had borne them, and so did the women, with no trace of shame. They are the most handsome men and women whom they had found up to then, so very fair that, if they were clothed and protected themselves from the sun and air, they would be almost as white as the people of Spain" (Ibid., December 16). Meanwhile, Vespucci described them as having no shame. He found it embarrassing to describe their lack of shame: "Todos van desnudos como nacieron sin tener ninguna vergüenza, que si yo hubiese de contar cuán poca vergüenza tienen sería entrar en cosas deshonestas, y es mejor callar" (Vespucio, "Carta del 18 de julio de 1500").

dumbfoundedness about their living in a pure state of nature; repeated affirmations that the natives lacked any malice[85] while describing the lustful, libid-
inous, and sexually corrupt behavior of the women;[86] an astonishment at the
lack of sense of private ownership while at the same time condemning the
proclivities for local skirmishes with other tribes; descriptions of their peaceful
character while condemning their practices of anthropophagy; admiration for
their "free" natural existence in the wild yet insisting on the inferiority of their
lack of any form of government, law, or civil society;[87] and their fundamentally
idolatrous nature despite the fact that there was no "creed" known to them.[88]

---

85   Columbus, for instance, wrote that he considered these people free of wickedness. He
      wrote: "as I recognise ... these people have no creed and they are not idolaters, but they
      are very gentle and do not know what it is to be wicked, or to kill others, or to steal, and are
      unwarlike ..." (Columbus, *The Journal of Christopher Columbus*, November 12). In another
      instance we are told that the natives "do not bear arms, except some spears, at the end of
      which there is a sharp stick, hardened in fire ...."(Ibid., December 3).

86   In his account of the brief voyage of 1503, Vespucci reveals his misoginistic attitudes
      toward women by blaming them for corrupting Spanish men. He claimed that these
      women were anxious to copulate with the Spaniard. The native women were so lustful
      that they engaged in reprehensible sexual activities as a result of which many of their men
      have ended up becoming eunuchs. See Américo Vespucio, "El Nuevo Mundo: Américo
      Vespucio a Lorenzo Pier Francesco de Medici," in *El Nuevo Mundo: Viajes y documentos
      completos*, trans. Ana María R. de Aznar, notes by Fernández Navarrete, et al. (Madrid,
      España: Ediciones Akal, s.a., 1985), 61–62.

87   The interconnection between civil law and cultural concerns mixed with religions con-
      cerns for Vespucci. According to him, these people had no laws, no king, no borders. The
      fact that they had all things in common and shared everything with each other was fur-
      ther fascinating: "No tienen ni ley, ni fe ninguna y viven de acuerdo a la naturaleza. No
      conocen la inmortalidad del alma, no tienen entre ellos bienes propios, porque todo es
      común: no tienen límites de reinos, y de provincias: no tienen rey: no obedecen a nadie,
      cada uno es señor de sí mismo, ni amistad, ni agradecimiento, la que no les es necesaria
      porque no reina en ellos la codicia: habitan en común en casas hechas a la manera de
      cabañas muy grandes y comunes ..." (Vespucio, "Carta de 1502").

88   According to Columbus since these peoples had "No creed known to them ... they would
      be speedily converted to Christianity" (Columbus, *The Journal of Christopher Columbus*,
      October 16). Vespucci claimed that because they had no religion, the natives these
      people could not be called Jews or Moors. They were worst than gentiles because the
      natives were not seen by Vespucci or his travel companions to offer any religious sacri-
      fice or have a house of prayer. They were epicureans who lived without God and without
      morality. See Vespucci, "Letter of Amerigo Vespucci on the Islands Newly Discovered in
      His Four Voyages," in *The Letters of Amerigo Vespucci and Other Documents Illustrative
      of His Carreer*, trans with notes and Introduction by Clements R. Markham (London,
      UK: Hakluyt Society, 1894), 9.

These examples, among many others, demonstrate the kind of response elic-
ited from the Spaniards as they encountered and interacted with the peoples
of the "New Worlds." Columbus was so fascinated by what he saw that he found
himself at a loss for words:

> Your Highness may believe that in all the world there cannot be a people
> better or more gentle. Your highness should feel great joy, because they
> will presently become Christians and will be educated in the good cus-
> toms of your realms, for there cannot be a better people or country, and
> the number of the people and the extent of the country are so great that
> I no longer know how to describe them[89]

It is clear that Europeans were ill-equipped by their culture to make sense of
what they were seeing outside of their Eurocentric cultural frames. In a sense,
the sources of mythological stories, travelers' tales, the classical philosophers
and theologians, and the Christian tradition also unveil for us the monumental shift/crisis that took place in the European imaginary. The encounter with
the "New Worlds" changed their understanding of the world, themselves, and
perception and interaction with different peoples from other regions outside
Western Europe.[90]

At the outset, Western Europeans did not (could not, would not) understand the native peoples on their own merit or on their terms. It is possible
to conclude that at the beginning it was not so much an orchestrated refusal
to see the natives for who they were but a complex distorted process of (mis)
identification and (mis)recognition. Overtime however, through this *via negativa*, Europe came to be understood as everything the "New Worlds" were not.
In the "New Worlds" there were functioning societies, argues Hall; "what they
were *not* was 'European.' What disturbed western expectations, what had to
be negotiated and explained, was their *difference*."[91] Essentially, the natives
were non-Europeans; they were the negative "other" side of the European mirror. Europe became the cultural standard against which everything from the
"New Worlds" was measured. As the negative side of the Western European
mirror image, the natives of the "New Worlds" were reduced to little more than

---

89   Columbus, *The Journal of Christopher Columbus*, December 14.
90   The "New World" claims Lewis, left the Spaniards speechless. "La presencia de los nati-
      vos trajeron una crisis grande a la manera de concebir el mundo, la realidad y su misma
      existencia para los españoles y los habitantes de Europa" (Hanke, *El prejuicio racial en el
      Nuevo Mundo*, 21).
91   Hall, "The West and the Rest," 212.

animals in need of Western European salvation; they were "absolutely, essentially, different, *other*: the Other."[92]

Part of the Western European construction of the "New Worlds" was the creation of legends about natives who practiced anthropophagy. In 1580, Michel Montaigne commented that this practice should not be interpreted as enough evidence to view these people as "barbarians," considering that the Europeans had also practiced anthropophagy at different times, and were capable of greater "barbarous" activities than the natives of the "New Worlds."[93] Nevertheless, travelers like Vespucci told of their encounters with tribes that ate human flesh. Despite the fact that they used sign language and translators to communicate with the natives, he still insisted that he had met someone who claimed to have eaten 200 people.[94] One curious detail concerning cannibalism by the natives of the "New Worlds" is recorded by López de Gomara, who noted that during the time that the Spaniards were with the natives they did not offer human sacrifices.[95] Perhaps the most telling piece of information concerning the myth of cannibalism among the natives of the "New World" of the Americas is the Spanish mistranslation of the inhabitants of one of the Caribbean islands called Carib or Cariba. Late in 1492, Columbus encountered some of the inhabitants of this island and took Cariba to mean Caniba, and concluded that the inhabitants engaged in the practice of eating human flesh.[96]

Eventually, the inability to fit the natives into the European cultural and religious frames led to their marginalization and sometimes even erasure as "inferior savages," "uncultured-uncivilized," and as "unchristian"—the trifecta of ideas and factors informing European attitudes toward the rest of the world.[97] In the words of Hall, "these very different discourses, with variable statuses as—'evidence,' provided the cultural framework through which

---

92   Ibid., 216.
93   Michel de Montaigne, "Of Cannibals," in *Montaigne: Selected Essays*, ed. Blanchard Bates (New York, NY: Modern Library, 1949), 74, 77–79, 82–84.
94   Vespucio, "Carta de 1502."
95   López de Gómara, *Cortés*, Chapter 11.
96   Columbus, *The Journal of Christopher Columbus*, December 9–13. As Hall notes, the ethnic name Caribs came refer to anyone guilty of the practice of anthropophagy. The result is that we have the word "Cannibal" derived from the world "Carib." See Hall, "The West and the Rest," 214.
97   Hall comments that the Europeans were immediately struck by what they perceived as the lack of culture and absence of government and civil society—which for them was the basis of all "civilization"—among the peoples of the "New World." See Hall, "The West and the Rest," 211.

the peoples, places, and things of the New World were seen, described, and represented ..."[98] Conflating fact and fantasy these discourses came to be constituted as knowledge *about* the "New Worlds."[99]

The writings of the time reveal a concerted effort to show how the West was entirely different and therefore more culturally advanced than the rest of the world. They show how Western Europeans saw themselves having the divine, providential mandate to "share" their cultural superiority with whomever they encountered, no matter the methods. The invaders, quickly became heroes of civilization.[100] What developed, I argue, were Eurocentric cultural theologies. In the literature, the themes of: nakedness, the lack of social organization, civil structures and society; life in a pure state of nature; the lack of "culture;" the lack of "organized" religion; a proclivity for witchcraft; and an inability to engage abstract concepts appeared again and again over the centuries to justify conquest, colonization, and evangelization.

In what follows, I show how these multiple themes were woven into different written works from a variety of disciplines at different times, in order to demonstrate the breadth and extent of the discourse of the superiority of "Western" Christian cultural tradition and "civilization." Most importantly, I will show how these discourses of the superiority of the West appeared in relation to the "non-West." Here I follow Hall's argument that the idea of the "the West" must also be understood as constituting the processes of formation of "western" societies and their relation to the rest of the world.[101]

---

98   Hall, "The West and the Rest," 208.

99   Ibid.

100   In his massive social history in the nineteenth century, the Italian César Cantú celebrates civilization and the Spanish conquistadors as its agents. He wrote: "... civilization ... always advancing ... although sometimes through disasters, came to illuminate all of Europe. As she was set in motion for the search for new nations, she broke the chains of Hercules and with Vasco de Gama approached her birthplace, and with Christopher Columbus she planted the cross among the antipodes.... In [the conquistadors] is renewed the strength of the first Asian conquests: as it was in the latter, the victor seizes the land and to ensure its possession exterminates the inhabitants. How great are the names of Columbus, Amerigo, Pizarro, Cortés, Vasco and Alburquerque, adventurers turned heroes!" (César Cantú, *Tiempos Antiguos*, vol. I of *Historia Universal*, trans. D. Nemesio Fernández Cuesta [Madrid, España: Imprenta de Gaspar y Roig, Editores, 1854], XXXVII).

101   According to Hall, the European expansion coincides with the end of what we call the "middle Ages" and the beginning of the "modern age." As he writes:

    Feudalism was already in decline in Western Europe, while trade, commerce, and the market were expanding. The centralized monarchies of France, England, and Spain

As he claims, the ideas of the "the West" and "the Rest" of the world are thus two sides of the same coin.[102]

"Western Civilization" and the "New Worlds"
Background

Not long after Columbus' historic stumbling on the lands and continents that would later be called the Americas, the Spanish initiated their imperial move towards the establishment of Spanish colonies. They decided that in order for Spain to assert its sovereignty over and rights to the newly "discovered" lands a mechanism was needed to guarantee native submission to the Spanish Crown and the Catholic Church. The 1493 Bull of Donation by Alexander VI and those subsequently established by Julius II conferred Spain with the power to control both life in the Americas as well as the affairs of the church in the new lands.[103] As part of the process, the Spanish monarchs consulted theologians and jurists in order to morally and legally justify the Spanish conquest.[104]

----

were emerging ... Europe was on the threshold of a long, secular boom in productivity, improving standards of living, rapid population growth, and that explosion in art, learning, science, scholarship, and knowledge known as the Renaissance. (Leonardo da Vinci had designed flying machines and submarines prior to 1519; Michelangelo started work on the Sistine Chapel in 1508; Thomas More's *Utopia* appeared in 1516.) For much of the Middle Ages, the arts of civilization had been more developed in China and the Islamic world than in Europe (Hall, "The West and the Rest," 190).

102   Hall, "The West and the Rest," 187.

103   The *Bull of Donation* was the document issued by Pope Alexander VI, which effectively placed the new "found" lands under the jurisdiction of the Spanish Crown:

"Making use of the fullness of the apostolic succession and with the authority of Almighty God, which we have on this earth and which was given to blessed Peter, and as Vicar of Christ, and in this time, we give, cede and perpetually assignate to you and your heirs and successors in the kingdoms of Castile and Leon, all and each of the isles and lands which, known and unknown up to this moment, have been found by your emissaries and the ones to be found in the future and that right now are not under any other Christian lord"(Juan Manuel Pérez García and Francisco Javier Martínez Real, *In Evangelical Solidarity with the Oppressed: The Fifth Centenary Anniversary of the Arrival of the Order in America*, Official report by the General Chapter of Mexico [1992], 3, Http://www.domlife.org/2011Stories/files/anniv_garcia_martinez.pdf [Acessed February 14, 2015]).

104   The treatment of the natives of the Americas was an open question for the Spanish Crown since the initial encounter in 1492. As early as April 12, 1495 Bishop Fonseca had received the order from the Crown to sell some natives who had been brought

Meanwhile, opposition to the Spanish conquest and colonizing methods was mounting. Great controversy and disputes ensued, particularly after the sermon preached by Antonio de Montesinos (1511), in which he condemned the treatment of the natives as unchristian.[105] Also, the recently ordained (1512) Dominican Friar Bartolomé de las Casas condemned the colonizing measures of the Spaniards as immoral. Various juntas (meetings) took place debating the treatment of the natives by the Spanish forces: The Junta de Burgos (1512), the Junta de Valladolid (1513), and the Junta de Madrid (1516). The Junta de Burgos marked the issue of a series of ordinances created to "protect" the natives from bad treatment by the Spaniards. Effectively it was the creation of the *Encomiendas* system which, though initially designed to protect the natives, resulted in their exploitation, they were corralled like cattle for profit by the encomenderos.

The natives rebelled and resisted the Spanish military incursions, but representatives of the Spanish sought ways to insist on the "divine right" to conquer the newly-found lands; the declaration called "The Requirement" (*El Requerimiento*) was decreed in 1513. Drafted by the Spanish Jurist Juan López Palacios Rubio (an avid supporter of the monarchy's divine right to conquer) The Requirement—which the Spanish armies were required

---

from the Americas. But the next day, he received another document instructing him to save the money from the sale until "the theologians could provide satisfaction to the royal conscience concerning the morality of the act" (Lewis Hanke, "Introduction," in *Del único modo de atraer a todos los pueblos a la verdadera religión*, preface by Agustín Millares Carlo, introd. by Lewis Hanké [México, D. F.: Fondo de Cultura Económica, 1992], 41).

105   In his 1511 sermon, Montesinos condemns the bad treatment of the natives of the "New World" as unchristian. He berated his audience as follows:

Tell me, by what right or justice do you keep these Indians in such cruel and horrible servitude ...? By what authority have you declared such detestable wars on this people who were living, calmly and peacefully on their lands, where you have allowed an infinite number of them to be consumed in their sickness, resulting in death and destruction never heard of before? Through the excessive work you demand of them, they fall ill and die, or rather, you kill them with your desire to extract and acquire gold every day. And what do you care if someone instructs them in the Faith and that they know their God and Creator, are baptized, attend Mass, keep holy days and Sundays? Are these not men? Have they not rational souls? Are you not bound to love them as you love yourselves? (Pérez García and Martínez Real, *In Evangelical Solidarity with the Oppressed*, 7). See also Bartolomé de Las Casas, *Historia de las Indias*, vol. III, ed, prologue, notes, and chronology by André Saint-Lu (Madrid, España: Biblioteca Ayacucho, 1986), Chapter 4.

to read out loud before they went inland—demanded the natives to voluntarily submit to the Spanish crown. If they chose not to do it, then the Spanish forces would be justified to engage them into battle and destroy them. The Requirement affirmed the Spanish "divinely ordained right" to take possession of the new-found lands, and exploit both the lands and its inhabitants.

This document opened the door for many atrocities against the natives. Nevertheless, Spanish heinousness in the Americas did not go unchallenged. Criticisms against the abuses in Las Casas and Francisco de Vitoria's magisterial treatise *Des Indies*[106] elevated the significance of the debate to new levels,[107] eventually culminating in the historical debate between de Las Casas and Sepúlveda at Valladolid, Spain in 1550 organized by King Charles v.

Although these debates have enormous implications for "Just War theory," my interests here are simply to elucidate how at this early stage the ideas of "Western Christian Civilization" were already operative in these debates in the way many arguments were reasoned out in order to justify the Spanish invasion.[108] It will become apparent how the natives were seen as the negative counter-side of the "western" cultural imagination, and how the Spanish saw themselves as obligated to "civilize" and "Christianize" the natives of the Americas.

In what follows, I document the Spanish ideological and theological system of cultural and divine superiority against the "discovered" natives. In so doing I affirm the work of decolonial scholars who argue that the construction of the "west" and "modernity" begin at the turn of the sixteenth century, with

---

106   Vitoria, *Relecciones teológicas*, 1–87.

107   Vitoria had written his Des Indis in 1532, which constituted a legal indictment of the Spanish Crown's illegitimate claim to the lands of the Americas and the natives as its subjects. This document along with the persistent criticism of Las Casas who wrote his *Short Account of the Destruction of the Indies* in 1542, brought about the proclamation of the 1542 New Laws of Spain by King Charles V. The Laws were intended to effectively dissolve the *encomienda* system and prevent the exploitation of the natives by the Spaniards. However, the criollos in the Americas rejected the laws and continued their exploitation and enslaving of the natives. See Hugo Chumbita, *El secreto de Yapeyú* (Buenos Aires, Argentina: Emecé Editores s.a., 2001); Bartolomé de Las Casas, *A Short Account of the Destruction of the Indies*, ed. and trans. Nigel Griffin, introd. by Anthony Padgen (New York, NY: Penguin Books, 1992).

108   See Enrique Dussel, "Was America Discovered or Invaded?" *Concilium* 220 (1988): 126–34.

the conquest of the Americas and with a system of cultural otherization that is particular to those contexts.[109] Subsequently, I will connect these developments with similar cultural developments in the rest of Europe.

Juan Ginés de Sepúlveda

Spain was divided as to how to discern the best ways to deal with the natives, including their rights as people and the question of the ownership of the lands. On the side of humane treatment, Las Casas insisted that the evangelization of the natives needed to take place peacefully and that the Spaniards had no grounds to abuse them.[110] Vitoria went even further arguing that the Spanish Crown could not invade these people because they had a natural human right to the titles of the lands and the riches therein. Moreover, on those same bases, he insisted the Spanish Crown had no legitimate claim to impose itself over these peoples and govern them.[111]

However, many justified the Spanish invasion and conquest of the natives on the basis of the fact that they were non-Christian, "uncivilized," inferior peoples who practiced Cannibalism. According to Hanke, the Scottish theologian John Mair was the first to apply the Aristotelian doctrine of natural slavery to the natives of the Americas. Mair was also in favour of the deployment of force as "preliminary to the preaching of the faith."[112] But the central figure in this debate in terms of supporting the violent invasion of the Americas and the use of force against the natives was the theologian Juan Ginés de Sepúlveda.

Contrary to Vitoria and Las Casas, Sepúlveda argued that it was Spain's legitimate right to establish rule over the natives of the "New Worlds" of the Americas, wage war against them, and to force their evangelization. For his 1550 debate with Las Casas he wrote his *Apologia*, a document which is based on his more extensive discussion in *Demócrates Segundo*.[113] It is written in the form of an imaginary dialogue between fictional characters Leopoldo

---

109 Enrique Dussel, *El encubrimiento del Otro: Hacia el origen del "mito de la Modernidad,"* Collección Academia—Facultad de Humanidades y Ciencias de la Educación, Universidad Mayor de San Andrés (La Paz: Plural Editores—Centro de Información para el Desarrollo, 1994); Dussel, *The Underside of Modernity.*

110 Bartolomé de Las Casas, *Del único modo de atraer a todos los pueblos a la verdadera religión*, preface by Agustín Millares Carlo, introd. by Lewis Hanké (México, D. F.: Fondo de Cultura Económica, 1992).

111 See his *Des Indies* in Vitoria, *Relecciones teológicas*, 1–87.

112 Hanke, *El prejuicio racial en el Nuevo Mundo*, 28. Mair published his ideas in Paris in 1510.

113 Ginés de Sepúlveda, *Demócrates Segundo*. All the translations of this text are mine.

and Demócrates. Leopoldo represents those who consider the Spanish invasion unjust and Demócrates provides answers to their objections. Using this
method of disputation, Sepúlveda outlines four reasons in defense of Spain's
legitimate right to invade the natives of the "New Worlds" and subject them to
the dominion of the Spanish Empire.

First, Sepúlveda argued that the Spanish had the legitimate right to invade
the natives and take their lands because they had committed the sins of
anthropophagy and the offering of human sacrifices. This point was religious
in nature for Sepúlveda. According to him, the natives had committed the most
egregious sins by practicing the religion of cannibalism which he classified as
the "shameful genre of idolatry." For him, it was the crime that surpassed all
other crimes; their practices led him to conclude that their god was their stomach, a belief which resulted in a denial of the existence of God and choice to
live like beasts.[114] Furthermore, prior to the arrival of the "Christians," they had
the "nature, costumes, religion, and practices" of human sacrifices.

Once they had received the laws, education, and morality from the Empire,
which were "imbued with the Christian religion," he noted that many "differentiate from their primitive condition, as the civilized from the barbarians, those
who have sight from the blind, the inhuman from the meek ..."[115] Sepúlveda
strengthened his argument by drawing on the language of chosenness; just as
Israel had a legitimate cause to invade Canaan so also did the Spanish have
the divine mandate to invade the Americas.[116] He claimed that Spain had been
chosen as the agent of divine punishment against the natives for their great
sins.[117] For these reasons, it was, therefore, actually more just to subject these
peoples to their superior counterparts who were more prudent, more human
and more pious.[118] In the end, their supposed lack of laws and civic and human
"culture" was used to justify war against them.[119]

---

114   Ginés de Sepúlveda, *Demócrates Segundo*, 38.

115   Ibid.

116   Ibid., 39.

117   Sepúlveda acknowledges that "although the precepts [were given to] the children of
      Israel, nevertheless Godself declared that this was not only a divine law, but also of a
      natural law applicable to all peoples, when he [*sic*] was affirmed that he [*sic*] destroyed
      those sinful peoples for the same crimes" (Ginés de Sepúlveda, *Demócrates Segundo*, 40).

118   Ginés de Sepúlveda, *Demócrates Segundo*, 38.

119   Ginés de Sepúlveda, *Demócrates Segundo*, 39. For him, the pagans could not be invaded
      merely for being "pagan." But such a situation could not be compared to the Americas
      because in the latter case, their crimes, nefarious practices of human sacrifices and can-
      nibalism justified war against them. See (Ibid., 44).

Second, the Spanish had the "natural and divine right" to impose their dominion on the natives. Drawing on Aristotle's doctrine of natural slavery, Sepúlveda argued that their state of rudeness and uncivilization justified the obligation imposed on the natives to serve the Spaniards who were "naturally" their cultural superiors. To him, there were all kinds of expressions of dominion which rested on the doctrine of "natural right" including husbands over wives, masters over servants, magistrates over citizens, etc. Because of their turpitude, their inhuman and barbarous costumes, and their extreme natural state, the natives were "naturally inferior" and therefore destined to serve the Spaniards.[120] Thus, the Spanish "natural right" was also their divine right.[121] I want to emphasize that Sepúlveda did not understand the "natural" subjection of the natives as negative. Rather, it aimed to bring "perfection to imperfection, strength to weakness, and highest virtue to vice."[122] In other words, since the natives lived in this natural and inferior condition they *should* obey "others." If, on the other hand, they rejected the superior empire, then he averred that "there is no other recourse for them to be dominated but through weapons ..."[123] As far as he was concerned, such war was therefore *just*.[124]

Third, the Spaniards had the responsibility to invade the lands in order to ensure that the natives converted to Christianity and thereby save their souls. In stark contrast to the argument of Bartolomé de las Casas and the Dominican Friars, Sepúlveda argued that force was a necessary evil to ensure their conversion to Christianity.[125] He noted that the imperative for Spain to invade and use force on the natives rested both on the Christian obligation and the "natural" law (for human life) found in the Gospel imperative to love of neighbor and the Decalogue. The distinction was clear. For him, the natives were not being punished and forced against their will to accept the faith in Christ; they were punished because of their evil practices that ran opposite to the "natural" law.[126] He admitted that no nation was free from the possibility of breaking

---

120 Ginés de Sepúlveda, *Demócrates Segundo*, 20. In fact, he adds, "Can greater and clearer testimony exist, of the advantage that some men [*sic*] have over the others in ingenuity, ability, strength of courage and virtue? Is not this proof that they are servants by nature?" (Ibid., 36).

121 He asks, "is not that which is given by natural right that which God wants us to do, and is not that which we are prohibited to do what God prohibits?" (Ginés de Sepúlveda, *Demócrates Segundo*, 10).

122 Ginés de Sepúlveda, *Demócrates Segundo*, 20.

123 Ibid.

124 Ibid., 19.

125 Ibid., 45.

126 Ibid., 59.

the natural law, but it was also true that among the civilized nations such law tended to be observed. Thus, the use of force was a kind of "gratuitous help" that the Spanish provided so that the natives could accept Christianity.[127] Drawing on biblical imperatives, he argued that just as the Roman Centurion Cornelius needed help to convert and the cities of Sodom and Gomorrah faced divine punishment for their depravity, so also was it good and necessary for the natives to accept the Spanish empire and obey the "good" citizens of Spain, for they were "civilized and addicted to the true religion." He added, "the worst men, barbarians and impious, with the admonishments, laws and treatment of the [Spaniards] could achieve piety, civilization and salvation, with which the maximum Christian charity would be fulfilled."[128]

Fourth, Sepúlveda justified the invasion as a way to save the innocent lives of those who would die if the natives were not stopped from their evil practices. Once again Spain was imbued with messianic overtones being compared to Abraham. Spain was understood as the instrument of divine punishment against the evil of the natives thereby saving the lives of those who could be victims offered for sacrifice.[129] Paradoxically, Sepúlveda displayed no remorse for the loss of native lives by the Spaniards since they deserved to die for their evil deeds.[130] According to him, even the twenty thousand natives that Cortés was said to have killed, Sepúlveda insisted, were a "small price to pay." Cortés was the unequivocal hero of the story. Those he killed amounted to less than the amount the natives killed in any given year through their horrendous savage religion. More importantly, though, through their massacre he "guaranteed the salvation of the many others that will not die in those altars to their pagan gods."[131]

For these four reasons, the violent Spanish intervention was justified. At its root was a fundamental belief in the ultimate benefits that would be brought to the natives by preventing what could happen to them. In other words, The Spanish did not see themselves as doing harm to achieve the good. Rather, the goal was to *reduce* evil to its lowest degree, to prevent the natives from further sins; it was for their own good, after all.[132] The end goal of the just war, Sepúlveda claimed, was to live in peace and tranquility, with justice and virtue, "taking from the evil ones

---

127   Ibid., 55–56.

128   Ibid., 58.

129   Ibid., 61.

130   Ginés de Sepúlveda, *Demócrates Segundo*, 27. He writes that, "no nos debemos sentir mal por los nativos que mueren porque estos desde antes ya merecían morir por sus mismas maldades" (We should not feel bad for the natives that die because they already deserved to die for their own wickedness) (Ibid.).

131   Ginés de Sepúlveda, *Demócrates Segundo*, 61.

132   Ibid., 77.

the faculty to do harm and sin, and to watch for the public well-being of human-ity."[133] In his scheme, the Spaniards were like the good Samaritan; they had the obligation to help other peoples, not through punishment but by converting "the barbarians and almost humans, into civilized people in the degree to which they can be, from criminals into virtuous, from impious and slaves to the demons into Christians and worshipers of the true God in the new religion ..."[134] Summing it up, he affirmed that the "barbarians can be subjected to our dominion with the same right with which they can be compelled to hear the Gospel."[135] The circular logic (however contradictory) was complete: the Spaniards were fulfilling their Christian duty by imposing themselves upon the natives and forcing them to convert to Christianity. They were also following the divine mandate of love of neighbor by killing those who refused to accept the Spanish Crown and the gos-pel message. It was for the greater good.

With this sophisticated weave of "Western European" cultural and religious concerns, Sepúlveda articulated reasons for Spain to invade the lands and conquer the peoples of the "New World" of the Americas. The natives were constructed as the radical negative side of the superior Spanish Christians, "inferior" by nature and by divine "right" destined to be servants to the Spanish. In fact, the Spanish had the superior rights to this mandate even in Europe because they were the most prudent, just, and religious nation.[136] The justi-fiable invasion by the Spanish against the natives—on account of their lack of civilization and Christianity—was sanctioned in a decree from the "high Priest and Vicar of Christ," the Pope, to evangelize them.[137] The argument went to extreme lengths to justify not only violent domination but also rampant pillaging. Sepúlveda and his ilk saw their salvation and the Christianization of the natives along with many material and cultural goods brought to the Americas by the Spaniards as benefits of incalculable measure. The gold that the Spaniards took was in fact only a small payment for these "great" many benefits.[138]

---

133   Ibid., 15.
134   Ibid., 63.
135   Ibid., 65.
136   Ginés de Sepúlveda, *Demócrates Segundo*, 82. Here Sepúlveda is emphasizing that the Spanish are better than other European counterparts because only they display these characteristics of justice, prudence and Christianity.
137   Ginés de Sepúlveda, *Demócrates Segundo*, 83.
138   Ginés de Sepúlveda, *Demócrates Segundo*, 78–79. Sepúlveda comments that the gold that was taken cannot compare to all the things the Spaniards brought such as iron, horses, donkeys, bulls, sheep, goats, and pigs, and all the many kinds of fruit trees, things that the barbarians had never seen. See (Ibid.).

The conflation of Western European cultural elements and Christianity dis-allowed Sepúlveda and those in his camp from engaging the natives on their terms. As he unveiled his understanding of the natives of the "New World" of the Americas, he was simultaneously unveiling an emerging operating sys-tem of "Western European" cultural forces used to categorize, standardize, and subjugate the natives; their resulting status was as savages, as less than human beings. This system consigned them to a "natural" state of enslavement which, when rejected, was justifiably punished by annihilation and warranted a total rejection of their "evil" customs and practices along with their religious traditions. For him, there was no comparison between the Spanish and the natives; the natives were everything the Spaniards were not! Their "lack" of "culture," social structures, and religion simply confirmed their inferiority. The outcome of this constructed binary were two unrecognizable images both of which stemmed from these processes of (mis)identification and (mis)recogni-tion in the construction of the ideas related to "Western Civilization." On one hand, the natives were inferior savages, who were unchristian, uncivilized, and needed to be "guided" as minors. On the other hand, the Spaniards were from the "superior," civilized, and Christian nation divinely chosen for such a task.[139] Racialized cultural superiority was thus sanctioned by God.

"Western Civilization" and "The Rest" of the World

After the conquest of Latin America, including the Caribbean and large parts of today's United States of America, by Spain and Portugal, Western European nations went out to colonize the rest of the world. Gradually and despite of their internal differences, this group of cultures began to conceive of them-selves "as part of a single family or civilization"—"The West."[140] Like Spain before them, these countries went through their own processes of (mis)iden-tification and (mis)recognition as they encountered the different peoples throughout the world. Their own distorted, narcissistic, cultural imaginary and self-perception became the standard for interacting with and evaluating "the others" of the planet. As they engaged in multidisciplinary "studies" of these "others," they solidified their own self-perceived superior (cultural) identity by contrasting these other cultures and civilizations with their own.

As Said, Hall and others have documented, the result was the creation of a voluminous library archive which confirmed Western Europe's advanced and superior cultures, civilization and religion. Simultaneously, the Western European perception and colonizing gaze turned into created knowledge,

---

139   Ginés de Sepúlveda, *Demócrates Segundo*, 35.
140   Hall, "The West and the Rest," 197.

literature and evidence, which affirmed and enforced "the truth" about the "New Worlds," justifying rapacious European imperialism and colonization all over the globe. According to Hall, this archive had attached to it a family of ideas and a unifying set of values that were proven in various ways to be effective and "true."[141] It included a wide range of incontrovertible evidence that the peoples of the "New Worlds" were "inferior," "uncultured/uncivilized," "heathen/pagan" and "savages."

In what follows, I provide a small sample of the voluminous multidisplinary works produced by Western European and Euro North American authors right up to the beginning of the 20th century. Many of these authors became influential in shaping general ideas about "the West." As will become evident, they shared a set of assumptions and values about themselves which served as the prism through which they evaluated the various communities they encountered.

By the end of the sixteenth century, there was a proliferation of ideas about the natives of the "New Worlds." These ideas, constructed by Spanish and Portuguese, were not isolated instances; as the rest of Western Europeans started to engage in their own imperial projects, they also developed similar ideologies and cultural theologies. For example, in the seventeenth century, the English philosopher Thomas Hobbes wrote in his *Leviathan* that it was because of a lack of industry and the resulting lack of culture of agricultural knowledge (he called this "culture of the earth"), navigational knowledge or developed economies (he called this "use of commodities") that "the savage people in many places of America ... live at this day in [their] brutish manner."[142]

There were opposing views. For example, John Locke, a contemporary of Hobbes, in his first Treatise of Government countered political theorist Robert Filmer's[143] notion that the monarchy had a divine right to rule based on the patrimony of Adam. Filmer argued that the lineage continued to Noah's sons who each had the right to rule the world and from whom emerged all the kings of the earth.[144] But Locke showed gap problems in Filmer's proposal when he

---

141   Ibid., 206.

142   Cited in Hall, "The West and the Rest," 219.

143   Robert Filmer, *Patriarcha; or the Natural Power of Kings* (London, UK: R. Chiswell, 1680).

144   John Locke, *Two Treatises of Government*, A New Edition Corrected (London, UK: Whitmore and Fenn, Charing Cross; and C. Brown, 1821), 89, 155ff. According to Filmer, the kings of the earth derive their power and right to rule from the original dominion of Adam. Moreover, in support of the monarchy, he asks rhetorically: "what form of government God confirmed by His authority may be gathered by that commonwealth which He instituted among the Hebrews, which was not aristocratic (as Calvin says) but plainly Monarchical" (Filmer, *Patriarcha*, 8).

asked rhetorically: if we accepted this account and "Noah divided the world into Asia, Africa and Europe, portions for his three sons," are we, then, to say that "*America* ... was left to be his that could catch it"?[145] Locke's point was that the conquerors had no right to take the lands from the natives.[146] The discussion continued in his second Treatise of Government. In the chapter on property, he elaborated on the notion that the earth is given by God to all humanity to share in common; it was not to be owned by some through divine right but shared by all.

Though he was sympathetic with the natives, the pervasive construction of the superior European ideology is still evident. As he elaborated his perspective on property and the development of industry and technology to facilitate the extraction of goods from the earth, Locke arrived at the conclusion that in comparison with these European advances, the natives of the Americas did not yet have the cultural, the knowledge or the rational capacity. As far as he was concerned, "in the beginning, all the world was America, and more so that it is now; for no such thing as money was anywhere known."[147] In other words, America was for him, "a pattern of the first ages in Asia and Europe."[148] The operating assumption was that all civilizations follow the same (European) path to development, America signifying the starting point of this process. As Hall writes, "untilled, undeveloped, and uncivilized ..." for Locke America was the "childhood of humanity."[149]

In the seventeenth century, European travelers and explorers went all over the "New Worlds" and the reports from their expeditions continued to add to the formation of ideas about worlds outside of Western Europe. Among these travelers was the Italian Niccolao Manucci who wrote a three-volume *history of the Mogols* of India.[150] Another well-known traveler was the French physician Francois Bernier.[151] Bernier marks a crucial shift in the reorientation of Western Europe toward the rest of the world because he used race and racial categories. Often credited as the first to do so, this shift toward racial categories

---

145   Locke, *Two Treatises of Government*, 157.

146   Filmer, *Patriarcha*, 347.

147   Ibid., 228–29.

148   Ibid., 280.

149   Hall, "The West and the Rest," 219.

150   Niccolao Manucci, *Storia Do Mogor or Mogul India 1653–1708*, vol. I–III, translated with Introduction and Notes William Irvine, The Indian Texts Series (London, UK: John Murray, Albermarle Stree, 1907).

151   François Bernier, *Travels in the Mogul Empire A.D 1656–1668*, Second ed., translated, on the basis of Irvin Brock's version and annotated by Archibald Constable, rev. Vincent A. Smith (London, UK: Humfrey Milford, 1891).

is evident in his 1864 article "Nouvelle division de la terre par les différentes espèces ou races qui l'habitent" ("New division of the earth according to the different species and races that inhabit it") which classified the world racially and encouraged Europeans to view themselves as a "race" entirely different from the rest of the world.[152]

Anglo-Dutch philosopher Bernard Mandeville opens for us the eighteenth century with—much like Locke—a description of the central features of "good government."[153] Boasting of what good government (read European forms of government) looked like, he emphasized that the role of government was to provide the conditions that prevented humans from living like savages. According to him, only civilization could raise those in a "savage" state from their stupidity.[154] As he saw it, it would be impossible for humans to remain uncivilized if they found themselves in a country where the foundations of political government had been laid.[155]

Though earlier Spanish literature generally portrayed the natives as violent savages, there were also examples of idealized notions of the natives of the "New Worlds." This double image of violent and innocent was gradually perpetuated throughout Europe. For example, in the sixteenth century the French philosopher Michel Montaigne challenged ideas about the "barbarity" of the natives of the Americas, insisting that the French (and Europeans in general) practiced greater acts of barbarism compared with the "innocent Indians."[156] By the eighteenth century, idealized images of the natives had found their way in the Western European cultural imagination and ethos about the inhabitants of the "New Worlds." English adventurer Captain Cook repeats the same kind of paradisiacal portrayal as the Spaniards, though in reference to other regions and lands. In his account of his arrival to Tahiti in 1769, he writes "The women were extremely beautiful, the vegetation lush and tropical, the life simple, innocent, and free; nature nourished the people without the apparent necessity to work or cultivate; the sexuality was open and unashamed—untroubled by

---

152   As Bernier wrote, "I have observed that there are in all four or five Types of Race among men whose distinctive traits are so obvious that they can justifiably serve as the basis of a new division of the Earth" (François Bernier, "A New Division of the Earth," *History Workshop Journal* 51 [Spring 2001]: 247).

153   Bernard Mandeville, *The Fable of the Bees: Or Private Vices, Public Benefits. With an Essay on Charity and Charity-Schools. And a Search into the Nature of Society*, Sixth ed. (London, UK: J. Tonson, 1729).

154   Ibid., 160.

155   Ibid., 20.

156   Montaigne, "Of Cannibals."

the burden of European guilt."[157] Similarly, the French explorer Louis-Antione Bougainville after his travels to the Pacific said that Tahitians were "without vice, prejudice, needs or dissension and knew no other god but love."[158]

Romantic notions about the natives of the "New Worlds" prompted the emergence of the idea of the "noble savage," which—although it was coined by John Dryden in his *Conquest of Granada* (1670)[159]—owed its popularity in large part to the work of French philosopher Jean Jacques Rousseau. In an early essay, he reflected upon and justified the reasons for which there was inequality in the world. According to him, such inequalities were authorized by the law of nature.[160] He was convinced that there are two kinds of inequality: 1) Natural and physical, which was established by nature, and 2) moral or political, which was agreed upon by consensus in the political structures.[161] In both cases, he thought that the natives of the "New Worlds" were evidently inferior: they lacked the technology, industry, weaponry and civilization, as well as organized forms of civic and political government.[162] Most importantly—and here his sense of European global "superiority" betrays him—the natives lacked the arts of metallurgy and agriculture. According to Rousseau, these industries have helped Europeans be the most advanced and civilized region than the "other quarters of the world."[163]

In Rousseau, the "appreciation" of the natives was unambiguously mixed with his own ideas of the superiority of "Western European" civilization; it resulted in a simplistic reduction—an essentialized otherization—of the native cultures. For him, the natives' "rudeness," their uncivilized state, and their inability to engage in complex rational activities related directly to their immediate natural environment.[164] Because the savages were merely

---

157   Hall, "The West and the Rest," 210.

158   Cited in Hall, "The West and the Rest," 210.

159   According to Sharpe, the idea of the noble savage communicated the (romantic) idea that "virtue can and does flourish beyond the borders of Western urban civilization" (Eric Sharpe, "The Study of Religion in Historical Perspective," in *The Routledge Companion to the Study of Religion*, ed. John R. Hinnells [New York, NY: Routledge, 2005], 26). In an interesting twist, Rousseau extended this romantic idea insisting that Western "civilization" corrupted the human individual. See Jean Jacques Rousseau, *A Discourse Upon the Origin and Foundation of the Inequality Among Mankind* (London, UK: R. and J. Dodsley, 1761).

160   Rousseau, *A Discourse on Inequality*, B2.

161   Ibid., 6.

162   For Rousseau, the natives lacked laws, commerce, politics, agriculture, metallurgy and agriculture, all of which were important components of civilization. Rousseau, *A Discourse on Inequality*, 139–42.

163   Rousseau, *A Discourse on Inequality*, 120.

164   Ibid., 32–33, 40.

concerned with questions of survival, they lacked the desire to pursue knowledge because it had no practical purpose;[165] they were unable to appreciate beauty and consider abstract ideas of regularity and proportion; and they lacked the capacity to love because they had no passions.[166] Because they had not developed their rational capacity, the natives also did not have a "sense of wonder," and had no sense of future concerns or a developed society.[167]

Rousseau did not necessarily question the innate rational-biological capacity of the natives to engage complex and abstract ideas and to express passions. His essay, however, points in the direction of the need for education and civilization as the forces necessary for the development of the human rational capacity. For him, civilization provided humans with the needed rational "skills" and "abilities." At the same time, and in contrast, he thought that civilization was to blame for ruining humanity; civilization corrupted humans because it made possible selfishness and greed, of which the natives had none.[168] As he saw it, civilization was responsible for awakening and developing human desires and wants including the pursuit of knowledge.

---

165   To make the point, Rousseau asked: "In a word, tho' we were to suppose his [*his*] mind as intelligent and enlightened, as it must, and is, in fact, found to be dull and stupid; what benefit would the species receive from all these metaphysical discoveries, which could not be communicated, but must perish with the individual who had made them?" (Rousseau, *A Discourse on Inequality*, 47).

166   Rousseau, *A Discourse on Inequality*, 81–83. Rousseau argued that the natives are much like animals. They not only lack love but because they lack passion they only have "heat" seasons in order to reproduce like other animals. See Ibid., 85.

167   Rousseau, *A Discourse on Inequality*, 43. Rousseau's contempt for the natives is clear: He writes that in the Caribbean the people sell their cotton bed in the morning and come back in the evening with tears in their eyes to buy it back, "not having seen that [they] should want it again the next night" (Ibid.).

168   Rousseau certainly holds the European "advanced" civilization to account for much evil; in this he shares Montaigne's ideas about the "barbarity" of the European nations. For him, greed and selfishness are the resulting evils of civilization, and find themselves expressed in notions of private property:

> "The first man [*sic*] who, after enclosing a piece of ground, took it into his head to say, this is mine, and found people simple enough to believe him was the true founder of civil society. How many crimes, how many wars, how many murders, how many misfortunes and horrors, would that man [*sic*] have saved the human species, who pulling up the stakes or filling up the ditches should have cried to his fellows: be sure not to listen to this impostor; you are lost if you forget that the fruits of the earth belong equally to us all, and the earth itself to nobody!" (Rousseau, *A Discourse on Inequality*, 97).

In fact, for him, it was through the activity of the passions that human rational capacity improved.[169] But since the "savages" were only responding to
the impulses of their natural state, they were therefore "destitute of every
species of knowledge;"[170] they experienced no passions except those corresponding with their natural state.[171] In fact, their "desires never extend[ed]
beyond [their] physical wants ..."[172]

Two implications flowed from this perspective. First, because the natives
had not been "corrupted" by civilization and had not developed their passions, neither had they developed the tendencies to do evil. Here Rousseau
contradicted the Calvinist notion of "total depravity."[173] As far as he was concerned, the "savages" were neither good nor bad. Providence, he proposed,
provided what they needed to live in their natural state; it ensured that they
did not develop the kind of moral relations that would lead them to commit evil.[174] And second, the chasm between the Europeans and the "savages"
was a question of the "cultivation" of the mind; the development of cultural
and rational "superiority;" the development of civilization. The forces of the
"Western European" mind and education produced such differences that,

---

169 We covet knowledge, he says, "merely because we covet enjoyment, and it is impossible
     to conceive, why [those] exempt from fears and desires should take the trouble to reason.
     The passions, in their turn, owe their origin to our wants, and their increase to our prog-
     ress in science ..." (Rousseau, *A Discourse on Inequality*, 40).

170 Rousseau notes that the savages are consigned by nature to be creatures of pure
     instinct. As such, he also admits that they are "indemnified" for not having those most
     advanced faculties which would raise them a great deal higher. Rousseau, *A Discourse on
     Inequality*, 38.

171 Rousseau, *A Discourse on Inequality*, 40.

172 Ibid.

173 Rousseau, *A Discourse on Inequality*, 68–70. As far as Rousseau is concerned, the natives
     could not be considered to be bad because they did not know "what it is to be good"
     (Ibid., 70).

174 He explains,

     It was in consequence of a very wise providence, that the faculties, which he poten-
     tially enjoyed, were not to develop themselves but in proportion as there offered occa-
     sions to exercise them, left they should be superfluous or troublesome to him when he
     did not want them, or tardy and useless when he did. He had in his instinct alone very
     thing requisite to live in a state of nature; in his cultivated reason he has barely what is
     necessary to live in a state of society. It appears at first sight that, as there was no kind
     of moral relations between men [*sic*] in this state, nor any known duties, they could
     not be either good or bad, and had neither vices nor virtues (Rousseau, *A Discourse on
     Inequality*, 66).

when contrasted with the "savage mind," it was like the advantages a giant had over against a dwarf.[175]

In this romanticized portrayal by Rousseau, the natives of the "New Worlds" were "savages" by virtue of their lack of rational capacity, "culture," technology, and "civilization." The requirements of their natural state were such that they did not need to develop them.[176] In sum, the gentle and peaceful "noble savages" seemed, for Rousseau, to be better off without civilization, though they were also destined to remain "savages." If they wished to escape their "natural state," then they would have to adopt the culture/civilization of the "West." Rousseau's writings display the European construction of the "noble savage" as the reflection of a state from which Europe "escaped" long ago, even though it included the potential for greed and corruption.

The emphasis on travelling and exploring other cultures broadened over time. The literature began to cover many places from virtually all over the world. William John Burchell's account of his travels in South Africa provides a good example of the immense care and detail these ethnographic reports began to entail.[177] Still they were never free from their own culturally inherited assumptions, prejudices, and preconceived notions of the natives of the "New Worlds," many of which continued well into the nineteenth and early portion of the twentieth centuries. But by the nineteenth century, Western European notions of civilization and the cultural began to shift; they were taken to their logical next step. All those things Western Europeans brought to the "New Worlds": "civilization," "culture," "industry," "agriculture," "technology," "rule of law and government," "education," and "religion/Christianity," were racialized. Previously the concepts of civilization, culture, race, and Christendom functioned much more fluidly as loose categories which were almost used interchangeably. In the nineteenth century, however, they were consolidated under the rubric of the inherent *racial* superiority of Western Europeans. Many Western European and Euro North American authors from the nineteenth

---

175   He elaborates:

> Forces of the mind ... and education not only produces a difference between those minds which are cultivated and those which are not, but even increases that which is found among the first in proportion to their culture; for let a giant and a dwarf set out in the same path, the giant at every step will acquire a new advantage over the dwarf (Rousseau, *A Discourse on Inequality*, 88–89).

176   Ginés de Sepúlveda, *Demócrates Segundo*, 86–87.

177   William John Burchell, *Travels in the Interior of Southern Africa*, vol. II (London, UK: Paternoster-Row, 1824).

and early twentieth century contributed to the voluminous literature that produced "convincing evidence" of their superiority. A fuller analysis goes well
beyond the scope of this chapter. Here I only present a few samples to illustrate the kind of material that contributed to the complex and sophisticated
project of the construction of the myth of cultural, and later racial superiority,
of Western Europeans.

Let us begin with the U.S.A. physician Samuel Morton who systematically
organized Western Europeans and their descendants as the only people
capable of producing "advanced" cultures and civilizations.[178] He reproduced earlier notions that the natives of the Americas were warlike, had no
sense of law, were idolatrous nations, and had no moral constitution.[179] After
studying 400 crania, he concluded that these groups were inevitably racially
inferior.[180]

Morton anticipated the work of the twentieth century's German art critic
and ethnologist Wilhelm Worringer. In a kind of "de-orientalizing" and "de-
Africanizing" move, Worringer concluded that the founders/builders of the
Egyptian civilization in fact had Nordic characteristics and were therefore
"Indogermanic."[181] Greatly influenced by Leo Frobenius (see chapter 1), he
insisted that contrary to the feminine cultures of Africa, the Egyptian culture displayed a masculine virility of a foreign, i.e., non-African group.[182]
Unfortunately, and to their demise, the Egyptians regressed in their "evolution." They made the mistake of building their great civilization based on
"primitive" religious cults to animals, rife with savage superstitions and magic,
a fact that prevented them from moving to the next stage of advancement

---

178   Samuel George Morton, *Inquiry Into the Distinctive Characteristics of the Aboriginal Race*,
        Paper read at the Annual Meeting of the Boston Society of Natural History Wednesday,
        April 27, 1842 (Boston: Tuttle & Bennett, Printers, 1842).

179   Morton, *Inquiry Into the Distinctive Characteristics of the Aboriginal Race*, 10–11.
        According to Morton, the natives of the American continent were but one "race" with the
        exception of the Eskimo. "It is an adage among travelers that he who has seen one tribe
        of Indians, has seen all, so much do the individuals of this race resemble each other, not-
        withstanding their immense geographical distribution, and those differences of climate
        which embrace the extremes of heat and cold" (Ibid., 6).

180   Morton, *Inquiry Into the Distinctive Characteristics of the Aboriginal Race*, 7. See also
        Samuel George Morton, *Crania Americana; or, a Comparative View of the Skulls of Various
        Aboriginal Nations of North and South America: An Essay on the Varieties of the Human
        Species* (Pennsylvania, PA: J. Dobson, Chesnut Street, 1839).

181   Guillermo Worringer, *El arte egipcio: Problemas de su valoración*, trans. Emilio Rodríguez
        Sádia (Madrid, España: Revista de Occidente, 1927).

182   Ibid., 15.

as the Europeans did.[183] In the end, the implicit argument was that if the Egyptian had had a religion that resembled Christianity, they would have moved further in their development.[184]

Phrenology became the go-to pseudoscience that provided quantitative "evidence" for the "racial superiority" of Western Europeans. Unwittingly, the English naturalist and geologist Charles Darwin provided the material framework for understanding this "superiority" as part of the natural processes of human evolution. At the turn of the twentieth century, the USA physician Josiah Nott brought together phrenology with natural and biblical history as a way to classify humanity by different racial types in a hierarchical manner.[185] But it fell to the French aristocrat Arthur de Gobineau to make explicit the central tenets of notions of "racial superiority" in the third quarter of the nineteenth century. He used phrenology, but went quite a bit further to affirm that there were *de facto* inequalities between human groups with the Aryans being the inherently superior race of all.[186]

For Gobineau, the Aryan race was responsible to carry humanity to the next phase of development. As he saw it, many ancient civilizations had declined because they mixed with "inferior" groups.[187] Asserting what he called the

---

183   Ibid., 22–26.

184   Ibid., 30.

185   Josiah Clark Nott and George Robins Gliddon, eds., *Types of Mankind: Or, Ethnological Researches, Based Upon the Ancient Monuments, Paintings, Sculptures, and Crania of Races, and Upon Their Natural, Geographical, Philological and Biblical History; Illustrated by Selections from the Inedited Papers of Samuel George Morton; and by Additional Contributions from Prof. L. Agassiz; W. Usher; and Prof. H.S. Patterson.* (Philadelphia, PA: Lippincott, Grambo & Co., 1854); Josiah Clark Nott, *Types of Mankind: Or, Ethnological Researches, Based Upon the Ancient Monuments, Paintings, Sculptures, and Crania of Races, and Upon Their Natural, Geographical, Philological and Biblical History* (Philadelphia, PA: Lippincott, Grambo, 1855). These authors drew on each other's works to support their perspectives. For instance, in order to affirm the uniqueness of the American "race," Morton drew on the German geographer and naturalist Alexander Humboldt's affirmation that the "American race contains nations whose features differ as essentially from one another as those of the Caucasians, Moors and Persians" (Morton, *Inquiry Into the Distinctive Characteristics of the Aboriginal Race*, 8).

186   de Gobineau, *The Inequality of Human Races*, 205–7. For de Gobineau, careful attention to the differences between human groups on matters of physiology, language, intellect, development of civilization, and inventiveness demonstrated the hierarchy of those human groups. The Aryan race came out at the top of the pyramid as the strongest, most creative, most balanced intellectually and spiritually, as the most inventive "race" in the world.

187   de Gobineau, *The Inequality of Human Races*, 26–27.

"principle of repulsion," by which those of the superior groups display a "natural" repugnance to those who were inferior, he proposed intermixture with racially "inferior" groups had to be avoided;[188] it brought with it degenerative effects which included infertility.[189] For him, race mixture was the fundamental reason for the destruction and decline of earlier civilizations. Therefore, he argued that it was necessary for European civilization to preserve the purity of the "superior" Aryan race.[190]

The "superiority" of the Aryan race was inherent, argued Gobineau; it was in their blood. Neither civilization, nor government, nor national unity, nor democracy, nor climate differences had anything to do with the inequalities among human groups.[191] He wrote sarcastically:

> So the brain of the Huron Indians contains in an undeveloped form an intellect which is absolutely the same as that of the Englishman or the Frenchman! Why then, in the course of the ages, has he not invented printing or steam power? I should be quite justified in asking our Huron why, if he is equal to our European peoples, his tribe has never produced a Caesar or a Charlemagne among its warriors ...[192]

Assuming that all groups should follow the same developmental trajectory, he charged that the peoples of the Americas despite their many riches and an abundance of resources should have "advanced" and created "great" civilizations. As far as he was concerned, this failure to advance was proof of their racial inferiority.[193]

There is a connection with the religious sphere in Gobineau as well. Certainly, he wrote, Christianity was no guarantee for civilization. Christianity

---

188   de Gobineau, *The Inequality of Human Races*, 30–31. He explains that the contact with an inferior race "whose inferiority is shown not only by defeat but also by lack of attributes that may be seen in the conquerors. From the day the crossing begins, there appears a noticeable change in the quality in the blood of the masters. And as further conquests and crossings occur a new 'race' is developed but loses the strength of its ancestors" (Ibid., 31).

189   For Gobineau, when a race mixes with another its internal value is changed, therefore; it degenerates. Furthermore, civilizations fall when races mix. The effects, he thought, were worse if one race was "inferior" and another "superior." See de Gobineau, *The Inequality of Human Races*, 26, 35, 116.

190   de Gobineau, *The Inequality of Human Races*, 33.

191   Ibid., 19–22, 49–54.

192   Ibid., 37.

193   Ibid., 54–55.

elevated the "natural" virtues of the race, but it could not change "congenital" dispositions.[194] In other words, Christianity did "advance" the mind and the soul but "this is only true in so far as the soul and intellect to which it appeals are capable of being enlarged and elevated." He elaborated: "Most of the tribes of South America were received centuries ago into the bosom of the Church; but they have always remained savages, with no understanding of the European civilization unfolding before their eyes."[195] Ultimately, for Gobineau the capacity to build civilization was not merely a matter of cultural superiority but also of racial superiority. Still he argued that the cultural played a central role elevating the Aryan race into "full humanity."[196] Gobineau's scheme highlighted simultaneously the "superior" full humanity and culture of the Western Europeans and the "inhumanity" or the "lower" human stages and cultures of other groups, the non-Europeans.

Gobineau's treatise against intermixture caught fire and received many expressions.[197] The three better known were espoused by the United States of America lawyer Madison Grant, the British philosopher of science Herbert Spencer[198] and the German politician Adolf Hitler.[199] Grant promoted a policy of social Eugenics. Surprisingly reminiscent of Sepúlveda in

194   Ibid., 65–75.
195   Ibid., 69.
196   Gobineau insisted that humans can be called to be "civilized" in the first stage; the process of humanization can move humans out of their brute state. In the second stage, one finds the "cultured" human, the poet and the artist. But in the third stage, which is the highest expression of human development, one finds the "completely formed" human. See de Gobineau, *The Inequality of Human Races*, 83.
197   In Latin America, an entire generation of scholars dedicated their efforts to condemn and counter further levels of intermixture in the population. See Alberto Wagner de Reyna, *Destino y vocación de Iberoamérica*, prologue by Gonzague de Reynold (Madrid, España: Ediciones Cultura Hispánica, 1954); Carlos Octavio Bunge, *Nuestra América: Ensayo de Psicología social*, introd. by José Ingenieros (Buenos Aires, Argentina: La Cultura Argentina, 1918); Domingo Faustino Sarmiento, *Conflicto y armonías de las razas en América*, con una exposición de sus ideas sociológicas por José Ingenieros (Buenos Aires Argentina: La Cultura Argentina, 1915). Others celebrated intermixture, but saw it as an opportunity to "whiten" the population. See Justo Sierra, *Evolución política del pueblo mexicano*, 2d ed. (México, DF: La Casa de España en México, 1940); José Vasconcelos, *La raza cósmica: Misión de la raza iberoamericana*, Asociación Nacional de Libreros (México D.F.: Litografía Ediciones Olimpia, S.A., 1983).
198   Herbert Spencer, *On Social Evolution: Selected Writings*, edited, with an introduction by J. D. Peel (Chicago, IL: The University of Chicago Press, 1972).
199   Adolf Hitler, *Mein Kampf*, Sentry ed., trans. Ralph Manheim (Boston, MA: The Riverside Press, 1962).

Spain, he argued that the natives of the Americas were better off with the English invasion because it brought civilization.[200] According to him, the conservation of the "great" race was not "just a matter either of racial pride or racial prejudice" but "a matter of love of country ..."[201] He reminded his readers that the act of independence did not intend to say that "all men [*sic*] are created equal."[202] Resonating with Gobineau's resistance to the mixture of races, he argued against Democracy because it would "inevitably increase the preponderance of the lower types ..."[203] Countering the notion of "melting pot" pervasive at the beginning of the twentieth century in the u.s.a., he insisted that interbreeding between the "races" amounted to "race suicide."[204] Because miscegenation led to degenerative effects[205] and in order to preserve the purity of the "whites," he argued that "whites" could not live side by side with inferior groups.[206]

Articulating his sociocultural evolutionary theory, Spencer in turn saw the highest expression of "advance" and "development" among the French, German, English, Italians, and Russians.[207] Furthermore, for him war

---

200 Madison Grant, *The Passing of the Great Race or the Racial Basis of European History* (New York, NY: Charles Scribner's Sons, 1916), 8.

201 Ibid., IX.

202 Grant insisted that because the sentence in the act of the United States independence: "we hold these truths to be self-evident, that all men are created equal," was written by men who were slave owners, what they meant was that "they were just as Englishmen as their brothers across the sea. They did not intend to say that 'all men are created equal' " (Grant, *The Passing of the Great Race or the Racial Basis of European History*, XVI).

203 Grant, *The Passing of the Great Race or the Racial Basis of European History*, 5. Grant argued that civilization could not change the inherent inferiority of certain groups: "speaking English, wearing good clothes, and going to school and to church, does not transform a negro into a white man ... We shall have the same experience with the Polish Jew, whose dwarf stature, peculiar mentality, and ruthless concentration on self-interest are being engrafted upon the stock of the nation" (Grant, *The Passing of the Great Race or the Racial Basis of European History*, 14).

204 Grant, *The Passing of the Great Race or the Racial Basis of European History*, 43–44.

205 Grant used the Mexicans as evidence of the degenerative effects of intermixture between "inferior" and "superior" groups. In Mexico, he wrote, "the absorption of the blood of the original Spanish conquerors by the native Indian population has produced the racial mixture which we call Mexican, and which is now engaged in demonstrating its incapacity for self-government. The world has seen many such mixtures of races, and the character of a mongrel race is only just beginning to be understood at its true value" (Grant, *The Passing of the Great Race or the Racial Basis of European History*, 15).

206 Grant, *The Passing of the Great Race or the Racial Basis of European History*, 79.

207 Spencer, *On Social Evolution*, 147.

contributed to the advancement of humanity by "extirpating" the inferior groups.[208] Of course, he claimed, "after a certain stage of progress, instead of furthering the bodily development and the development of certain mental powers, [war] becomes a cause of retrogression."[209] Meanwhile, articulating his National Socialism, Hitler insisted that the great civilizations that had existed ceased to exist because they mixed with inferior foreigners. Blood mixture was the problem![210] His persecution and genocide of the Jews was therefore an act of German self-preservation.[211] He arrived at the conclusion that the segregation of species was not a racist act *contra-natura*. Rather, segregation was an activity that agreed with nature's own design to keep each species limited to their collective group. In a way, ethnic cleansing was, for him, a way to help nature.[212] He thought the benefits of the expansion of the Aryan race would be the spread of their civilization and overall cultural tradition, since they were a "culture bearing" that brought their culture with them and gave birth to *culture*.[213]

---

208   Ibid., Chapter 17.

209   Spencer, *On Social Evolution*, 171. The following quote summarizes his proposal:

> Severe and bloody as the process is, the killing-off of inferior races and inferior individuals, leaves a balance of benefit to mankind during phases of progress in which the moral development is low, and there are no quick sympathies to be continually seared by the infliction of pain and death. But as there arise higher societies, implying individual characters fitted for closer co-operation, the destructive activities exercised by such higher societies have injurious re-active effects on the moral natures of their members—injurious effects which outweigh the benefits resulting extirpation of inferior races. After this stage has been reached, the purifying process, continuing still and important one, remains to be carried on by industrial war—by a competition of societies during which the best, physically, emotionally, and intellectually, spread most, and leave the least capable to disappear gradually, from failing to leave a sufficiently-numerous posterity ... (Spencer, *On Social Evolution*, 173–74).

210   As he saw it, "Blood mixture as the resultant drop in the racial level is the sole cause of the dying out of cultures; for men do not perish as a result of lost wars, but by the loss of that force of resistance which is contained only in pure blood" (Hitler, *Mein Kampf*, 296).

211   Hitler, *Mein Kampf*, 93, 135.

212   Hitler, *Mein Kampf*, 168. Hitler wrote, "... nature looks on calmly, with satisfaction, in fact. In the struggle for daily bread all those who are weak are sickly or less determined succumb, while the struggle of the males for the females grant the right or opportunity to propagate only to the healthiest. And struggle is always a means for improving a species' health and power of resistance and, therefore, a cause of higher development" (Ibid., 285).

213   Hitler, *Mein Kampf*, 291.

Although the dangerous and painful effects of overt racialized classification are pervasive even today, by the first quarter of the twentieth century it had been largely discredited scientifically. Pseudo sciences like phrenology were abandoned and debates shifted again, with Western European superiority taking on explicitly cultural overtones instead.[214] Consider for example the works of English anthropologist Edward Burnett Tylor[215] and French philosopher and ethnologist Lucien Lévy-Bruhl.[216] Although not replete with the same sort of overt Eurocentric prejudices, these two scholars offer an approach that still asserts a superior European cultural theology.

Tylor, for instance states that his intention was to trace the development of humanity through "historical stages," but his work turns into more of a systematic comparison between the Western European culture/civilization and the rest of the nations of the world that he argued were in an earlier, "more primitive" state. Reviewing their customs, traditions, languages, and religious practices, he concluded that the reason these groups remained in such state was because they were in a "lower" mental state from their Western European counterparts.[217] In contrast to previous arguments however, he argued that such a low mental state was reversible with cultural development, and education.[218] He further argued that despite the hindering of the development of these groups because of war, famine, disease, oppression, and other mishaps, it was their inherited religious activities and practices that really kept them at a "lower" cultural stage. They would therefore need to outgrow them.[219]

The same religious connections appeared in Lévy-Brul's proposal. He argued that native traditions and customs did not point to an inferior rationality. As far as he was concerned, "primitive" groups had the ability to be trained. However, their context which included practices of idolatry and beliefs in the supernatural impeded their development. For both Tylor and Levy-Bruhl cultural education and redemption were the solution for elevating "primitive" groups out of their culturally "inferior" savage state.

---

214 Herein lies the porous boundaries between notions of "race" or "culture" as markers of distinct peoples. According to Paul Gilroy, "It is significant that prior to the consolidation of scientific racism in the nineteenth century, the term "race" was used very much in the way that the word "culture" is used today" (Gilroy, *The Black Atlantic*, 8).

215 Edward B. Tylor, *Researches Into the Early History of Mankind and the Development of Civilization* (Boston, MA: Estes & Lauriat, 1878).

216 Lucien Lévy-Bruhl, *Primitive Mentality*, trans. Lilian A. Clare (London, UK: George Allen & Unwin LTD., 1923).

217 Tylor, *Researches Into the Early History of Mankind*, 116–17.

218 Ibid., 117.

219 Ibid., 380.

Western European Imperialism: A Cultural Project

According to Paul Gilroy, it is important to challenge the credibility of a "tidy, holistic, conception of modernity." For him, the cultural history of blacks in the modern world has great bearings "on ideas of what the West was and is today."[220] By reading the "West" and "modernity" through the eyes of black peoples, he claims, we discover that we are dealing with a critical cultural apparatus of oppression that thrives on the exploitation of the other peoples of the world. Thus he, along with decolonial[221] and liberation[222] scholars, proposes a revision of the concept of "modernity."[223] More specifically,

---

220 Gilroy, *The Black Atlantic*, 45.

221 Decolonial scholars challenge the notion of "modernity" in light of its historical colonizing character and the communities that have been most directly affected by the Western European imperial impetus since 1492. Decolonial thinkers interrogate the Western European (and subsequently Euro North American) ideological apparatus and interwoven cultural factors by which they placed themselves at the center of the world, human history, and as highest expression of human civilization. See Dussel, "World-Systems and 'Trans-Modernity.'" As an alternative, these scholars insist it is necessary to reclaim the other forms of knowledge, histories, and civilizations of the world that until now have been obscured and silenced by the colonizing tendencies of the modern project. See Walter D. Mignolo, *The Darker Side of Western Modernity: Global Futures, Decolonial Options* (Durham, NC: Duke University Press, 2011); idem, "Epistemic Disobedience and the de-Colonial Option: A Manifesto" (2007), Waltermignolo.com/txt/Epistemic_Disobedience_and_the_Decolonial_Option_a_Manifesto.doc (accessed August 5, 2011); Dussel, "World-Systems and 'Trans-Modernity'"; idem, "Más allá del eurocentrismo."

222 Latin American liberation theologians emphasize the central protagonist role of those people who live in condition of economic poverty and oppression, and socially disenfranchised in understanding historical events. They also adopt the notion as the "preferential option for the poor and the oppressed" as the critical lenses for examining present social structures that privilege one sector of society over others. Over time LALT has changed to include the important ethnic and racialized forms of discrimination of Afrodescendants and Indigenous peoples. In the United States of America, liberation theological discourses include attention to social marginalization and discrimination because of ethnoracial and cultural background, gender, and sexual orientation. For a good sample of many of the liberation scholars and their theological contributions see Jon Sobrino and Ignacio Ellacuría, eds., *Systematic Theology: Perspectives from Liberation Theology* (Maryknoll, NY: Orbis Books, 1993); Deane William Ferm, *Profiles in Liberation: 36 Portraits of Third World Theologians* (Mystic, CT: Twenty-Third Publications, 1988); Deane William Ferm, *Third World Liberation Theologies: An Introductory Survey* (Maryknoll, NY: Orbis Books, 1992).

223 As he writes: "… the history of the African diaspora and a reassessment of the relationship between modernity and slavery may require a more complete revision of the terms in which the modernity debates have been constructed than any of its academic

he emphasizes that modernity needs to be apprehended through its counter-discourses.

With this kind of lens in mind, I have situated Western European notions of "advancement" and "modernity" in light of their larger history of oppression, despoliation, destruction, slavery, and exploitation of the peoples of the world. In other words, Western imperial projects (starting with Portugal and Spain at the end of the fifteenth century) were part of a larger cultural complex and processes that contributed to the construction of the Eurocentric cultural idea of "the West." As Hall and Gilroy, along with decolonial scholars like Dussel, argue, the cultural and ideological idea of "the West" "did not simply reflect an already-established western society."[224] "The West" as a cultural and ideological construct puts on display the cultural processes that formed "western" societies *in relation* to the world, "the Rest;" the Rest is in fact constitutive of the West. Or as Dussel would argue, any analysis of the West or modernity must be interrogated by its underside, by those outside of "modernity," or in this case by those outside of the West who actually made modernity possible.[225]

European imperial projects from the end of the fifteenth century up to today rested on a complex set of Western European cultural ideas about the rest of the world. It was the systematic organization of those ideas that informed Western European superior self-perception, its intellectual/conceptual framework, and its perception of other peoples. Western Europeans engaged in a systematic dehumanizing of the cultural groups of the "Rest" of the world: by naming the peoples of the "New Worlds" as "uncivilized," "inferior," "savage," and "heathens;" by promulgating the idea that they had inferior rational capacity, and had no technology or "advanced" forms of agriculture, or metallurgy, and no forms of recognizable government or laws; by arguing they had no history and had tendencies for violence and war; and finally by arguing they were inclined to magic and superstition and had no real religion, language, or morality. As we have seen, voluminous studies were produced that confirmed those prejudices. As Dussel argues, this system of ideas sometimes went so far that it actually negated alterity, erasing any final shred of humanity that might have been left intact.[226]

---

participants may be willing to concede" (Gilroy, *The Black Atlantic*, 46). See also Dussel, *The Underside of Modernity*; Dussel, *El encubrimiento del Otro*; Walter D. Mignolo, *The Darker Side of Western Modernity*.

224 Hall, "The West and the Rest," 187.

225 Dussel, *El encubrimiento del Otro*; idem, *The Underside of Modernity*; Idem, "Más allá del eurocentrismo."

226 Enrique Dussel, "Cristiandad moderna ante el Otro: De Indio 'Rudo' al Bon Sauvage," *Concilium* 150 (1979): 498–506, Http://www.enriquedussel.com/DVD%20Obras%20 Enrique%20Dussel/Textos/c/105.%201979/articulo.pdf (accessed January 25, 2015).

As I have argued, these ideas were deployed again and again at different times and in different situations. Their orchestrated manipulation provided the material justification for the invasions and imperial appropriation of the lands and resources of the peoples of the "New Worlds."[227] In the words of Hall, "Europe brought its own cultural categories, languages, images, and ideas to the New World in order to describe and represent it. It tried to fit the New World into existing conceptual frameworks, classifying it according to its own norms, and absorbing it into western traditions of representation."[228] Furthermore, earlier notions of the "savage" and the "primitive" were juxtaposed against notions of the Western European "civilized" Christian and were integral to understanding and framing "ethnic" differences. Over time, these categories became essential cognitive and aesthetic markers in the processes which generated a network of interconnected ideas and cultural symbols in which "Western European," "Christian" and other racialized attributes gave way "to the dislocating dazzle of 'whiteness.'"[229]

The orchestrated production of knowledge about the peoples of the "New Worlds" served various functions. All coincided, however, in deploying "civilization" as the cipher, metonym and discursive apparatus that displayed the (cultural and religious) superiority of Western Europeans over the "others" of the world. While the motivations for "studying" the peoples of the "New Worlds" were multiple, various and at times contradictory (actual curiosity, genuine desire to know and interact with them, search for evidence of their underdevelopment to justify destruction or enculturation, political and economic interests, etc.), the produced literature contributed to the creation of sophisticated processes of representation by which the colonial gaze became the measure, standard, and point of departure for the interaction between Western Europeans (and later Euro North Americans) with the peoples of the

According to Dussel, the effect of this systematic organization of ideas about the rest of the world meant that those "others" could be discarded; it amounted to a denied existence, which for him, it was the heart of the Enlightenment in its practical and cultural implications for the rest of the world. See Dussel, "Was America Discovered or Invaded?."

227   Hugh Honour notes in his study of European images of the Americas that there was the creation of a sophisticated system of representation based on stereotypes. There was also an ambiguity which can be seen in the way in which America was seen as "an idealized or distorted image of their own countries, on to which they could project their own aspirations and fears, their self-confidence and ... guilty despair" (Cited in Hall, "The West and the Rest," 215).

228   Hall, "The West and the Rest," 204.

229   Gilroy, *The Black Atlantic*, 9.

"New Worlds." The boundaries between the "civilized" and the "uncivilized" seemed clearly defined.

As I have been arguing, the platform of representation and interaction with the natives was first and foremost cultural in nature. As Western Europeans engaged with the natives of the "New Worlds," the complex process of Western European culturalization played a crucial role in the ways Europeans understood and interacted with the rest of the world. European cultural power was enacted so comprehensively in entire regions like the Americas and Australia that it went pass "representation" into the systematic eradication of the natives including the destruction of their cultural traditions, customs, practices, religions, and languages. It was not merely the imposition of one cultural tradition over another in order to "cultivate" the natives but it was culturecide.[230] In the words of Said, the imperial project was (and I would argue, continues to be) "an exercise of cultural strength."[231]

In what follows, I will be tracing some of the ways in which Western European and Euro North American scholars have engaged the question of the relationship of Christianity and the cultural. The scholars with whom I engage are really speaking about processes of culturalization, what I term *the cultural*, but consistently they inexorably write using the singular "culture." In part I suspect this is the case because they are so entrenched in the Western European cultural and intellectual tradition that they are unable to think the cultural in plural sense. I also posit that their use of "culture" reveals the "modernist" assumption of a fixed reality that can be studied and managed. With that in mind, in my discussion in the following three chapters (chapters 4 to 6), I preserve their use of the singular *culture* because to do otherwise would carry the potential of changing the content of their assertions. That said, in the introduction and conclusion of each of the chapters, I will be resorting to the use of *the cultural* as my preferred category in order to account for the complexity of the debates, the complex processes of culturalization, and the enormous diversity of cultural traditions as concrete expressions of such complex processes. To that we now turn.

---

230   Amilcar Cabral is correct insisting that culture is the focal point for any dominant power's attempt to keep people dominated; culture is systematically undermined and destroyed. See his "National Liberation and Culture."

231   Said, *Orientalism*, 40.

CHAPTER 4

The Cultural, Missions, and Mainline Protestants Theologians

The Caucasian has, in the cultural development of his race for many thousands of years, an advantage over the Ethiopian, by which he is superior to him as the man to the child, and wherever the consciousness of this superiority remains, there will also that advantage remain, however personally he may be ungifted in comparison with the acute children of nature.[1]

  DAVID LIVINGSTONE

• • •

Only ignorance or narrow-mindedness can question that in India the Government has not only abolished widow-burning and child-murder, but has also effected a far-reaching undermining of Hinduism by the introduction of European refinement and civilization, which must of necessity be favourable to the mission.... In like manner, it is manifest that the introduction of European culture into Japan, notwithstanding all the elements of unbelief and immorality which are rushing in along with it, is preparing a field for evangelical Christianity.[2]

  GUSTAV WARNECK

• • •

They [the missionaries] assumed that the most appropriate manner, texts, and instruments with which to worship God were those from Europe and America. They disparaged local music traditions they did not understand, undoubtedly because they felt them hopelessly

---

1 Cited in Gustav Warneck, *Modern Missions and Culture: Their Mutual Relations*, trans. Thomas Smith (Edinburgh, Scotland: James Gennel, 1883), 328.
2 Warneck, *Modern Missions and Culture*, 234.

culture-bound and therefore corrupted by the non-Christian world
they were seeking to overcome for Christ.[3]

GERALD HOBBS

Introduction

Spain and Portugal were not the only ones involved in imperial and colonial
endeavors at the turn of the sixteenth century; people from the other European
nations (France, England, Germany, Holland, etc.) participated as merchants,
explorers, indentured laborers, hired military support, etc., and benefitted greatly
from the Spanish and Portuguese conquests of the Americas. By the seventeenth
century, following Spain and Portugal in the previous century, Western Europeans
nations initiated their own imperial projects to conquer and plunder the "New
Worlds." These nations included Britain, Holland, Germany, France, Italy, Sweden,
Austria-Hungary, Belgium, and the Scandinavian countries, and later-on the
U.S.A. Each of these expressions of Western European imperialism drew on the
same family of ideas of European self-perceived superiority and providential chosenness; the peoples of the "New Worlds" were consequently understood to be
savages, uncivilized, heathen, and inferior beings.

As I demonstrated in the previous chapter, cultural expansionist interests
were at the heart of the imperial projects. Amilcar Cabral is correct that one of
the most important measures of the impact of colonial empires is how much
they managed to "destroy or at least, to neutralize and paralyze" the cultures
of the colonized.[4] As I have been arguing, a key part of the imperial cultural
project was the destruction of religious traditions and their replacement with
Christianity. The missionary movement played a crucial role in making this
happen. However, by the first half of the 20th century, missionary boards and
theologians began to realize that traditional approaches and attitudes toward
the cultures of the peoples of the world were no longer tenable. Western
European and Euro North American scholars began to rethink the connections
between Christianity and the cultural dimension.

My intention in this chapter is to chronicle major shifts in the debates on
Christianity and the cultural as a result of the enormous geopolitical changes

---

3   Gerald Hobbs, "Christianity and Music," in *Sacred Sound: Experiencing Music in World
    Religions*, Guy L. Beck (Waterloo, ON: Wilfrrd Laurier University Press, 2006), 82.

4   Amilcar Cabral, "National Liberation and Culture," 12. He added, "Imperialist domination
    being the negation of the true historical process of the oppressed people, it must necessarily
    be the negation of its cultural processes" (Ibid., 13).

during the latter part of the 19th and first half of the 20th century. Questions on the cultural came to occupy centre stage because of 1) the implications of those geopolitical changes on missionary work and 2) wide ranging theological reflections on the phenomena of cultures which were responding in turn to the geopolitical changes, especially in response to events in Europe. I divide this chapter in two parts; the first section shows in broad strokes how early missionaries and clergy saw their missionary enterprise as including two parts, Christian evangelization and cultural imperialism. In the second section, I show how Protestant theologians sought to rethink questions of the relationship between Christianity and the cultural especially in the middle of the twentieth century.

I want to reiterate that the scholars I will be discussing use the singular "culture" to speak of what I consider to be the processes of culturalization and the phenomena of the cultural, by which I mean the ubiquitous phenomena that define, shape, condition, and impact the ways humans engage life, and interact with their immediate environment, each other and the divine. In order to avoid confusion, I keep the use of the singular culture because these scholars did not think of the cultural in its plural expressions with the broad/richly diverse understanding I give it here. Besides, by changing "culture" into "the cultural" the meaning of what they are saying would be changed, unduly misleading readers, so I preserve the singular culture when quoting directly.

Protestant Missions and Evangelization as Extension of Empire

The theological cultures of Western Europe were fed by the Christian institutions that accompanied the forces of colonialism everywhere they went. Eurocentric Christian cultural theologies played a crucial role; in colonialism Christianity operated as the interpretive lenses for the history, reality, cultures, and, most important of all, the religions of the *other* peoples. In the words of Friedrich Hellwald from the middle of the 19th century, "Modern culture undeniably rests upon the view of the world derived from Christianity."[5] Like their Catholic counterparts (discussed in the previous chapter), Protestant clerics, ministers, and lay people in the Americas displayed imperial and colonizing attitudes and prejudices, and were convinced that European civilization and Christianization were two sides of the same coin for the foundation upon which empire was predicated. They were both heirs to similar theological cultures within which a perceived European "superior" cultural tradition was providentially tied to Christianity. As a result, European cultural superiority went hand-in-hand in the evangelizing project.

5   Cited in Warneck, *Modern Missions and Culture*, 3.

Protestant Christian clerics and missionaries contributed to the voluminous cultural written resources produced by Western Europeans (and later Euro North Americans) as part of what Said calls "the archive": the convoluted and copious production of studies and written material about the peoples of the "New Worlds." These materials provided distorted views of the cultures, traditions, values, and religious beliefs of originary inhabitants. Such writings were often deployed as evidence of the inferiority and cultural backwardness of Indigenous communities, and as justification for the need to civilize and Christianize them.

Just as Catholic missionaries had done in the Americas since the time of Christopher Columbus at the dawn of the sixteenth century, Protestant missionaries traveled to the various regions where empire had spread. Protestants did no better than the Catholics in their treatment of native communities, and adopted heinous methods of cultural imperialism and evangelization. Copious examples of how Protestant missionaries saw themselves as part of the imperial culture abound.

Andrew Porter insists that missionaries must be distinguished from the larger set of factors which constitute imperial cultural domination and control, and should not me mixed with other agencies of colonial oppression; they were part of the imperial culture and imaginary, but they were not as often explicitly interwoven with governmental structures.[6] That said, there is no doubt that Protestants also served imperial interests. They wrote "histories" of the New Worlds[7] and collected material for the study of Indigenous communities everywhere.[8] They also established schools

---

6   Andrew Porter, "Cultural Imperialism and Protestant Missionary Enterprise, 1780–1914," *The Journal of Imperial and Commonwealth History* 25, no. 3 (September 1997): 375.

7   One remarkable example here is the work of Samuel Purchas, who wrote a history of Asia, Africa and Latin America. See his *A Theological and Geographical Historie of Asia, Africa, and America, with the Ilands Adiacent*, vol. IV, *Purchas His Pilgrimage. Or Relations of the World and the Religions Observed in All Ages and Places Discovered, from the Creation unto This Present*. (London, UK: William Stansby, 1614). The five-volume collection was intended as an overview of God's creation from an Anglican perspective by someone who claimed to have travelled to those parts of the world. In reality, the work included the posthumous collection of papers written by Richard Hakluyt and a compilation of anecdotal material from sailors Purchas had met. See H.G. Rawlinson, *Narratives from Purchas His Pilgrimes* (Oxfor, UK: Oxford University Press, 1931), IX.

8   Gustav Warneck admitted that his writings on missions were primarily informed by reports by missionaries themselves. Many of his stereotypical perspectives stem from these reports. He insisted that though the reports needed to be critically adopted, "they must continue to be the main foundation of our representation" (Warneck, *Modern Missions and Culture*, 32). Many of the reports and studies written by missionaries constituted key material later used by anthropologists and other scientists concerning native

and literacy programs where Western European civilization would be taught along with Christianity.[9] They learned the local languages in order to translate the Bible to more effectively evangelize local communities, which often resulted in undermining local cultures and traditions.[10] And they introduced the Western European value system, along with sociocultural conventions as the only ways to live the Christian faith.[11] The blending of Western European cultural theologies and Christianity into the work of

peoples everywhere. An excellent example is the work of the well-known Anthropologist Lucien Lévy-Bruhl, whose *Primitive Mentality* is peppered with allusions to books, written and oral accounts, and anecdotal information by missionaries from many Christian traditions. The accounts by these missionaries—many of which are fantastic and exaggerated depictions of native peoples in many regions of the world—helped him bolster his claim of the "primitive" condition of many of these communities. He concludes that the people he writes about are not primitive because of the lack of intellectual ability but because their minds are hostage to beliefs in the mystical, the supernatural, and witchcraft. What they needed was to develop their minds and cultures. Thus, for him, this "underdevelopment" could be corrected by "education," "civilization," and "evangelization." See Lucien Lévy-Bruhl, *Primitive Mentality*.

9 Countering Jean and John Camaroff's assertion that by seeking mastery of local languages missionaries placed local cultures under their direct control, and in order not to concede that missions were part of the imperial project, Porter insists that schools, education programs, the printing press and books brought benefits for both the Protestant forms of Christianity that depended on literacy as well as the local peoples. According to him, local communities benefitted from the introduction of Western European cultures and languages. He correctly complexifies his analysis by acknowledging that imperial cultures encountered great resistance and profound processes of bargaining and negotiation which underlayed "all imperial arrangements." See Porter, "'Cultural Imperialism,'" 378, 383, 386–88. However, in order to negate the profoundly negative cultural and psychological impact of European missions in the New Worlds, Porter undermines the degree to which the introduction of Western cultural education, moral values, and construction of social relations contributed to the disarticulation of local cultures and their replacement with Western European cultures.

10 Although not willing to concede the profound cultural power and complicit with imperial projects, Porter admits that in British missions teaching English did mean a relative devaluation of vernaculars. See Porter, "'Cultural Imperialism,'" 376–77.

11 In the words of Harry Johnston, the missions "strengthen our hold over the country, they spread the use of the English language, they induct the natives into the best kind of civilization, and in fact each mission station is an essay in colonization." Cited in Porter, "'Cultural Imperialism,'" 369. Jean and John Camaroff have also quite explicitly cast the Wesleyan and Congregationalist missionaries in early nineteenth-century South Africa in the role, as they put it, of "agent, scribe and moral alibi" for the "colonizing project." Cited in Ibid., 370–371.

evangelization turned mission work into an effective mechanism for imperial and Western cultural expansion;[12] missionaries became prime agents of
these cultural imperial projects.[13]

Many missionaries boasted of their superior culture/civilization and even
went so far as to make cultural assimilation a required part of evangelization.[14]
As the famous U.S.A. missionary Rufus Anderson puts it in his 428th sermon:
"I should add that the civilization that the gospel has conferred upon our New
England is the highest and the best, in a religious point of view, the world has
ever seen."[15] Catholic and Protestant missionaries alike did not hold back in judging the spiritualities and religious practices of the peoples they encountered as
backwards and superstitious.[16] The Swiss missionary and ethnographer Henri
Alexandre Junod is a good example. He was convinced of the need to "initiate"
the South African Thonga people into "civilization."[17] As he saw it, the Thonga
were in a "state of utter degeneracy,"[18] needing to be freed from slavery to their
customs and traditions.[19] Building on Dudley Kidd's ideas of cultural eugenics, he
wondered whether it would not be advisable to develop a policy of segregation

---

12   The account by the Scottish Congregationalist missionary to Africa Robert Moffat is a
      good example of how Western cultural elements and values and views of "civilization"
      were imported into new regions by Western European missionaries. See his *Missionary
      Labours and Scenes in Southern Africa* (New York, NY: Robert Carter, 1843).

13   Porter, "'Cultural Imperialism,'" 367. While he acknowledges the complicity of missionar-
      ies with Empire, Andrew Porter rejects ideas that missions embodied a "concerted assault
      on values and the religious or spiritual sanctions" underlining the imperial project which
      constituted "the psychological basis for the politics of colonialism" (Ibid.).

14   In his account of his missionary work in British Guiana, William Henry Brett describes
      the natives as "children of the wilderness" who are "strangers to the habits of civilized life"
      (William Henry Brett, *The Indian Tribes of Guiana*, 6). Most important is his description of
      how the missionary work started. According to him, it was a long time after the discovery
      of the country before any effort was made "to bestow on its original inhabitants the bless-
      ing of Christianity and civilization" (Ibid., 37).

15   P. Beaver, ed., *To Advance the Gospel: Selection of Writings of Rufus Anderson* (Grand
      Rapids, MI: William B. Eermans Publishing Co., 1967), 73.

16   See Julius Jetté, "On the Superstitions of the Ten'a Indians (Middle Part of the Yukon
      Valley, Alaska)," *Anthropos* 6, no. 4 (1911): 699–723.

17   Henri Alexandre Junod, *The Psychic Life*, vol. II, *The Life of a South African Tribe* (Neuchatel,
      Switzerland: Attinger Fréres, 1913), 31.

18   Ibid., 539.

19   For Junod, the degree of knowledge of the Thonga people was as primitive as the time of
      the book of Leviticus. While they could not be called fully savages, they were semiprim-
      itive because of their lack of clear differentiation between magic, religion, morality and
      taboo. See Junod, *The Psychic Life*, 78, 278.

or relocation of the Thonga to tropical Africa for "their own protection."[20] As he wrote: "My conclusion is that the only salvation for the South African tribe is in a regeneration achieved by Christianity, education providing [sic], at the same time, the enlightenment of the mind which also is of primary necessity."[21]

One other prominent example provided by the missiologist Gustav Warneck who, writing at the time of the missionary movement, pointed out that Christianity was a cultural project. At the end of the nineteenth century, Warneck wrote his *Modern Missions and Culture*,[22] highlighting the particular ways in which he, along with many of his contemporaries, saw the correlation between (Western European and Euro North American expressions of) Christianity and Western European and Euro North American cultures/civilization.[23]

Warneck outlined the relationship he found between German culture and Christianity. He argued that German (for him European) culture and Christianity are not antithetical. In fact, he claimed, they complement each other because only a culture that models itself according to the principles of Christianity is a true culture.[24] He wrote, "… the gospel of Christ and culture hang together as cause and effect, as root and plant. While we lead the proof

---

20   Junod, *The Psychic Life*, 541. Dudley Kidd was an Anthropologist who promoted a form of social eugenics as an alternative that would "improve" the conditions of the African peoples. As he saw it, the western European culture and civilization were vital for the elevation of the Africans by supplying it with the necessary advanced cultural resources. Children, he argued, needed to be separated from African social environment and communities because those did not "provide an environment that will foster the new life they received" with Western European education (Dudley Kidd, *Kafir Socialism and the Dawn of Individualism: An Introduction to the Study of the Native Problem* [London, UK: Adam and Charles Black, 1908], 236).

21   Junod, *The Psychic Life*, 542. He continued stating that Christianity will lead the "weak and carnal Bantu savage to the height of the Christian ideal, thus victoriously replacing the non-moral religion and the non-religious morality of the Native" (Ibid.). William Brett expressed similar sentiments: "It may be that some tribes will expire in cold and gloomy heathenism, while others, as we hope and pray (and in part behold), may progress in Christianity and civilization, acquire our language, become useful to the community at large, and gradually forget their ancient distinctions and animosities in the common name of Christian" (Brett, *The Indian Tribes of Guiana*, 496).

22   Warneck, *Modern Missions and Culture*.

23   Although Warneck admits that civilization is too narrow a view of culture, he nevertheless opts to alternate his use of both terms. See Warneck, *Modern Missions and Culture*, 7.

24   For Warneck there was a convergence between the goals of culture and Christianity. As he saw it, the goal of culture was to achieve happiness. Thus, material and intellectual good had to be the objective of education. Only when these objectives were in harmony

that he [*sic*] who conducts a Christian mission plants culture also, we may also prove conversely that he [*sic*] who is a friend of culture must also be a friend of Christian missions."[25] More particularly, departing from the perspective of missions, he demonstrates the interwoven relationship between imparting "culture" and the task of evangelizing.[26] His boastful remarks betray the fact that he did not speak of "culture" in the abstract-universal sense meaning any cultural expression. Rather, by "culture" and/or civilization he means Western European and Euro North American cultures and civilizations.[27] He argued that these cultures had been providentially guided over millennia and now was being shared with the world via imperialism. The line of thinking continued by arguing that the superior cultures were far too advanced for more primitive cultures to handle; their very primitivity posed enormous obstacles to their own evangelizing.[28]

For Warneck, the connection between Christianity and Western civilization/culture was inevitable because the former presupposed the

---

did culture become ennobling. Meanwhile, he also thought that only those who adopt Christianity carry a truly honorable existence, enjoy happiness and reject evil. See Warneck, *Modern Missions and Culture*, 6, 14.

25   Warneck, *Modern Missions and Culture*, 17.

26   Warneck believed that a fundamental principle of mission was to proclaim the gospel to the heathen in their mother-tongue. As soon as possible the Bible ought to be translated into that tongue. It followed that the mission needed to teach the natives how to read, found schools, and provide them with literature. In so doing, mission "gives an entirely new impulse to the entire mental life" of the people. See Warneck, *Modern Missions and Culture*, 40, 124.

27   The connections with Macaulay place Warneck among those who thought that the Indigenous cultures had to be liquidated and substituted with the alien culture of a colonizing power via education. See http://en.wikipedia.org/wiki/Macaulayism (accessed April 25, 2015). He quotes Hellwald insisting that "our whole actual culture-development rests upon the Christianization of Europe" (Ibid., 36).

28   He noted: "In order that the hitherto heathen peoples of Europe might not have a comparatively completed culture indiscriminately thrust upon them, which doubtless would have been hurtful to them, physically and intellectually, the educative wisdom of the Divine government of the world arranged it so that they had to make, so to speak, a development of culture *ab ovo*, in which they advanced only step by step on the long and toilsome way of their own work. Upon this Divine pedagogic depends essentially the solid foundation, as well as the permanence, of the Western Christian culture; while—as we shall see further on—the almost immediate conveyance, to the heathen peoples of the present day, of this culture, which with us has grown gradually by development for more than a thousand years, forms one of the chief difficulties of the modern mission." (Warneck, *Modern Missions and Culture*, 37).

latter. To evangelize or engage in missionary work required that the recipients of the evangelizing work be also "civilized." Consequently, the missionaries were the "bringers" of "culture" as they laid the foundations for civilization to occur.[29] The rationale for the civilizing component of mission work was connected to the fact that Western European and White Euro North American cultures were far superior to those of the natives of the colonies.[30] Along with Rousseau in the previous century, Warneck thought that Western European civilizations were the best medium for the communication of the Gospel and, that therefore, "Christian nations have become the bearers of culture."[31] Civilization created the structures and conditions for people to receive Christianity[32] and it elevated the people morally by freeing them from their spiritual slavery and immorality.[33] Most importantly, for Warneck, in this interweaving of European culture and Christianity,

---

29   Warneck, *Modern Missions and Culture*, 38. He made his argument in condescending and patronizing ways: "Among savage peoples the missionary must be everything, teach everything, set the example of doing everything. He must be a father among children, the patriarch of a great family, the teacher among scholars, he must be architect and husbandman, merchant and artisan, road-maker and schoolmaster, councillor in the affairs of the community, and literateur! He must put his hand to axe and plough, and his wife must teach the native wives to use the broom and the needle. Among all uncivilized peoples the missionary labours at laying the foundation of culture" (Warneck, *Modern Missions and Culture*, 42–43).

30   In cultural terms, Warneck noted that missions during the time of the apostles were a fairly easy endeavor because the people they intended to evangelize shared the same culture. In the Middle Ages, missionary endeavors were complicated as medieval missionaries had levels of culture that were slightly higher than the people they intended to missionize. But in "modern" times, he noted that the difficulty is far greater because Western European civilization is absolutely superior to the other cultures of the world. Thus, in order to evangelize the people, they had to be introduced/enculturated into the Western European culture and civilization. See Warneck, *Modern Missions and Culture*, 36–38.

31   Warneck, *Modern Missions and Culture*, 13.

32   Warneck, *Modern Missions and Culture*, 13. For Warneck there was a humanizing effect that resulted from the intersection between Christianity and civilization. For him, the gospel in particular had a humanizing impact. But since the gospel and civilization go together, by giving the Indigenous peoples culture, civilization and the gospel, Western culture had the effect of humanizing them; it gave them honor, dignity and nobility. See (Ibid., 159).

33   As he observed, religion must be accompanied by morality. Where religion exists without morality it is only pretension. See Warneck, *Modern Missions and Culture*, 11.

Christianity was preeminent; Western European civilization/culture was an offshoot of Christianity and not the other way around.[34]

Warneck was certainly aware of the interconnection between empire and Christianity. His commitment to civilization and missions carried multiple implications. First, and as I have been explaining above, he advocated enculturation/Europeanization as the method most suitable for the evangelization of peoples. Included in this approach was the commitment to instill in the natives[35] Western European (here German) cultural views and moral values by teaching them the Christian demand for "purity" and "decency," among other things. Warneck saw the task of the missionaries as to "awaken" among the natives the sense of "modesty," which in some cases meant to insist on a "certain measure of clothing" to cover their nakedness.[36]

Second, he acknowledged that it was through the imperial forces and structures that Western cultures were introduced to the colonized.[37] As far as he was concerned, imperial expansion was good for missions since it increased the regions to which missionaries could take Christianity. Imperial expansion was also good culturally because it imported the Western European and Euro North American cultures, which elevated the host societies in which missions were key, and prepared them to be properly evangelized.[38]

Third, missions were good economically because of the expansion of imperial commerce in the colonies. On one hand, he thought that colonial powers should encourage evangelization because it was cheaper to

---

34   He wrote: "To us it seems that it is just the Gospel that gives the strength which awakens the required energy, and imparts the indispensable moral standing. We plant and promote civilization when we present" the Gospel, and we make the nature-peoples human by making them Christians. Christianity is not the bloom but the root; culture "is not 'the root' but a 'bloom of Christianity'" (Warneck, *Modern Missions and Culture*, 245).

35   Warneck is not referring here to a particular group of natives. Natives here refers to the local people of the places where empire has spread.

36   Warneck, *Modern Missions and Culture*, 44. Warneck did qualify his comments by noting that natives were not required to wear European clothing everywhere, except in those places where the people had no custom of wearing clothes. See Ibid.

37   For him, for example, culture permeated all aspects of the colonial structures of commerce, politics and travel. Warneck, *Modern Missions and Culture*, 38–39.

38   Warneck insisted that wherever the mission had gotten a foot-hold, the people's "miserable huts" with their "rude" furnishings were replaced by "more respectable and cleaner dwellings." With some degree of condescension, he added, "there an elementary architecture begins to spring up" (Warneck, *Modern Missions and Culture*, 57).

evangelize the natives than to spend money exterminating them.[39] On the other hand, the missions were a strategic post in the expansion of colonial commerce. As he saw it, the missions were an avant-guarde pioneer for commerce.[40] Although the trade was organized by merchants, missionaries were responsible for its emergence:[41] the missions created the need for civilized life and they were also a protective power in favour of commerce amidst the heathens.[42]

Warneck's cultural blinders did not allow him to see the complicity of Christianity with the violence of colonial invasions and cultural imperialism. In fact, ignoring the very issue of imperial invasion, he claimed that the presence of the missions hampered lawless people from plundering the natives.[43] He distances the missions from the larger phenomenon of unspeakable acts of violence against native peoples by imperial subjects by claiming that those acts were done by nominal Christians and that the missions were not involved.[44]

---

39   Warneck, *Modern Missions and Culture*, 62. Educating and Christianizing the natives turned them away from hostility to the colonial powers and into pacific people, Warneck argued. It elevated them and made it easier for them to be "won" for the gospel and meant that the colonial powers did not have to spend so much money on exterminating them. He wrote, "Without doubt it is a far more costly thing to kill the natives than to Christianize them" (Ibid., 60).

40   It is unclear whether Warneck was in support of slavery or of emancipation. He supported the education of slaves as constituting a cultural advance for colonial societies, but he also disapproved of the emancipation of the slaves on economic grounds. As he stated:

> It is incontestably true that the abolition of slavery has been, from a politico-economical point of view, a great misfortune both for the West Indies and for the Southern States of the American Union. It is just as true that the wholesale and entire emancipation of the slaves has not hitherto been any considerable cultural advantage. But it is not true that the mission bears the real blame of this *fiasco*. Certainly she is a sharer of the blame, in so far as she in her energetic agitation for the abolition of slavery, was deficient in wisdom respecting the necessary education—a charge, however, which is essentially palliated by the consideration that the slave-owners strenuously opposed all training of this sort (Warneck, *Modern Missions and Culture*, 95).

41   Warneck, *Modern Missions and Culture*, 48.

42   Warneck, *Modern Missions and Culture*, 49. The fact that the missions functioned as protection for commerce meant that they should not be opposed but rather seen as ally. See Ibid., 50–51.

43   Warneck, *Modern Missions and Culture*, 51.

44   Warneck mentions these criticisms of the colonial forces emerging from Africa, Oceania and other places. He includes a crucial critique by one Professor Gerland, who seems to

He chastised those who claimed that "the requirements of modesty are only conventional, a product of culture and fashion, an aesthetic, but not a religious necessity."[45] Instead, he emphasized the interconnection between Christianity and Western culture to such a degree that "the introduction" of clothing among the converts is so general a fact that to wear clothing and to be baptized, or to be a catechumen, are often synonymous.[46]

In the end, Warneck represents a good example of how Protestant missionaries understood (Western European expressions of) Christianity as intertwined with and inseparable from Western European and Euro North American cultures. It is no surprise that for him the question of culture and Christianity was a non-issue because he understood them as indivisible. The celebration of Christianity for Warneck inevitably meant the celebration of Western civilization and cultural accomplishments.[47] For all intents and purposes, the

---

be convinced that all colonial subjects, wholesale, are to be blamed for the bad treatment against the natives wherever the imperial forces have gone. He wrote.

> In the first place, it must be confessed that all cultured-peoples have conducted themselves in the same way, cruelly, recklessly, and unmanfully towards the nature-peoples who have come into contact with them—Spaniards, Portuguese, Dutch, English, French.... The almost always inhuman and murderous way in which the Europeans subdued the nature-peoples, and generally exceeded them greatly in savagery, compels us to an anthropological conclusion of no small importance, for we see clearly that 'the gulf which separates the civilized man from the barbarian is by no means so wide as is commonly supposed.' ... Let it not be said that the atrocities perpetrated by the Europeans were the doings only of individuals, and so that only the particular individuals should bear the blame of them; they were pretty equally practised by the whole colonial people, and were everywhere highly approved by them; yea. they are very far from being reprobated even now (Cited in Warneck, *Modern Missions and Culture*, 256).

45   Warneck, *Modern Missions and Culture*, 45.
46   Ibid.
47   In a proud and yet contradictory statement, Warneck celebrates the contributions of Christianity to Western civilization. For him, Christianity brought

> The right of individuality, the recognition of the dignity of man, and therewith of humanity, the equality of the sexes, the regeneration of marriage, of family life and the education of children, the gradual abolition of slavery, the moral esteem of labour, and therewith a new economical arrangement, with a whole range of new moral virtues, unselfish love, universal charity, beneficence, meekness, purity—all these are foundations of culture which the gospel of Christ was the first to lay, and which it laid not only in peculiarly favourable circumstances, but in universal human society, whose lowest strata indeed it elevated. (Warneck, *Modern Missions and Culture*, 35).

marriage between these two forces, including their political and economic implications, and their cultural impact on the colonized exemplified all the good brought to them. He boasted of the good brought by the empire:

> Other peoples have accomplished much more, but they required many centuries for their advances; we may well be proud of the attainments we have made in a half century. A heathen people has embraced Christianity; barbarians are half civilized; you find churches and schools in all directions; every kind of slavery is removed; a constitution has been granted; laws govern; courts of justice are in operation; various departments of administration are in action; roads intersect the whole country; shops are opening in every village; and all aids to civilization are beginning to beautify the land.[48]

He was aware that mission work is arduous and demands a serious commitment from those who contemplate becoming missionaries. However, there is little acknowledgement of the destruction of native cultures and traditions; he saw only the great *benefits* for the locals through their acceptance of the gospel and the many good things from the empire.

Contrary to Jacob Hobson, a contemporary of Warneck who sharply criticized the economically motivated British (and Western European) imperial agenda,[49] Warneck saw the missions as contributing to the establishment of branches of imperial economic interests. For him, the missions functioned as a crucial bridge that facilitated the import and distribution of imperial goods

---

The contradictory nature of this statements becomes obvious since neither Warneck nor his contemporaries nor the colonial powers sought to apply such "Christian principles" to the colonized populations. Moreover, it was not until the import of Western cultures that labour was commodified, slavery was instituted and turned into a very profitable industry, and hierarchies among human collectives were instituted.

48   Warneck, *Modern Missions and Culture*, 201.

49   J.A. Hobson, *Imperialism: A Study* (New York, NY: James Pott & Company, 1902). Like Warneck, Hobson's critique of the Western European project focuses on two important aspects, economics and culture. He highlights an explosion of imperialist / colonizing forces around the end of the nineteenth century (Germany, France, Italy, Portugal, Belgium, Holland, Russia, and the United States). See Ibid., 20–23. Much ahead of his time, he argued that Western European imperialism's real agenda was to expand all over the world in order to increase its sources of revenue and to "share" the benefits of Western European civilization. As he saw it, the excuse of the colonization of "lower races" disguised the goal of creating new centers of distribution and consumption of imperial goods. See Ibid., 52–57.

to the locals in the colonial societies. In this way, the missions became an extension of imperial economic efforts. As far as he was concerned, missions were economically beneficial to the empire because they converted people and therefore turned them away from being enemies of the empire. They also contributed to "good economics" because it was cheaper to convert the natives than to kill them. And finally, the missions operated as posts of colonial commerce; they protected commercial branches better than armed forces. In other words, the missions made sound economic sense.

(Re)Connecting Christianity and Culture (the Cultural) among Protestants

By the end of the nineteenth century, the violence and inhumanity of the Western European imperial project had been buried by historical amnesia. The memory of the destruction of Indigenous communities, cultures, and traditions by the Western European imperial projects did not register in the historical imaginary of Western Europeans and Euro North Americans. Western Europe boasted enormous advances in the sciences; European industrialization was in full swing; and new philosophical and cultural currents were burgeoning. The Western European hubris and cultural imaginary had created the myth that their advancement was the result of internal uninterrupted processes of historical development that spanned fifteen centuries.[50] But confidence in their "progress" was thoroughly shattered by the two world-wars.[51] Europe entered into a crisis from which it has not been able to recover to this day. In a kind of myopic paradox, Europeans took seriously the events that led to the Holocaust but they were not able to see that those events were part of a larger—then four-centuries long—history of rapacious imperial greed which had contributed to the destructions of entire civilizations and cultures all over the world.[52]

---

50   Although many Western European and Anglo North Atlantic authors repeat this idea in different ways, immediately after the second world war Emil Brunner was insisting that it took fifteen centuries for "Western Civilization" to be created. See Emil Brunner, *Foundations*, vol. 1, *Christianity and Civilisation* (New York, NY: Charles Scribner's Sons, 1948), 1.

51   As Van Til puts it, the old liberals have been chastened because the world wars "purged the leaven of their evolutionary faith" (Henry R. Van Til, *The Calvinistic Concept of Culture* [Grand Rapids, MI: Baker Book House, 1959], 161).

52   The sense of guilt and shame over the events that led to the Holocaust were seared in the Western European imaginary. Ironically, the violence of the Holocaust did not

It is impossible to adequately convey the depth of the crisis in which Western Europeans entered as a result of the world-wars and the multiple human atrocities that took place during that time. It is also impossible here to do justice to the multiple and diverse responses of Western Europeans and Euro North Americans as they sought to make sense of the fallout from this historical juncture. For many Christians, the problem of Western Europe was not merely political or cultural, it was also spiritual. Paul Tillich would call it the crisis of anxiety and meaninglessness. Many blamed the events that led to the world wars and the internal crisis in Western Europe on the widespread rejection of Christianity. Emil Brunner, for example, noted that the Enlightenment marked a crucial moment by which "civilization" was emancipated from the God of Christianity.[53] He wrote: "The last three centuries, seen from the spiritual point of view, represent a history in which step by step the central and fundamental idea of the whole of Western civilisation, the idea of the dignity of man [*sic*] was undermined and weakened."[54] He continued: "For more than a thousand years Western culture had been based on the Christian idea that man is created in the image of God.... With the Enlightenment, this idea, on which the whole structure of Western life was rested, began to be doubted."[55] Barely ten years after Brunner, Henry Van Til blamed the crisis and deep cultural changes in Western Europe, which resulted in the renunciation of Christianity, on the Renaissance, the Enlightenment, and the French Revolution.[56] According to

---

help retrieve the four hundred years of the violence, colonization and oppression of Indigenous communities everywhere and the enslaving of African peoples. I agree with Decolonial scholar Walter Mignolo who argues that "starting off from the refugees of the Second World War and the Holocaust means to ignore four-hundred years of history in which the refugees and the Holocaust are certain moments in a much longer chain of the disposability of human life and the violation of human dignity (not only of human rights)" (Walter Mignolo, "Epistemic Disobedience"). Mignolo continues, Moreover, Aimes Césaire claimed that "the crime of the White man in Hitler was that he dared to apply the logic of coloniality to fellow white men which until then he had reserved for the Arabs, Algerians, Coolies of India ... Niggers of Africa," and I would add the myriad Indigenous communities of the Americas (Ibid., 31).

53   Brunner, *Foundations*, 3. Brunner insisted that ideas such as evolution, idealistic humanism, positivist philosophy and the atheism of Friedrich Nietzsche and Karl Marx had contributed to undermining the influence of Christianity in Western European culture. See Ibid., 3–6.

54   Brunner, *Foundations*, 2.

55   Ibid., 3.

56   Van Til, *The Calvinistic Concept of Culture*, 215.

him, these three major historical events "brought the harvest of an inhuman, lawless, depersonalized collectivism."[57] Much like Brunner and many others, he placed much of the responsibility of Western Europe's cultural and spiritual instability on Existentialism and associated philosophers like Martin Heidegger and Jan-Paul Sartre, along with Nietzsche's nihilism, and the emergence of atheist communism, all of which, he insisted, affirmed the human individual independently of God.[58]

Responding to these issues, by the middle of the twentieth century, various Protestant theologians and Christian scholars began to reconsider the relation between Christianity and the cultural—the all-encompassing phenomena that define, shape, condition, and impact the ways humans engage life, interact with their immediate environment, each other and the divine. There were many scholars who from different perspectives engaged the complexity of these issues. In multiple ways, they reformulated how Christianity related to the larger cultural context confronting the pervasive influence of positivism, evolutionism, and the scientific method, and its application to multiple aspects of the Christian faith. They confronted many of the philosophical and theological challenges prior to and after the world-wars, in order to reclaim—to repeat Brunner—the "Christian foundation" of Western European Civilization.[59]

In what follows, I deal with some of these scholars in more depth and examine the particular ways in which they reflected upon the connections of Christianity and "culture."[60] Each of these authors wrote substantially and a thorough analysis of their work exceeds the scope of my comments here. My narrow focus pays attention to those writings in which the authors deal with the intersection of religion/Christianity and the cultural explicitly. I divide them into four groups to briefly sketch the connections and differences

---

57   Ibid.

58   Ibid., 174, 179.

59   Brunner, *Foundations*, 1.

60   In addition to the Protestant scholars I deal with here, other contemporary works are worth mentioning: John Baillie's, *What is Christian Civilization?*; Karl Barth's *Christengemeinde und Buergereinde; Church and State*; Nicolas Berdyaev's *The Destiny of Man*; Emil Brunner's *Justice and the Social Order*; Charles Norris Cochrane's *Christianity and Classical Culture*; Christopher Dawson's *Religion and Culture*; *Religion and the Rise of Western Culture*; T. S. Eliot's *The Idea of a Christian Society*; Jacques Maritain's *True Humanism*; Reinhold Niebuhr's *The Nature and Destiny of Man*; *Faith and History*; Arnold Toynbee's *Civilization on Trial*; *A Study of History*; Charles Kraft's *Christianity in Culture*; and the First Assembly of the World Council of Churches, *Findings and Decisions*. See H. Richard Niebuhr, *Christ and Culture* (New York, NY: Harper and Row, Harper Torchbooks/Cloister Library, 1956), 230 note 1.

between their various proposals. However, I will focus mainly on the three groups which intentionally engage questions of the cultural (they all use culture) in theological terms.

Connecting Culture and Religion: Arnold, Eliot and Frye

The first group was composed of cultural and social critics who approached questions of culture from a more "literary" perspective. These scholars conceived the relationship between culture and religion within their largely "secular" context. They insisted on highlighting the connection between culture and religious traditions. For example, cultural critic Matthew Arnold thought that culture was an effective defense against the spiritual impoverishment of "modern" life. He saw a correspondence between religion and culture, particularly exploring culture as the means by which the human pursuit toward perfection is achieved.[61] Culture was for him, a "pursuit of [humanity's] total perfection by means of getting to know ... the best which has been thought and said in the world."[62] Arnold saw the cultural as having an almost spiritual/religious character in its ability to "move humanity forward." Still, his understanding of "culture" as from the vantage point of the elite won the day. As Dawson explains, though Arnold criticized the middle class and while he was more "liberal" than the aristocracy, "his conservatism was unambiguous as he championed culture against the 'anarchy'" that he saw threatened "society by the rising working classes."[63]

Not too different from Arnold, literary and social critic T.S. Eliot sought to reclaim an understanding of the sacred character of culture.[64] And literary critic Northrop Frye examined the cultural impact of Fascism, Communism, and Nazism, and how they can be countered by Protestantism in the Euro North American context.[65]

Much more could be said about these authors, but not without digressing significantly from the main concerns of this chapter of exploring how Protestant theologians of the time reflected upon the relationship between Christianity and culture. Although evident in their writings is the influence of Christianity, in no way did they intend to respond theologically to the ways in which Christianity relates to the larger cultural context.

---

61   Matthew Arnold, *Culture and Anarchy: An Essay in Political and Social Criticism* (London, UK: Smith, Elder, and Co., 1890), VIII.

62   Ibid., 190.

63   Christopher Dawson, *Religion and Culture* (London, UK: Sheed and Ward, 1948), 496.

64   T. S. Eliot, *Notes Toward the Definition of Culture* (New York, NY: Faber & Faber, 1948).

65   Nortrop Frye, "The Church and Modern Culture," in *Collected Works of Northrop Frye*, vol. 11, ed. Jan Gorak (Toronto, ON: University of Toronto Press, 2003), 237–43.

The Cultural as Intellectual Endeavor: Herridge and Machen

The second group emphasized the "rational/intellectual" aspect of culture and included Presbyterian scholars such as the Canadian William Herridge and the U.S.A. theologian Gresham Machen. From their particular perspectives, they wrote in response to the deep impact of the larger "secular" culture upon Christianity among Euro North Americans; they were more concerned to provide (pastoral) advice to the church and church leaders. In 1888 in his "Christianity and Culture," William Herridge asserted the compatibility of the Christian faith with the larger cultural context. Countering what was understood as a dualism between piety (Christianity) and intellectual attainment (culture), he argued that culture as fundamentally formative must include all aspects of human life including the religious formations of individuals.[66] And since Christianity concentrates on the religious / moral dimension of humanity, that is, the human relationship with God through Christ, there must, it follows, be correspondence between the goals of culture and Christianity.[67] Mental-intellectual and moral elements cannot be separated.[68]

For Herridge culture needed to be anchored in God. Though he admitted the cultural advances of the Enlightenment were notable, he saw them as futile attempts since they were made independently from God.[69] Christianity ought to find its enlightenment elsewhere, in Christ.[70] Instead of rejecting

---

66   For Herridge, "Culture, when applied to man, must signify the proper development of everything sown within his nature which is capable of growth, and no definition can be adequate which ignores a single faculty. The cultured man is he who is thoroughly matured in every part, so as to be able to fulfill the purpose of his creation" (William T. Herridge, "Christianity and Culture," *The Presbyterian Review* IX [1888]: 389).

67   For Herridge, the belief in moral law rests on the unchanging truth of God as Father and humanity as the children made by his hands. Thus, a complete definition of culture must include the moral aspect of the human existence in relation to God, which finds expression and fulfillment in Jesus. See Herridge, "Christianity and Culture," 389–90.

68   Herridge, "Christianity and Culture," 399.

69   Herridge, "Christianity and Culture," 395. Herridge was also critical of Greek and Roman cultures which while great in their achievements had collapsed and disappeared. However, great their achievements, these cultures did not give adequate answers "to the great questions of the human soul." In contrast Christianity provides the best answers: "This is eternal life, to know Thee, the only true God, and Jesus Christ, whom Thou hast sent" (Ibid., 397).

70   Herridge, "Christianity and Culture," 398. He stated that if culture disposes of moral concerns, then culture has a mission "with which Christianity has no immediate concern" (Ibid., 390).

culture, he concluded that, "there is no real antagonism between culture and Christianity, but the aim of both should be identical."[71] Both (should) work toward developing the faculties of humans so that they can fulfill the destiny for which they were created which is to be in relationship with God. But the relationship between Christianity and culture needed to be re-defined according to Herridge: Christianity must dictate the orientation of culture since "Christianity is Culture brought to a true perfection, and Culture in its highest sense is impossible without Christianity."[72] In the end, he understood culture to be properly fulfilled only when it prepares humans for their relationship with God.[73]

Twenty-five years later, another Presbyterian, this time from the USA, wrote an article with the same title as Herridge. Gresham Machen wrote his "Christianity and Culture" in 1913, wrestling with the internal tensions in the Church concerning the greater cultural context. Like Herridge, he insisted that piety (Christianity) and intellectual endeavors (culture) were not antithetical. In fact, he claimed that religion and culture are not two entirely separate compartments of the soul; their union does not mean the destruction of both.[74]

Focusing more specifically on the implications of adapting the scientific method to theology and the study of the Bible, he proposed three alternative approaches to understand the relationship between Christianity and culture.[75] In the first approach, Christianity is subsumed to culture, resulting in a distortion of Christianity. In other words, if culture determines what Christianity is, then the very essence of Christianity is jeopardized; it becomes a human endeavor and is no longer truly Christianity. With the abandonment of the supernatural, reality becomes reclassified as an entirely human construct.[76] In Machen's second approach, culture is subservient to Christianity. The problem with this framework for him was that it prevented Christians from engaging the Christian

---

71   Herridge, "Christianity and Culture," 400.

72   Herridge, "Christianity and Culture," 401. For Herridge, Christianity ennobled and consecrated culture "because it comes a minister of righteousness, and takes its place in the school of Truth" (Ibid., 403).

73   Herridge, "Christianity and Culture," 405.

74   J. Gresham Machen, "Christianity and Culture," *The Princeton Theological Review* 11 (1913): 2, Http://reformedaudio.weebly.com/uploads/1/2/0/5/12058158/machen_-_christianity_and_culture.pdf (accessed May 1, 2015).

75   According to Machen, the intellectual endeavors of history, language, science, and philosophy had previously been engaged by Christians, and that needed to be corrected. So his article is a kind of proposal of how to engage these disciplines. See Machen, "Christianity and Culture," 2, 12.

76   Machen, "Christianity and Culture," 3.

faith with their intellect.[77] Since Christians are encouraged to engage their faith and the Bible intellectually, ignoring the intellect amounted to not engaging Christianity altogether according to Machen's interpretation of this line of thinking.[78] The third option that Machen articulated allowed for the coming together of both culture and Christianity, by which cultural elements and the intellectual task are consecrated to the service of God.[79] This was Machen's option. Christians, he stated, cannot be indifferent to any "branch of earnest human endeavor." But human endeavor "must all be brought into some relation to the Gospel."[80]

Like Herridge, Machen also upheld the ennobling character of Christianity. For him, dedicating human powers to God did not mean the end of culture, but its heightening.[81] In the final analysis, although Machen wanted to maintain a balance between Christianity and culture, he could not conceive culture except as subservient to Christianity: "Modern culture is a mighty force. It is either subservient to the gospel or else it is the deadliest enemy of the gospel. For making it subservient, religious emotion is not enough, intellectual labor is also necessary."[82]

Located well within Eurocentric debates on the supremacy of reason, this group of scholars understood culture as intellectual endeavor. Such a worldview assumed that Christianity was in tension with the larger cultural milieu, on one hand. On the other hand, they also understood culture to reach its fulfillment when guiding humans to God. At the same time, and although they show

---

77   Ibid.

78   Machen, "Christianity and Culture," 3–4. Machen emphasized that Christians cannot say that everything in the larger culture is evil since there are many resources in the larger culture, many of which are useful to Christianity. In one instance, he says that "Modern culture is not altogether opposed to the gospel. But it is out of all connection with it. It not only prevents the acceptance of Christianity. It prevents Christianity even from getting a hearing" (Ibid., 9). Later, he repeats: the "culture of today cannot simply be rejected as a whole. It is not like the pagan culture of the first century. It is not wholly non-Christian. Much of it has been derived directly from the Bible" (Ibid., 10). Interestingly, this emphasis supports the view that Christianity and Western European culture are inextricably bound.

79   Machen, "Christianity and Culture," 4. He wrote: "Instead of stifling the pleasures afforded by the acquisition of knowledge or by the appreciation of what is beautiful, let us accept these pleasures as the gifts of a heavenly Father." He added, "Instead of obliterating the distinction between the Kingdom and the world, or on the other hand withdrawing from the world into a sort of modernized intellectual monasticism, let us go forth joyfully, enthusiastically to make the world subject to God" (Ibid.).

80   Machen, "Christianity and Culture," 5.

81   Ibid., 7.

82   Ibid., 11–12.

an openness toward cultural activities, they place these under the authority of Christ, which meant that cultural endeavors were undermined significantly if they did not end up leading the person into relationship with God.

Culture as Service to God: Schilder and Van Til

In the third group, one finds an explicit theological argumentation of culture. Coming at it from a more Reformed perspective, these scholars insisted on a broad understanding of culture but with a narrow focus. The Calvinist Dutch Reformed Klaas Schilder and Henry Van Til are two examples from this group.

The Dutchman Klaas Schilder wrote his *Christ and Culture* at the beginning of the second quarter of the 20th century.[83] In it he attempted to go beyond earlier notions of the opposition between culture and religion. Like Herridge and Machen he claimed that the two concepts correspond and complement each other.[84] Unlike Herridge and Machen, Schilder defined culture broadly as the set of activities whose goal is to orient humans toward the service of God.[85] For him, culture was not external to divine activity or will but encompasses all aspects of human life.[86]

---

83   Klaas Schilder, *Christ and Culture*, trans. G. van Rongen and W. Helder (Winnipeg, MB: Primier Printing LTD, 1977), Http://www.reformed.org/webfiles/cc/christ_and_culture.pdf (accessed April 14, 2015). *Christ and Culture* is the English translation of Schilder's *Christus en Cultuur*. The original version was published in 1932 under the title "Jezus Christus en het cultuurleven," which was included in his collection of articles titled *Jezus Christus en het menchenleven*. In 1947 it was published as *Christus en Cultuur*.

84   Schilder, *Christ and Culture*, 15.

85   As he wrote, culture is the

> systematic endeavor toward the process wise acquisition of the aggregate of labour by the sum total of human beings as they belong to God, evolve themselves unto God in history with and for the cosmos, and are present at any historical moment, having assumed the task of disclosing the potencies lying dormant in creation and successively coming within reach in the course of the history of the world, of developing them in compliance with their individual natures, of making them subservient to their environment, both far and near, according to their cosmic relationship and in submission to the norms of God's revealed truth; and all this order to make the treasures thus acquired usable by man as liturgical creature, and, subsequently, to bring them, together with the now more thoroughly equipped man himself, before God and put them at his feet, in order that he may be all in all, and work may praise its master (Schilder, *Christ and Culture*, 54–55).

86   Schilder, *Christ and Culture*, 8, 55. As he writes: "Everyone has to deal with a temporally and locally determined phase of cultural life" (Ibid., 8).

Schilder dealt with a double meaning of culture as including "cult" and "cultivation." Humans, he claimed, engage in culture for two fundamental reasons: one, to "cultivate" human nature as made in the divine image, and two, to orient humans toward the service (cult) of God.[87] According to him, God wills that humans be "cultivated," that is, be oriented toward service to God. As part of the same dynamic, cultural activity is the human response to the divine mandate, a mandate proclaimed to humanity after creation. For him, the divine cultural mandate was encapsulated in Genesis 1:28 when God told Adam and Eve to "be fruitful and multiply."[88] Schilder thought that human cultural engagement and cultural activities are thus a divine vocation, which goal is to serve God.[89]

It must be emphasized that for Schilder, the divine cultural mandate was an infralapsarian event; consistent with his Calvinist convictions, he insisted that sin had not revoked the human ability to fulfill such a cultural mandate. He argued that culture is part of divine imaging in humans though sin prevented culture from fulfilling its mandate and prevented humans from listening to God.[90] In order to prevent humans from realizing the potential of their sinfulness, common grace has been imparted on humanity to serve as a restraining force.[91] Grace also operates in culture; it is found in the cultural activities of those who fear God.[92]

Schilder argued that any consideration about culture must be Christocentric. Reflecting the concerns of his time, he rejected the bifurcation of the Jesus of history and the Christ of faith. According to him, culture must be framed in light of

---

87   Schilder reminds us that the word culture is derived from the Latin *colere* which means "to cultivate," to "care for." See Schilder, *Christ and Culture*, 51.

88   Schilder, *Christ and Culture*, 55, 96.

89   Schilder, *Christ and Culture*, 111–14. For Schilder cultural activities of self-cultivation are also examples of service to God. The function of culture is to create in humans self-discipline so that they can fulfill their vocation of following and serving God. Moreover, he added, because humans are made in God's image, human "cultural work must be spontaneous [as] a matter of serving God as a representative of His [*sic*] supreme authority and consequently a matter of discovering God and causing Him to be found" (Ibid., 55). Human activities of self-development and self-cultivation are then not ends in themselves but matter of divine mandate. Human cultural activity has as its purpose to follow the divine moral commandment and to remain subject to the creator. See Ibid.

90   Schilder, *Christ and Culture*, 57.

91   Ibid., 60–64.

92   Schilder, *Christ and Culture*, 63. This is not a universal grace in culture, but it is bestowed upon all those that are God's. As such, grace has an effect on their cultural achievements. See Ibid., 64.

Jesus Christ as the divine incarnate visitation who embodies the divine love and salvation, and who was simultaneously the human cultural response to God. For this reason, Jesus' life, ministry, death and resurrection must be interpreted as a preeminently cultural event.[93] Christ's coming among humanity was a cultural event because it modeled what it means to serve God, what it means to fulfill the divine cultural mandate.[94]

Schilder held that there is no one thing that can be called a universal culture for people. Yet, the far-reaching effects of culture, as he saw them, impacted and shaped even human responses to God: anything designed to cultivate humans so that they can approach and serve the divine is cultural. In fact, people serve God in all of their daily activities.[95] Still, not all cultures are the same or equal. There is only one authentic culture and cultural activity. For Schilder, true / genuine / authentic culture exists only when it is designed for the service of God. As people labour and live the Christian life they engage in authentic cultural activities as long as they are directed toward the service of their fellow humans (to cultivate them) and to God (to fulfill their divine vocation).[96] Any cultural activity not designed for the service of God is in fact a corruption of culture's original purpose.[97]

While in some ways Schilder's view of culture was broad, it is also evident that he understood the purpose of culture as narrowly specific. In addition, by subsuming culture under an abstract notion of Jesus Christ out of history and time, Schilder reiterated traditional Protestant Reformed positions of Christ as transcending culture.[98] What he actually understood as *service to God* in his hyper-spiritualized and moralized paradigm of the relationship between

---

93   Schilder, *Christ and Culture*, 47.

94   Schilder, *Christ and Culture*, 48. For Schilder, Christ models what it means to carry out the Christian life and respond to God in cultural situations. Jesus Christ is the only one who "has acted and still acts upon cultural life." Christ is the only one who, because of his sinlessness, can react to cultural situations and complications fully, purely and according to culture's original purpose. See (ibid.).

95   Schilder, *Christ and Culture*, 92–93.

96   According to Schilder, the act of grace of bringing believers together into community and form *koinonia* has direct cultural significance. See Schilder, *Christ and Culture*, 84.

97   Schilder, *Christ and Culture*, 75. In fact, Schilder argued that anything not geared toward God is geared toward self or Satan. This kind of godless culture is not really culture at all. It is instead a kind of anti-culture and therefore not legitimate culture. See Ibid., 81.

98   In fact, Schilder claims that the Christ of the Scriptures speaks about cultural elements like music, arts, fashion and architecture only as *Christ*, as the one who "even before the birth of Jesus, dominated the history and culture of all the nations, and Who on the feast of Pentecost entered into His working period of "a thousand years" from Ascension Day and Pentecost until His second coming" (Schilder, *Christ and Culture*, 41).

Christ and culture remains elusive.[99] Not surprisingly, he emphasized faith as essential in cultural responses to God.[100] Yet, while he insisted that culture and Christ are not opposite forces, he diminished the impact of culture on religion (in this case Christianity) by subsuming it under the rubric of Christ or service to God. He insightfully argued for keeping religion (Christianity) and culture together as part of the original divine creative intent of "cultivating" humans to help them fulfill their divine calling though how he interpreted this proposal in his historical and social context remains unclear. Still, the implications of Schilder's broad reading of culture including its intimate connection to religious traditions is quite a progressive move, one with which contemporary theologians have yet to fully grapple.

Deeply influenced by the cultural work of Schilder and in conversation with Abraham Kuyper, Augustine and Calvin, Henry Van Til proposed a Calvinistic theological reflection on culture 25 years later, at the beginning of the second half of the twentieth century.[101] Much like Schilder, he posited that culture refers to the activity of humans, through which they fulfill the Genesis 1:28 divine covenant and "creation mandate to cultivate the earth, to have dominion over it and to subdue it" in the name of God.[102] He argued that culture does not belong to the "civilized" nations, but is the expression of all of humanity's activity as image bearers of the creator as they work to shape nature for their

---

99   Schilder does emphasize a support of ministry and missions as cultural activities, however indirectly. At times, he also alludes to people's everyday working context as the space in which they can serve God. But he does not clarify what falls under the purview of "service to God" and what does not. Admittedly, his admission that cultural activities may bring humans closer into the service of God could lift up culture as a locus theologicus, yet it remains unclear how this definition is understood in the social context.

100   Schilder, *Christ and Culture*, 85.

101   Van Til, *The Calvinistic Concept of Culture*, 10. Although he admits that his view is certainly not definitive, Van Til does contend that "Calvinism furnishes us with the only theology of culture that is truly relevant ..." (Ibid.). For him, Calvinism provided the most appropriate answers to the cultural questions the church was facing at the time.

102   Van Til, *The Calvinistic Concept of Culture*, 10. For Van Til, there is a close connection between being created by God and being God's regents in this world. Humans, he maintained, were "placed in this created world ... to bring to fruition and fulfillment this glorious cosmos, to rule over all for God's sake" (Ibid., 31). Humans serve an office in the eyes of God. This office has three facets: "prophet, priest and king, which can never function separately but only in unity and concert;" as prophets, humans know the truth; as priests, humans love their God; and as kings (queens), humans are called to "subdue the universe and to have dominion over it" (Ibid., 31). See also Ibid., 35.

purposes.[103] As covenant people in creation,[104] culture embodies the divine calling for humanity. Furtheremore, since humans are moral beings, culture cannot be amoral.[105] Van Til viewed culture as intrinsic to all aspects of human life.[106] But unlike Arnold (see above), for him religion as a category was more inclusive than culture.[107] Humans, he explained, precede culture and are the creators of culture. Culture is not an end in itself but the means to expressing one's religious faith in response to the divine mandate.[108] Religion, then, "does not so much consummate culture" as was the case with Schilder, rather it gives "culture its foundation, and serves as the presupposition of every culture."[109]

Van Til also used the double meaning of culture as *cultivation* (work) and *cult* (worship), but his emphasis on the totalitarian character of religion (cult) redefined the role of culture. For him, the conscious or unconscious relationship to God was what determined all human cultural activities; human "morality and economics ... jurisprudence and ... aesthetics, all are religiously oriented and determined."[110] He wrote that because of humanity's relationship to God then, culture and religion could not be separated. Within this framework, Van Til interpreted human sin as a falling away in which religion became apostate and culture lost its true divinely ordained purpose. Culture became instead the end of human endeavors. In Christ, he insisted, we are "restored to God

---

103   Van Til, *The Calvinistic Concept of Culture*, 27. Van Til is one of the few theologians to acknowledge the plurality of cultures in the world. Drawing from E.B. Tylor, he conceded that "Culture ... is not the achievement of our contemporary Western world alone" (Ibid., 26). All groups have their peculiar culture. Thus, humans are cultural creatures and "civilization is merely the external side of culture" (Ibid., 27).

104   By covenant, Van Til means the sense of the divine in humans that cannot be eradicated. See Van Til, *The Calvinistic Concept of Culture*, 235.

105   Van Til, *The Calvinistic Concept of Culture*, 10. Van Til argued that since humans are religious beings, then culture must also express the religious aspect of human existence. Culture is therefore religiously determined.

106   Van Til, *The Calvinistic Concept of Culture*, 25.

107   As indicated above, Arnold saw culture as the study of perfection. Van Til found Arnold wanting, because he conceived of culture and religion too narrowly. Moreover, he rejected Arnold's inclination to make culture more inclusive than religion. See Van Til, *The Calvinistic Concept of Culture*, 25, 27.

108   Van Til, *The Calvinistic Concept of Culture*, 28. Van Til noted that humans, as cultural creatures, are called to "re-create, to re-produce, to form artistically and to mould creation to his will, duty-bound to function in the realm of power, to seek harmony and beauty and to have dominion over the earth" (Ibid., 30). Human are magnificent creatures, a replica and analogues of the blessed Tri-unity who created them.

109   Van Til, *The Calvinistic Concept of Culture*, 39.

110   Ibid., 42.

as cultural creatures to serve their maker and to rule over the world" for God's sake.[111] In the end, sin does not invalidate the cultural mandate nor excuse humans from fulfilling their cultural task.[112] Humans, by which he meant elect believers, are then called to be in the world as "developer-exploiter of the good earth for God."[113]

Faith is central to Van Til's understanding of culture. On one hand, because there is no neutral terrain in culture, one is either for or against God.[114] And on the other hand, faith is key because culture presupposes God as a way to explain human existence.[115] Also deeply influenced by Kyuper, Van Til saw common grace as playing an important role. While Schilder underplayed common grace because he saw culture as God's gift, Van Til affirmed common grace as part of the divine act of regeneration which makes believers into new creatures led by the Spirit and thereby enabled to function in cultural ways.[116] He argued that believers have an important role with respect to culture; as creatures and image bearers, they are called to replenish the earth, subdue it and have dominion over it through cultural means. As new creatures in Christ, they are called to make disciples, teaching them to observe all that God has commanded.[117] Seen this way, evangelism was, for Van Til, also a cultural activity.

Although Van Til's religious framing of culture subsumed it to the religious dimension (Christianity), he claimed that the way to understand his proposal was by seeing Christ as transformer of culture.[118] Recognizing the potentially dangerous ecological implications of Schilder's proposal, Van Til does go beyond Schilder to emphasize creation along with the cultural nature of humanity. More emphatically than Schilder, he insisted that culture is not just part of human existence and activity but is part of being created in the image of God. Both Schilder and Van Til place the motivation and origin of human culture in Godself. The difference between them is that Schilder grounds

---

111   Van Til, *The Calvinistic Concept of Culture*, 46. Christ as king, he added, "restores humanity and command their allegiance to fulfill the service of God" (Ibid., 207).

112   Van Til, *The Calvinistic Concept of Culture*, 57.

113   Ibid., 222.

114   There is also an antithesis in those who do not follow Christ. He believed they are against Christ. See Van Til, *The Calvinistic Concept of Culture*, 188.

115   Van Til, *The Calvinistic Concept of Culture*, 172–76.

116   Ibid., 186.

117   Ibid., 223.

118   It is most likely that Van Til is drawing on Richard Niebuhr's categories here because he gave no indication of being aware of Machen's much earlier article with his three very similar options.

culture in the divine cultural mandate and Van Til connects it to being made in the image of God. Both leave little to no room for considering the impact of culture and cultural traditions on religion.

Christianity and Culture, the Enduring Debate: Tillich and Meland

Finally, in the fourth camp are the more familiar names of Paul Tillich, and Bernard Eugene Meland. (I include Richard Niebuhr in this group but his contribution has had a broader reach that I find the need to discuss him separately in the next chapter). This group of scholars from different theological schools (Socialist Christian, Neo-orthodox, and Liberal respectively) did not engage questions of culture from a theological perspective like the previous group. Tillich sought to provide an actual "cultural theology" and Meland inverted the debate by focusing on faith and how it relates to questions of culture. Much more intentionally than the foregoing groups, the writings of these authors reflect the sense of anxiety, despair, tragedy and confusion over the fallout from WWII, including Jewish Holocaust, the bombing of Hiroshima and Nagasaki, and the enormous death toll. They often alluded to aspects of these or other contemporaneous concerns in their writings.[119] For example, Tillich spoke of the shock left by the void of the war.[120] And Meland wrote about the "chastening fires of war, disillusionment, despair, and tragedy ..."[121] These authors were not so concerned with the larger questions of meaning of culture; rather they were responding to their own immediate cultural and contextual challenges. They were also very prolific. For our purposes, I focus on writings in which they deal with the intersection of religion/Christianity and culture explicitly.

In an attempt to redefine the terms of engagement between culture and Christianity, at the turn of the second half of the twentieth century

---

119   Even in his articulation of his cultural theological project, Tillich makes a connection to the impact of the wars. He wrote: "While after the first World War the mood of a new beginning prevailed, after the second World War a mood of the end prevails. A present theology of culture is, above all, a theology of the end of culture, not in general terms but in a concrete analysis of the inner void of most of our cultural expressions. Little is left in our present civilization which does not indicate to a sensitive mind the presence of this vacuum, this lack of ultimacy and substantial power in language and education, in politics and philosophy, in the development of personalities, and in the life of communities" (Paul Tillich, *The Protestant Era*, translated with a concluding essay by James Luther Adams [Chicago, IL: University of Chicago Press, 1948], 60).

120   Tillich, *The Protestant Era*, 60.

121   Bernard Eugene Meland, *Faith and Culture* (London, UK: George Allen and Unwin Ltd., 1953), 5.

Paul Tillich engaged in what he called a theonomous analysis of culture.[122] Although he stated that all of his writings wrestled with some or other aspects related to culture,[123] his work is too large for a detailed analysis here. My main concern is to highlight his theological reflections as they explicitly pertain to culture.

Unlike Catholics and Lutherans who had rejected the culture and secular movements of protest that had rejected religion, Tillich's intention was to bridge the gap, to find a common ground between religion and culture. Tillich did not view culture as monolithic. For him, there were three types of cultures: autonomous, heteronomous and theonomous. Autonomous cultures are those which function independently of religious concerns and do not explicitly express any ultimate concerns or appear to be grounded on something unconditional or holy.[124] The Renaissance and the Enlightenment are two expressions of autonomous culture.[125] Heteronomous cultures are those which privilege and emphasize ecclesiastical religion or political movements that follow the patterns of religious institutions.[126] As for the concept of a theonomous culture—his preferred alternative, it pointed to those cultures which

---

122 Tillich, *The Protestant Era.*

123 Paul Tillich, *Teología de la cultura y otros ensayos* (Buenos Aires, Argentina: Amorrortu Editores, 1974), 11.

124 Tillich defines "autonomous culture [as] the attempt to create the norms of personal and social life without any reference to something ultimate and unconditional, following only the demands of theoretical and practical rationality" (Tillich, *The Protestant Era*, 57).

125 He further explains,

> Autonomous culture is secularized in the degree to which it has lost its ultimate reference, its center of meaning, its spiritual substance. The Renaissance was a step toward autonomy, but still in the spiritual power of an unwasted medieval heritage. The Enlightenment quickly lost its Protestant and sectarian substance and became in some though not in many of its expressions completely secular. The later nineteenth century, with its subjection to the technical pattern of thought and action, shows the character of an extremely emptied and secularized autonomy in an advanced stage of disintegration. But even here the religious substance, a remnant of something ultimate, was noticeable and made the transitory existence of such a culture possible (Tillich, *The Protestant Era*, 58).

126 Tillich writes that "A heteronomous culture ... subjects the forms and laws of thinking and acting to authoritative criteria of an ecclesiastical religion or a political quasi-religion, even at the price of destroying the structures of rationality" (Tillich, *The Protestant Era*, 57).

display their ultimate concern and transcendent meaning as the ground for spirituality.[127]

The notion of a theonomous culture, Tillich claimed, provides the conditions for the reconciliation between religion and culture; it allowed him to claim the "mutual immanence of religion and culture."[128] In order to highlight the intimate connection/relation between culture and religion he gave his— now famous—dictum: culture is the form of religion and religion the content/substance of culture.[129] He viewed religion as being much more than a complex system of rituals, symbols, and rites directed toward a highest being. Rather, religion as "ultimate concern," is "the state of being grasped by something unconditional, holy, and absolute,"[130] which "gives meaning and depth to all culture and creates out of the cultural material a religious culture of its own."[131]

Like Van Til and Schilder, Tillich also considered Christianity /religion to play the greater role. Echoing Van Til, Tillich claimed that it is not culture but religion that includes and permeates all aspects of human existence. He argued that religion is not merely one aspect of human spirituality; it is "the dimension of profundity" in all the functions of human spirituality.[132] More specifically, culture attains its "highest expression where human existence is comprehended in its finitude and its quest for the infinite within the framework of a complete, autonomous form. Conversely, religion in its highest expression must include the autonomous form, the Logos ... within itself."[133] Tillich's understanding of the relationship between religion and culture is similar here to the proposals of Van Til and Schilder. He understood culture as the means by which religion finds expression. But in Tillich's concept of

---

127 Tillich, *The Protestant Era*, 57. Drawing on a circular logic, he proposes that "Theonomy asserts that the superior law is, at the same time, the innermost law of man himself, rooted in the divine ground which is man's own ground: the law of life transcends man, although it is, at the same time, his own" (Ibid.).

128 Tillich, *The Protestant Era*, 55.

129 Tillich, *Teología de la cultura*, 16–17.

130 Tillich, *The Protestant Era*, 59.

131 Ibid.

132 Tillich, *Teología de la cultura*, 15. What is this profundity of which Tillich speaks? he answers: It means that "the religious aspect points to that which, in the spiritual life of humans, is ultimate, infinite and unconditional. In the broadest and more fundamental sense of the term, religion is ultimate concern. And ultimate concern is manifest absolutely through all of the creative functions of the human spirit" (Ibid., 16–17).

133 Paul Tillich, *On the Boundary: An Autobiographical Sketch* (New York, NY: Charles Scribner's Sons, 1966), 70.

theonomous culture, the connection between culture and religion is more inti-mate; religion does still establish special dominion over culture but without entirely subsuming it.[134]

Tillich's proposal of theonomous culture allowed him to emphasize ele-ments of ultimate concern in all three expressions of culture—autonomous, heteronomous and theonomous.[135] Heteronomous cultures can be easily understood as having elements of ultimate concern; they are already religious in nature with those that are political in nature functioning in quasi-religious ways, for instance.[136] The greater challenges to his proposal of theonomous culture were autonomous cultures, which function independently of religious concerns and do not explicitly express any ultimate concerns. As he saw it, the challenge was to show how autonomous cultures which function without expressing ultimate concern, or something unconditional or holy, are actually inspired by them. For instance, he argued for ultimate concern in autonomous cultures, as in the case of revolutionary and protest movements.[137] As he saw it, the fact that those movements reject heteronomous cultures express an implied ultimate concern even as they reject Christianity or religion. Their ulti-mate concerns are made manifest *via negativa*, by way of what they reject.[138]

---

134   Tillich, *Teología de la cultura*, 45.

135   Tillich insisted that elements of ultimate concern could be found in all cultures and not during the time of theonomous culture such as high middle-ages of "our Western civiliza-tion." For instance, he argued that one can also find ultimate concern even during periods when heteronomy was victorious, as in the later Middle Ages and in Arabic and Protestant Orthodoxy. Likewise, the ultimate concern is still evident in times when autonomous culture dominated or even in secular epochs like classical Greece, the Renaissance, the Enlightenment, and the nineteenth century. See Tillich, *The Protestant Era*, 57.

136   Dismantling claims of the bifurcation between culture and religion by "ecclesiastical het-eronomy," he insists that "it is always possible to show that all the rites, doctrines, insti-tutions, and symbols of a religious system constitute a religious culture which is derived from the surrounding general culture from its social and economic structure, its character traits, its opinions and philosophy, its linguistic and artistic expressions, its complexes, its traumas, and its longings" (Tillich, *The Protestant Era*, 57).

137   Elsewhere, Tillich noted that contact with "the Labor Movement, with the so-called dechristianized masses, showed me clearly that here too, within a humanistic framework, the Christian substance was hidden, even though this humanism looked like a material-istic philosophy that had long since been discredited by art and science" (Tillich, *On the Boundary*, 62).

138   With the notion of theonomous culture, Tillich was able to show "the religious back-ground of the rebellion of the vital and unconscious side of man's personality against the moral and intellectual tyranny of consciousness; it was able to interpret the quasi-religious, fanatical, and absolutistic character of the reactions of the twentieth century

For Tillich, there was a false dichotomy in understanding the relation as primarily between religion and culture. Rather, the tension must be explained in terms of religious and secular culture.[139] However, taking a different direction from Schilder and Van Til—in their affirmation that non-Christian cultures still serve God but only in limited preparatory ways—Tillich emphasized that secular cultures display an undergirding ultimate concern. In other words, no culture can really be without religious concerns: "No cultural creation can hide its religious ground or its rational formation."[140]

It must be made clear that at the heart of Tillich's sense of religion (like the aforementioned scholars) were European cultural expressions of Christianity even though he employed new nomenclature to articulate his theological culture.[141] Furthermore, his sense of culture—as complex as it was—like those before him, really referred to Western European civilization and society.

----

as against the nineteenth. It was able to do all this without special reference to organized religion, the churches being only a part of the whole picture, but with a decisive reference to the religious element which was and is hidden in all these antireligious and anti-Christian movements" (Tillich, *The Protestant Era*, 58). It was evident that in these anti-religious and anti-Christian movements there is an ultimate and unconditional determining concern "something absolutely serious and therefore holy, even if expressed in secular terms" (Ibid., 59).

139   Tillich, *The Protestant Era*, 59. Still weighing in on autonomous and heteronomous cultures, he insisted that the religious must not be absorbed by the secular (as happens in autonomous cultures) nor the secular be absorbed by the religious (as happens with heteronomous cultures). Rather, religion/Christianity determines the meaning and substance of the culture while culture expresses the ultimate concerns of that culture (as his theonomous alternative).

140   Tillich, *The Protestant Era*, 57.

141   For Tillich, issues of ultimate concern can be found in all expressions of the Western European cultural world. In many ways, he followed the tradition of understanding Western European Anglo North Atlantic culture and civilization as impossible without Christianity. In this sense, he agreed with Emil Brunner. He took a different path, however, by emphasizing that ultimate concern is not an element that can be imposed on people. Rather, they have to be developed, emerging from the cultural community itself. It is for this reason that he ridiculed claims to objectivity and the idea that cultures could present themselves as absolute. See Tillich, *The Protestant Era*, 58; Tillich, *On the Boundary*, 65. He took this idea further, when he noted that since language—oral or written—marks the basic elements of a culture, the idea of sacred language must be rejected. Even biblical languages are not sacred. See Tillich, *Teología de la cultura*, 46–49. "What we have is a human language that is formed with the confrontation between humanity with reality; that changes throughout millennia, [and] that is necessary for daily life ... just as it is necessary for the expression and communication of our ultimate concerns" (Ibid., 50).

"Ultimate concern" described both human spirituality and its aspirations to an ultimate reality, which, for him was the Christian God.[142]

Tillich's engagement of religion and culture can be understood as emerging from an introspective analysis and response to post world-war-two challenges. Unlike Herridge, Machen, Schilder, and Van Til, Tillich tended to underplay sin. He blamed the horrors of war and the crisis of meaninglessness on the separation of culture and religion. He emphasized instead the estrangement of humanity from God, which he argued caused a rift between the sacred and the profane in human existence. But he was confident that the notion of theonomous culture did away with such a dualism. If indeed religion is the state of being dominated by ultimate concern, then the sacred spills out to all aspects of life; "The universe is God's sanctuary," he argued.[143] Similarly—and here one finds a sense of the eschatological dimension of culture in Tillich's work—the proof of the fall is found in the fact that there are both secular and religious cultures; since the gap between the profane and sacred cannot be bridged in time, space, and history, it should be overcome by the anticipation of a theonomous period, yet to come.[144] Since he found ultimate concerns to be present in all cultures—even in "secular" movements—whether they are autonomous or heteronomous, they are in some sense ultimately Christian.

Tillich's understanding of culture, however much it refers to Western European civilization, is subsumed, conditioned, and determined by the religious dimension and ultimate concerns. Unlike Schilder and Van Til, Tillich's theonomous culture does not find its origin in God but in the human response to the ultimate (God), which stems from human spirituality. His rejection of "absolute cultures" and objectivity left the door open to conceive the role and impact of culture on religion at deeper levels including the way in which the divine is at work in and through culture. With him, we gain the insight that culture is the means through which religious, and ultimate concerns are made manifest.

---

142   Though not very often, Tillich equated claims of ultimacy with the idea of God as articulated by Christians. He also spoke of the "absolute" and the unconditioned God as pointing to what traditional Christian language refers to as "the Majesty of God." See Tillich, *On the Boundary*, 69, 71. In this theology of culture he unambiguously refers to ultimate concern as contained in the name of God and Jesus Christ. See Tillich, *Teología de la cultura*, 44.

143   Tillich, *Teología de la cultura*, 45.

144   According to Tillich, this was the "kairos which we believed to be at hand was the coming of a new theonomous age, conquering the destructive gap between religion and secular culture" (Tillich, *The Protestant Era*, 59).

Expressing some of the concerns raised by Tillich, Meland shifted the debate by privileging faith. While Tillich and Niebuhr saw Christianity and culture almost as the two equal sides of the debate, Meland expressly privileged faith. Drawing from cultural anthropology and metaphysics he elevated the status of faith to being a cultural, psychic, or social energy. Meland's concern was to highlight the cultural import of faith, which for Western culture meant the cultural import of Christianity. For him, faith was a form of cultural psychic energy found in the history of any culture which arises from individual and social groups as they respond to the ultimate demands of living. Without faith, the history of any culture is inconceivable. However, Meland did not understand faith in a narrow personal and individual sense as prescribed by traditional forms of Protestantism since the Reformation, for instance. Rather, he understood faith as the cultural energy, the dynamic force that shapes individuals and entire societies. Human collectives and societies attest to the influence of faith through the symbols they have imprinted in their cultures.

Speaking in metaphysical terms, he defined faith as the phenomenon that emerges before speech and which gives rise to intellectual belief.[145] Faith is also the "indispensable ingredient" and resource of the human psyche that persists in a culture "in the form of a structure of experience," even after it is no longer a central aspect of that culture.[146] Taking "Western" culture as example, he focused on the impact of faith on culture;[147] since faith is expressed by way of structures of experience, the structures of experience in Western culture, he claimed, have been deeply shaped by the Christian faith. Meland preferred

---

145   Meland, *Faith and Culture*, 15.

146   Ibid., 20.

147   Meland does not provide a clear sense of what he means by culture in *Faith and Culture*. However, in his other works he defines culture in terms that are metaphysical as his definition of faith. For him, culture "connotes the total complex of the human association, expression its prevailing sentiments, style, and way of life ..." (Bernard Eugene Meland, *Fallible Forms and Symbols: Discourses on Method in a Theology of Culture* [Philadelphia, PA: Fortress Press, 1976], 155). He adds that, culture is

> The human flowering of existing structures and facilities, becoming manifest as an ordered way of life in the imaginative activities and creations of a people, their arts and crafts, their architecture, their furniture and furnishings, their costumes and designs, their literature, their public and private ceremonies, both religious and political. It is in their formative ideas, giving direction to their educational efforts and customs, as well as to their religious notions and practices, their social graces and manners; in their habits of eating and body care; in their modes of livelihood and the social organization that follows from them (Ibid.).

to speak of the Christian myth—as myth relating primarily to the human response.[148] He was convinced that it was the ineradicable myth of Hebraic-Christianity to which Western culture owed its formative process; this myth had such a profound cultural impact historically, and is still present within "Western" thought and symbolic structures.[149]

Thus, in a round-about sort-of-way, he affirmed that Western Culture cannot be understood outside / without / or separate from the Christian myth. He felt that subsequent generations do not perceive the degree to which Christianity has influenced their culture.[150] Even though the Renaissance and the Enlightenment represented a move away from the Christian myth, and the reformation signaled the reduction of faith to a private individual activity, still Western Culture reflects the deep Christian influence in its multiple expressions and symbols. Of those symbols the person of Christ as the central feature of the Christian mythos has impacted Western culture most directly. For him, Christ was both the summit of the West's cultural achievement and the focal point of the Christian myth.[151]

By speaking of *the structure of experience*, that is, the ways in which faith persists in culture, Meland brought together two important aspects: "the sense of depth and the notion of valuation." The former, he saw as a genuine dimension of existence beyond conscious existence, "which, when related to the conscious life, illuminates and enhances it in qualitative ways."[152] This dimension of depth emphasized the objective reality of God and Christ. The latter highlighted the interrelated working of humans and God or what he called the "creative passage," and exhibited subjective experience and activity. Together, these two aspects constitute the two extremes of the structure of experience.[153] Even psychic life, he noted, involves a regional character which can neither be eradicated nor cancelled out.[154]

According to Meland, the impact of faith on culture is such that "we are subconsciously molded as persons and as a society in the way that a mythos

---

148   Myth, he thought, was "the human response to actuality in its ultimate dimension" (Meland, *Faith and Culture*, 44).

149   Meland, *Faith and Culture*, 56. For Meland, the motif in Western culture, "which has set the pattern of faith within our structure of experience, can be said to be the *covenant relationship*" (Ibid., 50).

150   Meland, *Faith and Culture*, 55–56.

151   Ibid., 86.

152   Ibid., 39.

153   Ibid., 43.

154   Ibid., 84.

invariably imposes a distinctive character upon any people."[155] Additionally, faith is responsible for providing the structures of consciousness available in a culture. In this dialogical relation between culture and faith, Meland envisioned culture as the creative work of God, made possible through God's prior creation of these structures of consciousness. Unlike Schilder who attributed culture to God via the cultural mandate of Genesis and unlike Van Til who attributed culture to God because humans bear the divine image, Meland credited God with culture because of God's creative act forging humanity as a psycho-physical organism.[156] Despite the enormous impact of faith (or myth)[157] over culture in Meland's paradigm—even to the point of orienting a culture—still he acknowledged that faith expressions of what he called "mythical responses," are culturally conditioned,[158] a significant shift in reorienting the debates of faith and culture for these intellectuals.

Much more than the previous authors in each of the previous groups, Meland was able to pay attention to the communal formative character of faith and cultural processes in large part because he emphasized the impact of faith in culture. Humans are not only made for God, as Schilder and Van Til insisted from their Calvinist position, humans are also made for each other because faith operates as a communal cultural energy.[159] In the end, he noted, God approaches human beings through the sense of "absolute dependence" (borrowing from Schleiermacher), but does it through the symbols and processes of culture.[160] This insight, communicated as a revelation in Western culture, "reaches human consciousness in the very act of symbolization."[161] The opposite is also true: hidden in the Christian revelation is the meaning of contemporary Western culture.[162]

---

155   Ibid., 125.

156   Ibid., 84.

157   Meland, *Faith and Culture*, 95. He wrote that myth "is indispensable to a profound orientation of the human psyche in our culture, and the source of our most discerning insight" (Ibid.).

158   Meland, *Faith and Culture*, 84. Stated differently, he said, "Within our culture, the Christian faith is mediated in this structure of experience, rising out of the accumulative valuations of the culture in which its prophets and poets, its hopes and aspirations, its destructive and redemptive forces, have been persuasively at work" (Ibid. 97). In other words, culture and the social context play a crucial role in mediating the Christian faith.

159   Meland, *Faith and Culture*, 127, 136.

160   Meland tackled this question later on but from the perspective of methodology, and still within the Western European cultural and intellectual tradition. See Meland, *Fallible Forms and Symbols*.

161   Meland, *Faith and Culture*, 173.

162   Ibid., 136.

In the end, Meland did reiterate the sense of superiority of Western culture. While it is true that he insisted that neither Western culture nor U.S.A culture could serve as criterion for all cultures around the world, and he also dismissed any claim to a universal psyche or the establishing of a universal myth because all cultures are different and display different myths. Still, he insisted that some cultures deserve greater attention than others in the way they give witness to the work and activity of God.[163]

Despite this Eurocentric limitation and the fact that he under-emphasizes the impact of culture on faith, Meland sets the tone for a new appreciation of the culturally conditioned character of faith. In fact, he privileged faith and its cultural import to the degree that faith could change and reorient a culture / society. But he leaves the other side of the question unanswered: can culture impact faith in the same way that faith impacts culture? Despite this too-one-sided proposal, Meland, along with Tillich, did leave the door open for the possibilities that other cultures might enter the debate. Even more, by distancing himself from abstractions and universals more explicitly than his contemporaries, he signaled a deeper change in the way other cultural groups ought to be perceived and engaged. He even challenged Western culture to engage in a "relinquishing" of their cultural ego "in the effort to be receptive to meaning and value beyond the range of our restricted social experience."[164]

Reestablishing the Connections

My intention in this chapter has been to mark early-to-mid twentieth century shifts in the theological approaches to the relation between Christianity and the cultural. As I showed in the first section, the initial inspiration for this shift toward a more interwoven understanding of Christianity and the cultural was the interconnection between the task of evangelization and the exporting of Western European culture. Evangelization and civilization were understood as two sides of the same activity, as intertwined with the colonial projects.

In the second section, I followed the radical shift away from imperial notions of Christianity and other cultures toward internal theoretical analyses

---

163   Meland, *Faith and Culture*, 85, 116–17. As he puts it, "Without attempting to appraise the degree of psychical superiority which can be ascribed to the Christian culture of the West, it can certainly be said that it reveals a range and reach of sensitivity and of creative imagination which must place it high in the human venture wherein God's creative working is exemplified" (Ibid., 85).

164   Meland, *Fallible Forms and Symbols*, 116–17.

of the relationship between Christianity and—almost exclusively—Western European and Euro North American cultures starting at the end of the nineteenth century. Geopolitical shifts ushered in a new global reconfiguration signaled by the emergence of the United States of America as the "new Empire" replacing Western European imperialism at the end of the nineteenth century (1898) and the Russian Revolution of 1917. As I argued, when the Western European imagination and culture went into crisis a wide range of Protestant scholars took it upon themselves to respond to the cultural contextual challenges they were facing. Although most did not explicitly say it, their new perspectives on the cultural are tempered in no small part by the background of two terrible world wars which debunked the notion that Western Europe embodied the pinnacle of human and cultural evolution and advance. They were well aware that the "modern" project was crumbling around them; their theological approaches show their awareness of the monumental implications. Despite the various qualifications they articulated, each of these scholars assumed that *culture* generally functioned as synonymous with Western European civilization and "society." In the words of Niebuhr, to whom I return in the next chapter, "What we have in view when we deal with Christ and culture is that ... which now the name culture, now the name civilization, is applied in common speech."[165]

Nevertheless, it becomes evident that their concerns about "culture" increasingly correspond with what I identify as the cultural. Scholars like Eliot, Arnold, and Frye, made explicit the connection between the cultural and the religious. Meanwhile Herridge and Machen engaged the cultural more in terms of how the church and church-ministers ought to respond to the pervasive impact of the general "secular" culture; they were concerned with its impact on the church, and, in the case of Machen, its impact on theology and our understanding of the Bible. Schilder and Van Til represent an intentional attempt to think theologically about the cultural and how it fits within the gospel message. Finally, Tillich and Meland's main concerns were the actual construction of a theology of culture.

There are marked differences between these scholars. Schilder and Van Til understood the role of the cultural as cultivating humans to reach to God whereas Tillich and Meland saw a greater correspondence between the cultural and the religious. Herridge, Machen, Schilder and Van Til perceived an obvious antithetical relation between religion and the cultural and Tillich and Meland understood there to be a mutual fertilization, though for them the cultural was always subservient to religion / faith / Christianity. Still, I emphasized that

---

165   Niebuhr, *Christ and Culture*, 32.

these authors signaled a shift toward considering more carefully the impact of the cultural on religious faith.

However, while they acknowledged a variety of Christian expressions, they also operated under the assumption that Christianity is a coherent homogeneous whole, which was represented in the European expressions they knew. They also approached the cultural as a finished air tight human construct that was easily distinguishable from religious traditions. Although Arnold and Meland had insisted that religious faith was expressed though cultural artifacts, and Tillich insisted that the cultural mediated religious ultimate concerns, they spoke of it in terms of clear distinctions between what is cultural and what is religious. Moreover, the more conservative thinkers like Schilder and Van Til understood the "objective" revelation of God to be the sole arbiter in questions of the cultural. At the same time, for others like Tillich, the criteria for judging the cultural were a mixture of inherited Eurocentric philosophical and theological frames.

In the end, each of these authors remained within the Western European Euro North American intellectual camp and cultural tradition. It is from within this tradition that they sought for tools and solutions to respond to the challenges and crises they were confronting. Although they were beginning to accept the fact that all peoples in the world had cultures, other cultures did not figure as significant in these debates, if they figured at all. The task would be left to their theological heirs as will be seen in Chapter 6. Had they dared to look outside of the European intellectual and theological traditions for answers to the "problems" "modernity" was facing, "other" cultures might have been able to make rich contributions to theo-cultural debates much earlier.

CHAPTER 5

Richard Niebuhr and the Enduring Debate

'European culture' is a mere abstraction, an empty concept. Where does, or did, it actually exist in its entirety? In which nation? In which period? Besides, it can scarcely pose as the most perfect manifestation of man's culture, having—who can deny?—far too many deficiencies, weaknesses, perversions and abominations associated with it. Only a real misanthrope could regard European culture as the universal condition of our species. The culture of man is not the culture of Europeans; it manifests itself "according to place and time in every people."[1]

TIMOTHY GORRINGE

• • •

The Christian message is to be communicated to all nations. Such communication presupposes that preachers and teachers enlarge their horizons to include an accurate and intimate understanding of true culture and the language of the people they address They must grasp the virtual resources of that culture and that language, and they must use those virtual resources creatively so that the Christian message becomes, not disruptive of culture, not an alien patch superimposed on it, but a line of development within the culture.

BERNARD LONERGAN[2]

Introduction

Almost 40 years after Gresham Machen wrote his "Christianity and Culture" article[3] which provided three approaches for Christians to reflect on the relation

---

1 Timothy J. Gorringe, *Furthering Humanity: A Theology of Culture* (Burlington, VT: Ashgate Publishing Company, 2004), 186.

2 Cited in Maeve Louise Heaney, *Music as Theology: What Music Says About the Word* (Eugene, OR: Wipf and Stock, 2012), 17.

3 J. Gresham Machen, "Christianity and Culture."

between Christianity and culture (see previous chapter), and almost 20 years after Klaas Schilder wrote his book titled *Christ and Culture*, Richard Niebuhr wrote his famous book by the same title.[4] In the 1951 volume, Niebuhr provided not so much a theology of culture but rather a rubric for appreciating how Western Europeans and Euro North American Christians have dealt with the relationship between the Christian faith and their cultures at various points in history.

Although many see his work as the definitive approach to framing how Christianity and the cultural relate, Niebuhr did not intend to provide *the* answer to this "enduring problem." The book is really about ethical concerns; about the various ways Christians live in and interact with this world/broader culture/society. As such, he devised five paradigms as possible responses to the ethical connections between Christian life and "culture."

In this chapter, my intention is not to revisit/repeat Niebuhr's five paradigms; many other scholars have already engaged his proposal in greater depth. Rather, I consider his proposal in light of the central question of this book; how does Christianity/the gospel/Christ relate to the phenomena of the cultural, by which I mean, to repeat, the complex dynamic network of socially and historically inherited codes and segments of codes: that allow and make possible inter-human interaction in a given society; that provide the interpretive frame and lenses for reality; and that constitute the set of guiding principles by which humans and societies interact with their surrounding environment and the divine. As with the other authors already discussed, I preserve his use of "culture" in order not to alter the meaning of Niebuhr's original contribution. In the second half of this chapter, I exhibit how his work continues to be a source of inspiration for many scholars, including several from the Global South, many of whom seek to go beyond his proposal.

I argue, however, that these scholars tend to remain trapped in Niebuhr's paradigm and intellectual frame even as they attempt to reformulate it. I insist that they are caught in a moralizing understanding of "culture" which causes them to quickly dismiss the cultural,[5] thus maintaining a wedge between

---

4   Writing at the beginning of the second half of the twentieth century Niebuhr does not mention or engage any of the two previous works with the same title.

5   It will become evident that the authors I discuss including Niebuhr tend to discuss culture and society as synonymous terms. Herein lies the tension I identify as I insist that the cultural is broader than the larger social context though it includes it. As I explained earlier, I use the cultural to signal the enormous cultural diversity of the world; to highlight the wide range of activities and processes of culturalization that define, shape, condition, and impact the ways human collectives and individuals engage life, and interact with their immediate environment, make sense of reality, and engage each other and the divine.

Christ and the cultural, and painting a vision of a beleaguered church desperately seeking ways not to be co-opted by the *unredeemed world*.

Richard Niebuhr's Christ and Culture

As Niebuhr developed his paradigms—Christ against culture; the Christ of culture; Christ above culture: Synthesis; Christ and culture in paradox; and Christ the transformer of culture—there is some overlap with Machen and his categories. However, Niebuhr's understanding of the relationship between *culture* and Christ is much broader, although still within the Western European and Euro North American cultural and intellectual framing of the question. Others have discussed Niebuhr's categories at length, including useful critiques, to which we will return in the next chapter.[6] Here I limit myself to commenting on the general thrust of his argument and the implications of his approach to the issues at hand.

Niebuhr made sure to explain what he meant by both Christ and culture, in much greater detail than his contemporaries or those who have been discussed thus far. A brief explanation of their definition aids in understanding his five types. First, his understanding of culture is refreshingly broad. Like Tillich, he defined culture as the "total process of human activity," the "artificial, secondary environment" which humans impose upon the natural, comprising "language, habits, ideas, beliefs, customs, social organization, inherited artifacts, technical processes, and values."[7] For him, culture referred to what the New Testament identifies as "the world."[8] Thus the problem with which he was dealing is larger than the connection between Christianity and ("Western") civilization;[9] he was not concerned simply with a particular society. In fact, he underplayed those who, like Troeltsch, thought that "Christianity and Western culture [were]" so inextricably intertwined.[10] The "culture" with which he was

---

6   For example, Craig A. Carter, *Rethinking Christ and Culture: A Post-Christendom Perspective* (Grand Rapids, MI: Brazos Press, 2007); Gorringe, *Furthering Humanity*; D.A. Carson, *Christ & Culture Revisited* (Grand Rapids, MI: William B. Eerdmans Publishing Company, 2008).

7   H. Richard Niebuhr, *Christ and Culture*, 32, 259 pp.

8   Ibid.

9   Niebuhr, *Christ and Culture*, 11. Though Niebuhr viewed civilization and culture functioned as synonyms, his notion of culture was distinguished from that of civilization, which he argued pointed to a question of a higher degree of "advance, perhaps more urban, technical and even senescent forms of life" (Ibid., 32).

10   Niebuhr, *Christ and Culture*, 30.

concerned was "not a particular phenomenon but the general one" concretely expressed in multiple ways.[11] The scope of culture in Niebuhr's frame was large; he conceded the fundamentally cultural nature of the conditioned character of humans[12] as well as of the Bible.[13] For him, culture is that phenomenon without which humans cannot "function" since it encompasses the entire spectrum of human social and intellectual engagement.[14] Finally, by culture he included the wide diversity of cultural traditions represented by the nations of the world.[15] Despite of his own Western European, Euro North American assumptions and the intellectual tradition from which he drew his examples, he still insisted that "If Christians do not come to Christ with the language, the thought patterns, the moral disciplines of Judaism, they come with those of Rome; if not with those of Rome, then with those of Germany, England, Russia, America, India, or China."[16] By asserting a multiplicity of cultures, Niebuhr's proposal leaves the door open for the possibility of conceiving of culture in a much broader light than any other author of this period.

In contrast, his definition of Christ goes in the opposite direction; it is paradoxically narrow and vague while his definition of culture was exhaustive and broadly encompassing. Sometimes by "Christ" Niebuhr seems to mean Christianity while at other times he seems to have in mind some dogmatic set

---

11   Ibid., 29–44.

12   For Niebuhr, culture is the inescapable phenomenon that shapes and conditions all aspects of human existence. There is no room for cultural neutrality. In fact, no person "looks at the world with pristine eyes" (Niebuhr, *Christ and Culture*, 39).

13   Niebuhr, *Christ and Culture*, 104. Niebuhr chides those critics of the Christ and culture perspective, who urge a return to "biblical ways of thought." They forget, he stresses, that many cultures are represented in the Bible. Furthermore, there is no single "biblical language and no single Biblical cosmology or psychology." He adds, "The word of God as it is uttered to men comes in human words; and human words are cultural things, along with the concepts with which they are associated" (Ibid.).

14   Emphasizing what he sees as the mistaken view of those who claim to be able to exit culture, he points out that humans speak and think with the aid of language. The objective world has been "modified by human achievement." The forms and attitudes of the human mind, which allow people "to make sense of the objective world" have been given to them by culture. Humans cannot dismiss the "philosophy and science" of their society "as though they were external" to them; "they are in [them]—though in different forms from those in which they appear in the leaders of culture." Similarly, humans cannot rid themselves of the "political beliefs and economic customs by rejecting the more or less external institutions; "these customs and beliefs have taken up residence in" "their minds" (Niebuhr, *Christ and Culture*, 69).

15   Niebuhr, *Christ and Culture*, 69, 104.

16   Ibid., 69.

of assumptions about a cosmic Jesus Christ.[17] His assertion about the "objectivity" of Christ and the objective nature of gospels as accounts of the historical Jesus betray his own neo-orthodox perspective.[18] Even though Niebuhr was aware of multiple perspectives about Christ, he seemed to think that those differences could get resolved by affirming that in "these portraits [of Christ] he is recognizably one and the same."[19] Whether Christians emphasized the law or the grace of God, he wrote that, "they look to the Jesus of history or to the pre-existent and risen Lord, the virtues of Jesus Christ are the same."[20] It is this one "objective" and identifiable-by-any-Christian- tradition Jesus Christ that he had in mind. He believed that this Jesus Christ provided the answer—however indecipherable—to the question of the relationship between Christianity and culture.[21]

It becomes evident that Niebuhr's preferred paradigm is that of a Christ above culture, Christ the transformer of culture, a position only possible when the integrity of Christ is preserved.[22] He affirmed the dogmatic Reformed

---

17   Ibid., 13.
18   Niebuhr, *Christ and Culture*, 13. Concerning the Jesus of the Christian dogma, he notes, "whatever roles he plays in the varieties of Christian experience, it is the same Christ who exercises these various offices. The founder of the church is the same Christ who gives the new law; the teacher of truths about God is the same Christ who is in himself the revelation of the truth" (Ibid.).
19   Niebuhr, *Christ and Culture*, 13.
20   Ibid., 15.
21   The distinction between Christ's response and Christian responses to the "problem" of human culture needs to be made. For Niebuhr, while Christianity offers many answers Christ provides *the* proper response even though he had to express it through finite cultural material: "Christ as living Lord is answering the question in the totality of history and life in a fashion which transcends the wisdom of all his interpreters yet employs their partial insights and their necessary conflicts" (Niebuhr, *Christ and Culture*, 2).
22   The integrity of the transcendent nature of Christ makes a synthesis of "Christ of culture" and "Christ above culture" (synthesis) untenable. As he wrote:

> Apart from the specific objections to specific formulations of the synthesis, Christians of other groups will point out that the enterprise in and of itself must lead into an error. The effort to bring Christ and culture, God's work and man's, the temporal and the eternal, law and grace, into one system of thought and practice tends, perhaps inevitably, to the absolutizing of what is relative, the reduction of the infinite to a finite form, and the materialization of the dynamic. It is one thing to assert that there is a law of God inscribed in the very structure of the creature, who must seek to know this law by the use of his reason and govern himself accordingly; it is another thing to formulate the law in the language and concepts of a reason that is always culturally conditioned. Perhaps a synthesis is possible in which the relative character of all

position: Jesus is the cosmic being who makes concrete God's love and grace; he embodies the divine revelation; the whole universe lies under his authority and judgment; and, in the cross he reconciled the world to God.[23] In relation to the world/culture, Niebuhr saw Christ as superior; the world needs Christ and conversion to Christianity since the world can access God's grace only through faith in Christ. Moreover, the separation between God and humanity is explained as the result of sin. Human structures and projects are all corrupted by sin and therefore need the changing restorative love of God.[24] However, how such an understanding of Christ gets translated into the day-to-day social context remains unclear. The lack of clarity in his definition of Christ complicates the rest of Niebuhr's discussion of the five paradigms. There is little room left for the acknowledgement of the ethnocultural Jewishness of the historical Jesus and how that factors into our own understanding of Christ, for instance.[25] At some point, the historical Jesus dissipates in Niebuhr's work and the reader is left unhelpfully with a confessional cosmic (and acultural) Jesus Christ and God who stands absolutely outside of history.[26]

When Niebuhr discusses the five types he crafted, it is obvious that he intended these categories heuristically. He repeatedly states that they involve

---

creaturely formulations of the Creator's law will be fully recognized. But no synthesist answer so far given in Christian history has avoided the equation of a cultural view of God's law in creation with the law itself (Niebuhr, *Christ and Culture*, 145).

23   Niebuhr, *Christ and Culture*, 39.
24   In no other type but "Christ transformer of culture" does Niebuhr engage the impact of sin on Christian life. The result is that he points to the corrupted status of humanity and highlights the divine redemptive grace of Christ. See Niebuhr, *Christ and Culture*, 194–95.
25   Niebuhr, *Christ and Culture*, 2. Though he generally countered any attempt to undermine the importance of culture and Christianity, Niebuhr does also admit the tendency to reject culture altogether. For example, he writes that Rabbi Klausner suggested that Jesus did not reform culture, but rather ignored it. Again in his concluding chapter, he identifies a similar attitude in the overemphasis on the transcendent character of Christ. This time it is Kierkegaard's existentialism that posits that the culture problem is irrelevant to faith, not because it is existentialist and practical, but because it is individualistic and abstract. These two perspectives he modified by subsuming them in his model of culture under the authority of his cosmic Christ. See Niebuhr, *Christ and Culture*, 3, 244.
26   Niebuhr, *Christ and Culture*, 249. Not surprisingly, as he ends the section on the Christ of culture he concludes by dismissing this approach on the basis of his Christology. Even as he discusses the first of the three types of Christ above culture (synthesis), he concludes that there is really no room for synthesis because Christ's grace, law and reign cannot be institutionalized. The church is the recipient of the actions of Christ, "the free Lord." See (Ibid., 115. 146).

a hypothetical organization in which some of the authors can easily fit into more than one category.[27] Aware that many expected him to come up with *the* solution to this enduring "problem," he categorically denied the possibility of a definitive solution to the relation between culture and Christianity.[28] But as he explained, his was an inconclusive proposal because there is no one single "universal" response to this challenge; Christians, in their multiple expressions, will have to come up with their own distinct resolutions for such a complex, contested, and volatile relation.[29] Still, in the consideration of the proper ethical response to the phenomenon of culture, Niebuhr insisted that Christians will have to wrestle with questions of loyalty or disloyalty to Christ in the midst of cultural tasks.[30]

More recently some evangelical scholars have revisited Niebuhr's work and have identified key weaknesses, while remaining well within his framing of the debates. While seeking to reformulate Niebuhr's ideas, they remain trapped within an understanding of Christianity and culture (read large social context and society) as entirely antithetical.

Niebuhr's Christ and Culture *Reformulated?*

One of the particularities of the debates on the relationship between Gospel/faith/Christ/Christianity and culture is that most authors at some point revisit Niebuhr's work. The specter of Niebuhr's *Christ and Culture* looms large in almost every proposal one encounters. Most authors are caught in Niebuhr's paradigmatic ideas of culture as referring to the larger social context. Even those proposals that seek to go beyond the Christ and culture dualism find it necessary to allude to his work. Some scholars have

---

27   For example, he claims that Tolstoy does not fully conform to any of the types he mentions. His discussion of Paul, Augustine, and the gospel of John appears in different perspectives, illustrating the fact that these types are not meant to be interpreted as hard-and-fast frames. According to him, the "types" were not exclusive of each other. See Niebuhr, *Christ and Culture*, 231.

28   Niebuhr, *Christ and Culture*, 231.

29   Niebuhr, *Christ and Culture*, 230–33. As Niebuhr saw it, "no amount of speculative insight into the reasoning and believing of other men, and no continuation of consideration of the imperatives and values issuing from Christ and culture, can relieve the Christian individual or the responsible Christian community from the burden, the necessity, the guilt and glory, of arriving at such conclusions in present decisions and present obedience" (Ibid., 233).

30   Niebuhr, *Christ and Culture*, 248.

recently reopened the discussions about Niebuhr's proposal insisting on its usefulness for today.[31] Others have argued for a way to reclaim the Christ that seems to disappear in Niebuhr's work.[32] And yet others have attempted to redefine the interconnection between the notion of culture and the larger social context. For example, Frederica Mathewes-Green describes the relationship between the church and the larger social context as weathering a storm.[33] Meanwhile, John M. Frame considers culture to be a mixture of sin and righteousness, good and bad, love of Christ and hatred of Christ.[34] Focusing on culture as the human response in obedience to the divine cultural mandate, he insists that culture is a term broader than "the world." The world (the larger social context), he comments, is the bad side of culture.[35] The emphasis should therefore not be Christ against culture but Christ against the world.[36]

Anabaptist Rethinking of Christ and Culture: *Carter and Friesen*

In more mainstream approaches, scholars tend to find the need either to reconfigure Niebuhr's proposal or offer alternative ways for thinking about

---

31   Douglas F. Ottati, "*Christ and Culture*: Still Worth Reading After All These Years," *Journal of the Society of Christian Ethics* 23, no. 1 (2003): 121–32.

32   Glen H. Stassen, "It is Time to Take Jesus Back: In Celebration of the Fieftieth Anniversary of H. Richard Niebuhr's *Christ and Culture*," *Journal of the Society of Christian Ethics* 23, no. 1 (2003): 133–43. For Glen Stassen, the Jesus of Niebuhr's types grows thinner the farther one goes into the book. Exploring Niebuhr's larger corpus, he shows how Niebuhr seemed to adopt a watered-down view of Christ.

33   Frederica Mathewes-Green, "Loving the Storm-Drenched," *Christianity Today*, 1 March 2006, Http://www.christianitytoday.com/ct/2006/march/10.36.html (accessed November 7, 2015). She writes: "The culture ... is like the weather. We may be able to influence it in modest ways, seeding the clouds, but it is a recipe for frustration to expect that we can direct it" (Ibid.).

34   John M. Frame, "Christianity and Culture," Lectures given at the Pensacola Theological Institute (Pensacola, FL, 2001), 9, Http://thirdmill.org/files/english/hall_of_frame/Frame.Apologetics2004.ChristandCulture.pdf (accessed October 28, 2015).

35   According to Frame, culture can be said to be what which God makes through us. Culture for him points to all things that humans make with their hands and minds and it is directly connected to creation. But he is still able to see good in culture, and for this reason he adopts a kind of Manichean approach to his understanding of culture. See Frame, "Christianity and Culture," 1–5, 9, 12.

36   Frame, "Christianity and Culture," 13. Frame argues for a recovery of the Scriptures because they give us God's point of view on human culture, which for all intents and purposes is pretty depressing. The tension between God and the world, then, is that people rebel against God and end up practicing all kinds of wickedness. See Ibid., 22.

how Christ and culture should relate or not relate to each other. One good example is Craig Carter who engages in a reformulation of Niebuhr's famous book on the eve of its 50th anniversary. He writes to "correct" and "improve" the work.[37] His central concerns are twofold: One, to unmask and dismantle what he views as the wrong premise of Christendom that shaped and informed Niebuhr's formulations on how Christ and culture relate. And two, to propose alternative ways for conceiving the relationship between Christ and culture (read the influence of the larger social context) from a Post-Christendom vantage point.[38]

Although he sometimes makes unwarranted generalizations, Carter engages in a significant dismantling of Niebuhr's work. His objections can be organized under three main headings: Niebuhr took Christendom for granted; he neglected to take coercive violence into consideration; and he made wrong theological assumptions. Most importantly, Niebuhr's work should be understood as an apology for Christendom.[39] Carter chides Niebuhr for assuming that Western cultures (read Western societies) are Christian, which inevitably resulted in making Christians responsible for culture.[40] Moreover, Niebuhr was unable to take coercive violence as a crucial criterion for articulating his typological approach. By taking Christendom for granted, he left violent coercion unaddressed and as such he left the world's (sinful) rebellion unchallenged for its tendency to use violence.[41] It is for this reason that in his *Christ against Culture* typology, he wrongly lumped together groups that rejected violent coercion with those that accepted coercion as an appropriate means to resist

---

37   Carter, *Rethinking Christ and Culture*. See also his two previous articles: Craig A. Carter, "The Legacy of an Inadequate Christology: Yoder's Critique of Niebuhr's *Christ and Culture*," *Mennonite Quarterly Review* 77, no. 3 (July 2003): 387–401; Craig A Carter, "Rethinking Christ and Culture After Christendom," paper presented at The Evangelical Theological Society (San Antonio, TX, 2005), Http://reclaimingthemind.org/papers/ets/2003/Carter/Carter.pdf (accessed April 30, 2015).

38   Carter's proposal is very narrow in scope directed to the debates as they take place in the United States and Canada, and more particularly to those who consider the Anabaptists and Mennonite groups to have no social or cultural relevance in the region.

39   He explains: "I mean that it takes Christendom for granted as its starting point and assumes that Christendom is real, permanent, and on the whole a good thing" (Carter, *Rethinking Christ and Culture*, 56).

40   Carter, *Rethinking Christ and Culture*, 15.

41   Rather than actually transforming culture, Carter notes, by leaving violent coercion unaddressed Niebuhr confirms the violence of the world. As a result, his proposal does not lead to transformation, repentance and conversion. See Carter, *Rethinking Christ and Culture*, 30.

the larger social context.[42] In the same way, the proposal of *Christ Transformer of Culture* in Niebuhr resulted in conforming Christianity to the culture/larger society.[43] Niebuhr failed to account for the many groups who adopt violence as the means to bring transformation, and that there are many other groups who reject violent coercion but who have a transformative effect on culture/society.[44]

Carter's critical stance is broad ranging. He considers that from the time of Constantine to the present Christianity has operated under the framing of Christendom.[45] He argues that an examination of Christian history demonstrates that the emergence and preservation of Christendom has compromised the gospel message and made the church complicit with endless violence (the Crusades, the Inquisition, the judicial murder of heretics, the blessing of wars of conquest in the Americas, the justification of slavery, World War II, the Holocaust, the use of atomic weapons as tools of terror against civilians, in short the climax of all the evils of Western civilization). This is a sad history, he comments, and "should never have been part of church history. But it is

---

42   Taking John Howard Yoder critiques of Niebuhr as his springboard, Carter critiques the Niebuhr brothers for making many groups with pacifist traditions to feel "ashamed of their long heritage of peace." Carter is convinced that Niebuhr's work is an assault on the "Christ against Culture" type. He concludes that "The effect of *Christ and Culture* [typology] has often been to convince educated young people from peace church, charismatic-Pentecostal, pietistic, fundamentalist, evangelical and other non-mainstream traditions that their heritage of significant opposition to important aspects of the majority culture is something of which to be ashamed and which must be discarded if one is to become responsible and culturally engaged" (Craig A. Carter, "The Legacy of an Inadequate Christology," 388).

43   It is very difficult to identify how Carter arrives at this conclusion. Vaguely he argues that Niebuhr seems to call for engaging culture, but "Ironically, this engagement leads as often to cultural accommodation as it does to cultural transformation. The amount of accommodation to culture that occurs in the name of being 'transforming' and 'realistic' is little short of astounding" (Craig A. Carter, "The Legacy of an Inadequate Christology," 388).

44   Carter, *Rethinking Christ and Culture*, 30.

45   He understands Christendom as the

> concept of Western civilization as having a religious arm (the church) and a secular arm (civil government), both of which are united in their adherence to Christian faith, which is seen as the so-called soul of Europe or the West. The essence of the idea is the assertion that Western civilization is Christian. Within this Christian civilization, the state and the church have different roles to play, but, since membership in both is coterminous, both can be seen as aspects of one unified reality—Christendom (Carter, *Rethinking Christ and Culture*, 14).

part of our history—because of Christendom."[46] For him, Christendom was a perversion of the gospel and a parody of the church;[47] what makes this a bad history is that those terrible acts were carried out by people who knew Jesus, he claims.[48] The church did benefit from Christendom but in the process lost its way, and that prevented it from becoming a messianic community witnessing to the lordship of Christ.[49] For the church to be church in this post-Christendom era, Carter proposes, it will have to first repent of the whole Christendom project.[50] In his attempt to reclaim this "true" Christian church, Carter affirms that "only those movements of Christianity that follow Jesus in rejecting violence, practicing reconciliation and witnessing to the triumph of the Lamb can be said truly to be Nicene in nature."[51]

The deficiency in Niebuhr's proposal is then not just a matter of taking a Christendom as legitimate framing but in the failure to appropriately connect with the gospel message of his proposed solution—the transformation of culture.[52] Overall, for Carter, Niebuhr's theology was simply flawed! It had a

---

46   Carter, *Rethinking Christ and Culture*, 21. In an almost ironic move, Carter argues that the attacks of Darwin, Marx and Freud against Christianity were directed to the Christianity of Christendom. That is, "the Christianity of ruling elites and state churches, the Christianity of violent coercion and intolerance, the Christianity of power and privilege, the Christianity of racism, patriarchy and colonialism, the Christianity of the Inquisition and the Holocaust" (Carter, *Rethinking Christ and Culture*, 19).

47   Carter, *Rethinking Christ and Culture*, 30, 127. Carter is enormously critical of the many ways in which the church partook in the violence of Christendom. Yet, he does not regard all of Christian history from the fourth to the twentieth century as "a write off." Although Christendom was of no help to those who preached, and believed the gospel, still faithful witness to Christ did take place. The church, he insists, witnessed the gospel despite not because of Christendom. See Ibid., 30.

48   Carter, *Rethinking Christ and Culture*, 22.

49   Many are the aspects that show how the church was tangled up with Christendom. Yes, the church benefitted from the taxes that the state had imposed on the people, and which gave incentives to the church to support the political configuration. In addition, the church had to pledge its allegiance to the state, which is something it had renounced prior to Constantine. Since war was sanctioned by the rulers, Christian were expected to fight. Overall, argues Carter, Christendom marginalized Jesus and put the state in place of the church; it was a bad idea. See Carter, *Rethinking Christ and Culture*, 85–87, 108.

50   Carter, *Rethinking Christ and Culture*, 201.

51   Craig A. Carter, "The Legacy of an Inadequate Christology," 401.

52   The endorsement of Christendom in Niebuhr causes Carter's pacifist sensibilities to respond by stating that (Niebuhr's) methodology is not much different from those "cultural Germans" that Karl Barth adamantly opposed. Carter is referring here to the 93 German Christians who filled the ranks of those who supported the Kaiser's call for war

low Christology,[53] his sense of creation was problematic,[54] his doctrine of the Trinity was skewed,[55] his eschatology was non-existent,[56] and he was missing the doctrine of the Holy Spirit.[57] Basically, Niebuhr's theology did not live up to the standards of "orthodox" Nicene Christianity, and for this reason his typology should be reformulated.[58] Agreeing with John Howard Yoder, Carter places the emphasis not on the relationship between Christ and culture/society but

---

in 1914. He qualifies his statement by saying that Niebuhr did not support nationalism, but the question is whether his perspective would have had the theological resources to oppose it. See Carter, *Rethinking Christ and Culture*, 60.

53   For Carter, Niebuhr's view had no room for the Lordship of Christ and the church, the community of disciples who "live under that Lordship in joyous anticipation of the full coming of the reign of God" (Carter, *Rethinking Christ and Culture*, 60). Niebuhr's Jesus was an otherworldly, almost mythical figure who had no interest in the mundane things of life such as politics, family and social structures. His version of Jesus is so distant from material reality that one "could say that his feet barely touched the earth." See Ibid. 66). In the end, Carter adds, Niebuhr's Christ is docetic, and "can never become embodied in history" (Ibid., 125). See also Craig A. Carter, "The Legacy of an Inadequate Christology," 388–93.

54   Carter's critique against Niebuhr relates to his understanding of culture as the creation of humans, which means (for Carter) that culture still part of creation. But Carter contrasts creation with the gospel. In light of the New Testament, he says, culture refers not to the "unfallen" world but the sinful world. It is Niebuhr's failure to make this distinction that undermines (Carter thinks) his proposal. See Carter, *Rethinking Christ and Culture*, 68.

55   Carter is persuaded that Niebuhr attempts to locate his reluctance to make the lordship of the biblical Jesus decisive for Christian ethics in a doctrine of the Trinity that posits multiple ways to divine truth. He cites John Howard Yoder as his evidence of Niebuhr's faulty trinity. Yoder, he writes, "correctly discerns that Niebuhr's doctrine of the Trinity is a way of justifying ethical thought that does not spring from Christ by presenting the authority of God the Father as the basis for natural theology" (Carter, *Rethinking Christ and Culture*, 70).

56   Carter bemoans the lack of futuristic eschatology in Niebuhr in order to balance the sense of realized eschatology. As he sees it, Niebuhr's eschatology "is insufficient to prevent the development of a relaxed relationship to the existing social order and the settling down of the church into a pattern of accommodation to the world" (Craig A. Carter, "The Legacy of an Inadequate Christology," 400).

57   As he argues, "Niebuhr is missing a doctrine of the Holy Spirit and a conviction that the power of the Holy Spirit can make the separated church a community of equality rather than of authoritarianism" (Carter, *Rethinking Christ and Culture*, 161).

58   Having considered other alternatives, Carter concludes that his task is that of devising a new typology of Christ and culture that allows the church to imagine how to interact with culture in ways that avoid compromising our witness to the gospel. See Carter, *Rethinking Christ and Culture*, 75.

between the church and culture/society.[59] In view of the "failure" of Niebuhr's proposal, he then posits a new typology of Christ and culture, which "should aid us in the task of discerning how the church can engage culture without compromising its unity, holiness, catholicity, and apostolicity."[60]

Carter's typology uses the critique of coercive violence as the criterion to solve Niebuhr's shortfalls. Volunteering as the man for the job,[61] He proposes six redesigned typologies which somewhat resonate with Niebuhr's earlier work and which also operate as heuristic devices. Three of them are representative of Christendom and its use of coercive violence: 1) Christ legitimizing culture, 2) Christ humanizing culture, and 3) Christ transforming culture. The other three are representative of post-Christendom and a refusal to violence: 4) Christ transforming culture, 5) Christ humanizing culture, and 6) Christ separating from culture. He demonstrates the strength and weaknesses of each of the types, as well as their possible biblical bases, reminding us of Niebuhr's proposal. But his point is made clear, violent coercion is the "key dividing Christendom from non-Christendom types because it is at this point that the dividing line between the church and the world is either maintained or blurred."[62]

Carter's fundamental concern with the relationship between Christ and culture/society is simple, they are irreconcilable. He represents those who take a more extreme view of culture, meaning *the unredeemed world*, that stands diametrically opposite to the gospel message or Christ.[63] His solution

---

59   He asks: "If Niebuhr's question is the wrong question, then what is the right question? Yoder is correct to see that, fundamentally, the relationship between Christ and culture is not the place to start. One must start with the question of the relationship between the church and its surrounding society" (Craig A. Carter, "The Legacy of an Inadequate Christology," 396).

60   Craig A Carter, "Rethinking Christ and Culture," 10.

61   Carter makes clear that he is not siding with "liberal" or "conservatives" Christianity, though he surely resonates with the latter. He considers that both currents have been severely compromised by the Enlightenment project by adopting the autonomy of human reason and sciences and technology as the way to salvation. For him, both conservatives and liberals think that Christendom is not entirely dead although severely ill, yet, look for ways to revive it. See Carter, *Rethinking Christ and Culture*, 8, 20–21, 200.

62   Carter, *Rethinking Christ and Culture*, 114.

63   The contrast is obvious for him. Niebuhr focuses on the this-worldly aspects and he is oriented toward what is to come. What H. R. Niebuhr thought of as 'the real world' the biblical narrative exposes as a "temporary aberration—of creation in unsustainable revolt against the Creator and of a world in the process of passing away" (Craig A. Carter, "The Legacy of an Inadequate Christology," 398).

is to move into a Church and the world relationship, and place both under the Lordship of Jesus Christ as criterion for evaluating both.[64] In contrast to Niebuhr, his intention is not to suggest any typology as his preferred answer. However, his proposal loses steam when he tells us that his post-Christendom typologies show that there can be a similar range of engagements possible "by those movements that reject violence as well as those who embrace it."[65] He paints a picture of a beleaguered church condemned to the sidelines because of a fear to be "corrupted." Just as Jesus was confronted with the temptation to found Christendom, Christianity must now deal with the same temptation faced by the church in the fourth century.[66] Ultimately, the choice is between Christ and Constantine; "The vanguard of history is not the Communist Party, not Liberal Democracy, and not the United States of America. Rather, it is the messianic community, the church or, as Yoder put it, a 'New World on the Way'."[67]

Carter's evangelical commitment and his Anabaptist sentiments shape his reformulation of Niebuhr's work. By focusing on culture narrowly as *the unredeemed world*, he fails to see how culture as *way of life* (including Menonnites and Anabaptists) impacts the way people view the world, approach the divine, and interpret the Bible. With all that he condemns about Christendom, he uncritically deploys notions of a universal Christ, which he has inherited from the very Christendom that he loathes. More to the point, he does not account for the fact that Christendom and imperialism (which he appropriately condemns) were cultural projects; coercive violence also included the destruction of other peoples' cultures through the imposition of the Western cultures that came together with the preaching of the gospel.

Carter's critique of Niebuhr's can be turned in on itself and applied to his own typologies. I agree with his rejection of the violence of Christendom. In chapter 3 we showed how coercive violence served Europe's colonial imperial agenda. However, and as D. A. Carson points out, Carter reflects little on what he means by the gospel, sin, judgment and how these point to the cross and resurrection

---

64   Craig A. Carter, "The Legacy of an Inadequate Christology," 397–98. This is a way by which he conceives the culture of the church while participating in the larger non-Christian culture around it.

65   Carter, *Rethinking Christ and Culture*, 122. He comments that "there are ... no pure types, and all examples are only impure incarnations of them" (Ibid.). Even among those who would fall in the *Christ separating from culture* type, in reality "there never has been any Christian community completely cut off from culture" (Ibid.).

66   Carter, *Rethinking Christ and Culture*, 204, 211.

67   Craig A. Carter, "The Legacy of an Inadequate Christology," 398.

of Jesus.[68] Furthermore, while he holds the historical Jesus as antidote to both Christendom and Niebuhr's typological frame, he remains oblivious to the theological import of the historical and cultural specificity of Jesus as a first century Palestinian Jew. He does admit that Christ as a historical figure was culturally embedded, but he says nothing of how Jesus' own conceptions of the divine were culturally conditioned. Instead of opening the door for how lived everyday culture could play a crucial role in the way people conceive and approach the divine, Carter shuts the door and instead affirms just as seemingly acultural and (equally docetic) universal Christ as Niebuhr. In terms of the cultural, then, Carter is not nearly radical enough and far less radical than he claims.[69]

By insisting on "coercive violence" as the sign of Christianity gone wrong and criteria for his typologies, Carter creates, yet again, another reductionistic straight jacket for Christianity, the Church, and even our understanding of the Christ.[70] Carson helpfully points out that by focusing on "coercive violence" and not force, he refuses to acknowledge distinction in kind and use of force.[71] The biggest weakness in Carter is that he seems to think that the church is not affected (remains pristine) by the social issues in the broader cultural context. In discussing the tensions between the "already" and the "not yet," Carter seems to presume that all that one has to do is to reject coercive violence and the problem is solved.[72] It almost seems as if Carter thinks that racism, misogyny, sexism, and all cultural social evils cannot take place within the "true" "Christian" church. In my view, Carter repeats the same mistake for which he faults Niebuhr, by failing to explain why the typologies are necessary if so fraught with problems. He also develops categories of groups of people that could result in their not recognizing themselves (in his description of them) and as a result engages in the same game of reductionism for which he accuses Niebuhr.[73]

---

68 There is little in Carter's argument, says Carson that "convincingly puts together the entire story line of the Bible, including the great turning points in redemptive history" (Carson, *Christ & Culture Revisited*, 221).

69 Carter, *Rethinking Christ and Culture*, 7.

70 Carson tells us that Christianity has too often been domesticated, and Carter, it appears, wishes to domesticate it by his post-Christian pacifist ideals. He notes that by focusing on "coercive violence" and not force, Carter refuses to acknowledge distinctions in kind and use of force. See Carson, *Christ & Culture Revisited*, 220–21.

71 Carson, *Christ & Culture Revisited*, 220.

72 Ibid., 222.

73 This is the problem that Yoder finds with Niebuhr's typologies. For Yoder, "Niebuhr seems to want it both ways, in that he wants to admit that his 'pure' categories do not exactly fit the people to whom he applies them and, at the same time, he wants to criticize those people for not fitting the type perfectly!" (Craig A. Carter, "The Legacy of an Inadequate Christology," 391).

In his short article, Duane K. Friesen offers a different Anabaptist alternative that avoids some of the problems one finds in Carter's proposal.[74] His purpose is twofold: one, to demonstrate the inadequacy of the Christ-against-culture typology and two to provide a broader understanding of transformation, which is the central feature of Nieburh's fifth type. Written before Carter, he highlights that he does not recognize his own tradition in Niebuhr's typologies. Contrary to Carter, he pays greater attention to the encompassing character of cultural traditions, affirming Jesus' own cultural embeddedness—as a first century Palestinian Jew, who prayed in Aramaic and taught parables that fit his cultural context and people's own cultural embodiedness—as a person with flesh and bones who was integrally bound up with his/her cultural context.[75] For these reasons, he claims that Niebuhr's typologies fail because it is logically nonsensical to describe anyone as "against" or in "agreement" with culture;[76] the question should not be between Christ and culture but between contrasting cultural visions.

Friesen seems to want to move beyond fixed prescriptive categories by identifying cultures as fluid and complex and not as monolithic. He observes that within the Christian tradition there is a great deal of variety in the way churches deal with the larger social context. He makes allowance for the fact that even in working against social issues such as abortion, capital punishment, and war, one finds "strange bedfellows." On one issue people might agree and on another issue, they might disagree.[77] For some reason, however, Friesen backpedals when he comes up with his own typology. Carter's types echo Friesen's, and both establish Constantinianism (Carter uses Christendom) as a line of separation.[78] Friesen provides only an outline of his six types but with labels

---

74   Duane K. Friesen, "A Discriminating Engagement of Culture: 'An Anabaptists Perspective',"
      Journal of the Society of Christian Ethics 23, no. 1 (2003): 145–56.

75   Ibid., 147.

76   Ibid., 148.

77   Ibid., 149.

78   The similarity between Friesen and Carter's proposals is striking. For Friesen, the Church
      within the Constantinian stream means it "must cooperate with the dominant institu-
      tions of the world in order to shape a relatively just social order." Christians find them-
      selves living in a sinful world "'between the times' of God's revelation in Christ and the
      eschatological fulfillment of God's complete redemption." But sin is present in this world
      and has impacted the human condition limiting what can be achieved in history. Yet,
      "God providentially works through human cultural agents (e.g. civil authorities; govern-
      ment) to order society toward the common good." As a result, Christians are required "to
      cooperate in the use of the 'sword' to protect the good and punish the evil." As for the

in which "culture" is conspicuously absent.[79] By offering his new typology, he seems convinced he is providing an alternative solution that better accounts for the descriptions that Niebuhr lumped together in the Christ-against-culture category (Carter reiterates this concern years later).[80] Also, by using "transformation" in four of his types, he shows how many church traditions identify with the impetus of "transformation" despite their "cultural" differences, which also explains why people find themselves attracted to Niebuhr's fifth type: "Christ-transformer-of-culture."

Overall and helpfully, Friesen represents a move away from fixed and inflexible categories. He clearly recognizes the slippery character of identifying the larger social context as "culture" precisely because "culture" in its more proper sense, refers more directly to "everything humans do that is not determined by strictly biological forces."[81] His notion of embeddedness and embodied cultures is really helpful, but does not go as far as to include the impact of culture in the divine disclosure and mediation. He still leaves unresolved the question as to why the development of a new schema is necessary. Instead his sets of categories provide false paradigmatic choices when in reality, different church traditions cross boundaries according to the social and historical circumstances they face.

Reformed Evangelical Approach to Christ and Culture: *Carson*
The problem of the inadequacy of fixed categories to embody equal and independent alternatives is one of the reasons for which D. A. Carson wrote *Christ and Culture Revisited*.[82] Following a Geertzian approach, he defines "culture" as

<hr>

non-Constantinian types, Friesen views the church as a "disciplined community called to model an alternative cultural vision distinct from the dominant culture" (Friesen, "A Discriminating Engagement of Culture," 150).

79   His six types are: Christ as Founder of Ethical Communities; Christ as Model for Public Witness; Christ as Healer of the Nations. The name of the Constantinian streams: The Spiritual Christ who Legitimizes Social Structures; The Christ who Humanizes Social Structures; The Christ who Transforms Social Structures. See Friesen, "A Discriminating Engagement of Culture," 152–54.

80   Friesen, "A Discriminating Engagement of Culture," 154.

81   Ibid., 147.

82   Carson, *Christ & Culture Revisited*. Resonating with other earlier and contemporary scholars, he provides six reasons for the way in which he revisits the relationship between Christ and culture: 1) Richard Niebuhr cannot be ignored; 2) The emergence of different voices clamoring to dictate how the relationship between Christ and culture ought to take place; 3) changes in the global landscape due to communication technology, migration, and multicultural societies; 4) challenges concerning the relative merits of arguing one culture superiority over another; 5) the decline of Christianity in the West; and 6) long history of tensions and disputes between Church and state. See Ibid., 5–6.

denoting "an historically transmitted pattern of meanings embodied in symbols, a system of inherited conceptions expressed in symbolic form by means
of which men [sic] communicate, perpetuate, and develop their knowledge
about and attitudes towards life."[83] This semiotic all-encompassing view of
culture (the cultural) enables him to see that cultures are essentially communal and that human activity cannot take place outside the context of the
cultural. Conversations about Christ/Christianity and culture are incoherent
unless we account for the fact that all forms of Christianity are embedded in
cultural expressions.[84] Thus, much more than Carter, he is aware of the conditioning effects of the cultural.

However, that admission is also the extent of Carson's engagement with questions of culture as way of life and instead shifts to reflections on society. He spends
the rest of the time talking about Western cultures (read Western societies), and
the factors that force Christians to relate to the larger social context: democracy,
freedom, postmodernism, and power.[85] In order to respond to the central concern
about Christ and culture (read the larger society), he first engages in an evaluation of Niebuhr's work. Carson does not berate Niebuhr as much as Carter does.
Instead, he is more incisive concerning the weaknesses he finds in Niebuhr's work.
He agrees that the object of Niebuhr's *Christ and Culture* was to show that there
is no one "Christian answer;"[86] but he argues that his five typologies are merely
"illustrations" and not hard and fast archetypes, since no example fits perfectly
under a given category.

Delving in greater detail on Niebuhr's actual typologies, Carson dismisses the examples in *the Christ of Culture* pattern (Gnostics and liberal
Christianity) because they are of doubtful Christian authenticity and simply
have no basis in the Bible.[87] The *Christ above Culture* (synthesis) option he
finds dangerous in its capacity to absolutize the world and reduce to finite
form the infinite.[88] Meanwhile, he asserts that the *Christ Transformer of*

---

83   Carson, *Christ & Culture Revisited*, 2. Carson also draws on L Kroeber and C Kluckhohn's
      definition of culture as consisting of "patterns, explicit and implicit, of and for behavior
      acquired and transmitted by symbols, constituting the distinctive achievement of human
      groups, including their embodiment in artifacts; the essential core of culture consists of
      traditional (i.e., historically derived and selected) ideas and especially their attached val-
      ues; culture systems may, on the one hand be considered as products of action, on the
      other hand as conditioning elements of further action" (Ibid.).
84   Carson, *Christ & Culture Revisited*, 3.
85   Ibid., Chapter 3–4.
86   Ibid., 29.
87   Ibid., 34–36, 200.
88   Ibid., 22.

Culture type is found in restricted forms in the biblical text but certainly not in the purity in which Niebuhr described it.[89] In the end, Niebuhr will not do, writes Carson.[90] The five typologies offer idealized competing alternatives that need to be trimmed to reflect "the broader realities of biblical-theological developments."[91]

Carson uses this weakness to launch his own proposal: since Nieburh's five patterns are idealizations they rarely subsist in their pure form. In reality people most likely will merge disparate elements from two or more of these paradigms. So he wonders whether these five patterns are real individual alternatives or components of a bigger pattern. In order to be more consistent with the Bible's story line he asks: should we not be "attempting a holistic grasp of the relations between Christ and culture, fully aware, as we make our attempt, that peculiar circumstances may call us to emphasize some elements in one situation, and other elements in another situation"?[92]

For Carson, the objective is not to merely describe the relation between Christ and culture but to probe "what the relationship ought to be in the light of Scripture."[93] The Bible narrative provides a framework to focus specifically on what he calls the non-negotiable turning points in Christianity: creation, fall, incarnation, Jesus' death and resurrection, coming of the Spirit, and the final

---

89   Ibid., 39–40, 61.

90   As he writes, the fivefold typology that Niebuhr presents is not very effective at interacting with current discussions over post-modernism. "We find it lacking in an age when notions like 'the Christian west' cannot really be sustained, when multiculturalism has shaped many decisions of the Supreme Court, and when immigration patterns force us to think about the way non-Christian religions, notably Islam, are likely to view the typologies Niebuhr proposes. In short, as influential as it has been in the past, Niebuhr's fivefold typology now seems parochial" (Carson, *Christ & Culture Revisited*, 200–201).

91   Carson, *Christ & Culture Revisited*, 60.

92   Carson, *Christ & Culture Revisited*, 43. Elsewhere he adds, "We will be wiser if we refrain from distinguishing discrete patterns or paradigms or models of the relations between Christ and culture, and think instead of wise integration, with different aspects of the whole clamoring for more attention from time to time. Better put, if for any reason we continue to think of different models of the relationship between Christ and culture, we must insist that they are not alternative models that we may choose to accept or reject. Rather, we shall ask in what sense they are grounded in the Scriptures and ponder their interrelations *within* the Scriptures, and how and when they should be emphasized under different circumstances exemplified in the Scriptures" (Ibid., 62).

93   Carson, *Christ & Culture Revisited*, 87.

judgment and consummation.[94] This metanarrative (or later worldview)[95] is not only his attempt at countering the postmodernism strategy to undermine the authority of the biblical message in the broader cultural context,[96] but is also his way to emphasize that the larger society can only be understood in the light of eternity, "of a hell to be feared and a new heaven and new earth to be gained."[97] The reason for the impasse between culture and Christ according to him is sin, which is the aspect of human social reality that causes this radical separation; it means defiance of God.[98] In ways that are reminiscent of Calvin's notion of "total depravity," he describes sin as "so warping that it corrodes every facet of our being, our wills and affections, out view of others and thus our relationships, our bodies and our minds."[99] Its effect is such that while culture-society discloses that we were made in the image of God, such image is mis-shaped and corroded by human rebellion against God.[100]

Carson takes a different route than Niebuhr or Carter. As he opines, it is more important to develop a schema that allows for multiple responses in the midst of the contested relationship between the church and state, always keeping in mind the subservient nature of the state (Caesar) to God.[101] Contra

---

94   Ibid., 85.

95   Adapting the notion of the Bible as providing a worldview Carson holds that

> ... a worldview must be comprehensive enough to address the question of deity (If there is a God, what is he like?), the question of origins (Where do I come from?), the question of significance (Who am I?), the question of evil (Why is there so much suffering? If things are not the way they're supposed to be, why not?), the question of salvation (What is the problem, and how is it resolved?). The question of *telos* (Why am I here? What does the future hold?). It does not purport to identify all the subatomic quarks; it does not claim to say all that might be said about God. It merely claims to cast a broad enough vision to be able to see the shape of the whole (Carson, *Christ & Culture Revisited*, 95–96).

96   Carson, *Christ & Culture Revisited*, 87–113.

97   Ibid., 206.

98   As he reflects on the nature of sin, Carson agrees with Niebuhr, identifying "culture as devoid of Christ" or "the world" as seen in the New Testament. He adds that the tensions between Christ and culture "from a Christian perspective...find their origin in the stubborn refusal of human beings, made in God's image, to acknowledge their creaturely dependence of their Maker" (Carson, *Christ & Culture Revisited*, 207).

99   Carson, *Christ & Culture Revisited*, 48.

100   Carson, *Christ & Culture Revisited*, 49. Because of God's common grace, says Carson, we still see glimpses of the goodness among us.

101   See Carson, *Christ & Culture Revisited*, Chapter 5.

Niebuhr, Carter and the like, he concludes that there are no better or worse examples of how these tensions might play out. In fact, they will differ in different contexts. The best way forward is to talk about a *Christ and culture* position, but as shorthand for the possible relationships in which Christians might engage with non-Christians. The broader culture will refuse Christ's authority, even if it cannot escape it. In such context, sometimes the

> culture ... ignores Christ and Christians; sometimes culture explicitly contradicts Christ and Christians; sometimes culture persecutes Christ and Christians; on occasion culture very selectively approves and disapproves Christ and Christians. And the responses of Christians correspondingly adapt (sometimes wisely, sometimes unwisely) to such varying cultural stances.[102]

One needs to keep in mind, though, that for Carson, all these are varying responses of a larger pattern based on the biblical text.

Carson quite convincingly argues against independent typologies as options for understanding and engaging the relationship between Christ and culture/society. Much more than any of his contemporaries, he showed the importance of the biblical text in these debates and in some modest way accounted for the cultural diversity of the world, which inevitably leads to an acknowledgement of diverse expressions of Christianity.

But his strengths also mark the limits of his proposal. First, he discusses the richness of the biblical text but he does not identify the impact of cultural conditioning within the biblical text itself. He seems to think that the Bible has not been influenced by cultural concerns and that the reading of the Bible does not need to account for such cultural conditioning. Second, while creating space for other cultures, Carson leaves out Jesus' own cultural particularity, and how that shaped his understanding of God. It appears that for him revelation is either *acultural* or *transcultural*; either way such view is problematic as it does not allow for the cultural specificity of the historical Jesus, nor the cultural specificity of his own understanding of God and the Bible narrative. And third, while starting with an anthropological-semiotic definition of the phenomena of cultures, he quickly moves to an understanding of culture as society and civilization. His understanding of culture as system wrongly communicates ideas of consistency and clearly defined borders while undermining the lived character of people's cultures. At the same time, his view of culture as society-civilization remains caught in his Western European intellectual

---

102   Carson, *Christ & Culture Revisited*, 64.

tradition, and sees other cultures as merely different ways of looking at the world. He fails to see other cultures as embodying entirely different epistemologies that demand more intimate discussions of the relationship between Christ and lived culture.

A Methodist Theological Proposal: Long

D. Stephen Long wrestles with the conditioning effect of the cultural in theology. Though designed as an introduction to the debates, his initial argument that "culture" is a metaphor is quite promising.[103] His reflections on culture are very specific, focusing primarily or almost exclusively on human language. The metaphor culture carries for him the implications for his "linguistic turn;" language is in large part what he means by the metaphor culture.[104]

Based on this approach, he disagrees with Niebuhr's five typologies. His problem with Niebuhr's proposal is that Niebuhr considers both Christ and culture as 1) clearly defined realities; 2) easily identifiable; 3) related to issues of citizenship and civilization; and 4) within a Eurocentric system of thought.[105] Instead, Long finds culture (read the cultural) to be much harder to define and slippery; for him culture is based on human activity and functions like a totalizing frame. His awareness of cultural plurality leads him to wonder whether God is anything other than a "product of culture and language." Of course, Long does not think so, but the consideration helps him explore the conditioning role of culture in theological assumptions.[106] In keeping with his culture as metaphor idea, he posits that the language we use to speak about God is more like a "rule of grammar" than an exact mental description. Cultures are internally inconsistent frames that provide unstable identities; stable identities do not exist except when differences are being forced to fit into "the strictures of a single interpretation."[107]

Long sees culture and theology as inextricably linked because language is crucial for theology. But they must be kept separate as well since they are utterly distinct. The best guidelines he can muster to explain the relationship between theology and culture (or Christ and culture for that matter) is to be

---

103   Stephen Long, *Theology and Culture*, 8–9.

104   Ibid., 23.

105   Long, *Theology and Culture*, 63. Long thinks that Niebuhr was immersed in his own European intellectual tradition, so much so that without his influences—Throeltsch and Wever, his theology of culture could not have been possible. See Ibid., 62.

106   Long, *Theology and Culture*, 38–39.

107   Ibid., 99.

found in the incarnation, where God in human form existed as one person, human and divine, without mixing and without separating the human and divine natures. Thus, we are back to the Christ and culture question, which for Long results in a radical distinction of these two despite their interconnectedness. The implication is that if cultures are nothing but the result of human activity, then culture is distinct from grace, from God's transcendence. He elaborates this distinction, as "'culture' is not a gift to be received from God outside of immanent human activity; it is only one we humans create and do."[108]

The radical distinction between the two does not prevent culture and theology from interacting, says Long. In fact, discussing Tillich's understanding of culture as the expression of religion, He explains how he sees that these two are interwoven. As he views it, culture poses questions which theology then answers, but such answers are given in cultural form, which then again raise further questions. In this interactive cycle, the theological responses are themselves cultural artifacts.[109] But the difference remains between culture and Christ: there is a difference between the way we talk about God and that about which we talk, i.e., God. The former is a cultural artifact![110]

In dealing with culture as metaphor, and by emphasizing his linguistic turn, Long signals a move away from culture as referring merely to questions of civilization and the larger social context. Though he does engage issues of modernity and postmodernity, he surprisingly and too quickly dismisses contextual theologies[111] and liberation currents that oppose European dominant versions of theology and epistemologies.[112] As I explained above, he is deeply aware of the conditioning effect of the cultural context. His awareness of the dynamic interaction between theology and culture is certainly refreshing and creative. But his theology becomes the very obstacle to furthering his understanding of the cultural and how it relates to Christ because he sees them as radically distinct. He simply cannot stomach Tanner's idea (below) that Christian theology and Christian faith both use the material from the culture/society of which

---

108   Ibid., 66.

109   Ibid., 73–74.

110   Ibid., 74.

111   Although there is great debate among notions of contextual theologies, generally these scholars insist that theologies emerge from and must respond to people's economic, social, political and cultural contexts. In other words, all theologies are contextual. See Angie Pears, *Doing Contextual Theology* (New York, NY; London, UK: Routledge, 2010); Stephen B. Bevans, *Models of Contextual Theology* (Maryknoll, NY: Orbis Books, 1992).

112   Long, *Theology and Culture*, Chapter 10.

they are part.[113] His fear of "syncretism as relativism" and the assumption that there are truth claims that can be established without the cultural and without conversation with other cultural groups betray his cultural framing. He is blind to the fact that his views of God, faith, Christ, etc., are deeply conditioned and shaped by his own Euro North American cultural tradition, which he cannot escape. Somehow, his Christ turns into something that transcends the cultural and is not in any way impacted by cultures.

Christ and Culture *in the Global South: Trimiew, Fujiwara and Fukue*

Niebuhr's *Christ and Culture* has also had enormous influence outside the Global North: Euro North America (United States of America and Canada), Western Europe, Australia and New Zealand. Scholars from the Global South have offered their own insights as to how we can understand the relation between Christianity and the cultural,[114] many of them still alluding to Richard Niebuhr's classic work since it first was published. A fuller discussion would require a book length project. One instance is Darryl Trimiew's reflection from an African American perspective. He contends that Niebuhr's work remains a useful heuristic device but it needs to be "relativized, particularized and trans-mogrified" by those communities who experience oppression.[115] To that end, he engages in a rethinking of Niebuhr's Christ-transformer-of-culture typology from the perspective of the oppressed. The two key issues here are the agency of the oppressed and the nature of the transforming Christ. For Trimiew, these two meet in a critique of Niebuhr when he asserts that the oppressed "have a different conceptualization of Christ and of culture" than Niebuhr's picture of Christ permits. More to the point, Niebuhr did not see the oppressed as playing a significant transformational role as cultural agents.[116]

---

113 Ibid., 100.

114 For other contributions dealing with questions of Christ and culture see John S. Mbiti, "Christianity and African Culture," *Journal of Theology for Southern Africa* 20 (1977): 26–40; Virgilio Elizondo, *Christianity and Culture: An Introduction to Pastoral Theology and Ministry for the Bicultural Community* (Huntington Indiana: Our Sunday Visitor Inc., 1975); Yang Hullin, *China, Christianity, and the Question of Culture* (Waco, TX: Baylor University Press, 2014); Mikka Ruokanen and Paulos Huan, eds., *Christianity in Chinese Culture* (Grand Rapids, MI: William B. Eerdmans, 2010); Ke Joon Lee, *Theology of Korean Culture* (Seoul, Korea: Christian Literature Society of Korea, 2002).

115 Darryl M. Trimiew, "Jesus Changes Things: A Critical Evaluation of *Christ and Culture* from an African American Perspective," *Journal of the Society of Christian Ethics* 23, no. 1 (2003): 158.

116 Ibid.

But not all transformative cultures are the same, and the tendency toward creating hierarchies among them is a clear and present danger. Indeed, certain Christian practices were generated or upheld by certain Christian communities as morally superior to others.[117] For Trimiew, many of these practices point to specific Christologies. He engages in a historical retrieving which emphasizes oppressive practices like genocide, violent segregation, and religious intolerance. He brings the point home by stating that "the Christ of the Afrikaner apartheid-supporting church" at one point was seen as a "transformative Christ" but it was also a Christ of oppression, brutal and unjust.[118] It is in this space of competing Christs that Trimiew reclaims the Christ-against-culture type for African Americans, as a way to bring about transformation. His blending of two categories stems from his realization that Niebuhr's types are merely signposts of how Christian communities might act in the world with regard to specific circumstances. Most assuredly, he adds, "no black churches act monolithically within any one typology."[119]

Trimiew weaves questions of Christ and the cultural together in ways that are both theologically and culturally challenging. While drawing from Niebuhr, he demonstrates the limitations of conceiving hard-and-fast categories as initially perceived by Niebuhr. He shows that the vantage points of the oppressed provide levels of meaning as yet uncovered in debates on Christ and culture. Still, Trimiew remains subject to Niebuhr's demarcation of the debates. His experience as an African American proves helpful, yet he leaves his African American cultural background and theological view of Christ disengaged, in terms of how they impact the ways he (and other African Americans as well) understands and expresses his faith in God.

Atsuyoshi Fujiwara is yet another instance of the powerful influence of Niebuhr's work among other ethnocultural groups. His is a contribution toward a theology of the cultural from the context of Japan.[120] In dialogue with what he calls "authentic theology in the West," and engaging the works of Niebuhr,

---

117   Ibid., 159.

118   Ibid.

119   Ibid., 162.

120   Atsuyoshi Fujiwara, "Theology of Culture in a Japanese Context: A Believers' Church Perspective," Ph.D. dissertation (Durham, UK: University of Durham, 1999), Http:// etheses.dur.ac.uk/4301/1/4301_1821.pdf?UkUDh:CyT (accessed November 9, 2015). See also the book form of his dissertation: Atsujoshi Fujiwara, *Theology of Culture in a Japanese Context: A Believers' Church Perspective*, Princeton Theological Monograph Series (Eugene, OR: Pickwick Publications, 2012) and Atsuyoshi Fujiwara, "A Fresh Encounter with Jesus," *Christianity Today*, 25 July 2013, Http://www.christianitytoday.com/ct/2013/ july-august/fresh-encounter-with-jesus.html (accessed November 9, 2015).

Yoder, and Hauerwas, he reflects on the status/reception of Christianity in Japan.[121] He states his purpose is to undertake "a theological inquiry into what might constitute and authentic and vibrant Christianity for Japan through an analysis of the Christian faith and culture."[122] He is clear that his "theology of Japan" is not theology in Japan, Japanese theology, or theology for Japan, but a "theology which studies, considers, and understands *Japan* from a theological viewpoint."[123] Fujiwara does not want to create what he considers disdainfully an "Asian Christianity," by fusing Oriental traditions and Christianity. It appears that he assumes an acultural understanding of Christianity or that the Christianity he has inherited does not have (Western European) cultural baggage. His theology is a unique contribution to the debates on Christ-and-culture and is a self-directed critique of Japan's nationalism.[124]

Despite his particular critical focus on Japanese nationalism, Fujiwara still emphasizes the broad range of the cultural including the totality of all human products and the common understanding of a people. While he generally sides with fundamental aspects of Yoder's and Hauerwas's theologies, he also is critical of their positions, particularly for the lack of taking seriously the human component of revelation in the former, and the failure to adequately explain the adoption of pacifism as the only criteria for identifying communities as legitimately Christian in both.[125] There are other critiques that Fujiwara casts against these scholars, but the most important one for the purpose of this conversation is against Yoder's inability to give sufficient attention to the human dimension in the reception of divine revelation and in the production and the interpretation of the Scriptures. The human dimension is crucial! Yoder, he states, is preoccupied with discussing how the Bible can be of value to us today in our situations at the expense of the human contribution. Instead, Fujiwara highlights the "interwoven transformational grammar" to claim that Jesus is Lord. Yoder presumes, he writes, that "every Christian can read the Scriptures 'correctly and in the same way as he does'."[126] He continues: "Both Yoder and Hauerwas seem to believe that they know the truth on which everyone should agree at the end, which appears to be quite arrogant."[127]

---

121 Atsuyoshi Fujiwara, "Theology of Culture in a Japanese Context," 1.

122 Ibid., 13.

123 Ibid., 284.

124 Ibid., 304.

125 Ibid., 116–26.

126 Atsuyoshi Fujiwara, "Theology of Culture in a Japanese Context," 125. While Yoder critiques Niebuhr's position on the Trinity, Fujiwara accuses Yoder of falling into a monotheism of the Son.

127 Atsuyoshi Fujiwara, "Theology of Culture in a Japanese Context," 88.

While Fujiwara attempts to chart his own path, the influence of the Western European Christian tradition remains unexamined and cannot be undone even as he engages three notable Japanese theologians. On one hand, he tells us that Kazoh Kitamori was the most self-consciously Japanese theologian— "affirming the indigenization of the Gospel, using Japanese concepts such as *higeki* [tragedy], *tsurasa* [pain, bitterness, or sadness], and *tsutsumu* [embracing or enfolding]."[128] On the other hand, he critiques the tendency to indigenization because it prevented Kitamori from critiquing Japanese culture with the Christian faith. Again, it seems that Fujiwara thinks of Christianity as an acultural phenomenon since he still celebrates Kitamori for not "amalgamating the Christian faith with Japanese culture."[129] He is less critical of Yasuo Furuya who pays more attention to questions related to the reception of Christianity in Japan. And he sides with Hideo Ohki's critical stance against liberation theologies,[130] because he (Ohki) thought that these currents overused the language of theology. Resonating with traditional critiques of liberation theologies, Ohki argued that these streams placed themselves as subjects of theology, something which is only reserved for God. Fujiwara celebrates Ohki for his move, and emphasizes again that his goal is to consider "Japan" from the viewpoint of "God."[131] Overall, it is very clear that for him his Japanese cultural tradition is of little significance, in comparison to how he sees Christianity. While he sees the cultural as broad and fluid, he does not think it plays a significant role in revelation. His own Western European theological training (and conditioning) shapes his approach and blinds him to the (Western European) cultural content of his own version of the Christian tradition.

Hitoshi (Paul) Fukue offers yet another attempt to deal with the question of Christ and the cultural.[132] In conversation with Niebuhr and Geertz, and

---

128   Ibid., 279.

129   Ibid., 280.

130   As I explained earlier, liberation scholars emphasize the central protagonist role of those people who live in condition of economic poverty and oppression, and socially disenfranchised in understanding historical events. They adopt the notion of the "preferential option for the poor and the oppressed" and interrogate present social structures as they privilege one sector of society over others. In terms of theology, liberation scholars affirm that theology must include a critical engagement of and response to the social, political and economic context in which people find themselves with especial attention to the poor and marginalized in society.

131   Atsuyoshi Fujiwara, "Theology of Culture in a Japanese Context," 304.

132   Hitoshi (Paul) Fukue, "Beyond Christ and Culture," *The Mediator* 3, no. 2 (2002): 1–10, Http://www.apnts.edu.ph/resourcecenter/mediator/Fukue_Behind%283.2%29.pdf (accessed, November 3, 2015).

in contrast to Fujiwara, in a brief article he categorically states that there
is "no single absolutely right expression of faith which applies anywhere
anytime."[133] In dialogue with other Japanese intellectuals, he recounts an
instance in which the novelist Shusaku Endo "confessed that he felt as if
he put on western clothes which did not quite fit him." Likewise, priest Yoji
Inoue commented on the foreignness of the Christian faith and wished "to
find a faith which touched the heart of the Japanese sentiment."[134] Unlike
Fujiwara, he welcomes the liberationist impetus. Together with c.s. Song he
encourages Asian Christians to attend to the Bible with "our minds and hearts
in our cultural context."[135] For Fukue, the central concern is to discover the
meaning of the Word of God but without the people having to relinquish
their cultural, intellectual and religious legacies. Fukue shows the complexity of these issues. Indeed, the connection with Western Christianity cannot
be set aside as it reveals human weaknesses in religious wars, exploitation
and colonialism carried out in the name of God. Yet, it was through their
witness and missional passion that Asians came to know Christ. The solution, he claims, is the adoption of an "interpenetrating approach" that will
enrich both Asian and Western Christians. Asians and Western Christians
will interpenetrate each other with their own unique understanding of faith
and greatly contribute to each other.[136] Wanting to move beyond the Christ
and culture tensions, Fukue appropriately pushes for an appreciation of
Japanese culture and traditions. The specter of Western theological influence appears yet again though when he makes sure not to "fall into religious
syncretism."[137]

Bridging the Debates on the Cultural

More than any other author of his time, Niebuhr was aware of the tensions,
complications, complexities, and multiple factors involved in discussing the

---

133   Ibid., 5–6.
134   Ibid., 4.
135   Ibid., 7.
136   Fukue, "Beyond Christ and Culture," 8. In the interpenetration approach, "Asian Christians
      will continue to learn greatly from the western understanding and history of Christian
      faith but at the same time attempt to explore Asian expression of faith with keen sensi-
      tivity to Asian culture and history. In this approach, western Christians and theologians
      will also learn from Asian expressions of faith and perhaps find fresh perspectives in their
      understanding of faith" (Ibid.).
137   Fukue, "Beyond Christ and Culture," 5.

relationship between Christianity and the cultural sphere. Still, the cultural/ culture and Christ remain separated in his work because they are perceived as inhabiting two different existential planes. I propose that one of the key reasons for which Niebuhr and some of his contemporaries—discussed in the previous chapter[138]—conceived this relation as an "enduring problem" is because they saw Christ, the Gospel, and God as wholly other, something transcendent and entirely out of this world.[139] In contrast, the cultural dimension is viewed by them as something entirely from this world.

In my view, such an understanding of God and Christ displays left over vestiges of quasi-platonic tendencies that do not allow us to explore the imminent character of Christ in the incarnation and through the Spirit. The position does not allow us to view culture as closely connected to God. Still, even in the midst of his narrow Christology—and unlike Schilder, Van Til, Herridge, Machen, Tillich and Meland—Niebuhr hinted at the possibility of other perspectives. Although it is uncertain whether he already had cultural diversity in mind, he, like Tillich, rejected any tendency to absolute statements on the matter.[140] Furthermore, he emphasized the fragmented character of our faith and the role of the historical community in exploring the relation between Christianity and the cultural.[141] At the same time, and like his contemporaries, Niebuhr left little room for considering the impact of the cultural dimension on our understanding of the Christian faith and Christ. He does go as far as affirming the connection between the cultural and humanity: no one person is purely a natural being;[142] they always become human in "culture" and are penetrated

---

138 Niebuhr is well aware of the many authors who have engaged these questions of Christianity and culture during or prior to his time. It is from this perspective, I argue, that he views the relation of Christianity and culture as an "enduring problem." See Niebuhr, *Christ and Culture*, 230 note 1.

139 As he wrote: "... belief in Jesus Christ by men [*sic*]in their various cultures always means belief in God. No one can know the Son without acknowledging the Father. To be related in devotion and obedience to Jesus Christ is to be related to the One to whom he undeviatingly points" (Niebuhr, *Christ and Culture*, 27–28).

140 Niebuhr, *Christ and Culture*, 239.

141 Niebuhr, *Christ and Culture*, 244–45. It is worth noting that Niebuhr leaves the door open for the possibility that the relation between Christianity and culture can be configured differently depending on the community of which one is part. This aspect is crucial because, for him, no single historical group can be "said to constitute the church to the exclusion of others." See Ibid., 256.

142 According to Niebuhr, "we cannot escape culture any more readily than we can escape nature, for 'the man of nature, the *Naturmensch*, does not exist ...'" (Niebuhr, *Christ and Culture*, 39).

by "culture."[143] Nevertheless, how cultural conditioning impacts the Christian faith still remains unaddressed.

I propose that Niebuhr's project marks a shift toward broader considerations of the relation between Christ and the cultural, not so much for what it proposes but because of its limitations; the limitations point towards the ways in which the debates need to be opened up. The trajectory of the debates concerning the relationship of Christ and the cultural has changed significantly. While Niebuhr's work continues to be a useful frame for thinking about these questions for some, it appears that for others it has also become the very obstacle to moving the debates forward.[144] The limitations of Niebuhr's typologies have become too problematic to continue using them in the process of advancing theological reflections on the relationship of Christ and the cultural.[145] Those who adopt Niebuhr's framing find themselves trapped in the predicament of attempting to advance a false dualism that is no longer sustainable or adequate. (I do not think it ever was adequate). Many other Christians in the world are reclaiming their cultures as an appropriate prism for celebrating and expressing their faith. They are abandoning inherited Eurocentric totalizing perspectives like Niebuhr's and its accompanying permutations in Carter, Frame, Friesen and Carson.

In light of present constantly shifting global contexts and especially of growing multicultural societies, it is understandable that there is need to open up the debates to include other cultures in the conversation as Trimiew, Fujiwara, and Fukue have attempted to do. But their uncritical adoption of an acultural vision of Christianity and Christ blinds them to further possibilities. Trimiew and Fujiwara reclaim human agency in these conversations, but neglect to recognize that all human agency is also cultural agency. Long and Fukue move ahead in creative ways by acknowledging the conditioning role of the cultural (Long) and by establishing a crossfertilization between cultural traditions (Fukue), but their goal is curtailed because their inherited Eurocentric theologically motivated concerns of "syncretism."

---

143   Niebuhr, *Christ and Culture*, 69.

144   For other works that draw on Niebuhr as springboard to wrestle with issues of missions see Santosh Thomas, *Christianity and Culture* (New Delhi, India: Mittal Publications, 2005); Charles H. Kraft, *Christianity in Culture: A Study in Dynamic Biblical Theologizing in Cross-Cultural Peerspective* (Maryknoll, NY: Orbis Books, 2005); Xongxia Song and Richard J. Mouw, "Christ and Culture in Contemporary China: Exploring Theological Options," Ph.D. dissertation (Pasadena, CA: Fuller Theological Seminary, 2011).

145   For other works that drawn on Niebuhr as springboard to wrestle with issues of missions see Thomas, *Christianity and Culture*; Kraft, *Christianity in Culture*; Song and Mouw, "Christ and Culture in Contemporary China."

All the authors here mentioned are haunted by a moralizing tendency and overemphasis on the impact and presence of sin in the cultural. To repeat, this moralizing tendency contributes to their quick dismissal of the cultural, to maintain a wedge between Christ and the cultural, and to paint a vision of a beleaguered church desperately seeking ways not to be co-opted by the *unredeemed world*. As a result, these authors are unable to find in the cultural a place of divine outworking and theological reflection. Particular about these authors is the move away from a Niebuhrian framing toward a reconsideration of the multiple points of intersection between Christianity and the cultural. Such move allows them to reconfigure our understanding of the cultural in ways that more deliberately acknowledge the complexity of these debates while considering cultural diversity. In what follows, I discuss other approaches that endeavor to deepen our understanding of Christ/Christianity/gospel and the cultural, which add further complexity to these conversations.

CHAPTER 6

Reviving the Debates on Christ and Culture in Contemporary Protestantism

"The culture" appears to be an aggressive challenger to "the church," and Christians keep worrying what to do about it. You soon get the impression that Church Inc. and Culture Amalgamated are like two corporations confronting each other at a negotiating table. Over there sits Culture—huge, complex, and self-absorbed. It's powerful, dangerous, unpredictable, and turbulent. Church is smaller, anxious; it studies Culture, trying to figure out a way to weasel in.[1]

FREDERICA MATHEWES-GREEN

• • •

The church in Latin America in the context of poverty and oppression must proclaim liberation and good news to the poor; the church in Asia in the context of religious pluralism and caste must speak of dialogue and human dignity ...; The church in Africa in the context of traditional religions must draw on traditional wisdom and deal with the spirit world ...; and the West must challenge its growing secularism.... The global church needs to develop vital theologies that incorporate a rich diversity of theological approaches emerging out of varied experiences throughout the world.[2]

PAUL HIEBERT

Introduction

Theological reflections on the cultural multiplied at the end of the twentieth and beginning of the twenty-first century. Christians from different

---

1 Frederica Mathewes-Green, "Loving the Storm-Drenched.
2 Paul G. Hiebert, "Gospel and Culture: The WCC Project," *Missiology: An International Review* XXV, no. 2 (April 1997): 203.

cultural contexts and traditions have been reexamining earlier positions on
the relationship between Christianity/ the Gospel and the cultural. Intentional
explorations of the impact of cultural background on our understanding of
Christianity have increased awareness of the plurality of cultures and cultural groups in the world. In addition, the ending of many colonial regimes, a
renewed commitment "not to repeat the mistakes of the past" in the missionary movement, the accelerated growth of globalization, the desire for Christian
unity, and the emergence of local movements of resistance can be cited as
forces energizing this new wave of interest in these debates. With the greater
participation of the peoples of the world in these discussions another shift is
taking place; their contributions unveil new dimensions and challenge earlier
notions of the relationship between Christianity and the cultural.

In this chapter, my goal is to provide a brief sampling of the diverse set of
recent scholars who are rethinking the role of the cultural in the Christian
faith. To repeat, I use *the cultural* to signal the complex set of inherited codes
and activities passed down from generation to generation through processes
of culturalization that define, shape, condition, and impact the ways humans
engage life, and interact with their immediate environment, each other and
the divine. By using *the cultural*, I also highlight the fact that all human collectives and individuals engage in cultural activities and participate in the construction of cultural elements and traditions.

In some sectors, the World Council of Church (WCC) has acted as catalyst
for deeper worldwide local undertakings to understand how local cultures and
communities make sense of the intersection of Christ and the cultural/cultural
traditions. How the WCC has shifted more attention toward issues of the cultural is the content of the first part of this chapter. In the second part, I discuss
how a new generation of scholars go beyond Niebuhr's opus and offer new
directions for considering the dynamic interconnections between "Christ" and
"culture." In the work of each of these authors a dualism can still be detected;
the cultural seems to be conceived of as incompatible and at times simply
irreconcilable with Christ. I argue that to go beyond inherited approaches,
there is a need to think more critically about how the most basic aspects of
the cultural operate in shaping the way people understand and approach the
gospel and God, and how God can be imagined as active in the cultural sphere.

A slippage of interwoven multiple meanings will become abundantly evident
in every one of the authors I consider in the ways they deploy and reflect on the
dualism of Christ and the cultural. As with previous chapters, I preserve their
use of the singular "culture." I hasten to add, however that despite their use of
the singular culture, there is a multiplicity of meanings: 1) sometimes referring
to a socially plural context, Christ and culture really mean the relationship of

the church to the larger (secularized) social context; 2) in a context of cultural plurality, Christ and culture refers to the gospel in the process of evangelization of the cultures of the world; and 3) in a context of cultural plurality religious plurality is often assumed, so Christ and culture also point to Christianity in relation to other religions. It is this ambiguity in the use of the singular *culture* that I find problematic, but for the sake of this discussion I preserve it. Notwithstanding their use of the singular "culture," in most instances these scholars are writing about the complex processes of culturalization I dub "the cultural."

The WCC and the Rethinking of Gospel and Culture

The ecumenical movement played a key role in redirecting the debates on Christ and the cultural. Prior to World War II the tendency was to contrast the gospel/Christianity and other religions; the cultural was assumed as the outer expression of different religions. The move toward a reconsideration of the cultural preceded the founding of the WCC; small pockets of cultural engagement and resistance against European supremacy began popping-up in the nineteenth century. For instance, as early as 1821 an African Independent Church was formed in Sierra Leone because of people's discontent with white missionaries. By 1890, similar churches began being formed in Nigeria. Today they are a major sector in African Christianity.[3] Let us consider another example. In 1938, the International Missionary Council at Tambaram, India, focused on two main questions: How Christians should relate to non-Christians and how missionaries should respond to the fact that the young churches around the world were copies of the Western churches that planted them and therefore foreign to their own contexts?[4] In yet another instance, Humphrey Waweru reports how the 1955 meeting in Accra, Ghana, argued for a continuity between African religions and Christianity. Finally, in 1969, in the Third All-African Conference of Churches held in Abidjan, Ivory Coast, African theologians recommended the indigenization of liturgies and Africanization of doctrine.[5]

With the founding of the WCC (1948) ideas started trickling down, that the gospel needed to adopt values from other people's cultures.[6] Paul Hiebert

---

3 These churches were formed in order to express Christianity in ways more appropriate to the African experience and context. See Humphrey Waweru, M, *The Bible and African Culture: Mapping Transactional Inroads* (Eldoret, Kenya: Zapf Chancery, 2011), 50.

4 Hiebert, "Gospel and Culture," 199.

5 Waweru, *The Bible and African Culture*, 58.

6 Emilio Castro, "On Evangelism and Culture: Some Reflection," *International Review of Mission* 84, no. 335 (October 1995): 265–378.

writes that the "bewildering" variety of people and cultures that the missionary movement has encountered, the reemergence of identities and rise of nationalism around the world, and the personal encounters and experiences of missionaries with the people they ministered corresponded with the shift toward rethinking the role of culture in Christianity.[7] As he puts it, these multiple encounters contributed to the denigration of the term "civilization" as arrogant and ethnocentric and its replacement with "culture."

Hiebert points out that the change of words reflects a profound shift in the way Western Europeans and Euro North Americans viewed other peoples. Citing Bernard McGrane, he posits that the adoption of the concept "culture" has brought about the democratization of differences. The twentieth-century concept has "rescued the non-European other from the depths of the past and prehistory" and reasserted them in the present.[8] From a missionary perspective, all cultures came to be considered of unquestionable value, capable of receiving and embodying the gospel. The idea of a "pure gospel" that remained untainted by the cultural and could therefore be injected into the messy field of the cultural became unsustainable.[9]

The shift in the perception of other cultures was mirrored by the changing focus of the WCC conferences. The East Asia Conference (Bangkok, 1949) and the all Africa Conference of Churches (Ibadan, 1958) focused on the African and Asian cultural contexts respectively, calling missions to "present the gospel in the voices of the traditional cultures."[10] The 1962 conference in New Delhi affirmed the gospel not only as disruptive of the cultural but more importantly as a saving force of the deepest values of a cultural tradition. The Bangkok East Asia Christian Conference Assembly (1964) called for "self-emptying foreign ways in order to reclaim the Indigenous traditions;"[11] and the Bangkok 1973 meeting concluded that "culture shapes the human voice that answers the voice of Christ."[12]

The Nairobi summit in 1975 celebrated plurality as an opportunity for exchange between cultures. They also confirmed that the notion of "Christian culture" was fraught with cultural imperialism.[13] In ways that resonated with the Vatican II insights, they affirmed that "no culture is closer to Jesus than

---

7   Hiebert, "Gospel and Culture," 199.

8   Ibid., 200.

9   Michael Paul Gallagher, *Clashing Symbols: An Introduction to Faith and Culture* (Mahwah, NJ: Paulist Press, 1998), 62.

10   Hiebert, "Gospel and Culture," 200.

11   Ibid., 203.

12   Gallagher, *Clashing Symbols*, 60.

13   Ibid.

any other culture."[14] In this conference the idea of contextualization entered the ecumenical vocabulary. As Gallagher explains, "instead of the Barthian approach of judgment of culture by the gospel," the Council "diagnosed a more politico-cultural source of conflict in the 'unthinking imposition of Western customs' due in turn to the identification of 'Christian culture' with the West."[15] Hiebert adds that local churches challenged their Christians to live more actually in the cultures of their own people and to see their non-Christian neighbors not as "other peoples" but as "their peoples."[16]

The impetus toward embracing the culturally diverse human communities and churches in the Global South gained prominence in Vancouver (1983) as the Council's strong ecclesial focus could not avoid dealing with the multiple expressions of worship in the church. Meanwhile, the question of how the gospel should be experienced by local cultures came to the forefront in Cranberra (1991) when Professor Chung Hyun-Kyung invited the participants to listen to "the cries of creation and the cries of the Spirit within it."[17] And in 1996, the WCC Central Committee chose the topic of the Conference on World Mission and Evangelization to be held in Salvador, Brazil: "Called to One Hope: The Gospel in Diverse Cultures." The central concern was to redress the effects of early colonizing missionary approaches. Out of this study it became apparent that the gospel was still perceived as foreign. The displacement approach to missions had caused people to become estranged from their own older customs and adopt the customs of the missionaries.[18]

As Hiebert finds, the growing concern in the WCC and its national and local branches is "taking the gospel to people in their cultures rather than calling them to reject their old beliefs and practices."[19] However, welcoming other cultures is not the same as their wholesale acceptance. In fact, all cultures are believed to have negative factors that degrade humans and block the hearing of the Word. But they also have positive elements, "the human zone of

---

14   Gallagher, *Clashing Symbols*, 60. The Council rejected Western Culture and version of
      the gospel as the only acceptable Christian expression. The wanted to prevent the gospel
      from becoming hostage to any culture. See Ibid., 61.

15   Gallagher, *Clashing Symbols*, 60.

16   Hiebert, "Gospel and Culture," 200.

17   Cited in Hiebert, "Gospel and Culture," 200.

18   The First Nations in Canada and the case of the residential schools is a good example of
      how the gospel was imposed and local cultures destroyed. Another example is how the
      African clergy in South Africa were forbidden to wear native clothes and instead were
      instructed to wear European apparel. See Hiebert, "Gospel and Culture," 201–2.

19   Hiebert, "Gospel and Culture," 202.

imagination most capable of fostering new languages of faith ..."[20] Critical to this understanding is the general affirmation of the presence and activity of the Holy Spirit in the Christian Church, human history and various cultures.[21] The belief is that just as the gospel casts new light on each human situation, so also those human situations can also release different dimensions of the gospel into new life.[22]

Many other significant insights stem from the shift that took place in the ecumenical movement like the belief that a Christian unity ought not to be pursued at the expense of Christian particularity.[23] Greater recognition for contextual differences has become a central focus in ongoing conversation to the point that even theological reflection is now conceived as inextricably tied to particular contexts.[24] For Rino, it is clear that "if we take seriously the theological assumptions of the gospel transforming cultures from within, and if the gospel cannot be considered independent from its various cultural expressions," then there are no single universally applicable criteria for engaging these complex questions.[25] It is nevertheless important to keep in mind that the binomial "Christ" and "culture" refers to the tensions between gospel and larger social-cultural context, revelation and reception, and the encounter between the divine and the human. It does not often include questions of the gospel and other cultural traditions or in relation to the gospel and the more complex processes of culturalization.

Various authors respond to these questions in ways that clearly go beyond Niebuhr's proposal and in many ways, conceive the relationship between the cultural and the gospel much more closely. To that I now turn.

---

20   Ibid., 66.

21   Jeffrey Gros, "Word and Spirit, Church and World. The Final Report of the International Dialogue Between Representatives of the World Alliance of Reformed Churches and Some Classical Pentecostal Churches and Leaders 1996–2000," *Pneuma* 22, no. 1 (Spring 2001): 16.

22   Hiebert, "Gospel and Culture," 104.

23   The WCC's Uppsala assembly in 1968 reported that "Christ has to be responded to in a particular situation" (Hiebert, "Gospel and Culture," 203).

24   As Hieber writes, "The church in Latin America in the context of poverty and oppression must proclaim liberation and good news to the poor; the church in Asia in the context of religious pluralism and caste must speak of dialogue and human dignity (Selvanayagam 1996; Massey 1996); the church in Africa in the context of traditional religions must draw on traditional wisdom and deal with the spirit world (Pobee 1996); and the West must challenge its growing secularism (Davies 1996; Wessels 1996). The global church needs to develop vital theologies that incorporate a rich diversity of theological approaches emerging out of varied experiences throughout the world" (Hiebert, "Gospel and Culture," 203).

25   Cited in Hiebert, "Gospel and Culture," 205.

Rethinking the Role of the Cultural in the Christian Faith

Christianity and Culture, A Fluid Relationship: Tanner and Gallagher

Well ahead of her theological peers, Kathryn Tanner offers a twofold post-modern proposal which both challenges "modern" understandings of "culture" and responds to postliberal theological perspectives on the relation between Christianity and the larger cultural context. Discussing the question of Christian discipleship and Christian life, or whether it can be said that there is one set of practices that apply to all peoples everywhere, she insists on the cultural relational character of Christianity. "Modern" anthropology, she claims, dismantled ideas about differences between groups as grounded on racial or genetic variation that were in fact the result of cultural differences.[26] She reminds us of the origins of the Western European contemporary notion of culture with its roots in the debates and developments from England, Germany, and France.[27] Drawing from anthropology, she proposes a postmodern analysis which does away with cultural hierarchies or claims to cultural superiority.[28] Here is where she departs from "modern" views of anthropology: "culture," she points out, is an abstraction drawn from the concrete facts of socially significant behaviors.[29] But for anthropologists, cultural elements must cohere and be integrated preventing them from seeing the contingent character of culture.[30] They are too preoccupied with preserving the internal

---

26   Kathryn Tanner, *Theories of Culture*, 3.

27   According to her, each of the countries emphasized the notion of culture differently. For example, Germans had two notions to speak of culture: *Kultur* and *Buildung*; the former referring to the network of social institutions and advances while the latter referring to the "cultivation" of the individual. Meanwhile in France, it referred to the entire body of protocols and rule-patterns regulating human interaction, most often identified among the "upper" classes' fatidious observance of rules of conduct. And in England, it referred to the primacy of social influence on individuals, but which was articulated in evolutionary terms of superiority over other groups and individuals. For a fuller discussion see Tanner, *Theories of Culture*, 3–24.

28   Tanner, *Theories of Culture*, 3. According to her, Anthropology provoked a levelling effects by affirming culture as a human universal; culture was affirmed as constitutive of human nature. But since social groups are diverse and cultures are the product of social groups, diversity is inherent to the anthropological project on culture. See Ibid., 25–29.

29   Tanner, *Theories of Culture*, 31. To her, "the plastic character of human biology, cultural diversity, and the vagaries of human history combine to suggest strongly the contingent character of culture" (Ibid., 28).

30   Tanner, *Theories of Culture*, 32.

consistency of their interpretive frames of culture as texts or works of art, and as a result underestimate the evidence of inconsistencies, unevenness, and tensions at the everyday.[31]

Tanner charges that modern views of the cultural are vitiated with "nationalism, colonialism, and the power plays of intellectual elites."[32] One of the key problems with these notions of the cultural is the presumption that cultures are finished products and therefore consistent wholes.[33] In this position, every aspect of "culture" becomes "readable" and "decipherable." However, she insists that the interrelationship among cultures is far messier than they appear in abstract theory. Cultures are partly continual and integrated and partly fragmented. The demand for internal consistency seems to be an aesthetic demand from high culture rather than an anthropological one.[34] But the fundamental flaw in such notions is the separation of the cultural from its historical agents, from people's activities. Moreover, cultures are not air tight systems but are permeable making it difficult to define boundaries.[35]

Tanner's postmodern view of cultures spills over into her view of Christianity.[36] In contrast to postliberal positions which claim a clearly definable version of Christianity and Christian culture, she correctly describes Christianity as participating in a borrowing relationship of elements from the larger cultural context. In the same way, theological descriptions of missions, that is, the spread of Christianity by evangelization should be seen as the study of "enculturations."[37] These are, she muses, a series of processes

31   Tanner, *Theories of Culture*, 38. Anthropologists, she notes, have also ignored the conflicting evidence of presumptions of stasis of consensus. In fact, "determinacy, closure, and consistency are no more to be expected in the tacit cultural forms of every day life than they are in formalized and explicit ones" (Ibid., 39).

32   Tanner, *Theories of Culture*, 38. She goes further stating that the "way an anthropologist describes a culture is ideological in the sense that it disguises the unequal workings of power both within the society studied and between the anthropologists and his or her subjects" (Ibid., 40).

33   Tanner, *Theories of Culture*, 42.

34   Ibid., 44.

35   Ibid., 53–56.

36   Consistent with her postmodern understating of culture, she outlines her own view of Christianity: Christian communities are not self-contained nor self-sufficient; Boundaries between Christian and non-Christians are permeable; what Christians have in common has nothing to do with the practices themselves (the forms). For this reason, what unites Christians is the concern for true discipleship. See Tanner, *Theories of Culture*, 150–53.

37   Tanner, *Theories of Culture*, 62.

by which Christianity adopts elements from other cultures. In sync with her postmodern critique, she argues that there is no such thing as Christian culture that can be easily identified or have its boundaries demarcated. Christianity does not have a unique social system and can be compared to anyone other "way of life"/culture. When it comes to interacting with the larger social context, Christianity manages to encompass a fuller range of human functions only by incorporating institutional forms from elsewhere. For example, in order to become a social alternative to the Roman Empire, Christian social practices had to borrow cultural elements from the very society they opposed.[38] In a very real sense then, Christianity is dependent on other cultures and social practices. Christian social practices are essentially parasitic; Christianity "has to establish relations with other ways of life; it has to take from them, in order to be one itself."[39] For these reasons, she concludes, it is more adequate to think of Christianity as a subculture. Moreover, contrary to the influential views of Richard Niebuhr, she argues that in the Christian case relations with the wider cultural context are never simply relations of accommodation, opposition or radical critical revision, "but always some mixture."[40]

Tanner's postmodern corrective posits that the postliberal claims which uphold the notion that there are sharp differences between Christian social practices and those of others are a futile endeavor. There are no clearly definable boundaries between Christianity and the larger society; Christianity is a composite of Christian and non-Christian social practices which form a voluntary association within a wider society, rather than a separate society in and of itself.[41] Christian communities are neither self-contained nor self-sufficient; Christian identity is therefore not "a matter of unmixed purity, but a hybrid affair established through unusual uses of materials found elsewhere."[42] The postliberal idea that a Christian way of life is self-defining and can be therefore properly analyzed is mistaken and seems to be motivated by an apologetic "laudable goal of keeping a Christian way of life from being simply subsumed by some other ..."[43] Because Christianity is always borrowing materials in order

---

38   Tanner, *Theories of Culture*, 98. She provides another example affirming that "Christianity simply does not have a school system of its own in that sense: it takes one over from elsewhere, and shapes it to its own needs, or does without" (Ibid.).

39   Tanner, *Theories of Culture*, 113.

40   Ibid., 119.

41   Ibid., 103.

42   Ibid., 152.

43   Ibid., 111.

to make up Christian words and deeds, there is strictly speaking no such thing as a "Christian something," independent from the wider society. Christians do not generate cultural artefacts all of their own. Rather, they have to make do "with materials that they do not themselves produce; they create meaning through a process of consumption."[44]

Thus, for Tanner, the attempt to "purify" Christian practices from outside influences out of the fear of possible corruption of the faith are futile. Even the most "distorted" Christian practices, she claims, are already beneficial, as reminders of errors that should be avoided.[45] Consistent with her view of diversity in cultures, Tanner upholds the diversity of Christian expressions and theologies. Diversity is for her the antidote to the postliberal presumption of a universal Christian identity and one Christian culture. She writes: "Christian identity does not mean in any strong sense that all Christians share a common set of beliefs and values. Contrary to the famous Vincent of Lerins, all Christians have not everywhere and at all times believed the same things."[46]

Latino scholar Rubén Rosario welcomes Tanner's goal not to eliminate the modern understanding but to "de-centre" dominant conceptualizations in order to give greater attention to the role of humans as culture creating agents.[47] Her theological proposal disrupts current perspectives which maintain a wedge between the cultural and Christianity and the cultural and theology. Her proposal also counters ideas about single universally applicable notions of Christianity and theology. As far as she is concerned, because Christianity borrows elements from cultures and adapts them to its own interests, the theological task is therefore also a cultural activity.[48] She closes the logical circle: since cultural activity is a characteristic of being human, to say that theology is a part of the cultural is a way to talk about theology in terms of what it means to be human.[49] Drawing on semiotics (and echoing Geertz), she writes that "culture refers to the whole social practice of meaningful action, and more specifically to the meaning dimension of such action—the beliefs, values, and orienting symbols that suffuse a whole way of life."[50] She prefers

---

44   Ibid., 112.
45   Ibid., 113, 155.
46   Ibid., 124.
47   Rubén Rosario Rodríguez, "No Longer Jew Nor Greek but *Mestizo*? The Challenge of Ethnocentrism for Theological Reconstruction," Ph.D. dissertation (Princeton, New Jersey: Princeton Theological Seminary, 2005), 135.
48   Tanner, *Theories of Culture*, 63.
49   Ibid., 64.
50   Ibid., 70.

to speak of the Christian theologian as a "postmodern Bricoleur," recognizing the activity of the theologian in making use of existing materials, pulling them apart and then putting them together in new creative ways.[51]

Tanner's treatment of the relation between Christianity and the cultural advances the debates significantly by identifying a dynamic fluid relation between the two. However, she does not help us in further understanding that relationship in theological terms. She reiterates the connection between the cultural and humanity, but does not go beyond such affirmation. Understandably, her postmodern project centres on the (her) Western European and Euro North American intellectual tradition, but she pays little attention to how notions of *culture* in France, Britain, and German (the countries she analyzed) were intimately woven within the imperial projects of these countries. Her postmodern perspective proves fruitful in her critique of "modern" notions but she does not critique her own Eurocentric vantage point foreclosing an engagement with notions of the cultural outside her own intellectual tradition.

Another postmodern perspective on the relationship between the cultural and faith is found in the work of Michael Paul Gallagher. Although he is an Irish Jesuit Priest, his proposal coincides with the Protestant views I am discussing here. It is for this reason that he is included in this section. Gallagher appropriately reminds us that, theologically speaking, culture (the cultural) is that important aspect that has been neglected and which only recently has taken centre stage.[52] Although he does not explicitly articulate a theology of culture, he does contribute important theological insights. He rehearses some of the developments in the relationship between faith and culture that have taken place among Catholics, specifically Vatican II and Pope John Paul II, and among Protestants, specifically the World Council of Churches. It is the official documents from these two important traditions of Christianity that he uses to express his own position.

Gallagher acknowledges that part of the increasing interests in Christ and culture debates relate to the global demographic shift of Christianity, growing outside of the richer countries of the Western European and Euro North American regions amidst increasing globalization of world communications. The demise of modernity and the emergence of postmodernity take a prominent role in his proposal, but only as markers of the cultural dynamics of the contemporary culture of secularization taking place outside the context of the Church.

---

51   Ibid., 166.

52   Gallagher, *Clashing Symbols*, 1–2.

Adopting a Geertzian approach,[53] he defines culture as

> the human learning space where the child develops its open-ended
> potentials for growth. And, unlike the animals, this adventure of cultural
> learning is 'not simply about behaviour. It is also about ideas', involving
> patterns of meaning, embodied in symbols, and subject to considerable
> evolution and even conscious change.[54]

With this broad definition, he situates his position insisting that cultural
activity is fundamentally related to human beings. There are three important
theological aspects here in relation to the question faith and culture. First, to
speak of culture is to speak of the very being of humanity. Any approach to
culture, then, cannot identify (read reduce) it only to specific cultural products or activities.[55] Consistent with *Gaudium et spes* he also affirms humans as
the architects of culture. Yet he goes further, drawing from Pope John Paul II's
statement that humans are the architects of culture, in which he (the Pope) is
not thinking of a "contemporary sensibility but of something in the very constitution of humanity."[56] In other words, there is an intimate connection between
being human and cultural activity: to be human is to create culture. Stated
differently, culture is " 'the second nature' of human beings in their social relations," as Konrad Raiser would say.[57] Culture, is the space where human beings
become more human. The plurality of cultures then means "different ways of
facing the question of the meaning of [human] existence."[58]

Second, for Gallagher culture relates to the transcendence of human beings.
Cultures are never a private matter but involve the common good of each people; it is always in community. It is in this sense of the collective nature of cultures that Gallagher suggests the possibilities of a Christian culture. Together
with Fernando Miguens, he is not promoting "a single Christian culture"
but many possible versions. Here again, he does not mean that Christianity

---

53   He is well aware of the many definitions of culture to his disposal. In fact, he reflects
      on the origins of the term culture tracing it back to Edward Tylor's *Primitive Culture* in
      1871 and he then discusses A. L. Kroeber and Clyde Kluckhohn (1963) *Culture: A Critical
      Review of concepts and Definitions*, which he classifies under six key categories: Descriptive
      accounts, historical dimension, normative elements, psychological function, structure of
      meaning, and genesis of culture. See Gallagher, *Clashing Symbols*, 14–15.

54   Gallagher, *Clashing Symbols*, 6.

55   Ibid., 49.

56   Ibid., 50.

57   Ibid., 57.

58   Ibid., 48.

can be stand-alone cultural phenomena, but that "different cultures can be Christianized."[59] His concern for Christian cultures relates more broadly to human interconnectedness. The cultural is that aspect which brings people together and places them in relationship with one another. Again, drawing on Pope John Paul II he asserts that culture unites humans "in what is most truly theirs, their common humanity."[60] In fact, he argues, the entire future of humanity is intimately linked with whatever happens in the field of culture. Most importantly, culture is also a space of human transcendence because of its role in the encounter with God. That is, culture plays a central role in "mediating the faith for people in diverse contexts of receptivity for the gospel."[61]

For this reason, one cannot conceive the gospel outside of the human dimension of the cultural. Together with the World Council of Churches, Gallagher agrees in this third point that, there is no timeless position of the gospel. Christianity, he says, requires embodiment.[62] "The one Christ now has many faces and all faith embodiments are cultural."[63] Chiding even some theologians of inculturation, he writes:

> Some theologians of inculturation talk as if there were an ahistorical 'essence of Christianity' waiting to be incarnated, which 'is to ignore the fact that Christianity never existed, not even in its first days, without being expressed in some cultural forms'; instead the adventure of Church history always means a 'meeting of cultures in search of a new and original expression of the one faith.'[64]

Tensions are inevitable in his proposal as he sees the gospel as universal and cultures as particular and local. These are not equal for him; cultures are subsumed to the gospel. Yet Gallagher wants to hold in each on his hands: the cultural embodiment of the gospel and its "transcultural independence." He finds it necessary to highlight the transcendent nature of the gospel while simultaneously affirming that it (the gospel) is "never accessible apart from specific cultures."[65] Siding with the Vatican's notion of inculturation, he argues that since all cultures are human constructs, they remain a source of ambiguity and in need of purification.

---

59   Ibid., 54.
60   Ibid., 52.
61   Ibid., 78.
62   Ibid., 83.
63   Ibid., 58.
64   Ibid., 103.
65   Ibid., 62.

We have come full circle now, as Gallagher considers more intentionally how culture and the gospel relate in relation to modernity-postmodernity's cultural developments. For him, modernity—that is, the outside culture of secularization—ought to be countered.[66] Here is where Gallagher's understanding of culture runs into difficulties. While on one hand he speaks of cultures as referring to the lived cultures of the world, in the same breadth he speaks of modernity-postmodernity as "cultures." It appears that, for him, modernity and now postmodernity are Western Europeans and Euro North American cultural embodiments. But it seems to me that he is conflating the idea of culture as a way of life, consistent with his own definition cited earlier (which coincides with my proposal of the cultural), with the philosophical range of intellectual schools behind the ideas of modernity and postmodernity within Western European and Euro North American cultures. It almost seems as if he does not consider the "West" to have any other cultural traits outside of modernity-postmodernity discourses.

Nevertheless, for him culture (read modernity and secularization) is "simply sick." Any attempt to view it positively will only lead to false compromises.[67] At times Gallagher seems to gravitate to a radical separation between Christianity and culture (read larger social context) because of the surreptitious negative effects of culture (read modernity). He even ponders the possibilities of bracketing one-self out of culture. Thus, adopting a kind of cultural ghettoism, he encourages believers to "protect themselves from cultural pollution by maintaining strong Church loyalty as a defense against this invading world of superficiality."[68]

In the end, Gallagher proposes three alternative responses to the current contemporary cultural situation of secularization: tense hostility, innocent acceptance, and discernment and creation of culture, which easily correspond with three of Niebuhr's paradigms: Christ against culture, Christ of culture, and Christ transformer of culture.[69] He seems to prefer the discernment option. But for him, the best alternative for the present cultural context is the

---

66   Gallagher is hesitant to date the beginning of modernity. He revisits some of the important instantiations of modernity in order to show its long lasting historical effects: The Renaissance, the Protestant Reformation, the emergence of the printing press with Gutenberg, Descartes and rationalism and subjectivism, the scientific revolution, the Enlightenment and the industrial revolution. See Gallagher, *Clashing Symbols*, 68–70.

67   Gallagher, *Clashing Symbols*, 117.

68   Ibid., 117.

69   Ibid.

development of a spirituality of culture.[70] He argues that while one cannot dismiss "contemporary culture," the "discernment of culture ... hinges on one's own spiritual disposition, and the resultant tone of one's dialogue with the culture."[71] All in all, while starting with great theological promise in terms of the human component in the relationship between the cultural and faith, Gallaguer loses steam, and in doing so reverts to a defensive position in the relationship between the Church and the larger cultural context. While he begins identifying the enormous possibilities of divine activity in the culture, his great concern about the negative impact of secularization-modernity and his inability to see it as fundamentally the product of particular European cultural streams, force him to find solutions by proposing the development of a spirituality of culture/the cultural without developing the larger social implications of such a proposal.

The Wholly Otherness of the Sacred and the Secular: Metzger

Paul Louis Metzger offers a perspective on the cultural based on his exploration of the work of Karl Barth. He draws on Barth in order to reframe debates on the relation of Christ and culture. Quite refreshingly, he presents Barth's theology as a response to a specific historical context, and as culturally conditioned.[72] Right from the beginning he tells us that Barth's theology undergoes profound changes, particularly after his disillusionment with the ninety three "cultural Christians" who supported the war policy and politics of Kaiser Wilhelm II and Chancellor Bethmann-Hollweg.[73] Barth's disenchantment related to the fact that they saw a close relation between German culture and Christianity, and saw in the "Nazi revolution an act of divine redemption and a source of divine revelation."[74] And it is in light of this ideological confrontation that Barth saw the need to rethink his own theology.

---

70   By spirituality of culture, Gallagher means, the development of a disciplined life that highlights people's experiences of faith, fosters growth in contemplative and committed love, and teaches practical skills to nourish a conscious relationship with God through prayer and other exercises. See Gallagher, *Clashing Symbols*, 138

71   Gallagher, *Clashing Symbols*, 123.

72   Paul Louis Metzger, *The Word of Christ and the World of Culture: Sacred and Secular Through the Theology of Karl Barth* (Grand Rapids, MI: William B Eerdmans Publishing Company, 2003), 153.

73   Metzger, *The Word of Christ and the World of Culture*, 10. According to Barth, Argues Metzger, these cultural Christians identified the kingdom of God with the Third Reich, position which was supposedly based on a second source of revelation and not the Scripture. See Ibid.

74   Metzger, *The Word of Christ and the World of Culture*, 29.

As part of this shift in his theological frame, Metzger avers, Barth critiqued Schleiermacher for his belief that there was continuity and close identification between Christ and (German) culture. In Schleiermacher, the ultimate affirmation of culture was its union with the divine.[75] Meanwhile, while Harnack had not accepted cultural ideas naively, he still saw the Gospel as the "fulfillment of all that is truly good in [German] culture."[76] These "German Christians," Barth said, deployed a natural theology through which they defended and justified the rise of the Third Reich, as the providential expression of a superior humanity. This theology inevitably turned Christ into "the midwife, helping humanity bring forth what has always been there within it, albeit implicitly, namely, its own participation in the divine nature."[77]

According to Metzger, as Barth returned to the biblical text, he realized that the critical theological move had to focus not on the human words about God but on God's word about humans. The theological orientation was, for Barth, that of divine descent rather than human ascent to the divine.[78] The shift for Barth had to be the affirmation of the *wholly other* character of God in relation to creation, humanity, and human culture(s). Contrary to attempts at deifying humanity, Barth argued that humanity has no capacity for the divine. Even the "human nature of Christ does not possess a capacity for the divine nature and its attributes."[79] Knowledge of the wholly other God did not depend on the human capacity to bring it to mind via a process of discursive reasoning. Rather, it depended upon God's self-revelation, which for Barth meant a dialectic move whereby God is revealed in hiddenness,[80] a hiddenness in history by which God assumed humanity (anhyspostatic-enhypostatic). Stated differently, "the eternal Word reveals himself [*sic*] in history through the otherness

---

75   Ibid., 35.

76   Another key figure critiqued by Barth because of their overt deification of German culture and humanity was Hegel, who insisted that God or Spirit required human consciousness to attain self-consciousness. For Hegel, God became conscious of himself through human consciousness through the course of history. Metzger, *The Word of Christ and the World of Culture*, 61.

77   Metzger, *The Word of Christ and the World of Culture*, 67.

78   Ibid., 8, 13.

79   Ibid., 49.

80   Metzger, *The Word of Christ and the World of Culture*, 31. According to Metzger, Barth upheld a notion of indirect revelation. For him, the Word was revealed in history only to be hidden again. God was unveiled and veiled in the historical person of Jesus Christ. See Ibid., 34.

of creatureliness."[81] Thus, in highlighting the Word's assumption of humanity, Barth was able to speak both of the transcendence and the immanence of God.[82]

According to Metzger, Barth's notion of revelation as concealment ensured the dedivinization of the world, nature and history. In this framing, God is wholly other, the world is not an extension of God, and nature and humans are not on their way to divinity.[83] The nature of the church is then crucial to define in this framing, which for Barth meant separation from the world. This separation (*diastasis*) between Church and the world ensured the church's freedom to witness Jesus Christ to the state. As Metzger sees it, Barth was too much of a modernist to want a return to Christendom, so he was all too happy for the dismantling of the *corpus christianum*; its fundamental problem was assuming that European society was thoroughly Christian.[84] The separation between church and the world did not mean for Barth that the church had no role in the world or that the divine was disconnected from the world.[85] Rather, by emphasizing *diastasis* the church was freed to confront the world with the gospel; its *secular* function is to bear witness to the state.[86] The church and the state each have their unique function. While the role of the church is exemplification and proclamation in the political realm, the state is called to govern society in a just manner befitting the kingdom. For this reason, sometimes the church may be called to speak out against an existing state for the sake of the true cause of

---

81   Metzger, *The Word of Christ and the World of Culture*, 37.

82   For Barth, notes Metzger, "The humanity of Christ, although it is body and soul, and an individual, is nothing subsistent or real in itself. Thus it did not exist prior to its union with the Logos. It has no independent existence alongside or apart from him.... The human nature of Christ has no personhood of its own. It is anhypostatos—the formula in which the description culminates. Or, more positively, it is enhypostatos. It has personhood, subsistence, reality, only in its union with the Logos of God" (Metzger, *The Word of Christ and the World of Culture*, 44)

83   Metzger, *The Word of Christ and the World of Culture*, 63.

84   Ibid., 85.

85   Barth preserves the tension between the world and the divine. "The creaturely reality known as humanity comes forth through the free act of creation by God and is taken to God in the event in which God takes humanity to himself in and through the eternal election of Jesus Christ. In and through God's election in Christ, the world, including human culture, is integrally related to God, but in a manner free of confusion" (Metzger, *The Word of Christ and the World of Culture*, 91).

86   When the church demands privileges from the state, noted Barth, it goes beyond its mandated role and abandons its freedom to witness to the state. See Metzger, *The Word of Christ and the World of Culture*, 177.

the state. When the state acts in an anti-Christian manner, "putting itself as the kingdom, the church must speak out against it."[87]

For Barth, argues Metzger, the church and humanity are inseparably related to Christ, although differently. While the Word did not identify with any creature, because of the incarnation, it enfolded and indwelled all creaturely reality, including human culture.[88] It is because of the humanity that the Word assumed, which cannot have existence apart from the Word, that all those possessing humanity are elect, and by analogical extension, so also are the Church and human culture.[89] That is, the elect are constituted as truly human persons,[90] after the Jesus Christ in whom God is revealed (however indirectly) and also true humanity is revealed. The highlighting of the incarnation of God in a concrete human, writes Metzger, allowed Barth to ensure that humanity and human culture would not be completely absorbed in God's word.[91] By the same token, it enabled him to steer clear from deifying / divinizing humanity and human culture.[92]

In Barth's incarnational theology, the historical particularity of Jesus Christ cannot be overemphasized. As he saw it, confirms Metzger, the Word is not amorphous but incarnate. As incarnate, the word is not generic humanity but Jewish flesh. More to the point, the Word is not simply incarnate but also enculturated.[93] And this enculturation did not take place in the abstract. For Barth, clarifies Metzger, one cannot retain Jesus Christ if one severs his Jewishness. This is the crux of the matter in terms of how the gospel relates to other cultural groups. However, one cannot stop at Jesus' Jewishness

---

87   Metzger, *The Word of Christ and the World of Culture*, 180. For Barth, observes Metzger, even when the church must go against culture, "it is because it seeks to exhort human culture to be fully human—to be what it is called to be" (Ibid., 95). For this reason, the gospel that the church preaches must have political implications and must speak to the issues of its time. See Ibid., 177.

88   Metzger, *The Word of Christ and the World of Culture*, 173.

89   Barth, explains Metzger, makes the distinction between the *de jure* election of the world, by which all are called, and the *de facto* election of the world by which some respond favorably to God's calling. Metzger also tells us that at times Barth so emphasizes the *de jure* election that it tends to overwhelm the *de facto* so much as to becoming itself *de facto*. See Metzger, *The Word of Christ and the World of Culture*, 96.

90   Metzger, *The Word of Christ and the World of Culture*, 64, 88. Humanity stands in distinct though inseparable relation to Jesus Christ, who is both true God and true human. See Ibid., 90.

91   Metzger, *The Word of Christ and the World of Culture*, 41.

92   Ibid., 64.

93   Ibid., 151.

either. The incarnation did not exhaust the Word! It is therefore opened to take form in other cultural contexts; it is transcultural.[94] But here Metzger reminds us that since for Barth the finite is incapable of the infinite,[95] there is nothing inherent in language or culture that enables it to witness to the Word. Rather, it is through the divine act of grace that God's Word stands in, with and over the "word" of culture, elevating it to "participate in the life of the Word."[96] God *elevates* the words of secular culture by giving them the function to witness to the Word even without transforming them in the process.[97] The Word in Jesus Christ enables other words to bear witness to him and take form in other cultures, again without being overwhelmed by those cultural forms.[98]

Barth's dedivinization and desecularization of the cultural, comments Metzger, also dismantle any idea of a universal amorphous Christianity. In this sense, both the enculturation and transcultural reality of the Word, in Barth's incarnational theology, make space for the church in every cultural tradition

---

94   Ibid., 154.

95   Metzger himself disagrees with Barth's idea that humanity could not reveal the divine. He counters Barth's ideas by stating that even the very humanity reveals God just as God reveals humanity. See Metzger, *The Word of Christ and the World of Culture*, 148–50.

96   Metzger, *The Word of Christ and the World of Culture*, 141.

97   As he says, "When God's Word becomes present to culture's word, it is not a matter of God's Word becoming culture's word or of culture's word becoming God's Word, except in a virtual sense." Later he adds,

> The word of culture can never be viewed as becoming the Word of God. It does not ascend to the Word whereby it is perfected and transformed into *the* Word....God does not perfect or transform the internal properties of words and their meanings, but rather, gives them, *new* meaning, *elevating* them to bear witness to the Word while preserving them in their creaturely integrity (Metzger, *The Word of Christ and the World of Culture*, 141).

98   In this theological dialectic, Barth seeks to preserve the sovereignty of the Word over against the human dimension. As Metzger clarifies,

> The incarnation is a dialectical reality. By entering the human sphere, the Word is not thereby fused with a particular culture, not even the culture in which the Word entered time and space as a human being, but is sovereign in relation to culture. Thus, not only is the Word enculturated but also it is transcultural. The enculturation of the Word does not lead to the overwhelming of that same Word by a particular culture. The Word transcends culture even in its enculturation (Metzger, *The Word of Christ and the World of Culture*, 154).

to bear witness to the Word through its cultural forms. As Metzger sees it, the implication is that no cultural group has a corner on the Word; it remains sovereign. He comments,

> Only by fostering and being aware of a national gospel can one be open to a truly international gospel, one that welcomes the particular manifestations of the gospel in diverse cultural fields, while, at the same time, critiquing them in light of the Word. An amorphous Christianity, on the other hand, gives rise to the subsuming of Christ, and other Christian subcultural construals of Christ, under a particular form.[99]

The only international gospel for Barth, notes Metzger, is one that accounts for the incarnation of the Word in the plethora of particular cultures. The denial of such enculturation of the Word runs the danger of absolutizing one's own particular appropriation of the Word.[100] He adds, "a supposedly non-enculturated, amorphous, international Christianity is in danger" of being an imperialistic Christianity.[101]

Metzger is correct that by virtue of his theological dialectics Barth cannot be easily placed in any of Niebuhr's Christ and culture paradigms. For Barth, argues Metzger, the Word is simultaneously *against* culture and *for* culture. The Word stands against culture by critiquing it, and yet "the divine critique gives way to the divine confirmation" of culture. Further, "the Word of Christ is the transcendental ground and goal of culture, making its existence possible, even to the extent of providing limits within which culture glorifies God in its sheer otherness from God."[102] However, the insistence of the wholly otherness of God for Barth (and Metzger for that matter), disallows a more crucial role of the cultural in human existence.

If we accept with Barth that because of the incarnation the secular dimension is included in the sacred sphere, and if we agree that the humanity

---

99   Metzger, *The Word of Christ and the World of Culture*, 156.
100   Metzger incisively notes that "Western peoples come to understand better their own enculturated gospels and perceive more clearly how to speak the gospel to their culture, realizing, too, that the gospel is not limited to their Western conceptions, but rather, transcends them" (Metzger, *The Word of Christ and the World of Culture*, 154–55).
101   Metzger, *The Word of Christ and the World of Culture*, 156.
102   Metzger, *The Word of Christ and the World of Culture*, 239. According to Metzger, "For Barth the Word of Christ radically critiques culture, but only for the ultimate confirmation of culture as eschatological promise" (Ibid.).

of Christ included his Jewish cultural particularity, then, did not the very mode of divine disclosure drawing on the cultural particularity of Jesus' Jewishness turn the cultural into a central feature without which the divine self-disclosure could not have taken place or without which it could not be conceived? Moreover, if the Word was enculturated yet not exhausted, do other enculturations of the Word among other cultural groups not create the possibility for *new* revelatory understandings of the divine—the incarnate Word and its relation to humanity—in which case the cultural becomes once again a central feature in the divine self-disclosure? These are the kind of questions that Metzger via Barth leaves unresolved, and which I intend to explore in the last chapter.

Culture and the Long Revolution: Gorringe

Influenced profoundly by the works of Johann Gottfried Herder (1744–1803) and Karl Barth (1886–1968), Timothy Gorringe articulates his theology of culture (read of the cultural). The central principle of his theology is that the role of all human cultures (and religions) is to further humanity.[103] Like Kathryn Tanner (see above), he reminds us that contemporary notions of "culture" can be traced back to the German notion of *Kultur* and *Bildung* which were later elided with French and British notions of "civilization."[104] Similarly, he also reminds us that the use of "culture" as a "way of life" can be traced to the publication of E. B Tylor's *Primitive Cultures* (discussed in Chapter 3).[105]

That said, Gorringe sets out to articulate an assault on modernity and *laissez-faire* capitalism and to promote what he calls—borrowing from Raymond Williams—the "long Revolution," which for him—in contrast to Williams but in agreement with Herder—it is a way to view the whole of

---

103   Timothy J. Gorringe, *Furthering Humanity.*

104   See Gorringe, *Furthering Humanity*, 3–22. As he explains, *Kultur* pointed to the network of social institutions often spoken of as social achievements, and which once conflated with the British and French notion of "civilization" were used to refer to those aspects of cultural production such as the arts, music, and architecture. As to *Buildung*, it is related to the agricultural metaphor of cultivation and which also conveys the idea of formation in this case more related to the individual. According to Gorringe, *Kultur* was bound with the rise of the middle class in Germany and functioned to self-differentiate from the court and the proletariat.

105   As I explained in Chapter 3, Tylor's *Primitive Cultures* shows a Eurocentric orientation in conflating notions of culture from "upper" class such as art and music, and notions of culture as social achievement like education and law. The actual people's traditions get lumped together under the category of magic and superstition.

human history in its journey toward—borrowing from Herder—the "fur-thering of humanity."[106] The long revolution is the process by which people become and remain human.[107] In theological terms, for Gorringe, this long revolution refers to culture as the "whole process in the course of which God does what it takes ... to make and to keep human beings human. Culture in this sense is, under God, 'the human task'."[108]

Gorringe's theological reflection corresponds with his idea of culture as the totality of the human creative effort and as being concerned with the ethical and intellectual significance of the material world.[109] Culture, he claims, relates to the "cultivation" of humanity which is intimately bound with the activity of God.[110] It should not be understood as one homogeneous universal whole. Drawing on Barth, he argues that it should be understood as the realization of humanity. In fact, together with Herder, he acknowl-edges the ambiguity and indeterminacy of the term; since culture describes everything we do as humans, it is inevitably irreconcilably plural.[111] Taking his cue from Herder, he writes that the affirmation of the plurality of cul-tures must also be accompanied with the recognition of the irreducible dis-tinctiveness of each cultural tradition. Such distinctiveness, he adds, is a divine gift which cannot be compromised. This affirmation encompasses Gorringe's position about culture: "Not a man [sic], not a country, not a peo-ple, not a natural history, not a state, are like another. Hence the 'True, the Good, the Beautiful in them are not similar either.' Each image of human-ity is unique and *sui generis*."[112] Stated more succinctly, no culture alone embodies the kingdom.[113]

---

106 Williams called the "long Revolution" to the development of economic, political and cultural changes that began in the eighteenth century and were wedded to no Promethean doctrine of inevitable progress. Of course, claims Gorringe, Williams remained commit-ted to the possibility of a more humane and more just fulfilling future, while he looked at socialism to deliver it. See Gorringe, *Furthering Humanity*, 17.

107 Gorringe, *Furthering Humanity*, 261.

108 Ibid., 4.

109 Elsewhere he also comments that the word culture referred to what human beings make of their world materially, intellectually and spiritually. See Gorringe, *Furthering Humanity*, 105, 172.

110 Here Gorringe wants to preserve the idea of "culture" as comparative to the agricultural metaphor of cultivation. He cites Cicero's famous phrase *cultura animi* to speak of educa-tion as the "cultivation of the mind." See Gorringe, *Furthering Humanity*, 3.

111 Gorringe, *Furthering Humanity*, 13.

112 Ibid., 80.

113 Ibid., 19.

Gorringe sees the divine Spirit as active in culture, in its preservation and upholding of life. To destroy cultures is to counter the divine intent for life. Several implications intersect in Gorringe's theological discussion on culture. First, culture is that one inescapable aspect of human existence.[114] He is not positing a romantic view of cultures; all cultures are deeply marked by imbalances of power along gender, racial and class lines structured in ways that a group in the population remains at the bottom.[115]

Second, to describe culture as human "creative achievement" binds culture with power.[116] This aspect is perhaps the most critical for Gorringe's proposal, and the one on which he spends most time in the book, daring to critically unmask the ways in which power in culture both has operated in the past in Christianity (even to wrestle with cultural wars in the Bible) and how it operates today in the various expressions of capitalism.[117] Unlike most theologians of culture, Gorringe confronts head-on the Christian legacy of imperialism and colonialism. He categorically argues that we cannot write a theology of culture without taking into account the "Church's collusion with imperialism, patriarchy and racism."[118]

In the same way, Gorringe envisages the failure of capitalism and modernity as cultural in nature. He challenges ideas about "modernity's" cultural imperialism as resulting from its strength over against "weak" cultures. Rather, its growth can be described more like a form of cancer spreading its cultural decay.[119] The present reality of cultural imperialism, the commodification

---

114   For Gorringe it is impossible to operate outside of culture. He agrees with Barth's recognition that we can no more speak outside of culture than we can pump out of our own skin. See Gorringe, *Furthering Humanity*, 43.

115   Gorringe, *Furthering Humanity*, 45.

116   Here Gorringe draws heavily from Michel Foucault's understanding of power. Instead of describing power in binary terms between those who have it and those who do not, Gorringe argues that "Power circulates or can be understood as a chain. 'It is never realised here or there, never in anybody's hands, never appropriated as a commodity or piece of wealth. Power is employed and exercised through a net like organisation'" (Gorringe, *Furthering Humanity*, 152).

117   Gorringe tends to speak of capitalism in the singular, which is problematic in terms of the various permutations that capitalism has taken in various places in the world.

118   Gorringe, *Furthering Humanity*, 19–20. According to him, the reality of colonialism is what led Herder to protest against missions and their colonizing implications (Ibid., 81).

119   What we see in fact, is not the "invasion of weak cultures by strong ones but almost the opposite—a sort of cultural decay spreading from the West to the rest of the world" (Gorringe, *Furthering Humanity*, 94). Speaking of capitalism's obsession for growth he adds, "Growth for the sake of growth is a form of cancer. 'In the long perspective of history, it would be difficult to deny that the exuberant capitalism of the past two hundred and

of life,[120] the production of mass cultural products,[121] the preservation of ideologies of power and dominance, the upholding of ideas of racialized superiority, the asymmetrical distribution of the world's wealth,[122] and the destruction of the earth, all are expressions of the present culture's idolatry that places its confidence in the present system of capitalism; these expressions culminate in the reality that capitalism is threatening both the planet and the survival of local cultures.[123] As far as he is concerned, Capitalism's "right to dominate, what today we view as neocolonialism," is not just a matter of markets, but of science, technology, economics, and the values of unlimited progress.[124] Supported by military forces everywhere especially the United States of America,[125] the present system leads to cultural homogenization,[126] the emergence of a new transnational class,[127] and ultimately "deculturation,"

---

fifty years will be diagnosed in the future as a desperately dangerous case of cancer in the body of human society'" (Ibid.).

120   According to Gorringe, "A consumer culture puts he emphasis on the cultural dimension of the economy, and therefore on the subsumption of meaning and value to profit" (Gorringe, *Furthering Humanity*, 68–69).

121   Gorringe spends a bit of time discussing the importance of distinguishing mass culture and popular culture. At the end, his concern is more with what he calls (borrowing from Herder) "residual culture," by which he means the rejection of the ideas of "outmoded" or "obsolete" cultural traditions. See Gorringe, *Furthering Humanity*, 52–66.

122   Gorringe takes a liberationist perspective here emphasizing the need of the Church to take a stance for the poor. Much in sync with liberation theologians he argues that poverty leads to the premature death of peoples. For him, the class system is the biggest killer in Britain. Citing Davies, he notes that "The effect of poverty on health in Britain ... is the same as a plane crashing and killing 115 passengers every year. Yet, since the abandonment of socialism as a realistic political option, it is unremarked, and accepted as fate, replaced by the fiction of a classless society" (Gorringe, *Furthering Humanity*, 157). See also Jon Sobrino, "Poverty Means Death to the Poor," *Cross Currents* 36 (1986): 267–76.

123   Gorringe, *Furthering Humanity*, 17.

124   Ibid., 89.

125   Gorringe mentions Thomas Friedman's insight that the "hidden hand of the market will never work without a hidden fist ... And the hidden fist that keeps the world safe for Silicon Valley's technologies to flourish is called the US Army. Air Force. Navy and Marine Corps" (Gorringe, *Furthering Humanity*, 88).

126   The philosopher Roy Weatherford is happy to see English displacing all other languages as a result of the dominance of the USA as a military, economic and entertainment superpower. In his view, it means that we are finally about to become One World, One Government, One Culture. See Gorringe, *Furthering Humanity*, 88.

127   He writes, "The growth of a transnational class comprised of intellectuals, bureaucrats, politicians, business people, journalists and diplomats is part of the same process. They share procedures, working practices and organizational cultures, 'there is a 'global culture',

the destruction of primary cultures and the creation of a cultural emptiness.[128] Gorringe's theological point is simple yet complex. Modernity and capitalism prevent the furthering of humanity and for this reason they must be countered and resisted. Capitalism must be resisted because of its power to turn us into "modern cannibals" who eat other people and leave "unattractive, rude specimen[s] of humanity, out of harmony with" themselves and those with whom they have to live.[129]

It is the unqualified use of the term culture, the inability to deal with questions of power, and the failure to confront the present capitalist economic systems that lead Gorringe to abandon Niebuhr's proposal.[130] According to him, in his discussion of the relation between Christ and culture, Niebuhr elides anthropological notions of culture with those of "high" culture. But a careful awareness of the plurality of cultures causes his theoretical framework to fracture and collapse.[131]

Third, for Gorringe, the gospel proves to be a great cultural force for resisting cultures of death and providing the ideological alternative of life. The incarnation plays an irreplaceable role. Christ, says he, became flesh but not as an avatar. The taking on of "flesh" by God, as spelled out by John's gospel, points to the course of Jesus' mediation, meaning culture—food, world symbols, the way in which we cherish our bodies.[132] The incarnation provides the grammar for divine cultural engagement: "The doctrine of the incarnation claims that God took flesh at a particular time and place, taught in a particular language, and was tortured to death under particular laws."[133] Thus, the purpose of the incarnation was the redemption of history, the offering of interpretive clues for teasing out the "meaning of the whole historical process, what we have called the long revolution."[134] Intrinsic to the long revolution and the incarnation is

---

remarks Anthony King', it is that which enables 'an increasing number of scientists, academics, artists and other elites ... of widely different nationalities, languages, ethnicities and races to communicate more easily with each other than with others of their own ethnic or national background' " (Gorringe, *Furthering Humanity*, 90).

128   Gorringe, *Furthering Humanity*, 92.

129   Ibid., 181.

130   As far as Nieburh was concerned, Gorringe writes, he tried to elide anthropological notions of culture with those of "high" culture. As soon as he did that, his typology started to fail. In the same way, as soon as we attempt to nuance the notion of culture we find the need for a richer understanding of the Church and culture than one finds in Niebuhr. See Gorringe, *Furthering Humanity*, 15.

131   Gorringe, *Furthering Humanity*, 12–16.

132   Ibid., 18.

133   Ibid., 100.

134   Ibid.

the rejection of the culture of "modernity" and capitalism in its multiple per-mutations in the destruction of cultures, the manipulation and impoverish-ment of societies, and the promotion of a culture of consumption. The role of the incarnation in culture/the cultural is, then, the furthering of humanity.

Gorringe wants to make clear that the incarnation is not a philosophical first principle. The incarnation is the highest expression of God's grace in Christ, opening the opportunity for humans to know God. "It is a way of reading a particular historical event, the life and death of a first century Jew, as revelatory of the Wholly Other. It is the claim that the hidden God reveals Godself here in this life and death."[135] In other words, if the taking on of "flesh" by God is true, then bodies and what we do with them, all the issues of housing, food, clothing and housing are also declared as decisively important. Culture in each of these senses "is command, because culture is the record of what we do as ensouled bodies, or bodily souls, from cuisine to quartets, from poetry to pottery."[136] By the same token, the particularity of the incarnation prevents claims to uni-versality, since that means the elimination of difference.[137] The gospel comes to all cultures in their own terms.[138] God's self-revelation can be conceived beyond and through all cultural systems "if it is to amount to anything more than ethnocentrism."[139] For this reason, "no cultural policy informed by incar-nation can be chauvinist."[140] And the resurrection encompasses the promise of meaning and purpose, the anticipation of reconciliation for all people.[141]

Gorringe does not only want to uphold the Bible as the Word of God and then provoke dissonance with respect to every ideology especially challenging hege-mony.[142] He also does not only want to present the kingdom of God as a hegemonic alternative of subalternity. What his theology of the cultural seeks is liberation, a liberation that promotes release from injustice and poverty, but also release from "inner compulsions of violence, patterns of domination, and ultimately death."[143] The commitment for liberation also demands the rethinking of the question of

---

135   Ibid., 126.

136   Ibid.

137   As he sees it, "What the Church calls 'sin' is the refusal of gift, the attempt to take one's human gender or group as the measure of all things" (Gorringe, *Furthering Humanity*, 166).

138   Gorringe, *Furthering Humanity*, 101.

139   Ibid., 210.

140   Ibid., 101.

141   After the resurrection, Gorringe posits, "Christ belongs to all cultures and can identify with them through the proclamation of the Good News" (Gorringe, *Furthering Humanity*, 201).

142   Gorringe, *Furthering Humanity*, 212.

143   Ibid., 213.

missions; missions cannot be colonizing! For Gorringe, we must also uncover the colonizing impetus of capitalism, which is not only an idolatrous system, but also a colonizing missionary faith. Certainly, missions as expressions of European cultural hegemony were a departure from the Bible. As a result, the new mission must be one that follows a natural process of inculturation which "can never be induced artificially." Instead, inculturation is the "by-product of an involvement with a people rather than the conscious target of a programme of action. For it is a people that creates a culture. It is, therefore, from the people with whom one becomes involved that one understands and acquires a culture."[144] It is not difficult to see here how Gorringe's concern of preaching the gospel connects with the Catholic definition of inculturation, but he goes beyond it by including the social, political and economic aspects of cultures. Not surprisingly, he quickly dismisses as irrelevant the key questions in the minds of "inculturationists," namely, whether a particular church is inculturated, or why it is not inculturated, and how it could be inculturated. Those, he claims, are not what is important, but rather the struggle against economic injustice, sexism, and racism.[145]

For Gorringe, to be committed to liberation means to be committed to cultural revolution as part of the Church's task. What is at stake in this struggle and task of the church is the humanity of all. Still, it behooves the Church to recognize that "the power for change is located decisively in weakness ..."[146] The Church's role is to support a culture that stands for life and against death.[147] But it ought not to automatically have to respect other cultures; good examples of this point are Nazi culture, Afrikaner culture and caste culture.[148] At the same time, the Church ought to strive for a multicultural society.[149]

---

144   Ibid., 200.

145   Ibid.

146   Gorringe, *Furthering Humanity*, 172. He expands stating that "No liberation theology can claim to be rooted in the word of God if it does not hold together the two biblical axioms of the irreconcilable antagonism between God and mammon and the irrevocable Covenant between God and the poor" (Ibid., 209).

147   Gorringe draws from Hans Küng's cultural directives for the church to strive toward: "a culture of non-violence and respect for life; a culture of solidarity and just economic order; a culture of tolerance and a life of truthfulness; and a culture of equal rights and partnership between women and men" (Gorringe, *Furthering Humanity*, 225–26).

148   Gorringe, *Furthering Humanity*, 234.

149   Thinking of multiculturalism, Johann Baptist Metz argues that if "Western Christianity is to mature into a culturally polycentric World Christianity, then it must realize its biblical heritage as the ferment of a hermeneutical culture, a culture of the acknowledgement of others in their otherness, which in its heart is freed from the will to power" (Gorringe, *Furthering Humanity*, 253).

While the examples of England and the United States of America prove that "the melting pots do not melt" and instead only reproduce ethnic and racial divisions, it is the celebration of cultural diversity, as in the event of Pentecost, that must guide any society and church. Since all cultures mediate and reconstitute human nature in their different ways, and since moral life is always culturally embedded, he contends that "no vision of the good life can be based on an abstract conception of human nature alone."[150] Theologically, the task of the Church finds its origin in both the resurrection and Pentecost, spreading the good news of overcoming alienation and the possibility of a "new human community not marked by class, gender, and race divides."[151] He rejects any attempts at cultural homogeneity and monocultural hegemony. In fact, "every culture represents a different embodiment of the divine Spirit and therefore to eliminate cultures, or to preach the superiority of one over another, is to fly in the face of divine purpose."[152] The Church must articulate a theology that values diversity and real difference, but also represents a response to the one Spirit, having unity as its underlying motif.

To sum up in relation to our concern about the relation of culture and gospel, and coinciding with the notion of the cultural, it is evident that Gorringe sees both "gospel" and "culture" co-working toward the common goal of furthering humanity. For him, the gospel is at the heart of the very idea of growth of our true humanity, but such growth cannot be accomplished by the gospel alone. As he proposes, culture in the sense of creative achievement plays its part.[153] He also sees the divine and culture as much closer than previous scholars we have considered. Not only is the divine involved in culture, but cultural activity can also be a response to the divine Spirit, insofar as it seeks to preserve life. In other words, theology of culture is also a theology of the Spirit. All that is life affirming in cultures and other religions is therefore a response to the Spirit of God.[154] It is this framing from which Gorringe moves to reject

---

150 Gorringe, *Furthering Humanity*, 236.

151 As Michele Wallace puts I, "multiculturalism is not the promised land but it stands for something worth pursuing, namely the recognition of the significance of cultural diversity and of integrating the contributions of minority groups into the fabric of society" (Cited in Gorringe, *Furthering Humanity*, 247). In the same breadth, Gorringe also says that the idea of "equality" is not a Western concept but part of the liberationist struggle. See Ibid., 165.

152 Gorringe, *Furthering Humanity*, 8.

153 Ibid., 172.

154 Gorringe, *Furthering Humanity*, 258. In this sense, comments Gorringe, a theology of culture "is a theology which understands the full implications of the gospel claim that I meet God in my neighbour" (Ibid.).

modernity and capitalism as cultural expressions opposite to the divine intent for life. Instead of arguing for culture as irreconcilable with the gospel, he views these two as cooperating in their role to further humanity in its multiple expressions.

With Gorringe issues of the de-Europeanizing of the cultural emerge forcefully along with the confrontation with Christianity's colonial past which are taken seriously. Unfortunately, he does not elaborate further on how cultural diversity can be conceived as a gift of God or whether he would understand the cultural as a divine gift as well, and not merely a useful element in the furthering of humanity. He is correct to say that a theology of culture is also a theology of the Spirit, but he does not extrapolate the concrete implications for revelation. That said, his proposal opens the door for thinking pneumatologically about the dynamic relationship between the cultural and the Christian faith.

Beyond Christ and Culture? A Postcolonial Proposal: Rieger

Joerg Rieger's *Christ & Empire* is an eloquent articulation of a postcolonial proposal that claims to take a different trajectory from that of Niebuhr.[155] Right from the beginning Rieger tells us that the primary context for his proposal is "never 'culture.'" Much like Gorringe, he reminds us that contemporary scholarship teaches us of the perils of reflecting on the cultural independent from issues of power. For him, it is more useful to reflect on Christ in the context of empire, by which he means "the large and ever-changing conglomerate of power that are aimed at controlling all aspects of our lives, from macropolitics to our innermost desires."[156] Rieger is correct in pointing out that there is no such thing as "pristine forms of Christology;" that is, where it would be independent from the "metamorphoses of empire." By the same token, he shows that despite its impressive power, empire has never been able to co-opt Christology altogether.[157] It is this historical tension in terms of the relationship of Christology to empire and the function of imperial power in its ability or inability to impact all aspects of life, including Christology, that occupies Rieger. He concludes, the typologies as deployed by Niebuhr do not provide useful material for engaging such fundamental questions.

I applaud Rieger's bold engagement of *empire* as a critical category for exploring the multiple ways in which Christology has been shaped by empire and how he was simultaneously able to tease out aspects of a Christology that

---

155   Joerg Rieger, *Christ & Empire*, vii.
156   Ibid.
157   Ibid.

stands in opposition and resistance to empire. Skillfully, he demonstrates how particular Christological interpretations when viewed through the prism of empire show a degree of "ambivalence" (he discusses Paul, the Councils of Nicea and Chalcedon, Anselm of Canterbury and Friedrich Schleiermacher).[158] Such affirmations of Christ, he shows, can easily be understood as instruments of empire for the purposes of oppressing peoples and preserving the status quo. But at the same time, he highlights that the optic of empire allows us to see how those Christological interpretations put on display a "Christological surplus," a residual understanding of Christ that instead of supporting empire, runs diametrically opposite to it and provides material to resist it. This "play" between ambivalence and surplus in Rieger's work helps us understand the insidious and seductive character of empire. But Rieger provides yet a deeper dimension of the festering character of empire by demonstrating that even those who seek to deliberately and explicitly oppose empire often find themselves serving empire (see his discussion of Bartolomé de las Casas, Gustaf Aulén and Matthew Fox).[159] He shows that without a self-critical stance, people's blinders prevent their "good intentions" from contributing to the liberation project that he so espouses.

Rieger's proposal, however, seems trapped in the semantic space between "culture" and "empire." It is my view that these terms share more than Rieger is prepared to admit. He is correct that the cultural is not unilateral phenomena, and that it is heavily connected to issues of power. But there is ambiguity in his perspective because the concept, category and reality of empire are cultural constructs. It is a mistake to pretend that the idea or concept of empire, while powerful in its capacity to organize lives and societies, does not instead and more precisely describe questions of culture. Moreover, in terms of the reality of empire, by insisting that empire is an all-encompassing reality, Rieger seems to think that there is nothing outside of the tentacles of empire. Rieger simply gives empire more power than it actually has. He seems trapped in his own web of empire power that prevents him from engaging those cultures and communities that have successfully rejected empire or are actively involved in the struggle. Furthermore, his view of empire is deficient because he cannot see that for those who were colonized, empire was a fundamentally cultural event.[160]

---

158   Ibid., Chapters 1–3, 5.
159   Ibid., Chapters 4, 6–7.
160   Enrique Dussel, "Cristiandad moderna ante el Otro: De Indio 'Rudo' al Bon Sauvage," *Concilium* 150 (1979): 498–506, Http://www.enriquedussel.com/DVD%20Obras%20 Enrique%20Dussel/Textos/c/105.%201979/articulo.pdf (accessed January 25, 2015).

By contrast, Néstor García Canclini argues that the natives of the south of Mexico have successfully found ways of entering and exiting the present reality of capitalism and modernity (and I would say empire) precisely because of the fluidity of their cultural traditions.[161] According to Gary Sparks, for these peoples, it is not merely empire or economics but the preservation of their cultures that plays a fundamental role.[162] Moreover, by insisting on the depiction of Christ and empire in the way he does, Rieger runs the risk of perpetuating traditional (empire) interpretations that emphasized the incompatibility between Christ and (other) cultures, which led to the destruction of other cultures by empire, in the first place.

As can be seen, the shift away from Niebuhr's work has produced a wide range of proposals which have contributed exciting theological insights. With Tanner, we learn that the relationship of "Christ" and "culture" is much closer and more intimate than previously held. We can move away from fixed, airtight, and clearly defined cultures, and instead see them as fluid and inconsistent wholes. Most importantly, Tanner helps us understand how the church's relationship of cultural dependence means that the Church also reflects internally the same social issues and maladies found in the larger cultural context. Gallagher shares much with Tanner insofar as he reclaims the human component of the Christ and culture/society relationship. Unfortunately, the larger "secularized" social context distracts him and compels him to preserve the radical distinction between them. Metzger intensifies the distinction between Christ and culture by adopting Barth's focus on the divine wholly otherness. Admittedly, such a move allows him to emphasize divine grace and enables him to situate the incarnation as the point of contact between divine disclosure and human response. But in his paradigm, Christ immediately subsumes cultures unto himself and as a result the cultural sphere becomes of peripheral concern in terms of its contribution to our understanding of the divine activity or divine revelation. For his part, Gorringe provides a reinterpretation of Christ and culture arguing that they are collaborators in the furthering of humanity. In his proposal, the Christ event is also a cultural event in the divine advancing of humanity. As such, it allows him to uphold, celebrate, and struggle for life against the present capitalist system of the commodification of life. The

---

161 Néstor García Canclini, *Hybrid Cultures: Strategies for Entering and Leaving Modernity*, trans. Christopher L. Chiappari and Silvia L. López, foreword by Renato Rosaldo (Minneapolis, MN: University of Minnesota Press, 1995).

162 Gary Sparks, "Constructing Hyperlocal Theologies: Ethnohistorical Contextualization of 'Indian Theology' and JTatik Samuel's Legacy," *Journal of Hispanic/Latino Theology* 19, no. 1 (November 2013): 33–53.

insightful implication he offers us is that the Christ event resists the commodification of life. Insightfully, he helps us see how the Christ-as-cultural-event unveils divine grace and receives its fuller expression in the event of Pentecost.

Conclusion

As with the scholars in the previous chapter, the idea of "culture" still comes charged with notions of civilization, the world, and immediate social context. However, in this chapter the concept "culture" gains added levels of meaning such as a way of life, a philosophical current, and a national identity. This is the slippage that I mentioned at the beginning. Sometimes it is hard to gauge the meaning or meanings ascribed to the notion of "culture" by the authors. However, the Church and Christianity continue to be conceived of as otherworldly realities, making it difficult to consider the conditioning role of the cultural in people's experiences of faith and their reception of the divine disclosure, especially theologically.

It is impossible to discuss in a comprehensive way the multiple voluminous proposals on the relationship of Christ and culture. The review of the authors in this chapter, however, demonstrates a significant shift away from static understandings of the cultural and from the cultural as entirely separated from the reality of the divine. They shift towards more pluralized—and admittedly incipient—understandings of *cultures* and toward perceiving cultures as fluid and dynamic phenomena. The relation between Christ and cultures begins to be described not in antithetical terms but as dynamically interacting. The Christ event plays a central and pivotal role, although understood differently. In some cases, the incarnation becomes the bridge by which the distance (the radical difference) between God's wholly otherness and culture's this worldliness is preserved. In my view, such radical separation and distinction between Christ and the cultural strikes of docetism if not Nestorianism. In other instances, the incarnation functions as grammar for understanding the relationship between the divine (Christ) and the human (the cultural) in greater intimacy. And yet in other cases, the incarnation becomes a window through which to conceive divine activity in the cultural.

Those perspectives that focus on the radical separation of Christ and the cultural tend to focus on the nature and impact of sin in cultural phenomena; they emphasize debates on Christ and "culture" as primarily having to do with evangelization; they view Christ as transcultural though enculturated; and they focus on guarding the church and the gospel from cultural corruption. Yet, there is a growing list of other scholars who emphasize a closer relationship between Christ and a broader understanding of culture, which resonates with my proposed notion of the cultural—as the complex, open-ended processes of culturalization that define, shape, condition, and impact the ways humans engage life, and interact with their immediate environment, each other and the divine. These scholars tend to envision grace as the catalyst which enables the possibilities of divine activity in cultural traditions. They also emphasize the cultural particularity of Christ more intentionally and envision the possibility of cultures as sites of divine disclosure. The latter group helps us to create a platform for considering the role of the cultural in terms of divine pneumatological activity and in the light of the event of Pentecost. These two themes will be a central feature of the last chapter. In the following chapter, my intention is to trace the debates of Christianity/Christ/the gospel and culture/the cultural in the Catholic church, pointing specifically to the reconceptualization of their relationship as inculturation.

CHAPTER 7

Inculturation, the Catholic Church and the Cultures of the World

Never as in our days are major cultural groups of humanity felt and which want to defend their cultural uniqueness, together with their own character, language, art, symbolism, labels, and their general way of life: American, Indian Svadharma, Weltanschauung, or negrutide, which used to be source of shame but now are brandished like a proud banner.[1]

JOSEPH MASSON

• • •

Evangelization loses much of its force and effectiveness if it does not take into consideration the actual people to whom it is addresses [*sic*], if it does not use their language, their signs and symbols, if it does not answer the questions they ask, and if it does not have an impact on their concrete life. But on the other hand, evangelization risks losing its power and disappearing altogether if one empties or adulterates its content under the pretext of translating it...[2]

EVANGELII NUNTIANDI

Introduction

From the turn of the twentieth century, the Catholic Church has been undergoing radical shifts in the ways it views the ethnocultural groups (henceforth cultures) of the world. The complexity of interrelated global issues at the turn of the twentieth century forced Christians to rethink the implications of

---

1 Joseph Masson, "L'Eglise Ouverte sur le Monde," *Nouvelle Revue Théologique* 84, no. 10 (1962): 1038, Http://www.nrt.be/docs/articles/1962/84-10/1791-L'%C3%89glise+ouverte+sur+le+monde .pdf (accessed August 20, 2015).
2 Paul VI, *Evangelii Nuntiandi* [*Encyclical Letter on the Evangelization of the World*] (1975), 63, Http:// w2.vatican.va/content/paul-vi/en/apost_exhortations/documents/hf_p-vi_exh_19751208 _evangelii-nuntiandi.html (accessed June 23, 2015).

the relationship between the cultural[3] and faith. I focus on shifts in Roman Catholic thinking in this chapter. Two interrelated points are worth noting at the outset. First, the church was confronted with its own past and complicity with Western European colonial projects and the colonizing nature of missionary enterprises. And two, the church finally realized that most Catholic Christians live(d) in the southern hemisphere, outside the centres of power in Western Europe and Euro North America. I agree with Joseph Masson's insight that this realization of the global breadth of Christianity, or what he calls "*planétisation*," opened the church to become truly Catholic for the first time.[4]

In this chapter, I intend to briefly articulate some of the ways in which the Catholic Church has shifted its perception and degree of openness towards the other cultures of the world. This chapter is not intended as an exhaustive analysis of the complex and multiple theological streams within the Catholic Church. In broad strokes, I examine some of the important moments/key official documents that have contributed to shaping the Catholic Church's position on the relation between the Christian faith and the cultural,[5] as well as the theological implications of these moments. While the Second Vatican Council (Vatican II) is often understood as the crucial climactic moment which sets the tone for many of these changes, I also bring to bear prior and later developments in this discussion including the reception of these documents in Latin America and recent pastoral letters and encyclicals by Pope Francis. I draw on all these documents to demonstrate how the church's position has shifted. The notion of inculturation has become a central category in describing how the Catholic Church imagines/describes the relationship between the cultural and faith. This shift leads to an enriched theological

---

3   As a form of a reminder, "the cultural" points to multiple all-encompassing aspects by which human collectives codify the world. Make sense of reality, and engage in the complex processes of culturalization of life, relationships, the environment, and their understanding of the divine. The cultural highlights that all peoples engage in cultural activities and participate in the construction of cultural elements and traditions.

4   Masson, "L'Eglise Ouverte sur le Monde," 1033.

5   As stated earlier, by the cultural I mean the complex set of inherited codes, segments of codes and activities passed down from generation to generation through processes of culturalization that define, shape, condition, and impact the ways humans engage life, and interact with their immediate environment, each other and the divine. The cultural also identifies the broad range of rich, complex, changeable, unfinished/open-ended, dynamic, contested, fluid, and interconnected processes of culturalization that are part of the human experience in its greatly diverse multiplicity of concrete cultural traditions and expression and their intimate relation to experiences and expressions of (religious) faith and religious traditions.

understanding of humanity and divine disclosure through the welcoming of the cultures of the world. Because inculturation is defined in myriad ways, I pay specific attention to some of the nuances as expressed in official documents. My goal is to highlight the richness and promising nature of the term as well as to uncover some of the weaknesses that haunt the term's ability to go beyond its colonial past and accompanying Eurocentrism, and toward the construction of a culturally inclusive truly *catholic* Church. This discussion will certainly add to the theological understanding of the interconnectedness of faith and the cultural being developed in this volume. However, even though Catholics tend to perceive other cultures as enriching the Church, and the Gospel as having the potential to transform/ennoble other cultures, yet there are still lingering questions about how much Catholics will allow the cultural to impact the Gospel which I also explore.

Until now the discussion in previous chapters has tended to revolve around the language of religion/Christianity and culture. Among Catholics, however, the language of Gospel/faith and culture is preferred. Still, the range of issues and concerns coincide. In this chapter I opt for Catholic terminology in order not to bring added confusion to an already complex debate. As in previous chapters, I still preserve the use of the singular "culture." I preserve it both not to change the content of the author's writings as well as not to veer the conversation in a different direction as that intended by the writers I revisit. That said, I do think that many of the issues discussed coincide with the concerns of the broader understanding of the processes of culturalization and concrete expressions in the phenomena of cultures as I am proposing in the notion "the cultural;" when I think it is appropriate I use this language.

Evangelization and Assimilation

The same prejudices expressed by Protestants concerning the self-perceived superiority of Western Europeans viz-a-viz native peoples were also displayed by Catholic missionaries. There can be no doubt that the Catholic Church contributed to and at times supported the colonial project of cultural genocide and the colonization of the peoples of the world under the guise of evangelization.[6] Although there were some sensibilities that encouraged cultural

---

6   Marcello de Carvalho Azevedo, *Inculturation and the Challenges of Modernity*, vol. 1, *Inculturation: Working Papers on Living Faith and Cultures*, ed. Ary A. Roest Crollius (Centre "Cultures and Religions"—Pontifical Gregorian University, 1982), 20.

exchange during evangelization,[7] still the Catholic task of missionizing was also *de facto* a task for civilizing the natives, whether intentionally or unintentionally, as we have seen in previous chapters. Catholic missionaries inevitably became agents of the empire and promoters of Western European cultures including the later missionary movements in the United States of America.[8]

"Education" was one of the most effective and in some cases most sinister tools of Christian indoctrination; it was the medium through which the cultures of the natives where effectively ridiculed, undermined, and eradicated.[9] As I showed in chapter 2, Catholic missionaries, in their complicity

---

7   In 1659, Michael Paul Gallagher unburies an early instance the Congregation for the Evangelization of Peoples (formerly known as the Congregation for the Propagation of the Faith) in which missionaries are given important guidelines to be careful not to force unnecessary cultural changes in the people they were about to evangelize. They were told:

> "Do not bring any pressure to bear on these people to change their manners, customs and practices, unless these are obviously contrary to religion and morality. There is nothing more absurd than to want to bring France to China—or to bring Spain or Italy or any part of Europe. Carry none of that but rather faith which neither despises nor destroys the way of life and the customs of any people, when these are not evil things. In the contrary, faith desires that these traditions be conserved and protected" (cited in Michael Paul Gallagher, *Clashing Symbols*, 101–2).

8   Speaking of the Catholic Church, Marcello de Carvalho Azevedo writes:

> "Here was a substantial, perduring identification of the Church an institution with the cultural assumptions and frame of western civilization and with many of its detailed expressions. Thus, the structures for the communication of the Christian message were increasingly shaped in accordance with *western symbolic systems* and western intellectual patterns and trends of thought. When announced in the context of other cultures, the gospel was presented and received as a western package in both its theological-liturgical formulation and its social organization" (Azevedo, *Inculturation and the Challenges of Modernity*, 26).

9   Among the native communities of North America, the establishment of schools cannot be separated from the creation of reservations and the forced removal of children from their native homes in order to "educate" them and indoctrinate them into Western European cultures. The cases are too well documented to ignore. See two small examples: Bev Sellars, *They Called Me Number One: Secrets and Survival at an Indian Residential School* (Vancouver, BC: Talonbooks, 2012); Daniel L. Hawk and Richard L. Twiss, "From the Good: 'The Only Good Indian is a Dead Indian', to Better: 'Kill the Indian and Save the Man', to Best: 'Old Things Pass Away and All Things Become White!': An American

with empire, also contributed to the creation of the "archive," the collection of documents that were used by many scientists to highlight the "primitive" state of the Indigenous peoples of the world and used as the justification to dominate them. In the Americas, some of the most detailed naturalist, anthropological, and ethnological studies were written by Spanish Catholic missionaries in their attempt to facilitate the mission work of evangelization. Some of the most prominent Spanish Catholic missionaries who participated in the production of such works were: The Franciscan Friars Juan de Torquemada[10] and Bernardino de Sahagún,[11] the Dominican Diego Durán,[12]

Hermeneutic of Colonization," in *Evangelical Postcolonial Conversations: Global Awakenings in Theology and Praxis*, ed. Kay Higuera Smith, Jayachitra Lalitha, and Daniel L. Hawk (Downers Grove, IL: IVP Academic, 2014), 47–60. Meanwhile in Latin America, the creation of *reducciones*—communities where the natives where brought together "for their own protection" and where they would be "encouraged" to work—was part and parcel of attempts to "educate" and "civilize" the natives. In some cases, Jesuit missionaries also took children away from their parents to "civilize" and Christianize them. In other cases, missionaries organized incursions into native territories searching for slaves and returned with children, women, and elderly people. See Ángel Rosenblat, *El mestizaje y las castas coloniales*, vol. II, *La Población Indígena y el Mestizaje en América* (Buenos Aires, Argentina: Editorial Nova, 1954), 145.

10   Juan de Torquemada wrote the multivolume *La Monarquía Indiana*, which was the product of much research and what he claimed to be actual interviews with the Indigenous peoples. At one point considered the definitive history of the various ethnic groups that inhabited New Spain, today many question his (native) sources accuse him of plagiarizing material from other extant accounts of the time. For fuller debate see José Alcina Franch, "Juan de Torquemada, 1564–1624," in *Guide to Etnohistorical Sources: Part Two*, vol. 13, *Handbook of Middle American Indians*, ed. Howard C. Cline and John B. Glass, general editor Robert Wauchope (London, UK: University of Texas Press, 1973), 259–75; Franch, "Juan de Torquemada, 1564–1624."

11   Sahagún dedicated more than half of his life studying the religious traditions of the Nahuatl peoples. See his three volumes entitled *Historia general de las cosas de Nueva España* (Mexico, D.F.: Editorial Pedro Robredo, 1938). He devoted much time to learning native languages and cultures, and finding connections between Aztec religious themes and symbols and Christianity, all to help in the task of evangelization. See his *Bernardino de Sahagún's Psalmodia Christiana (Christian Psalmody)*, trans. Arthur J. O. Anderson (Salt Lake City, UT: University of Utah Press, 1993). Despite his extensive enumeration of the religious traditions of the natives of New Spain, he spared no opportunity to condemn some of their religious practices as being from the devil. See his *Historia general de las cosas de Nueva España* (Mexico, D.F.: Editorial Pedro Robredo, 1938), II:182, 241, 281, 284.

12   Diego Durán, *Historia de las Indias*.

and the Jesuit José de Acosta.[13] Despite his opposition to the exploitation of the natives,[14] the Dominican Bartolomé de las Casas also contributed to the production of ethnographic and historical material of the peoples of the Americas,[15] and was convinced of their *need* to be evangelized/enculturated into Christianity, the *true* religion.[16]

Though I cannot adequately summarize these authors and their views of the natives, I highlight that these materials fed into the systematic (mis)representation of the natives in the Americas and their eventual decimation. Their writings were often cited to bolster colonizing attitudes within which local native cultures and religious traditions were targeted for eradication, to be replaced with a version of Christianity that included compulsory assimilation into Western European cultures. As we have seen, by engaging in the cultural projects of producing "histories" and other types of studies of the natives of the New World as part of fulfilling their own sense of vocation for evangelization— which was accompanied by Spanish and Portuguese language and culture instruction—these Spanish and Portuguese missionaries ensured the success of the Spanish imperial projects on the ground. As with the Protestant counterparts, for Catholic missionaries Christianity and Western European cultures went hand-in-hand. Generally, evangelization meant assimilation into Western European cultural traditions and understandings of Christianity. As Claudio Esteva Fábregat notes, the missionaries were the ones responsible for popularizing Spanish culture. They contributed to the destruction of Indigenous cultural structures and institutions and participated in the invasion of the structures of family and community. He states pointedly that the missionaries were "the most effective agents of acculturation."[17]

It must be noted that there were numerous Catholic priests who resisted the worst of these imperial impulses by working incessantly against the abuses

---

13   Joseph de Acosta, *Historia Natural y Moral de las Indias* (Sevilla, España: Casa de Juan de Leon, 1590); José de Acosta, *Predicación del evangelio en las Indias*, Http://ecaths1.s3.amazonaws.com (accessed January 22, 2015).

14   Bartolomé de Las Casas, *A Short Account of the Destruction of the Indies*.

15   Las Casas also wrote his own multivolume history of the New World. See his 5 volume *Historia de las Indias* (Madrid, España: Imprenta de Miguel Ginesta, 1875). There was great negotiation and contestation as to the most reliable sources for the history of the natives of the Americas. Las Casas for example despised Fernández de Oviedo's *Historia General* because for him it "contained as many fictions almost as pages" (William Henry Brett, *The Indian Tribes of Guiana*, 38 note 2).

16   Bartolomé de Las Casas, *Del único modo de atraer a todos los pueblos a la verdadera religión*.

17   Claudio Esteva Fábregat, *El mestizaje en Iberoamérica* (Madrid, España: Editorial Alhambra, S.A., 1988), 23.

exacted on the originary communities of the world. For example, Dominicans have a long-standing tradition of working for justice and against the oppression of the Indigenous peoples in the Americas. This commitment was confirmed by the Dominicans in Latin America when they observed the fifth centenary of the arrival of the order to the Americas.[18] Accompanying documents provide instances of the multiple ways many friars worked tirelessly to improve the condition of the Indigenous communities by denouncing and actively opposing the encomienda system which enslaved and exploited the Indigenous peoples.[19] In the same vein, Enrique Dussel lists a number of the names of priests and bishops who were committed to countering the abuses against the natives of the Americas.[20] Still, without undermining the efforts of those priests and friars, Jorge Presmanes points out, from the beginning the church justified the colonization effort by presenting the "bloody conquest of the Americas ... as a Christian mission." He adds "what prevailed was a process of evangelization that imposed" a western symbolic structure as a condition for Christianity.[21]

---

18   Juan Manuel Pérez García and Francisco Javier Martínez Real, *In Evangelical Solidarity with the Oppressed: The Fifth Centenary Anniversary of the Arrival of the Order to America* (2011), Http://www.domlife.org/2011Stories/files/anniv_garcia_martinez.pdf (accessed August 20, 2015).

19   Ibid., 4, 12, 13, 20, 23.

20   Dussel mentions several names along with an assertion of the level of their commitment:

> Bartolomé de Las Casas, bishop of Chiapas (1544–47), Antonio de Valdivieso, of Nicaragua (1544–1550), Cristobal de Pedraza of Honduras (1545–1583), Pablo de Torres of Panama (1547–54), Juan del Valle, of Popayan (1548–63), Fernando de Uranga of Cuba (1552–56), Tomas de Casillas of Chiapas (1552–97), Bernardo de Alburquerque of Oaxaca (1559–79), Pedro de Angulo ofVera Paz (1560–62), Pedro de Agreda of Coro (1560–80), Juan de Simancas of Cartagena (1560–70), Domingo de Santo Tomas of La Plata (1563–70), Pedro de la Pena of Quito (1666–83), and Agustin de la Coruna of Popayan (1565–90). These bishops risked everything: they were committed even to failure; were expelled from their dioceses, imprisoned, expatriated and suffered death for the Indians ... The idealists—if we may use the expression—of the liberation of the Indians were the theologians of the Convent of San Esteban in Salamanca....only three of the bishops mentioned above were not Dominicans (Cited in Pérez García and Martínez Real, *In Evangelical Solidarity with the Oppressed*, 23).

> Among those priests who worked hard toward the abolition of slavery one could also mention the Capuchin friars Francisco José de Jaca and Epifanio Moiráns.

21   Jorge Presmanes, "Inculturation as Evangelization: The Dialogue of Faith and Culture in the Work of Marcello Azevedo," *U.S. Catholic Historian* 30, no. 1 (Winter 2012): 61.

Over the years, the church has changed enormously in terms of how it deals with issues related to its involvement and complicity with colonization. Unthinkable in earlier times, today the Catholic Church has officially acknowledged that the missionary enterprise also contributed to the destruction of the Indigenous population, their cultures, traditions, and ways of life.[22] For example, the 34th General Congregation of the Society of Jesus has unequivocally admitted the need to free the Gospel from the colonial legacy which has undervalued the native cultures of the world.[23] Theologian Karl Rahner also expressed that the "potency" of the church as a world church could only be "actualized in the course of an extensive historical process whose origins go back to the beginning of European colonialism and the modern world-mission of the church in the sixteenth century."[24] And theologian Robert Schreiter adds that: "Western European forms of Christianity were mediated through a dubious colonial heritage."[25]

Moreover, the acknowledgement of the Catholic Church's involvement in the destruction of the traditions and cultures of the originary peoples of the world were expressed in the apology by Pope John Paul II "for the 'pain and suffering' caused during the 500 years of the church's presence in the Americas, during a 1992 visit to the Dominican Republic."[26] More recently, Pope Francis followed suit during his recent visit to Bolivia stating "I humbly ask forgiveness, not only for the offenses of the church herself, but also for crimes committed against the native peoples during the so-called conquest of America."[27] Unfortunately, he did not go far enough in renouncing the so-called "doctrine of discovery."

There is no need to belabor the Church's complicity with colonization other than to highlight the kind of shift more recent acknowledgements represent

22   Pérez García and Martínez Real, *In Evangelical Solidarity with the Oppressed.*
23   Society of Jesus, "Decree 4: Our Mission and Culture," Published Conference Proceedings of the General Congregation 34 (1995), 84, Https://www.gonzaga.edu/about/Mission/docs/GC34Decree4OurMissionandCulture.pdf (accessed August 10, 2015).
24   Karl Rahner, "Towards a Fundamental Theological Interpretation of Vatican II," *Theological Studies* 40 (1979): 717.
25   Robert Schreiter, "Faith and Cultures: Challenges to a World Church," *Theological Studies* 50 (1989): 744.
26   Nicole Winfield, "Pope Apologizes for 'Serious Sins' During Colonization of Americas," *National Post*, July 2015, Http://news.nationalpost.com/news/world/pope-apologizes-for-serious-sins-during-colonization-of-americas (accessed August 27, 2015).
27   Ibid.

for the Catholic Church today.[28] It signals a move, a kind of "openness" to the peoples of the world who were directly impacted by European imperialism and colonization. No doubt, an important aspect of such change is the Catholic Church's defensive attempts to clean up its image in relation to its collusion with colonization. But other changes have taken place that have also contributed to the Catholic Church's self-perception and "opening up" to the cultural mosaic of the world.

Geopolitical Shifts and the Cultures of the World

As we saw in the previous chapter, mainline Protestants experienced a profound crisis as they wrestled with the enormous cost of the First and Second World Wars. In Catholic writings one also finds that the world wars and the great depression in the 1930s called for a new type of dialogue in the theology of the church.[29] Yet, in terms of questions of culture/civilization, I would argue that other broader geopolitical changes taking place in Africa and Asia, and later in Latin America—and how those connected to the history of colonialism—caused in the Catholic Church a sense of urgency in rethinking its position and relation to the non-European world, and to redefine the relation between faith and the cultural.[30] These challenges made the response of the Catholic Church more direct/practical/ oriented to the people.

---

28   The Catholic Church has not yet denounced the infamous "Doctrine of Discovery" which provided Western European colonial powers (at the end of the 15th century, and the United States at the beginning of the nineteenth century) with dispensation to seize lands, territories and resources, through the conquest, colonization, and exploitation of non-Christian nations. By "Doctrine of Discovery" I refer to two specific papal bulls: the 1452 Bull by Pope Nicholas issued to King Alfonso v of Portugal in which he declared war against all non-Christians; and the 1493 *Inter Caetera* pronounced by Pope Alexander vi in which he divided Latin America between the Spanish and Portuguese colonial powers. The doctrine has also been reformulated and expanded by the United States, most concretely expressed in the Monroe's doctrine of Manifest Destiny during the middle of the nineteenth century.

29   Azevedo, *Inculturation and the Challenges of Modernity*, 22.

30   For example, Manuel Marzal writes that certain social events have made it necessary for the magisterium of the Church to begin to deal with the problem of ethnicity. Among those issues he lists the decolonization of Africa with its concomitant affirmation of the African identities; the growing presence of the peoples of the third world; the resurgence of ethnic issues in the first and second world; and the need for the affirmation of differences in light of the growing homogenization of the world

We have seen that European imperialism (Great Britain, France, Spain, Portugal, The Netherlands, and Germany) was at its zenith in the early part of the nineteenth century and had spread its tentacles throughout the world. But in the early twentieth century, Western European colonialism began to decline for three important reasons. First, the new geopolitical configuration of the global landscape began to change with the emergence of the new imperial "kid on the block"—the United States of America. Its neocolonial status and theological ideology of "manifest destiny" was first expressed during its war with Mexico in 1848. With the Monroe doctrine, the United States of America's status as the new global imperial power was then solidified during its 1898 war with Spain, as a result of which Cuba, Puerto Rico and the Philippines fell under its "protectorate." Subsequently, the expansionist aspirations of the United States of America received concrete expression through a policy of interventionism that sought to spread its power and control all over Asia, Africa, and Latin America. Western European imperialism was being effectively succeeded/replaced by the United States of America.

Second, the first and second world wars and the accompanying Great Depression confronted all of Europe and the Euro North American with serious economic, political, social and cultural challenges. Though Russia's communist revolution had taken place in 1917, it was not until after the dust settled from the world wars that the conditions for the Cold war were cemented. By the middle of the twentieth century, NATO (North Atlantic Treaty Organization) (established in 1949) and WarPac (also known as the Warsaw Pact, the East European defense treaty under Soviet leadership in response to NATO, established in 1955) had become emblematic of the two opposing political and economic systems—each of which had enormous military resources at their disposal. Europe was divided and the rest of the world became a battleground on which to "resolve" rivalries.[31] The tensions were exacerbated with the United States of America's proclamation of the Truman Doctrine of 1947, offering military and economic assistance to all countries for maintaining independence, a policy which went well beyond

---

because of technology and culture and consumption. See Manuel Marzas, "Identidad peruana y doctrina social de la Iglesia," in *Identidad cultural y modernización*, vol. II, ed. Carlos Galli and Luis Scherz, América Latina y la doctrina social de la iglesia: Diálogo latinoamericano-alemán (Buenos Aires, Argentina: Ediciones Paulinas, 1991), II:194.

31   Cuba, Nicaragua, Vietnam, Korea, and Congo are good examples of how the Cold war was played out in the global scene.

John Foster Dulles' foreign policy of military alliances and aid to "roll back" communism.[32]

Third, as Western European imperialism declined many African and Asian countries seized the opportunity and obtained their independence, around the same time that the cold war was initiated. Many of these anticolonial movements which resulted in independent nations reacted strongly against historical Western European and Euro North American social, political, economic, cultural, and religious imposition and sought for ways to redress the effects of colonialism in their countries including within the Christian Church.

Most of the newly independent nations of Africa and Asia convened in 1955 in Bandung, Indonesia, to provide a third *neutral* alternative. They were unwilling to side either with the Western capitalist or with the Atheist Soviet Bloc. Triggered by the Bogor conference of 1949, the goal of Bandung was to solidify the social and political ties that corresponded with the history of colonialism among these countries.[33] Although Robert Young concludes that the "non-aligned alternative" was not able to transform into a positive, separate political identity, and never really developed "a common economic and political philosophy distinct from capitalism and socialism ...,"[34] it was significant that many of those present came together no longer as activists and leaders of local anticolonial movements (such as Ho Chi Minh of Vietnam and Kwame Nkrumah of Ghana) but as politicians in power. Most importantly, during the conference, the leaders of these countries spoke in support of anti-colonial movements (and their leaders) taking place in other neighboring countries not yet independent.[35]

By the time of the Tricontinental conference in Havana, Cuba, in 1966, the situation had radically changed. Whereas the countries that participated at Bandung insisted on a "politics of neutrality,"[36] in Havana they had become militant nations. According to Young, during the Bandung conference communism was seen as an evil that had to be uprooted and the United States

---

32   Robert C. Young, "Postcolonialism: From Bandung to the Tricontinental," *Historein* 5 (2005): 13, Http://www.nnet.gr/historein/historeinfiles/histvolumes/histo5/historein5-young.pdf (accessed August 24, 2015).

33   Bandung is generally thought of as originating the "Non-aligned Movement." However, the Non-Aligned Movement was actually formally initiated in Belgrade in 1961, a few years after the Bandung conference. See Young, "Postcolonialism," 11.

34   Young, "Postcolonialism," 13.

35   According to Young, "all the 29 countries signatories had the experience of colonialism and were supportive of anticolonial struggles and current countries under colonial rule" (Young, "Postcolonialism," 12).

36   Young, "Postcolonialism," 13.

of America had been perceived since 1945 as "bringing freedom across the world."[37] But during the Tricontinental, the roles had shifted; "the Soviet Union was regarded as the major ally, and the United States [of America] characterized as the global imperialist power that had to be resisted at all costs."[38] The shift brought enormous geopolitical implications: the envisioned non-alignment, notes Young, turned into alignment, and "the political philosophy of non-violence had moved to one of violence."[39] The radical shift also corresponded with the U.S.A. imperialist ambition. It had adopted a paternalistic role by engaging in numerous interventions, providing active military support to dictatorships, and overthrowing democratically elected governments in Guatemala, Brazil, Bolivia, South Vietnam and Egypt, for instance.

The significance of the Tricontinental conference cannot be overestimated. It was the first time that the countries of Asia, Africa, and Latin America gathered to reflect on their shared experience of European and United States of America colonialism. Particularly symbolic was the Cuban revolution of 1959. Across continents, countries found themselves with a common enemy.[40] Most importantly, many of the leaders of the countries present were deeply influenced by anticolonial thinkers such as Aime Césaire (Martinique), Franz Fanon (Martinique-Algeria), Léopold Sédar Senghor (Senegal), Che Guevara (Argentina-Cuba), among others. A central theme shared by these thinkers was the reclaiming of ethnic and cultural roots and history, and a widespread rejection of Western European and Euro North American cultural influence.

---

37   Ibid., 17.
38   Ibid., 14.
39   Ibid.
40   According to Young, "The Tricontinental brought together the anticolonial struggles of Africa and Asia with the radical movements of Latin America, and marked the initiation of a global alliance of the three continents of Africa, Asia and Latin America against imperialism." Young adds, the Tricontinental brought together the three continents of the South, and the "two different time-schemes of the postcolonial world: the newly liberated and the about-to-be-liberated, with the long-time liberated nations which were struggling for the second liberation of establishing true national sovereignty and autonomy" (Young, "Postcolonialism," 19). Because of these cross-alliances, Cuba and Vietnam particularly, found themselves having the United States as a common enemy, or, in the words of Young, "two Davids against a Goliath" (Ibid.,). In Latin America, other anticolonial movements like FMLN (Frente Farabundo Marti para la Liberación Nacional) in El Salvador, the FSLN (Frente Sandinista para la Liberación Nacional) in Nicaragua, and the URNG (Unión Revolucionaria Nacional Guatemalteca) in Guatemala were already growing and drawing inspiration from the Cuban revolution.

Not surprisingly, Christianity was perceived as having more than a cozy relationship with colonialism.[41] For example, in the Catholic context, the Society
of Jesus found that in many places people distrusted the church because of its
inseparable linkage with Western culture.[42] As a result, many countries pro-
ceeded to nationalize lands including mission schools and projects and move
toward the nationalization of the church, and its leaders.[43] Also, not surprising, the Catholic Church's response sided with the Western European and the
Euro North American countries and their capitalist systems, in response to
the professed atheism of the communists and their now growing allies. This
dynamic contributed to the church's rejection in those communist countries.

My intention in revising this incredibly complex period of history is not
merely to rehash the events, noting the key players, central themes and concerns. Rather, I want to emphasize how this general backlash against Western
European and Euro North American cultures and colonial legacy in Asia,
Africa, and Latin America[44] had a direct impact on the Catholic Church, to the
point of causing significant shifts in its structures and theologies.

In light of this complexity of issues I reiterate that multiple factors fed
directly into the Second Vatican Council. I argue that from the perspective
of the majority world, the church's legacy of colonization lead to a number of impulses: the impetus toward reclaiming their own cultural expressions and epistemologies; the decentering/provincialization of Europe

---

41   Both Catholics and mainstream Protestants lost ground in Africa during this process
      of nationalization in Sudan, Malawi, and Ghana. The negative effects of colonialism in
      Africa were evident. According to Elizabeth Isichei, "African Christendom, like Africa in
      general, is divided by language barriers. Indeed, one of the most lasting and pernicious
      results of colonialism is its division of Africa into English-, French-, and Portuguese-
      speaking countries." Not surprisingly, she adds "These divisions go deeper than lan-
      guage" (Elizabeth Isichei, *A History of Christianity in Africa: From Antiquity to the Present*
      [London, UK: SPCK, 1995], 332).

42   Society of Jesus, "Decree 4: Our Mission and Culture," 81.

43   Isichei, *A History of Christianity in Africa*, 334.

44   Young argues that the Tricontinental conference embodied a real

          "proletarian internationalism," a globalisation of solidarity between the human family,
          working for "a world that is really for all, without hunger or poverty, without oppres-
          sion or exploitation, without humiliations or contempt, without injustice or inequal-
          ities, where everyone might live in full moral and material dignity, in true liberty." In
          affirming these values, the Tricontinental positioned itself firmly against those forces
          in the world that sought to impose forms of domination and exploitation on the
          poorer peoples of the earth (Young, "Postcolonialism," 19).

and European theology;[45] the move to the nationalization of the church with indigenous leaders; and the realization that Christianity's presence was shifting toward the Global South. All of these factors pressured the Catholic Church's structures at Vatican II into *supporting* more contextual expressions of Christianity, *encouraging* new approaches to evangelization different from those during colonization, and *promoting* a theological understanding of the church to encompass the other cultures of the world. Looking at Vatican II from the perspective of Western Europe and the Euro North American regions, there were also a number of factors. Avery Dulles notes that there were a number of forces that contributed to the Council's actual occurrence, including: the demise of European colonialism; the statistical growth of Christianity outside of Europe; the decline of the classical culture that provided the "critical apparatus for European Catholicism, ... its displacement by the new scientific and technological mentality;" and the collapse of the Christian culture that had permeated the public life of Europe.[46]

These interconnected factors help us understand how the Catholic Church has articulated the relationship between the gospel and the cultural since the turn of the twentieth century, and how those issues have changed the church's own perception and theology. Conspicuously, even the very nature of the Church's catholicity was being redefined. On the eve of Vatican II, Belgian Jesuit missiologist Joseph Masson anticipated the reconfigurations when he claimed that the church's openness to the multiplicity of cultures would be an evident postulate of its catholicity.[47]

Vatican II did mark a radical turning point in the way the Catholic Church redefined itself and how it articulated the relationship between the cultural and the Christian faith. However, it was not the starting point. Even prior to the Council there were animated discussions concerning the question of how the gospel related to other cultures among theologians, popes, and missionaries and they have continued ever since. With that in mind, in what follows, I discuss some of the official documents from pre, during and post Vatican II

----

45   As the Society of Jesus document explains, in many places in Africa there is a "great desire to create a truly African Christianity" (Society of Jesus, "Decree 4: Our Mission and Culture," 84).

46   Avery Dulles, "The Emerging World Church: A Theological Reflection," paper presented at the Thirty-ninth Annual convention, Catholic Society of America (Washington, DC, 1984), 2, Http://ejournals.bc.edu/ojs/index.php/ctsa/article/view/3179/2792 (accessed August 3, 2015).

47   Masson, "L'Eglise Ouverte sur le Monde," 1038.

eras, in order to trace the development of these debates. Again, this discussion is not meant to be exhaustive; it is not the definitive word on how the Catholic Church has dealt with how the gospel relates to the cultural. It is rather a sample of some of the most important documents on these debates, illustrating the "progression" and current "openness" of the Vatican in relation to the cultures of the world. It also exemplifies how these shifts have meant a theological reconceptualization of the Catholic Church itself along with its very sense of Catholicity.

The Culturalization of the Church: Evangelization, and Inculturation

Pre-Second Vatican Council

Just as the creation of the World Council of Churches in 1948 signified a change of attitudes toward the other cultures of the world among mainline Protestants, so also the Second Vatican Council signified a similar shift within the Catholic Church. In the Catholic Church, these shifts had already been fermenting for some time and the Vatican gradually sought ways to maintain a "balance" between the gospel message and the influence of the multiple cultures of the world.

Already in 1944, when Pope Pius XII promoted missionary work in Africa, he acknowledged the cultural diversity of the region and emphasized the Gospel's elevating function of local cultures.[48] At this early stage the Vatican was already promoting the importance of indigenous/native clerics and a somewhat surprising insistence that the local traditions and native customs must remain untouched, with the caveat: "as long as they remain compatible with the divine law."[49] In an official capacity, Pope Pius XII showed a "cautious openness" to and acknowledgment of "the validity of a plurality of cultures" inhabiting the world.[50]

The unexamined complicity between colonization and evangelization and the recognition of the reality of other cultures co-exist in the writings

---

48   Pius XII, "Speech to the Directors of the Pontifical Missionary Work in Rome," *AAS* 36 (1944): 207–11, Http://www.vatican.va/archive/aas/documents/AAS-36-1944-ocr.pdf (accessed August 26, 2015).

49   Pius XII, "Speech to the Directors," 210. "di qui il principio che l'indole, le tradizioni e i costumi nativi debbono rimanere inviolati, in quanto sono conciliabili con la legge divina."

50   Schreiter, "Faith and Cultures," 748.

of Pope Pius XII. His neglect of the terrible results of colonization becomes obvious when he celebrated the missionaries who took the gospel to other parts of the world since the sixteenth century without acknowledging that it coincides with the emergence of Western European imperialism.[51] And yet, for him Christianity and Western European culture were evidently interconnected. In fact, he wrote that "Christian civilization" did not stifle nor weaken the healthy elements from the various native cultures. Rather, it gave those cultures standards of morality and very solid foundations of true peace, social justice and brotherly love between all members of the human family.[52] Unfortunately, left over paternalistic views and attitudes of superiority from the colonial legacy imbue his ideas about other cultures. For example, he defended the position of the Catholic Church in his *Evangelii Praecones*:

> ... the Catholic Church has neither scorned nor rejected the pagan philosophies. Instead, after freeing them from error and all contamination she has perfected and completed them by Christian revelation. So likewise the Church has graciously made her own the native art and culture which in some countries is so highly developed. She has carefully encouraged them and has brought them to a point of aesthetic perfection that of themselves they probably would never have attained. By no means has she repressed native customs and traditions but has given them a certain religious significance; she has even transformed their feast days and made them serve to commemorate the martyrs and to celebrate mysteries of the faith.[53]

Pope Pius XII's apparent promotion of respect for and celebration of local cultures and leaders is exposed for its disingenuousness when the other cultures are (implicitly) cast as inferior. These cultures continued to constitute the missionary field, and they were understood to need the (Western European expressions of the) Catholic Church to be "perfected," "elevated," and "transformed," code words that reflect the Western European understanding and adoption of Catholicism.

---

51   Pius XII, "Speech to the Directors," 208.

52   Pius XII, "Nuntius Radiophonicus," *AAS* 36 (1944): 250, Http://www.vatican.va/archive/aas/documents/AAS-36-1944-ocr.pdf (accessed August 26, 2015).

53   Pius XII, *Evangelii Praecones* [*Encyclical Letter on Promotion of Catholic Missions*] (1951), 58, Http://w2.vatican.va/content/pius-xii/en/encyclicals/documents/hf_p-xii_enc _02061951_evangelii-praecones.html (accessed August 26, 2015).

By the 1950s, however, the imminent threat of the independence of many former European colonies became part of the preoccupations of the Vatican. The church was forced to reflect practically on issues like the indigenization of local leaders and the potential challenges-changes of the new nationalisms, locally and for the church more broadly. There were pressures for "more independent modes of thought" and consequently independent theologies.[54] In order to deal with some of those concerns, Pope John XXIII in his *Princep Pastorum* restated-quoted Pope Pius XII and his position which distanced itself from Western culture in his *Evangelii Praecones*.[55] At the same time, by citing Pope Piux XII, Pope John XXIII strategically deflected attention away from the church's colonial legacy, but left the door opened for the conceptualization of a multicultural church.

Further, in his 1959 letter to the participants at the Second World Congress of Negro Writers and Artists, Pope John XXIII maintained that the church "cannot be identified with any culture, not even the Western culture, with which its history is closely mixed."[56] The rationale he provided was simply that the mission of the church is of another *order*, namely, the salvation of humanity. He went further and pronounced the church's openness to the "renewal breath of the Spirit," remaining "ready to recognize, welcome and even animate ... the intelligence of the human heart from other shores of the world, of which the Mediterranean basin was the providential cradle of Christianity."[57] Again, by adopting a posture of openness Pope John XXIII contributed to the painstaking process of reconfiguring the church as a mosaic of cultures.

Not surprisingly, Masson was deeply motivated to challenge the church to take the emergence of the cultures of the world as an opportunity to build,

---

54   Schreiter, "Faith and Cultures," 748. Schreiter confirms that even structurally, together with political independence, these "mission fields" were elevated to dioceses, thus experiencing certain ecclesial autonomy and in turn changing the configuration of the Church. See Ibid., 749.

55   John XXIII, *Princepts Pastorum* [*Encyclical Letter on the Missions, Native Clergy, and Lay Participation*] (1959), 522, Http://www.papagiovanni.com/sito/images/vita/princepspastorum _en.pdf (accessed August 25, 2015).

56   John XXIII, "Letter to the Participants at the Second World Congress for Negro Writers and Artists," *AAS* 51 (1959): 260, Http://www.vatican.va/archive/aas/documents/AAS-51 -1959-ocr.pdf (accessed August 26, 2015).

57   John XXIII, "Congress for Negro Writers and Artists," 260. "Mais l'Eglise, pleine d'une jeunesse sans cesse renouvelée au souffle de l'Esprit, demeure disposée à reconnaître, à accueillir, et même à animer tout ce qui est à l'honneur de l'intelligence et du cœur humain sur d'autres plages du monde que ce bassin méditerranéen qui fut le berceau providentiel du christianisme."

for the first time, a truly *Catholic* Church.[58] His invitation was timely since Vatican II was on the verge of taking place. As far as he was concerned, the church had to be opened to modernity in order to be present, but also had to welcome the multiplicity of possible expressions of Catholicism throughout the world. "Western culture itself," he wrote, "if it is a Christian culture (which can largely be doubted in the face of modernity) is by no means the only possible Christian culture; It is even dangerous that she considers itself as such."[59] Masson was acutely aware that "spatial catholicity" or the presence of the church everywhere would be of little importance if the church remained closed to the changes that were taking place.[60] Still, unable to overcome his own paternalism, he concluded that those cultures have the right to love God with their hearts, customs, and habits, while European cultures had the responsibility to help them achieve it.[61]

For the purpose of this chapter, Masson was the first to deploy "inculturation" acknowledging the then "polymorphous" (and I would argue multicultural) expressions of Catholicism in the world. Michael Sievernich insists that Masson's used inculturation to "describe how the Christian message could take root in, or be grafted onto, non-Christian cultures."[62] Yet, it seems more accurate to conclude that for Masson the concern was not so much evangelization or missions as the inclusion of those cultural groups that had already embraced Christianity, who already had their own culturally conditioned *Catholic* expression of faith, but that had not been included in traditional understandings of the church. For him, what was at stake was the redefinition of the church and its catholicity in a way that included all the peoples of the world.

Masson's article provides a glimpse into the kinds of issues that were floating around among the leaders of the church prior to the Vatican II. Those issues were obviously front and centre in the discussions during the Council and they found themselves reflected in the final documents. To that we now turn.

Second Vatican Council

One could ask: what makes the events of Vatican II so significant? Theologian Karl Rahner contended that the Council marked a monumental shift which

---

58   Masson, "L'Eglise Ouverte sur le Monde," 1033.

59   Masson, "L'Eglise Ouverte sur le Monde," 1039. "la culture occidentale, même si elle est encore une culture chrétienne (ce dont on peut largement douter pour son visage moderne), n'est en aucun cas *la* seule culture chrétienne possible; il est même fort dangereux qu'elle se regarde comme telle ..."

60   Masson, "L'Eglise Ouverte sur le Monde," 1036.

61   Ibid., 1039.

62   Michael Sievernich, "Jesuit Theologies of Mission," *The Way* 42, no. 1 (January 2003): 45.

can only be compared to the changes that took place in the separation between Gentile and Jewish Christians in the early Church.[63] The shift in Vatican II, claimed Rahner, was so fundamental that it marked the first incontestable self-actualization of the Church *as* a world church in a fully official way.[64] In practical terms the Council created the conditions for phasing-out Latin from the liturgy and admitted the vernacular languages of the people; it encouraged the full, active conscious participation of the people. It also provided for the establishment of the International Synod of Bishops and "gave new status to regional and national bishops' conferences."[65] And in terms of evangelization, it endorsed the principle of missionary "accommodation." The affirmation of the emergence of this "world church," claims Dulles, suggests that the period when "Catholicism as a whole could be equated with its expression in the forms of Graeco-Roman, Mediterranean, or European culture" had come to an end. In the words of Dulles: "We are witnessing the birth of a new multicultural Catholicism in which all the regional churches may be expected to interact, mutually criticizing and enriching one another."[66]

The implications of Dulles' comments are enormous. He offers a much more optimistic perspective than Masson—with his cautious foresight prior to the Council—or Rahner not too long after it. I propose that his positive outlook is informed by official documents to which neither Masson nor Rahner had access. Still, it begs the question as to whether the documents of Vatican II really warranted this positive outlook. Though this conclusion is largely taken for granted, I suggest that the jury is still out, since different scholars have interpreted these documents differently. Certainly, for our purposes, some of the documents contain important affirmations that should not be taken lightly

---

63   According to Rahner, the shift "means that in the history of Christianity the transition of Christianity from one historical and theological situation to an essentially new one did happen *once,* and that now in the transition from a Christianity of Europe (with its American annexes) to a fully world religion it is starting to happen for a second time" (Rahner, "Fundamental Theological Interpretation," 722).

64   Rahner, "Fundamental Theological Interpretation," 717–18.

65   Dulles, "The Emerging World Church," 2.

66   Dulles, "The Emerging World Church," 1. According to Dulles, the novelty of the present situation can be illustrated by contrasting the period from 1500 to 1900, the "great epoch of missionary expansion." In that period, he writes, "Christianity, though it was disseminated to all parts of the globe, remained an essentially European phenomenon, exported in European form. Christians of other continents took European names, used European languages in their worship, studied the religious history of the West, and learned their theology from European textbooks" (Ibid.). Although he admits that this period has not entirely come to an end, it is gradually loosing strength.

in terms of the debates on "Christianity/faith" and "culture." Let us examine key sections in light of the themes I consider.

Lumen Gentium—one of the only two dogmatic documents produced by Vatican II—affirms the mysterious character of the church. The proclamation is pivotal, presenting the church both as partly human and partly divine dependent on Christ, for its existence, Christ as the mystery of the incarnate Word. The church's mission is to serve the divine Word, and as such it is a "living instrument of salvation."[67] In a very interesting move, the document also endorses the social structures of the church as serving the Spirit of Christ, appearing to ensure the preservation of the present configuration of the church. In terms of issues of how cultural traditions relate to the Christian faith, there is an intentional ploy by which the church's catholicity is affirmed on the basis of the church's constituency of believers from all over the world.[68] Moreover, the universal church is constituted by a "communion of churches."[69] Such an apparent unequivocal statement is tempered however, with a second declaration emphasizing the church's "purifying" and "perfecting" role of people's customs.[70] This statement brings to mind Pope Pius XII's comments earlier in *Evangelii Praecones*, and it also resonates with earlier civilizing attitudes toward non-European cultures. As a result, there are some unresolved tensions in the document.

This second statement appears once again in *Sacrosanctum Concilium*, and this time connected to issues of (doctrinal) error and superstition. The document establishes definitive changes in which local communities can incorporate some of their cultures and customs in the way they celebrate and express their faith by way of changing liturgical books, for example.[71] The intention, it seems, is to leave an open space for some liturgical documents to be adapted according to different groups, regions and peoples and not to impose uniformity.[72]

---

67   Vatican Council II, "*Lumen Gentium* [Dogmatic Constitution of the Church]," in *Vatican Council II, Constitutions, Decrees, Declarations: The Basic Sixteen Document with a Completely Revised Translation in Inclusive Language*, gen. ed. Austin Flannery (New York, NY: Costello Publishing House; Dublin: Dominican Publications, 1996), 8.

68   Ibid., 14.

69   Schreiter, "Faith and Cultures," 749.

70   Vatican Council II, "*Lumen Gentium*," 12, 17

71   Vatican Council II, "*Sacrosanctum Concilium* [The Constitution on the Sacred Liturgy]," in *Vatican Council II, Constitutions, Decrees, Declarations: The Basic Sixteen Document with a Completely Revised Translation in Inclusive Language*, gen. ed. Austin Flannery (New York, NY: Costello Publishing House; Dublin: Dominican Publications, 1996), 38–40.

72   As it reads: "Even in the liturgy the church does not wish to impose a rigid uniformity in matters which do not affect the faith or the well-being of the entire community" (Vatican Council II, "*Sacrosanctum Concilium* [The Constitution on the Sacred Liturgy]," 37).

But here again, the tension appears. The document is presented as an invitation to include only certain elements from people's ways of life, "provided they harmonize" with the general doctrine and practices of the church.[73] The "sympathy" of the church can be expected only for those cultural aspects, traditions, and customs which do not embody "superstition" and "error," notions fraught with Western European colonizing ideas about the other cultures of the world. The negative remarks seem to be almost contradictory given the fact that *Ad Gentes*[74] and *Nostra Aetate*[75] appear to stimulate respect and in fact promote dialogue with other religious traditions, while still upholding the task of evangelization.

Curiously, despite their subject matter, in *Nostra Aetate* (on non-Christian religions) one does not find substantive discussion on matters related to culture. Being one of the most contested aspects in the debates of faith and cultural traditions, the document is very selective in that it emphasizes so-called "world-religions" and even more selectively focuses particularly on the other two so-called "Abrahamic religions." The cultures, religious traditions and spiritualities of the former colonies remain absent. The fact that the document does not take these traditions seriously is highly problematic, since it is those popular religions and religious practices, those which are most distinctly interwoven with people's cultures, which were deemed demonic by the colonial forces.

Similarly, it is also surprising that *Dei Verbum*[76] does not deal with the connection between cultures and divine revelation. It focuses particularly on the hermeneutical aspect of the biblical text. By so doing, cultural issues figure

---

73   Vatican Council II, "*Sacrosanctum Concilium* [The Constitution on the Sacred Liturgy]," 37. It also affirms traditional European practices like Gregorian chant and the use of certain instruments over and above certain other instruments.

74   Vatican Council II, "*Ad Gentes Divinitus* [Decree on the Church's Missionary Activity]," in *Vatican Council II, Constitutions, Decrees, Declarations: The Basic Sixteen Document with a Completely Revised Translation in Inclusive Language*, gen. ed. Austin Flannery (New York, NY: Costello Publishing House; Dublin: Dominican Publications, 1996), 443–97.

75   Vatican Council II, "*Nostra Aetate* [Declaration on the Relation of the Church to Non-Christian Religions]," in *Vatican Council II, Constitutions, Decrees, Declarations: The Basic Sixteen Document with a Completely Revised Translation in Inclusive Language*, gen. ed. Austin Flannery (New York, NY: Costello Publishing House; Dublin: Dominican Publications, 1996), 569–74.

76   Vatican Council II, "*Dei Verbum* [Dogmatic Constitution on Divine Revelation]," in *Vatican Council II, Constitutions, Decrees, Declarations: The Basic Sixteen Document with a Completely Revised Translation in Inclusive Language*, gen. ed. Austin Flannery (New York, NY: Costello Publishing House; Dublin: Dominican Publications, 1996), 443–97.

prominently only in relation to the authors and not the readers because it does not account for the impact the reader's cultural background in the act of reading the text. It furthermore gives no acknowledgement of the cultural particularity of the revelation as it took place in Jesus in the first century Palestinian context. There is also no recognition of how (or whether) cultures impact the "revelation" itself and how it is communicated and received.

An almost entirely different spirit seems to animate *Ad Gentes.* Most particularly, the history of missions has been one of the most (if not the most) contested issues in discerning the relation of the church to the rest of the world and the relation of the gospel to other (non-European and Euro North American) cultures. To repeat, in the former colonies, it was when missionaries carried the task of evangelization that the cultural traditions of the myriad Indigenous peoples of the world were destroyed. This is the single most crucial point in which evangelization and colonization, the church and empire, intersected and worked together.

The decree does not shy away from this conundrum. While it does not explicitly acknowledge the church's complicity with empire, an omission it shares with all the other documents of the Vatican II, *Ad Gentes* does provide important insights that reveal a change in attitudes concerning the other peoples of the world and their cultural traditions. The first aspect I highlight is the advice to missionaries that, if they are to be witnesses of Christ, they should immerse themselves and "share in [the] social and cultural life" of the people.[77] This recommendation is a clear departure from previous approaches in which missionaries sought to reproduce/export the European social and cultural world wherever they went. Second, because the document dedicates a good portion to the establishments of local churches, it is important to note that the decree emphasizes that those communities be "endowed with the cultural riches of its own nation,"[78] which potentially creates the conditions for new local churches to truly reflect their immediate cultural context.[79] And third, the document goes to great length to establish a minimum training through which missionaries ought to become familiar with the social structures, customs, cultures, histories, languages, and religions of the people and nation where they might be sent.[80] They are

---

77   Vatican Council II, "*Ad Gentes,*" 11.

78   Ibid., 15.

79   Vatican Council II, "*Ad Gentes,*" 19. In fact, as missionaries think about establishing/ implanting local churches, the assumption is that those communities will be "rooted in the social life of the people and to some extent conformed to its culture ..." (Ibid.).

80   Vatican Council II, "*Ad Gentes,*" 26.

instructed to treat the people they encounter with respect and "hold their [cultural] inheritance, language, and way of life in high esteem."[81]

In the end however, *Ad Gentes* mandates that Bishops and local priests should preserve their communion with the "universal church." Bishops and priests are instructed to "graft" elements from the tradition of the church on to the local cultures in order to preserve the intimate communion with the church.[82] Even though the decree pushes toward a model mildly suggestive of reciprocity and mutuality, it falls short of empowering local communities to use their cultures as agents in the building of the life of the mystical body that is the (universal) church.

I close my reflections on the documents of Vatican II with a brief discussion of *Gaudium et spes*. *Gaudium et spes* is more intentionally designed to address some of the gaps concerning debates on faith and culture in the other documents produced by the Council. And it certainly goes beyond any official document written on the subject matter until then. As its title indicates, the main thrust of the document is to spell out the pastoral role of the church in view of modernity's advances. Not so clear in the title, but certainly evident in the content of the document is the theological repositioning (even reconceptualization) of the church in relation to human cultural collectives.

Addressed to the human family, the introduction sets the tone for the entire document outlining the multiple social, economic, political, cultural, and technological challenges facing the church, and its responsibility to respond thoughtfully for its constituency. The newly independent (African and Asian) nations are specifically welcomed as they, along with other developing nations, are acknowledged as the new actors in world affairs.[83]

Three things stand out: the first is a "political" strategic move by which the church is depicted as an institution dedicated only to its God-given mission of evangelization. In fulfilling its universal mission, the church is therefore not committed to any one cultural tradition or to any political, economic or social system.[84] Resonating with Pope John XXII,[85] and in even less ambiguous terms, the church is described as not "tied exclusively and indissolubly to any race or nation,

---

81   Ibid.

82   Ibid., 19.

83   Vatican Council II, "*Gaudium et spes* [Pastoral Constitution on the Church in the Modern World]," in *Vatican Council II, Constitutions, Decrees, Declarations: The Basic Sixteen Document with a Completely Revised Translation in Inclusive Language*, gen. ed. Austin Flannery (New York, NY: Costello Publishing House; Dublin: Dominican Publications, 1996), 9.

84   Ibid., 42.

85   See John XXIII, "Congress for Negro Writers and Artists," 260.

to any one particular way of life, or to any set of customs, ancient or modern."[86] The document presents the church as remaining faithful to her Christian tradition while cognizant of her universal mission. And it is from this vantage point that she enters into communion with other cultural modes.[87] I note however that there is no hint at acknowledging her complicity with colonial regimes. The second facet is the open acknowledgment of the sociological-anthropological-empirical reality of cultural diversity in the world. Although the document connects with some of the earliest understandings of "culture"—as cultivation of humanity—such views get conflated with notions of *civilization*; the church recognized that different life styles represent different value systems, ways of practicing religion, ways of working and self-expression, developments in science and the arts, and laws and juridical institutions.[88] The role of people as cultural agents cannot be set aside here. Humans, claims the document, are the architects and molders of their communities' cultures.[89] The implications for the church are enormous, since it would need to reconsider both how the task of evangelization, and the way people choose to live their lives and express their faith, are intimately linked to their cultural contexts and traditions.

Relatedly, the third point I want to raise is the portrayal of the church as having a long-standing record of working with and drawing from the cultures of the peoples to whom it has announced the gospel message. Again, with virtually no allusion to the role of past missionary practices in the destruction of local Indigenous cultural communities, we are told that "early in its history" the church learned to express the Christian message "in the concepts and languages of different peoples and tried to clarify it in the light of the wisdom of their philosophers."[90] The church's presence through time

---

86   Vatican Council II, "*Gaudium et spes*," 58. Gallagher tells us that this phrase may be connected to a comment by Cardinal Lercado, who during the council insisted that the "church should embrace a certain cultural poverty....the Church should explore the languages of contemporary culture and its emerging values" (Gallagher, *Clashing Symbols*, 41).

87   Vatican Council II, "*Gaudium et spes*," 58.

88   Vatican Council II, "*Gaudium et spes*," 53. According to Gallagher, paragraph 53 draws on the older meaning of culture, as a "field of human growth and of intellectual or aesthetic achievement—with the more empirical sense of culture (or cultures) as embodied in social structures and in historically diverse approaches to life" (Gallagher, *Clashing Symbols*, 39).

89   Vatican Council II, "*Gaudium et spes*," 55.

90   Vatican Council II, "*Gaudium et spes*," 44. This admission seems to refer to the initial ways in which early Christians drew from Greek philosophy to articulate the gospel message, but it certainly does not refer to the missionary project from the sixteenth to the end of the nineteenth centuries.

is tied to the transcendent Word. Just as God spoke "in the context of the culture proper to each age," so also the church throughout the centuries "has utilized the resources of different cultures to spread and explain the message of Christ ..."[91] One important feature of the interaction of the church with other cultures is a relationship of mutual enrichment and exchange.[92] It is for this reason that the church encourages dialogue between groups and nations, careful not to destroy traditional wisdom and endangering people's native characteristics.[93]

These three points make up what I consider the call of the Council for preserving the delicate balance between the integrity of the Gospel and safeguarding local cultural traditions and customs. The task is the transformation of the methods of evangelization:

> The move is for inculturation insisting for suitable forms of expressions and in conformity with liturgical requirements: ... the knowledge of God will be made more widely available; the preaching of the Gospel will be rendered more intelligible and will appear more relevant to people's situations.... the faithful ought to work closely with their contemporaries and ought to try to understand their ways of thinking and feeling, as these find expression in [their] current culture[s].[94]

It is important to note, however, that these three points are subsumed within a response to larger questions of "modern culture." This document is first and foremost a full-fledged "new humanism" enshrined in its support of modernity, and connected to the growth of technology, with the hope that it will aid in the development of a new humanity.[95] Framed within it is an Augustinian paradigm of the two cities: the worldly city, *culture* (the earthly and material realm where humans reject God) is articulated in the singular; without qualifications it refers to modernity, the sciences and technological advance. And the *City of God*, the universal church (embodying human desire to follow God) that is united but is also described as being culturally diverse. Although the declarations about modernity mark yet another shift away from anything that might look "obscurantist" in the church, the document nevertheless turns

---

91   Vatican Council II, "*Gaudium et spes*," 58.
92   Ibid., 44, 58.
93   Ibid., 56.
94   Ibid., 62.
95   Ibid., 56; Gallagher, *Clashing Symbols*, 39.

Eurocentric in its premise and goals.[96] Drawing on the Enlightenment, the council deploys a notion of *culture* which is in line with Western European notions of *civilization*: culture is described as flowing from "humanity's *rational* and social nature, has continual need of proper *freedom* of *development* and a legitimate possibility of *autonomy* according to its own principles."[97] (Italics mine) Indeed, the Council admits, technological advance should lead to fruitful dialogue between cultures, but it also has the potential to disrupt the life of communities and destroy their traditional forms of wisdom.[98] As a form of safeguarding this disruption and destruction from happening, the council insists that the growth of "culture" must be subordinated to the development of the human person, the good of the community and entire humanity.[99] Simultaneously, and quite romantically, the document announces that since humans are creators of culture within their own communities, such an act of creation (should) inaugurates a new universal culture of human solidarity.[100]

The confrontation between the earthly city and divine city is noticeable at this point: all people have the right to culture (read right to the benefits of modernity, technology and scientific advance),[101] and they are encouraged to engage in any cultural activity they please, yet, they must still ensure such activity does not violate the moral order.[102] Moreover, the challenge in developing this culture will be to harmonize the enormous progress of science and technology with *classical studies* from various traditions.[103] This emphasis does not seem to point to the other cultures of the world but the vigilant support of "modern culture." Echoes of earlier civilizing missionary projects thus surface. "Modernization" makes it possible to remove the "curse of ignorance" from most of the human race. This is a task most pertinent for Christians, in

---

96   Here there is a clear distancing from documents such as Pope Pius IX Syllabus of errors. See Pius IX, *The Syllabus of Errors* [*Encyclical Letter*] (1862), Http://www.papalencyclicals.net/Pius09/p9syll.htm (accessed August 10, 2015).

97   Vatican Council II, "*Gaudium et spes*," 59.

98   Ibid., 56.

99   Ibid., 59.

100   Ibid., 55–56.

101   This point is made at the beginning, where the "developing" and independent nations are depicted as "anxious to share in the political and economic benefits of modern civilization." Further, the juxtaposition between the cultures of the world and "modern culture" becomes evident: "Now for the first time in history people are not afraid to think that cultural benefits are for all and should be available to everybody" (Vatican Council II, "*Gaudium et spes*," 9).

102   Vatican Council II, "*Gaudium et spes*," 59.

103   Ibid., 56.

order to ensure that there is "sufficiency of cultural benefits available to every-body, especially the benefit of what is called 'basic' culture ..."[104]

Gaudium et spes is considered by many to be the *magna carta* when it comes to debating the Vatican II's treatment of culture.[105] Drawing on this document, Sievernich applauds Vatican II for its bold recognition that claims that all races have the capacity to express the message of Christ in their own fashion.[106] And Schreiter tells us that although the document did not wish to reduce culture to only an empirical or sociological concept, it clearly embraced this approach by stressing the plurality of cultures.[107] Schreiter also tells us that *Gaudium et spes* is the first place that culture is embraced at the highest level in a Catholic context. But as I have shown, the deployment of "culture" creates some confusion. Interwoven within it, one encounters several meanings of culture that do not receive equal treatment. For instance, one use of the term "culture" points to social philosophi-cal trends and phenomena like secularism.[108] In instances like this, the document expresses the sense of despair that Christianity has been replaced and that it no longer has as much social clout or influence. *Culture* as civilization is the one use which overshadows others. In these cases, culture really points to an instrumental and utilitarian notion of the production of cultural elements that make it possi-ble to advance and facilitate human existence on earth, including through the shaping of societies and social structures. Unfortunately, it is this meaning and its multiple connections to modernity, technology and the sciences, that dominates the document. It is for this reason that the almost antithetical tension between culture and church is preserved in this document.

As to how Christianity relates to other cultures, the central concern remains evangelization. Culture becomes a kind of shorthand to include all the peoples of the world under the rubric of cultural groups. This meaning of culture is the least developed in the pastoral document since it says little about how these different cultures represent decidedly different "visions of the universe" (cos-movisions not worldviews), ways to interact with nature and the environment, epistemologies, psychological and rational modes of living life, and ways to express faith in God. All these concerns are left untouched and unaddressed. In fact, with its excessive emphasis on culture as modernity, the other cultures

---

104   Vatican Council II, "*Gaudium et spes*," 60. The text continues: "lest any be prevented by illiteracy and lack of initiative from contributing in an authentically human way to the common good" (Ibid.).
105   Gallagher, *Clashing Symbols*, 43.
106   Sievernich, "Jesuit Theologies of Mission," 46.
107   Schreiter, "Faith and Cultures," 750.
108   Vatican Council II, "*Gaudium et spes*," 43.

of the world become yet again the recipients of (Western European and Euro North American) civilization, and "modern" Christians have a duty to help them advance. By virtue of this Eurocentric framing, the document falls short of uncovering or even remotely questioning the myth of modernity.[109] It also does not speak about the possibility that "progress," scientific development, and technological advance in ther capitalist expressions are or are not in fact desirable for all of humanity and the world.

Considering the documents of Vatican II, one cannot but conclude that in many ways it was a response to the accelerated growth of the church outside the Western European and Western North American regions. Such growth changed and is changing the balance of presence and political strength within the Church. The reconfiguration of Christianity signaled by Vatican II was not so much the result of intentional work by the Council, however. Rather it was caused by the social development and move-expansion of Christianity to the rest of the world (1) and simultaneous de-Christianization of Europe (2). For this reason, I suggest that Vatican II fell short of being a call to conversion for the Western European and Euro North American churches; a conversion to finally abandon colonizing attitudes and embrace the rest of the world as constitutive part of the *Catholic* Church.

Can we say that Vatican II went far enough? Did the shift that was so anticipated and celebrated in fact take place? Rahner himself did not seem convinced. At best, he stated, the Council was an "ecclesiastically official *beginning*," a fundamental caesura from the dominant Western European and Euro North American cultural and theological character of Christianity.[110] It would be a mistake to conclude that Vatican II went far enough in creating the conditions for a truly world Church. Certainly, there was an increased representation from church leaders from the majority world, but their participation and impact were minimal. The cultures of the peoples did figure prominently, but what resulted was a proposal of a "transformation" that continues to privilege the present Western European configuration of the Church's liturgy, theology and culture. Dulles admits that Vatican II took "cautious steps in the direction of de-Europeanizing" Christianity, but such affirmations seem to be contradicted by the situation on the ground at the meeting.[111] For example, Rahner himself held that

---

109   Enrique Dussel, *The Underside of Modernity*.

110   Rahner, "Fundamental Theological Interpretation," 711, 723.

111   Dulles, "The Emerging World Church," 2.

during the Council different rites were presented but one could not see any African dances.[112] In terms of morality, he incisively enquired: "Must the marital morality of the Masais in East Africa simply reproduce the morality of Western Christianity, or could a chieftain there, even if he is a Christian, live in the style of the patriarch Abraham? Must the Eucharist even in Alaska be celebrated with grape wine?"[113]

One cannot overestimate the fact that these various documents entail a significant change within the Catholic Church of monumental proportions. Contrary to the history of missions in which Western Christianity was the imperial benchmark for cultures, the shift invited the church to take some important "risks" in order to usher-in a real new beginning.[114] What was at stake was the possibility of a real de-Europeanization of the Catholic Church at the most fundamental level in its liturgy, theology and structures. Dulles correctly affirms that the present transition toward the inclusion of the cultures of the world in the church will have to involve a comprehensive pastoral strategy as well as the formation of new structures and methodologies.[115] But Rahner goes further! For him, "either the Church sees and recognizes these essential differences of other cultures for which she should become a world church and with a Pauline boldness draws the necessary [theological] consequences from this recognition, or she remains a Western Church and so in the final analysis betrays the meaning of Vatican II."[116]

Post Second Vatican Council

Vatican II had and continues to have an immeasurable impact on the Catholic Church as a whole. According to Sievernich, the Vatican II documents are a kind of foundation charter for the development of contextual theologies.[117] Yet, Elizabeth Isichei notes that, while Vatican II encouraged more contextualized versions of Catholicism, other expressions such as folk-Catholicism were never mentioned in the final documents, leaving millions of peoples throughout the world feeling troubled and alienated.[118] At the very least, it left the door open for local communities to begin to think theologically from their own cultural vantage points. More specifically,

---

112   Rahner, "Fundamental Theological Interpretation," 718.
113   Ibid.
114   Ibid., 724.
115   Dulles, "The Emerging World Church," 3.
116   Rahner, "Fundamental Theological Interpretation," 724.
117   Sievernich, "Jesuit Theologies of Mission," 46.
118   Isichei, *A History of Christianity in Africa*, 327.

Vatican II set the tone for beginning to think about effective new ways for evangelization that were not based on a partnership with European and U.S.A. expansionism.

In this section, I explore some of the most recent developments in Catholic official documents as they pertain to the phenomena of cultures. Post Vatican II documents reinforced and further developed the ideas initially expressed at Vatican II and opened the crack a little wider for a fuller acceptance of the pervasive significance of cultures in the way the church understands herself and the Christian tradition.

Building on the legacy of Vatican II, Pope Paul VI issued *Evangelii Nuntiandi* in 1975. Written on the ten-year anniversary of the Second Vatican Council, this encyclical centred on the primary mission of the Church: evangelism in the modern world. It draws from the work of the Third Ordinary General Assembly of Bishops (1974),[119] which focused specifically on the meaning of evangelization and its multiple facets.[120]

According to Schreiter, this encyclical stands as the best statement from papal magisterium on this issue.[121] There are three governing questions in the document: one, what happened to the hidden energy of the Good News; two, what is the extent to which the evangelical force can transform the people of the twentieth century; and three, what are the methods that should be followed in order that the power of God in the gospel can have its transforming effect.[122] The document goes beyond *Gaudium et spes* on a number of issues. I limit my reflection to those issues important in the discussion of the relationship between faith and culture.

First, the document spoke in greater detail concerning the relation of the gospel to the cultures of the world. The gospel and "culture" are clearly distinguished here, although the former is articulated as independent from all cultures. But the gospel and cultures are not presented as incompatible with each other, the gospel is described as capable of "permeating them all without becoming subject to any one of them."[123] Two, it deepened our understanding of the interconnectedness-interwoven character of the gospel to cultural traditions. The gospel is lived by people who are deeply linked to a culture. Similarly, the building of the kingdom cannot avoid "borrowing the elements of human

---

119   Paul VI, *Evangelii Nuntiandi*, 5.
120   The bishops present were from all over the world and included representatives from Asia, Africa and Latin America.
121   Schreiter, "Faith and Cultures," 751.
122   Paul VI, *Evangelii Nuntiandi*, 4.
123   Ibid., 20.

culture or cultures."[124] Unlike other documents, this encyclical connected the effectiveness of evangelization to the degree to which the gospel accomplishes "inculturation." Evangelization is now understood to entail a process of immersion into the cultures of the peoples to whom it is addressed. Evangelization must use the languages, and cultural signs and symbols of the peoples of the world, otherwise it will not be fruitful; it must respond to their concerns and challenges in order to have any impact on their concrete lives. Quite originally, the document asserted the role of the local communities in the difficult task of "inculturating" the gospel. They are the ones most capable of "assimilating the essence of the gospel and of transposing it ..."[125] And three, the document made cultures and not only individuals the object of evangelization. Although it is unclear whether Western Europe and Euro North American cultures are included here, the notion of the evangelization of cultures emphasized the necessary encounter of all cultures with the transformative power of the gospel. Quite refreshingly, one finds the recognition of the need of the church to be evangelized herself.[126]

Evangelii Nuntiandi established some clear guidelines for carrying out the task of evangelization. It went beyond merely affirming respect of other cultures as earlier documents did, and instead made those cultures themselves a vital ingredient for effective evangelization. By implication, says Schreiter, the document's attention to cultures underlines how humans are cultural beings and how cultures should play a central role in any theological reflection.[127] That being said, the document also put at bay other expressions that are not considered "true" expressions of Catholic Christianity. (Although they are not mentioned, one cannot but wonder if here the Council means certain expressions of popular Catholicism.) At the beginning of the document one encounters the strong statement that the Gospel does not permit indifference, syncretism, or accommodation.[128] The intention no doubt is to highlight the delicate dynamic between the gospel and cultures. For the magisterium, the "danger" is the corruption of the gospel. Evangelization itself may lose its effectiveness altogether "if one empties or adulterates its content under the pretext of translating it."[129] What seems to be at stake here is the preservation of the "integrity" of the gospel as an entirely otherworldly phenomenon.

124   Ibid.
125   Ibid., 63.
126   Ibid., 15.
127   Schreiter, "Faith and Cultures," 751.
128   Paul vi, *Evangelii Nuntiandi*, 5.
129   Ibid., 63.

In the debates concerning faith and culture, *Evangelii Nuntiandi* veered the conversation towards inculturation. Subsequent documents contributed to clarifying this approach and providing examples of what the magisterium meant by using such a neologism. In his apostolic letter *Africae Terrarum* (1967), Paul VI went a long way to celebrating the upholding of human dignity and deep sense of family in African cultures, values that resonate with the gospel message.[130] As he put it, the goal of the Church is to uplift the cultural legacy of the African peoples as well as to bring renewal to their cultures.[131] Most impressive in the document was the open recognition of the manifestation of the divine mystery in African cultures. God, claimed the document, is expressed differently in every culture.[132] Such recognition by the magisterium facilitated the articulation of an African theology that is based on the experience of faith and expressions of the African people.[133]

Schreiter is correct that this pastoral letter is significant because it is the first instance of the "application of some of the general principles affirmed at the council."[134] As I see it, it is a concrete example of what the Catholic Church means by inculturation.[135] Consistent with *Evangelii Nuntiandi*, in *Africae Terrarum* Paul VI introduced instances where culture came to be

---

130   Paul VI, *Africae Terrarum—The Land of Africa* [*Apostolic Letter to the Bishops of Africa*] (1967), Http://w2.vatican.va/content/paul-vi/it/apost_letters/documents/hf_p-vi_apl_ 19671029_africae-terrarum.pdf (accessed August 25, 2015). The document states: "The Church regards with great respect the moral and religious values of the African tradition, not only for their meaning, but also because it sees them as the providential basis on which to transmit the Gospel message and start construction of the new society in Christ" (Ibid.).

131   Paul VI, *Africae Terrarum*, 13.

132   God, says the letter, "si esprime in modo assai diverso da cultura a cultura" (Paul VI, *Africae Terrarum*, 8).

133   According to Schreiter, the letter identifies a "number of positive values in African cultures (pervasive concept of God, concern for human dignity, profound sense of the family) that may form the basis of an African theology that would be both genuinely African and authentically Catholic" (Schreiter, "Faith and Cultures," 750).

134   Schreiter, "Faith and Cultures," 750.

135   John Paul II provides another example of what the council means by inculturation in his Encyclical *Slavorum Apostoli* in 1985. Celebrating the lives and evangelizing work of Saint Cyril and Methodius, he notes that the work of evangelization they carried into the Slav peoples, "contains both a model of what today is called "inculturation the incarnation of the Gospel in native cultures and also the introduction of these cultures into the life of the Church" (John Paul II, *Slavorum Apostoli* [*Encyclical Letter on the Apostles of the Slavs*] [1985], 21, Http://w2.vatican.va/content/john-paul-ii/en/encyclicals/documents/hf_jp-ii_enc_19850602_slavorum-apostoli.pdf [accessed August 25, 2015]).

considered an essential aspect of Evangelization, and where the recognition of the "seeds of the Word" in other cultures were explicitly recognized among African cultures.[136] In the same vein, the role of local communities and leaders was emphasized in facilitating this complex process,[137] noting that doctrinal terms and liturgical forms must correspond "to the mentality of the African people."[138]

John Paul II made huge advances both in clarifying what inculturation meant as well as in creating the structures for the advance of inculturation, although not without inherent contradictions. During his tenure as pope he focused strongly on "orthodoxy"—which led him to appoint Josef Ratzinger (who became his immediate successor as Benedict XVI) as the Prefect for the Doctrine of the Faith, who carried out repeated witch-hunts against theologians (for example Gustavo Gutiérrez, Leonardo Boff, Ivone Gebara, Jacques Gaillot, Roger Haight, Hans Küng, etc.) who dared to disagree with papal teachings or speak the gospel in culturally non-Eurocentric ways.[139]

Notwithstanding, in his letter to the National Congress of the Ecclesial Movement of Cultural Commitment (1982), he solidified the connection between the cultural aspect and faith. In fact, he wrote, the synthesis between culture and faith is not only a demand of culture, but a demand of faith as well.[140] Building on the work of Paul VI, he reiterated the need for the evangelization of cultures and the fact that the faith does not identify with any culture (read cultural tradition). But he went further than his predecessor by

---

136   The Vatican II documents emphasized the idea that in the cultures and customs of the peoples there were "seeds of the Word" that function as preparation for evangelization. See Vatican Council II, *"Lumen Gentium,"* 17; *"Ad Gentes,"* 15.

137   The document credits the leadership of the Catholic Church for initiating the placing of local African leaders. It claims that it did not do so as a reaction to nationalist movements. "La Chiesa, infatti, non ha atteso i movimenti nazionalisti per avviare gli Africani a posti di responsabilità nel sacerdozio e nell'episcopato, grazie alle sapienti norme impartite dai Romani Pontefici, specialmente dagli immediati Nostri Predecessori" (Paul VI, *Africae Terrarum*, 23).

138   Paul VI, *Africae Terrarum*, 32.

139   Numerous were the Catholic theologians who were disciplined by the Vatican during the papacy of John Paul II. See Editor's note, "List of Theologians," *National Catholic Reporter*, 15 February 2005, Http://natcath.org/NCR_Online/archives2/2005a/022505/022505h .php (accessed July 27, 2016).

140   "A síntese entre cultura e fé não é só uma exigência da cultura, mas também da fé" (John Paul II, "Discurso aos participantes no i Congreso do Movimiento Eclesial de Empenho Cultural" [1982], 2, Https://w2.vatican.va/content/john-paul-ii/pt/speeches/1982/january/documents/ hf_jp-ii_spe_19820116_impegno-culturale.html [accessed September 10, 2015]).

emphasizing that "a faith that does not become culture is not fully received, not entirely thought through, nor faithfully lived."[141] Later that year, on May 20, he founded the Pontifical Council for Culture, of which one of its mandates is to continue the work toward the inculturation of the gospel.[142] The task of inculturation of the Council for Culture is reaffirmed when in, 1993, Pope John Paul II merged the Pontifical Council for Dialogue with Non-Believers (founded in 1965 by Pope Paul VI) with the Pontifical Council for Culture as described in *Inde a Pontificatus.*[143] As he plainly stated in his speech to the assembly of the Council for Culture: "The inculturation of the faith is the other major task of your Dicastery."[144]

But the single most important document on inculturation written by Pope John Paul II was his *Redemptoris Missio* written in 1990. Articulated as a continuation of Vatican II's *Ad Gentes* and in the spirit of Pope Paul VI's *Evangelii Nuntiandi*, this encyclical sought to renew the church's mission of evangelization to the peoples (*ad gentes*). Pertinent to issues of culture and faith, the letter specifically promoted the "insertion of Christianity in the various human cultures."[145] This time, we are told of the breadth of the transformation the council is seeking. "Inculturation" is a profound all-embracing process which involves all aspects of Christianity including the Christian message, and the

141 John Paul II, "Discurso do Papa João Paulo II," 2.
142 In this letter addressed to the Cardinal Secretary of State, he expresses that the relation between the Church and the cultures of the world is an issue that occupied his mind since the beginning of his pontificate. There he also stresses that his commitment to culture is expressed in other earlier speeches. As a result, he initiated a consultation with the members of the Sacred College of the Cardinals in Rome, which eventually led to the creation of the Council for culture. See John Paul II, "Foundation Letter of the Pontifical Council for Culture" (1982), Http://w2.vatican.va/content/john-paul-ii/es/letters/1982/documents/hf_jp-ii_let_19820520_foundation-letter.html (accessed July 10, 2015).
143 John Paul II, *Inde a Pontificatus* [*Apostolic Letter Given Motu Propio: The Pontifical Council for Culture and the Pntifical Council for Dialogue with Non-Believers Are United*] (1993), Http://w2.vatican.va/content/john-paul-ii/en/motu_proprio/documents/hf_jp-ii_motu-proprio_25031993_inde-a-pontificatus.html (accessed August 20, 2015).
144 John Paul II, "Address to the Plenary Assembly of the Pontifical Council for Culture" (1994), 3, Http://w2.vatican.va/content/john-paul-ii/en/speeches/1994/march/documents/hf_jp-ii_spe_18031994_address-to-pc-culture.html (accessed September 10, 2015).
145 John Paul II, *Redemptoris Missio* [*Encyclical Letter on the Permanent Validity of the Church's Missionary Mandate*] (1990), 52, Http://w2.vatican.va/content/john-paul-ii/en/encyclicals/documents/hf_jp-ii_enc_07121990_redemptoris-missio.pdf (accessed September 9, 2015).

Church's reflection and practices.[146] Nothing is left out! Missionaries are expected to immerse themselves in local cultures and learn of the traditions and customs of the host country through direct experience; they must enter "the cultural milieu of those to whom they are sent, moving beyond their own cultural limitations."[147] According to the document, to be immersed in a culture does not mean that missionaries renounce their cultural identity. Rather, it requires a more in-depth understanding, appreciating, fostering and evangelizing of the local culture in order to equip themselves to communicate the Gospel effectively. It is only by immersing themselves into the culture of the people that they can communicate the gospel and adopt a manner of living that corresponds with the culture of the people and remains faithful to the gospel.[148]

John Paul II further argued that the role of the community could be ignored because cultural activities are never private but are shared. Inculturation must therefore emerge from within and not without.[149] Only as local ecclesial communities develop can the gospel be expressed in "original ways and forms consonant with people's cultural" traditions.[150] It is the people that are best equipped to fulfill the task of "translating the gospel" into legitimate local cultural expressions. For this reason, although inculturation is a slow journey, it includes the whole people of God.[151]

Much more than other documents, this encyclical emphasized the mutual enrichment that exists between the church and the cultures of the world. Through inculturation the church makes the gospel incarnate in different cultures while at the same time introducing the people—all of particular cultures—into her own larger universal community. She takes her values and shares them and at the same time takes the good elements from their cultures and renews them from within their cultures. By allowing herself to be open to

---

146   Ibid.

147   Ibid., 53.

148   Ibid.

149   Behind the notion of inculturation, claims Gallagher, is the hope that "evangelization can take place from within the culture being evangelized ... Inculturation involves more than changing a receiving culture from outside: it implies that the gospel will be fully and permanently rooted only when it has been received, felt, celebrated and lived within the deep language of a local culture" (Gallagher, *Clashing Symbols*, 104).

150   As Paul VI said in Kampala, inculturation will "require an incubation of the Christian 'mystery' in the genius of your people in order that its native voice, more clearly and frankly, may then be raised harmoniously in the chorus of other voices in the universal Church" (Cited in John Paul II, *Redemptoris Missio*, 54).

151   John Paul II, *Redemptoris Missio*, 52–54.

cultural renewal, the church more effectively reflects the mystery of Christ.[152]
The twofold fundamental principles of inculturation become evident here.
For Pope John Paul II however, the complex dimension of multiple cultural
exchanges that take place during inculturation must remain compatible with
the gospel and in communion with the universal church.[153] In other words, the
emphasis on "mutual enrichment" actually means that cultures are subsumed
to the gospel message.

Though the implementations vary, the ethos of inculturation has been welcome
in the majority world. In broad strokes in Latin America, for example, the documents from the Vatican II provoked a rethinking of evangelization, of the praxis
of the church, and of its social teachings. Marcello Azevedo claims, however, that
although pontifical documents advanced the social conscience of the Church,
attention to the cultural dimension was not incorporated in its social teachings.[154]
It is only more recently that the church has received a call for greater sensibility
to the relation between faith and (the phenomenon of) culture.[155] Although the
conference of Latin American Bishops (CELAM) at Medellín, Colombia (1968)
started the process of rethinking the Vatican II's call to the global church and its
implications for Latin America, it would not be until the conferences at Puebla,
Mexico (1979) that the implications for the *evangelization of cultures* and the relation between faith and the cultural took centre stage.[156]

---

152 Ibid., 52.

153 Ibid., 54.

154 Marcello de Carvalho Azevedo, "Comunidades eclesiales de base en Brasil: ¿posible
mediación para la inculturación de la fe?" trans. Silvia Sinoott and Eduardo Sinnott, in
Identidad cultural y modernización, vol. II, ed. Carlos Galli and Luis Scherz, América
Latina y la doctrina social de la iglesia: Diálogo latinoamericano-alemán (Buenos Aires,
Argentina: Ediciones Paulinas, 1991), II:234.

155 Azevedo, "Comunidades eclesiales de base en Brasil," 238. Some of the documents to
which they allude most frequently are *Rerum Novarum* (1891), *Gaudium et spes* (1965);
Evangelii Nuntiandi (1975), *Catechesi tradendae* (1979). There is also special mention of
the Synod for the "Evangelization of the modern World" (1974), which greatly influenced
the text of *Evangelii Nuntiandi*. See also Carlos Galli, "Introducción: Identidad cultural
y modernización en América Latina," in *Identidad cultural y modernización*, vol. II, ed.
Carlos Galli and Luis Scherz, América Latina y la doctrina social de la iglesia: Diálogo
latinoamericano-alemán (Buenos Aires, Argentina: Ediciones Paulinas, 1991), II:8.

156 Galli, "Introducción," 8. Galli explains that, since Puebla "culture" appears as the addressee
of evangelization, and the cultural is presented as the platform for articulating the religious and the social. In an attempt to implement such an option, CELAM has created
the section for culture (Sección para la cultura SEPAC); it has promoted the creation of a
national commission for the evangelization of culture and has supported diverse encounters in order to reflect on related themes.

The Puebla document is in line with the Vatican push for inculturated evangelization but it reinterprets it.[157] Evangelization for the Council means both a forceful reclamation of the cultures of the peoples of Latin America and a rejection of the foreign pressures from the richer countries.[158] The document reads like a cultural manifesto rejecting what they perceive are destructive negative cultural foreign influences.[159] The Puebla document is shaped along the lines of *Evangelii Nuntiandi*, focusing on Paul VI's call to the evangelization of cultures. Thus the document displays a great awareness of the totalizing character of culture and the role of evangelization to reach the very roots of the cultures.[160] Yet, for the Council, the cultural dimension is also essential and defining because it is the site where people affirm or deny their "connection with God."[161] The Puebla documents affirm

---

157   Pope John Paul II's inaugural speech at Puebla locates cultural concerns within the scope of evangelization. As he wrote: "from within the church we are capable of penetrating culture with the gospel; transform the hearts, humanize systems and structures." (Juan Pablo II, "Discurso Inaugural pronunciado en el Seminario Palafoxiano de Puebla de los Ángeles, México," in *Documentos de Puebla: III Conferencia General del Episcopado Latinoamericano*, Documento Conclusivo [Biblioteca Electrónica Cristiana, 2008], I.5, Http://www.celam.org/doc_conferencias/Documento_Conclusivo_Puebla.pdf [accessed August 23, 2016]).

158   Consejo Episcopal Latinoamericano, "Mensaje a los pueblos de América Latina," in *Documentos de Puebla: III Conferencia General del Episcopado Latinoamericano*, Documento Conclusivo (Biblioteca Electrónica Cristiana, 2008), 8, Http://www.celam. org/doc_conferencias/Documento_Conclusivo_Puebla.pdf (accessed August 23, 2016). The official Puebla document also celebrates the emergence and re-valuing of the Indigenous cultures even while condemning external destructive influences upon them. See Consejo Episcopal Latinoamericano, *Documentos de Puebla: III Conferencia General del Episcopado Latinoamericano*, Documento Conclusivo (2008), 1.2.3.51–53, 2.2.2.234, Http://www.celam.org/doc_conferencias/Documento_Conclusivo_Puebla.pdf (accessed August 23, 2016).

159   The Council insists that evangelization must also include the promotion of the Latin American communities accompanied with a critical stance to those "ideologies and politics that condition the fate" of the nations of Latin America. They list a number of elements that need to be rejected and condemned as destructive to the communities' ways of life and culture: individualism, consumerism, deterioration of family values, economic dependence and the transnational corporations. See Consejo Episcopal Latinoamericano, *Documento de Puebla*, 1.2.55–58, 2.164.

160   Consejo Episcopal Latinoamericano, *Documento de Puebla*, 3.2.2.1.385–88.

161   Consejo Episcopal Latinoamericano, *Documento de Puebla*, 3.2.2.1.389. The document states that all the various aspects of cultures are responsible for inspiring either religious devotion or irreligion.

the particularity of the various cultures of Latin America. Cultural activity is understood as a creative activity through which humans respond to God's vocation to perfect creation.

I am suggesting that there is an incipient recognition of the correspondence between the cultures and the gospel message in these documents. That is, the gospel can only be lived in the context of a specific culture. More importantly, the construction of the Reign of God can only occur by incorporating elements from human cultures.[162] The important insight that Puebla gives us is that we cannot think about humanity without the cultural. It is precisely because all people are born within a particular cultural tradition that, the evangelization must include the cultural dimension; it is a social and historical reality.[163] Unfortunately, Puebla stopped short by going no further than inculturation, with a tinge of greater appreciation for aboriginal and Afro-Latin American cultures. Still, evangelization meant not the destruction of their cultural values, but the affirmation and transformation of those values within cultural traditions that resonate with the gospel message.[164]

Subsequent conferences of CELAM would not further the discussions on the relationship between the cultural traditions of Latin America and the gospel message; they would remain well within the scope of the framework of inculturation. For example, in the Santo Domingo conference of 1992, the Lady of Guadalupe is posited as the "perfect example of an inculturated evangelization" because in her "authentic indigenous values were incarnated."[165] Surprisingly, in the CELAM documents, there is little recognition of the complicity of the church in the colonial projects.[166] In fact, in the inaugural letter to the Santo Domingo conference, Pope John Paul II unambiguously portrayed

---

162 Consejo Episcopal Latinoamericano, *Documento de Puebla*, 3.2.2.3.400–401.

163 Ibid., 3.2.2.1.390–92.

164 Ibid., 3.2.2.4.409–15.

165 Juan Pablo II, "Nueva Evangelización, Promoción Humana, Cultura Cristiana," in *Documento de Santo Domingo: IV Conferencia Episcopal Latinoamericana*, Documento Conclusivo (1992), IV.24, Http://www.celam.org/doc_conferencias/Documento_Conclusivo_Santo_Domingo.pdf (accessed August 23, 2016).

166 In fact, allusions to the Western European (Spanish) colonial expansion in the documents condemn the enslaving of the African peoples and destruction of Indigenous communities and cultures, but leave unchallenged the role the Catholic Church played in colonial projects. See Consejo Episcopal Latinoamericano, "Mensaje a los pueblos de América Latina," in *Documento de Santo Domingo: IV Conferencia Episcopal Latinoamericana*, Documento Conclusivo (1992), 2.3.2.246, Http://www.celam.org/doc_conferencias/Documento_Conclusivo_Santo_Domingo.pdf (accessed August 23, 2016).

the Catholic Church as "the tireless defender of the Indigenous, protector of the values in their cultures, promoting their humanity in the face of the abuses by the colonizers ..."[167] Nevertheless, as with Puebla, there is an insistence on highlighting (reclaiming) what is "deeply human and humanizing" among Indigenous and afro-Latin American cultures.[168] Yet these communities and peoples remain the object of evangelization. Though the documents do not move beyond inculturation, they do focus on the present destructive cultural shifts caused by neoliberal capitalism and the foreign push for the adoption of globalizing market economies,[169] as in the documents of the conference at Aparecida (2007), for example.

Meanwhile, discussions on the relationship between the cultural and the gospel were advanced when Latin American bishops and theologians sought to make explicit the connections between the social teachings of the church and the cultural dimension.[170] In the words of Luis Gera, "the social doctrine of the Church must take into account" the plurality of cultures ...[171] They engaged

---

167   Juan Pablo II, "Nueva Evangelización, Promoción Humana, Cultura Cristiana," I.4.

168   Among those cultural aspects he listed, "their vision of life, the way in which they recognize the sacredness of the human being, their profound respect for nature, their humility, simplicity and solidarity will stimulate the efforts to carry out a true inculturated evangelization" (Juan Pablo II, "Nueva Evangelización, Promoción Humana, Cultura Cristiana," IV.22). The council goes as far as offering themselves as ministers of the gospel to the Indigenous and Afro-Latin American communities. See Consejo Episcopal Latinoamericano, *Documento de Santo Domingo: IV Conferencia Episcopal Latinoamericana*, Documento Conclusivo (1992), V.38.

169   Consejo Episcopal Latinoamericano, *V Conferencia General del Episcopado Latinoamericano y del Caribe: Aparecida 13–31 de Mayo de 2007*, Documento Conclusivo (Bogotá, Colombia: Editora CELAM, 2007), 13, 35, 37, 45, 51, Http://www.celam.org/aparecida/Espanol.pdf (accessed August 27, 2016).

170   Galli, "Introducción," 10. According to Galli, evangelization must include the whole human being. He argues that an analysis of "culture" is often viewed as if it is a distraction from social issues. A mistaken dichotomy is presented which views cultural and social issues as entirely unrelated. Meanwhile, Azevedo argues that attention to cultures is important because "There exists in humanity a specific biological unity, which is lived in a social and cultural diversity almost inexhaustible" (Azevedo, "Comunidades eclesiales de base en Brasil," 233).

171   Lucio Gera, "Evangelización y promoción humana," in *Identidad cultural y modernización*, vol. II, ed. Carlos Galli and Luis Scherz, América Latina y la doctrina social de la iglesia: Diálogo latinoamericano-alemán (Buenos Aires, Argentina: Ediciones Paulinas, 1991), II:200. And Galli adds, "a theology of culture and a social theology underlie the evangelization of culture and the development of the social doctrine of the Church ..." (Galli, "Introducción," 10).

the relation between faith and the cultural by reflecting on the ways in which people live their faith.[172] These theologians saw the preferential option of the poor as intertwined with the proposal for the inculturation of the faith in Latin America.[173] For them, linking the social doctrine of the Church with the cultural identity of the people becomes necessary precisely because of the need to inculturate the gospel.

Latin American theologians have made a point to emphasize that inculturaltion is a process which involves a deep sense of mutuality and dialogue. They have gone beyond prevailing notions of inculturation by arguing that it must assume the dynamic interaction between lived faith and lived culture.[174] And here they abandon the singular "culture" and opt for its plural usage stating that inculturation assumes an interaction between faith and cultures just as cultures exist in lived spaces, as part of dynamic processes.[175] They argue that, inculturation was implied in the full relation between faith, (a) culture, and (a given) society. Diego Irarrázaval's body of work, for example, shows greater attention to the role of the cultural in the way people live their faith,[176] even as he explores the deeper implications of inculturation as interreligious engagement.[177]

---

172   Azevedo insists that we cannot conceive evangelization unless it makes specific the relation between faith and culture. In the same way, he comments that we cannot ignore the experience of the small Christian communities where the relation between faith and society is made explicit. See Azevedo, "Comunidades eclesiales de base en Brasil," 236. We find echoes of this perspective in the way popular religious traditions are celebrated in the document of Aparecida, as in, for example: "popular piety is a legitimate form of living the faith, a way to be part of the church and a way to be missionary, where the deepest vibrations of the "deep America" (read indigenous communities) are gathered." "Popular piety," the Council adds, "is part of an 'historical cultural originality'" of the poor of this continent, and fruit of a "synthesis between the cultures and the Christian faith." (Consejo Episcopal Latinoamericano, *V Conferencia General*, 264).

173   Gera, "Evangelización y promoción humana," 66. As Galli puts it, "one cannot make abstractions of the historical situation of the nation in the process of liberation, nor can one attack the cultural identity of the people" (Galli, "Introducción," 11).

174   Azevedo, "Comunidades eclesiales de base en Brasil," 240.

175   My translation/paraphrase does not show the shift they make both preserving the singular *culture* but simultaneously hinting at the plural use of *cultures*. The original in Spanish reads: La inculturación supone interacción de la "fe con la(s) cultura(s) tal como ésta(s) existe(n) en lo vivo, en su proceso dinámico" (Azevedo, "Comunidades eclesiales de base en Brasil," 240).

176   Diego Irarrázaval, *Rito y pensar cristiano* (Lima, Perú: Centro de Estudios y Publicaciones, 1993); idem, *Cultura y fe latinoamericanas*.

177   Diego Irarrázaval, *Inculturation*.

Critical of traditional approaches to evangelism, Latin American liberation theologians expanded the notion of evangelism by affirming that it is not just the transference or the modification of languages, methods, rites, and symbols—in short, the reorganization of external norms and ways of being. Rather, it must go deeper through inculturation by reaching the foundations, the roots of a given culture and impacting the vision of the world and the sociocultural praxis of a given human group.[178] As Azevedo puts it, the intention of the evangelizer is to provide the members of the given cultural group with elements of sociocultural self-reflection for them to carry out the necessary transformations. For him, the agents of change are the members of the given cultural group; this is the fundamental difference between evangelization and inculturated evangelization.[179] Much more could be said to show how Latin American scholars have dealt with questions of inculturation or reflected upon cultures as they relate to the gospel message. A fuller analysis is also needed that will include how notions of inculturation have been received in Asia, Africa and other contexts. My limited discussion here is meant to illustrate some of the nuances in the ways notions of inculturation have been received outside of the Western European and Euro-North American contexts using Latin America as an example.

The Catholic Church in the Twenty-First Century
More recently it has been the task of Pope Francis to bring further clarity by sharpening the Vatican's understanding of the relation between the phenomena of cultures and faith, especially through the notion of inculturation. His recent encyclical *Laudato Si*, specifically focuses on the cultural dynamics and detrimental effects of modernity and present pervasive global market economic structures in the world, but does not explicitly add much of significance

---

178 Azevedo, "Comunidades eclesiales de base en Brasil," 241. Azevedo continues the argument by stating that an inculturated evangelization is much more than mere transmission of knowledges, practices, rites and disciplines. He argues that people must be considered within the entire complex of their day-to-day universe, with their social and cultural roots that encompass all the religious and sapiential dimensions as well as the economical and political ones. See Ibid., 251.

179 Azevedo warns that while the danger and possibility of foreign participation is not removed, the limited role ascribed to the evangelizer ensures that the people will be the protagonists in their own evangelization process. An inculturated evangelization is precisely the dialogue and interaction between the Christian message at the level of the people's own cultural roots, resulting in cultural transformations initiated by the members of a given culture, and the expressions of faith be done in their own terms. Azevedo, "Comunidades eclesiales de base en Brasil," 253–54.

to the debates on faith, cultures and inculturation.[180] However, his earlier pastoral letter *Evangelii Gaudium* addressed these questions at greater length,[181] expanding on previous documents by his predecessors, particularly the work on culture by Pope John Paul II. I would argue that his *Evangelii Gaudium*[182] serves as preparation for his later *Laudato Si*, but the issues raised get fuller attention in the earlier document.

Along with a wide range of other issues related to the renewal of the mission of evangelization of the church, *Evangelii Gaudium* articulates even further the church's view on inculturation and by extension on the relation between the Christian faith and culture. Much along the lines of Pope John Paul II's *Redemptoris Missio*, in this exhortation, Pope Francis highlights the immense importance of the phenomena of cultures.[183] For him, the people of God, who are incarnate in the peoples of the earth, each have their own culture. For him, "culture" is a useful category for "grasping the various expressions of the Christian" life present in God's people.[184] There is an ethos of humanizing culture here; cultures receive great attention by Pope Francis because they relate to "the lifestyle of a given society, the specific way in which its members relate to one another, to other creatures and to God." In no uncertain terms, he affirms culture as pointing to "the totality of a people's life;"[185] this resonates with the notion of the cultural I am proposing.

With this totality in mind, Pope Francis takes a more radical and critical four-fold stance concerning the interaction between the gospel and cultures and inculturation. First, the interrelationship between the gospel and culture stands out here. In contrast to earlier documents, culture is described as a dynamic reality, which people create and recreate over time and across generations. The people among whom the Gospel has been inculturated become the

---

180   Francis, *Laudato Si* [*Encyclical Letter on Care for Our Common Good*] (2015), Http://w2.vatican.va/content/francesco/en/encyclicals/documents/papa-francesco_20150524_enciclica-laudato-si.pdf (accessed September 3, 2015).

181   *Evangelii Gaudium* discusses issues of consumerism, globalization, the destruction of the environment, and modernity and it cultural effects, but all of these issues receive greater attention and a more sophisticated elaboration in his *Laudato Si*. For some instances of these themes in the document see Francis, *Evangelii Gaudium* [*Pastoral Exhortation on the Proclamation of the Gospel in Today's World*] (2015), 60, 62, 84, 178–91, 202, 214, 218., Http://w2.vatican.va/content/francesco/en/apost_exhortations/documents/papa-francesco_esortazione-ap_20131124_evangelii-gaudium.pdf (September 11, 2015).

182   Francis, *Evangelii Gaudium*.

183   Ibid., 68.

184   Ibid., 115.

185   Ibid.

collective subject and agents of evangelization. As they transmit their culture to the next generation they also transmit the faith in renewed forms.[186] As a result, the Gospel and culture are interconnected because people are always situated in a culture. The goal is for the gospel to become flesh in the culture of those who receive it.[187] By the same token, there is a cultural exchange in the process of evangelization. If the Gospel is embedded in a culture, the message is now transmitted with that cultural content. The implication here is that the gospel is always mediated through culture. The ultimate end of evangelization (and I would add inculturation), therefore, should be that "the Gospel, as preached in categories proper to each culture, will create a new synthesis with that particular culture."[188]

Second, for inculturation to take place Christianity must be de-Europeanized. As he puts it, over the centuries countless people have embraced Christianity and have made it their own in their daily lives, and "handed it on in the language of their culture."[189] Christianity does not have one cultural expression nor can it be circumscribed by the limits or understanding of the Gospel in any one culture. As he categorically states, "It is an indisputable fact that no single culture can exhaust the mystery of our redemption in Christ."[190] For this reason, evangelization cannot mean the demand that people everywhere imitate the modes of expression of the Christian faith which European nations developed at a particular moment in their history.[191]

Third, inculturation means diversification. According to Pope Francis, it would be an injustice to the logic of the incarnation if we thought of Christianity as monocultural. Rather, remaining true to the proclamation of the Gospel and

---

186   Ibid., 122.
187   Ibid., 115.
188   Ibid., 129.
189   Ibid., 116.
190   Ibid., 118.
191   He continues stating that

> While it is true that some cultures have been closely associated with the preaching
> of the Gospel and the development of Christian thought, the revealed message is not
> identified with any of them; its content is transcultural. Hence in the evangelization
> of new cultures, or cultures which have not received the Christian message, it is not
> essential to impose a specific cultural form, no matter how beautiful or ancient it
> may be, together with the Gospel. The message that we proclaim always has a certain
> cultural dress, but we in the Church can sometimes fall into a needless hallowing of
> our own culture, and thus show more fanaticism than true evangelizing zeal (Francis,
> *Evangelii Gaudium*, 117).

its tradition, the Church reflects the "different faces of the cultures and peoples in which it is received and takes roots."[192] In other words, the face of the church is a kaleidoscope of the cultural faces that make up the Church. Cultural diversity is a quality of the Church and not a problem to be resolved; as the Church "shows forth the beauty of her varied face," she expresses her own catholicity.[193] Most important is the connection that the pope makes between inculturation and revelation. In agreement with *Redemptoris Missio,* Pope Francis reiterates that through inculturation the Church brings specific cultures and peoples into her own community. He expands this enrichment of the church by affirming that the positive values that other cultures contribute to the Church "can enrich the way the Gospel is preached, understood and lived."[194] It is in the Christian customs of evangelized peoples that the Holy Spirit shows the church "new aspects of revelation."[195] The implications are monumental; the document supports the idea that the Church's view of the Gospel, the mystery of incarnation, or the divine disclosure is incomplete without the inclusion of the other faces of Catholic Christianity.

And fourth, consonant with *Evangelii Nuntiandi*, this exhortation focuses attention on the need for the evangelization of cultures as well.[196] The document shifts its attention significantly, though away from primarily paying attention to the evangelization of non-Christians and those cultures that have entered a profound process of secularization (de-Christianization is the term used in *Redemptoris Missio*) and toward the evangelization of (Catholic) popular cultures.[197] To my knowledge, this is the first papal document that explicitly explores the connection between popular cultural expressions and the Church while also giving them a privileged role in the task of evangelization. Instead of condemning them to silence as the Vatican II (and many subsequent papal) documents did, and without expressing the deep-seated fear of the potential corruption of the gospel,[198] Pope Francis welcomes popular cultural traditions as part of the Catholic Church.

---

192   Francis, *Evangelii Gaudium*, 116.

193   Ibid.

194   Ibid.

195   Ibid.

196   He wrote: "It is imperative to evangelize cultures in order to inculturate the Gospel" (Francis, *Evangelii Gaudium*, 69).

197   Francis, *Evangelii Gaudium*, 68–69.

198   The pope addresses the fear of corrupting the integrity of the gospel by noting that inculturation is indeed a slow process. At the same time, he chides those that because of doubt and fear do not take creative initiatives but remain comfortable and make no progress. See Francis, *Evangelii Gaudium*, 129.

He approaches them in a two-fold manner. On one hand, these traditions need to be evangelized. Just as all cultures are marked by sin, so also the popular cultures of the Catholic people display deficiencies, which need to be healed by the gospel message, "such as machismo, alcoholism, domestic violence, low Mass attendance, fatalistic or superstitious notions which lead to sorcery, and the like."[199] On the other hand, because of their wisdom and values of faith and solidarity, popular cultures once evangelized, are "capable of encouraging the development of a more just and believing society."[200] In fact, "popular piety itself can be the starting point for healing and liberation" from its own deficiencies.[201] Popular piety is a "true expression of the spontaneous missionary activity of the people of God" and therein lies its importance.[202] He goes even further by positing that popular piety is the most concrete example of what the Vatican means by inculturation. He writes that genuine forms of "popular religiosity" are incarnate; they are born from the incarnation of the Christian faith in popular culture.[203] And later he adds, "popular piety enables us to see how the faith, once received, becomes embodied in a culture ..."[204]

Much more can be said about Pope Francis' treatment of the relation between faith and culture. He remains within the parameters of the tradition insofar as he builds on earlier papal documents, but pushes for a more intentional diversification of the understanding of inculturation. He also makes a theologically significant connection between inculturation and revelation. His approach shifts toward empowering the people to do their own interpretation of the faith and theology, a *teología del pueblo* (theology of the people), which moves outside of the inherited frames in terms of understanding revelation. And although I did not elaborate on it here, Pope Francis emphasizes the Spirit as the principal agent in the process of inculturation.[205] As expected all of these documents have generated a great deal of debate. In what follows I mention some of the scholars involved in this ongoing discussion as they help us to further understand how the Catholic Church continues to deal with the relationship between the gospel and the cultural.

---

199   Francis, *Evangelii Gaudium*, 69.
200   Ibid., 68.
201   Ibid., 69.
202   Ibid., 122.
203   Francis, *Evangelii Gaudium*, 90. Citing the Document of *Aparecida* he elevates popular piety to a "spirituality incarnated in the people" (Ibid., 124).
204   Francis, *Evangelii Gaudium*, 123.
205   Ibid., 122.

Gospel and the Cultural: Theological Implications

As I have shown, discussions on the relationship between faith/gospel and culture (read the cultural) in the Catholic Church have undergone a series of changes corresponding to internal shifts within the institution as well as significant outside forces.[206] One can detect a progression both in the understanding of the relation between faith and the cultural as well as in the Church's openness toward conceiving itself within complex cultural dynamics and exchanges. In Protestant contexts both Nieburh's five paradigms of the relationship between "culture" and "faith/gospel/Christ"[207] and Tillich's understanding of culture as the form of religion[208] are often quoted or deployed almost uncritically. But as I have demonstrated, "inculturation" gradually has become the predominant term for defining and describing this relation in Catholic contexts. What the term means, however, is not agreed upon within the Church itself.[209] The

---

206   Dulles is correct in stating that it is arbitrary to place Vatican II as marking point of the enormous changes the Church has been undergoing. See Dulles, "The Emerging World Church," 1. As I have shown, there have been a series of shifts within the Catholic Church that when seen retrospectively can appear fairly sudden and radical. At the same time, many of the changes that we today see within the Catholic Church would not make much sense if it were not because of the initial breakthrough of the Vatican II documents. Although not without great tension, and still heavily Eurocentric in tone, it was Vatican II that set the tone for the subsequent opening of the Church toward the cultures of the world in later documents by Pope John VI and John Paul II, and even Francis. According to Andrés Tornos it would be *Evangelii Nuntiandi* that would flesh out those changes, although many of those changes were already incipiently present in *Gaudium et spes* and *Ad Gentes*. He mentions four: One, the change from the use of "culture" to "cultures;" two, the emphasis on the transcendence of the gospel; three, issues of culture have to do with local churches and not only with the universal Church or individual believers; and four, the lived character of cultures

207   See Dulles, "The Emerging World Church," 4; Frans Seda, "The Task of the Catholic University in the Dialogue Between Faith and Culture in a Plural Multireligious Society," in *Faith and Culture: The Role of the Catholic University*, vol. XI, *Inculturation: Working Papers on Living Faith and Cultures*, ed. Ary A. Roest Crollius (Rome: Centre "Cultures and Religions"—Pontifical Gregorian University, 1989), 102.

208   See Schreiter, "Faith and Cultures," 744.

209   Part of the difficulty in defining inculturation is that there are a wide range of terms that have been deployed over the years, many of which have fallen out of use and others which simply do not seem to catch the imagination of the Church. Some of the labels that I encountered in different documents related to this discussion were: adaptation, incarnation, assimilation, indigenization, and translating. Other less desirable labels were: transculturation, transposing, and transplanting, enculturation, and aculturation.

origins of the term are variously traced. Dulles traces it back to the public message issued by the Synod of Bishops in 1977, and notes that Pope John Paul
II used it frequently, notably in *Catechesi tradendae* (1979)[210] and *Familiaris
consortio* (1981).[211] Meanwhile Sievernich tells us that the term was first used
during the thirty-second General congregation of the Jesuits (1974–1975).[212]
He also mentions the letter by Pedro Arrupe to the Society of Jesus in which he
defined inculturation.[213]

However one articulates the changes that led to the affirmation of inculturation, for my purposes, what is crucial is the radical shift that points to
the development of a new theology of the cultural in official Catholicism.
Intentionally—although not entirely abandoning inherited Eurocentric
categories and perspectives—the Vatican seems to come closer to reflecting and understanding what entire communities have understood for centuries. Such new theology of the cultural views the relation between the
gospel and cultures in much more fluid terms. The cultural in its multiple
expressions becomes understood as the all-encompassing aspect of human
experience designed to advance humanity and which can effectively mediate the gospel message. It is no longer only that "suspect" element that must
be transcended, superseded, eradicated or resisted because it stands opposite to the Gospel and the Church. Rather, it ought to be celebrated so that

The label of contextualization apparently first used by a study team of the Theological
Education Fund in 1972 has also been used, but it seems to prevail among Protestants
while inculturation among Catholics. See for example, Stephen B. Bevans, *Models of
Contextual Theology* (Maryknoll, NY: Orbis Books, 1992).

210   Sievernich notes that in this letter the pope uses both inculturation and acculturation to
       speak of the same dynamic, but that his main concern is "how genuine catechesis 'takes
       flesh' in the various cultures and milieux" (Sievernich, "Jesuit Theologies of Mission," 49).

211   Dulles, "The Emerging World Church," 3.

212   Sievernich, "Jesuit Theologies of Mission," 45–47. According to him, inculturation has
       come to cover the same ground as older expressions such as "adaptation" or "accommo-
       dation." It was originally used to stress the mutual enrichment caused by the encounter
       of Christianity with a particular culture. Se Ibid., 45.

213   Arrupe's definition reads as follows: "Inculturation is the incarnation of Christian life
       and of the Christian message in a particular cultural context, in such a way that this
       experience not only finds expression through elements proper to the culture in ques-
       tion (this alone would be no more than a superficial adaptation), but becomes a princi-
       ple that animates, directs and unifies the culture, transforming and remaking it so as to
       bring about 'a new creation'" (Sievernich, "Jesuit Theologies of Mission," 47). The bishops
       of Latin American followed suit in their document titled "New Evangelization, Human
       Development, Christian Culture" (1992) and later Pope John Paul II in his *Redemptoris
       missio* although somewhat unselfconsciously. See Ibid., 49

cultural communities may respond to the divine calling from their own cultural vantage points.

There are many theological implications to this shift. Gallagher, for example, insists that discussions on inculturation (and I would argue the cultural) have direct implication for discussing creation, the incarnation, redemption and Pentecost, although he does not elaborate further.[214] I turn to these implications in the last chapter. It must be made clear that in the Catholic Church the reconfiguration of the cultural stems from a radical theological reconceptualization of what it means to be church especially with respect to how Catholicity is embodied and made concrete in the world. The changes lead to a new theology of the church as an ecclesiology of communion; the communion of local churches from various different cultural traditions. As such, inculturation called for the coordination of many charisms present in the community of churches to serve the local communities and the universal Church, "and in so doing points to the power and presence of Christ in the midst of a community of faith and culture."[215]

The radical shift toward a different apprehension of the cultural inherent in the proposal of inculturation has caused the pluralization of the category "culture." Whereas *Gaudium et spes* use of the singular "culture" displayed a lingering dependence on the Western European Euro North American perspective that privileges an elitist understanding of the term—and therefore excludes Africa, Asia and Latin America and marginalized cultures in the centres of global political power—the privileging of "cultures" by subsequent official documents as shown here signals the decentering of Europe as cultural referent in the "gospel and culture" debates. In fact, the affirmation of inculturation presupposes the "mutual critique and affirmation" as fundamental in the dynamic of evangelization between the culture of the evangelizer and the evangelizee.[216] On one hand, Europe (and its Euro North American extension)

---

214   Gallagher, *Clashing Symbols*, 106–7.
215   Presmanes, "Inculturation as Evangelization," 69.
216   Laurenti Magesa, *Anatomy of Inculturation: Transforming the Church in Africa* (Maryknoll, NY: Orbis Books, 2004), 5. Magesa correctly deduces that

> Christian proclaimers of the gospel anywhere do not preach "the Gospel," or "the message of Christ," or "revelation," or whatever other expression may be used to explain this task. The gospel as proclaimed is not a disembodied reality, a pure emanation from God. It is essentially a cultural reality. What Christian missionaries do, rather, is to transmit to their listeners their own understanding of the gospel. They bequeath to their converts the interpretation of Christ's message as it has developed in their own communities (Ibid.).

can no longer claim to "represent" *the faith*.[217] On the other hand, ironically, inculturation also includes the Western European and Euro North American regions as they can no longer be regarded as Christian.[218]

Seen from this vantage point, inculturation also signifies a liberative move for justice and toward a preferential option for the poor and the oppressed including oppressed cultures,[219] something which Latina/o theology has been doing for some time now.[220] It is a radical move of resistance against hegemonic and ethnocentric styles of evangelization that "prevailed in the historical period between the Jerusalem Council and Vatican II."[221] The liberative move embodies the identification of the cultures of the people as sites of theological reflection while simultaneously reclaiming the connection between the people's values and their lived cultural traditions.[222]

It is for this reason that Mario L. Peresson finds inculturation a helpful tool for highlighting the biogenetics in all cultures; that is, the force that engenders and defends life, as well as passionately seeks the full realization

---

    Along the lines of mutual enrichment, Gallagher views evangelization as inculturation and as including not just mutual engagement but an actual "two-way process of double conversions" (Gallagher, *Clashing Symbols*, 104).

217   Dulles provides the example of Hillaire Belloc, who equates Christianity with Europe in the dictum "Europe will return to the Faith, or she will perish. The Faith is Europe. And Europe is the Faith" (Dulles, "The Emerging World Church," 4).

218   Sievernich, "Jesuit Theologies of Mission," 47. Sievernich also includes the countries in the Eastern bloc under atheism. In other words, inculturation refers to the entire world where the inculturation of the gospel ought to take place.

219   According to Sievernich, inculturation requires us to witness with our very lives in whatever context we find ourselves, whether we are in the tribal cultures of Africa, in the postmodern societies of Europe, in post-communist China or in the religious pluralism of India. Justice requires of our witness a preferential option for the poor; sensitivity to culture requires us selflessly to risk ourselves within worlds that are unfamiliar; respect for other religions requires us to be able to live and work together. See Sievernich, "Jesuit Theologies of Mission," 57. See also Society of Jesus, "Decree 4: Our Mission and Culture," 81–84.

220   See Orlando O. Espín, *Grace and Humanness*; Orlando O. Espín and Miguel H. Díaz, "Introduction," in *From the Heart of Our People: Latino/a Explorations in Catholic Systematic Theology*, ed. Orlando O. Espín and Miguel H. Díaz (Maryknoll, NY: Orbis Books, 1999); Néstor Medina, *Mestizaje: (Re)Mapping Race, Culture, and Faith in Latina/o Catholicism* (Maryknoll, NY: Orbis Books, 2009).

221   Presmanes, "Inculturation as Evangelization," 60.

222   By implication this also means a move away from present ethnocentric prevailing theologies, a kind of de-Europeanization move. In order to celebrate the cultures and theologies of the world, Eurocentric expressions of theology will have to be provincialized.

of all of its virtues and potentialities.[223] For him, "an inculturated evangelization is ... in the first place, an act of recognition, humility and admiration that detects the divine presence and action in cultures, in all their dynamism and signs of communion, and in the life present in them."[224] Stated differently, inculturation points to the divine action and sacrament of life given by God that is present in all cultures. Gallagher adds that if all that is created is good, "human culture at its best seeks to start from that gift and to build our world with the same freedom and love."[225] The affirmation of the gift of life in cultures shows the need for a more developed theology of the presence and action of the Spirit in all cultures, issue which I intend to develop in the last chapter.

In light of this new theological understanding of the cultural, inculturation leads to new theological reorientation of our understanding of divine revelation and humanity. Consistently, church documents emphasize the connection between the cultural and the gospel. But by emphasizing inculturation, the Vatican has initiated a new understanding of revelation which is interwoven with the cultural. By entering into another cultural world, the goal of evangelization cannot be to merely find other cognate terms, words, rites, concepts, and symbols. Rather, the content of the Gospel needs to be thought through once again by the recipients of the gospel from the vantage point of their own cultural vantage point.[226] In the eloquent words of Paul Uche Nwobi concerning the Church in Africa,

> inculturation is not just something to think about /debate about or some liturgical translation into some local languages. Rather the African Christian faith, first of all, must be fully received in African cultures. Secondly, the faith must be thoroughly thought through in African cultures, and thirdly, the faith must be fully lived out in all African cultures. This is more than some intellectual debates and/or liturgical translations.... The priests and the lay faithful of Africa are to experience inculturation as a process by which Christ's life becomes African life, the Christian "faith becomes culture," and the Gospel presented and reinterpreted "in forms and proper terms" to African culture. Without a true inculturation process whereby "the Gospel challenges cultures, and

---

223   P. Mario L. Peresson, "Inculturación del Evangelio en un mundo pluricultural."

224   Ibid.

225   Gallagher, *Clashing Symbols*, 106.

226   Andrés Tornos, "La nueva teología de la cultura. Los cambios de lenguaje de los documentos oficiales de la iglesia, a partir del Vaticano II," *Estudios Eclesiásticos* 66 (1991): 21.

cultures relive the Gospel," evangelization may turn to be another form of "cultural domination, alienation or manipulation" ... a new cultural colonization in African Church.[227]

This affirmation bears great implications for understanding divine disclosure. I highlight three key points. The first and most obvious is that inculturation must necessarily lead to a radical unhinging of divine revelation from Western European cultures and their extensions in the United States of America. Divine disclosure cannot be contained nor exhausted by any one cultural tradition, as Pope Francis succinctly noted above.[228] Second, true inculturation inevitably leads to a new understanding of revelation. Presmanes is correct that the Apostle Paul's encounter with the cultures of the Gentiles became a locus of revelation. According to him, it led to a break with Old Testament salvation history as Paul had previously understood it.[229] (This is the radical caesura of which Rahner speaks in relation to Vatican II above.) Most importantly, maintains Presmanes, the result was a break with the early Christian Jews' understanding of revelation limited only to the Jewish people. And third, the cultural is reinterpreted as a dynamic aspect of life. The encounter between a *living* gospel and a *lived* culture inevitably leads to the evangelization of that one cultural tradition, by way of aligning it with the divine intent for life. Even more crucially, as people from other cultures live the gospel they elucidate, even amplify, our understanding of the gospel in ever new ways, which until now have been absent from predominant (Western European and Euro North American) expressions of Christianity. Presmanes writes: "The response of faith is not the response of someone, of a concrete human subject, unless it is given, lived, expressed in the flesh of a concrete [culturally bound] humanity."[230]

It is true that in discussing the encounter between cultures and the gospel, official Church documents allude to the fact that the cultures are enriched, healed, even ennobled by the gospel. However it must be emphasized

---

227   Paul Uche Nwobi, *Poor Formation as Principal Factor to the Crisis in Priesthood Today* (Bloomington, IN: AuthorHouse, 2012), 167–68.

228   In the words of Presmanes: "In Jesus Christ, God is revealed in culture. His preaching of the Reign of God in word and deed was enveloped in the patterns of meaning embodied in the symbols and social practices of first-century Palestinian Judaism. However, the culture through which God chose to be revealed was not made absolute. While the Incarnation was in itself an affirmation of culture, Jesus' preaching systematically called culture to conversion" (Presmanes, "Inculturation as Evangelization," 70).

229   Presmanes, "Inculturation as Evangelization," 71.

230   Ibid., 68.

that no true reciprocal-mutual relation is considered.[231] Let us reflect on Azevedo who tells us that inculturation is the only way in which local concrete communities can learn to articulate for themselves the fundamental "core" "content of the Christian message with the symbolic and normative apparatus of both communication and organization."[232] But then again he adds that this apparatus should be considered flexible and changeable enough to allow a reasonable reshaping of the message "according to the local, cultural patterns without a conflict with the really unchangeable contents of the message."[233]

It is this "unchangeable" "transcendent-transcultural" nature of the gospel that has come under attack lately. As mentioned earlier, the gospel and divine revelation are viewed as existing in a space which the cultural cannot inhabit. At the same time, as Peresson contends, there exist no Gospel in a "pure state," outside of the cultural.[234] Official documents seem overly preoccupied with ideas concerning the gospel being corrupted by anyone cultural tradition in this process. This is the concern Dulles expresses when he writes: "Under what conditions can the Church appropriate a particular human culture without impairing its fidelity to Christ and the gospel?"[235] But one must ask if the question is not rooted in the protection of "old" Eurocentric understandings of the gospel that have become standardized, rather than a genuine openness to the possibilities of new interpretive horizons of the gospel message in the encounter with other cultures.

The Society of Jesus has also interpreted Pope John Paul II as presenting inculturation as one of the fundamental aspects of the Church's total evangelizing mission and points to the *mutuality* between the Gospel and the cultures it engages. The Christian message is to be open to all

---

231   Dulles seems to favor an approach that draws on the notion of reciprocity when speaking about the cultural exchange enacted in evangelization. But his notion of reciprocity merely connects the exchange between cultures and not the exchange or process of reinterpretation of the gospel by any given culture. The gospel is assumed to exist outside of the sphere of culture and therefore there is no "real" contact between culture and the gospel except for the gospel to impact cultures. Any cultural impact on the gospel message is viewed by implication as a corruption instead of as part of the larger complex of interrelated dynamics within a reciprocal relation of Gospel and cultures. See Dulles, "The Emerging World Church," 8–9.

232   Azevedo, *Inculturation and the Challenges of Modernity*, 27.

233   Ibid.

234   Peresson, "Inculturación del Evangelio en un mundo pluricultural."

235   Dulles, "The Emerging World Church," 3.

cultures, bound to no single culture and made accessible to every human person through a process of inculturation, by which the Gospel introduces something new into the culture and the culture brings something new to the richness of the Gospel.[236]

In light of this emphasis on *mutuality*, I ask: is it possible to conceive that the exchange between the gospel and the cultural can in fact lead to a change in the gospel message itself? If indeed the gospel necessitated cultural garb to be manifested, if the revealing initiative of God and the faith which responds to God do not exist except in concrete cultural spaces, could we not say that in the cultural exchange assumed by inculturation of the gospel message, the message potentially changes as much as the local culture that receives it?[237]

   Laurenti Magesa, for example, questions the transmission process of evangelization. Drawing on Rufus M. Jones analysis of communication, he points out that in the exchange between the evangelizer and evangelizee the message is never left intact, a number of "transformations," "adjustments," and even "compromises" imperceptibly take place at various levels.[238] New converts will have a different outlook, context, interpretation, and slant of thought, "from those of the person who first proclaimed the message to them."[239] Those differences, he says, alter and reshape the content of whatever is transmitted. Thus,

---

236   Society of Jesus, "Decree 4: Our Mission and Culture," 76.

237   At the very least, this is the suggestive implication of Azevedo when he writes that: inculturation is "the dynamic relation between the Christian message and culture or cultures; an insertion of the Christian life into a culture; an ongoing process of reciprocal and critical interaction and assimilation between them" (Azevedo, *Inculturation and the Challenges of Modernity*, 11). Even more emphatically, following the writings of John Paul II, the Society of Jesus' stated that

> Pope John Paul II has presented inculturation as one of the fundamental aspects of the Church's total evangelizing mission and points to the *mutuality* between the Gospel and the cultures it engages. The Christian message is to be open to all cultures, bound to no single culture and made accessible to every human person through a process of inculturation, by which the Gospel introduces something new into the culture and the culture brings something new to the richness of the Gospel (Society of Jesus, "Decree 4: Our Mission and Culture," 76.).

238   Magesa, *Anatomy of Inculturation*, 6.
239   Ibid.

attention to those issues is important in order to prevent any kind of ethnocentrism from creeping into the process.[240]

Discussing these issues is also important because of the challenges of translatability and incommensurability in the very encounter between cultures.[241] According to Magesa, for example, even when equivalents terms for inculturation, namely, *utamadunisho* in Kiswahili, or *Gutaura Kirikaniro kuringana na muturire wa gitene* (literally, "interpreting the biblical message in an African perspective") in Kikuyu were proposed, "the problem of what the concept meant and implied in the life of the church remained substantially unresolved."[242]

Andrés Tornos further points out that the tension in determining the transcendence of the gospel relates to whether other cultures are viewed as being merely other forms of looking at the world rather than other modes of perceiving and conceptualizing reality. He notes that if cultures are simply different ways of looking at the world, then it is easy to understand in what ways the gospel is transcendent. That is, evangelization would be a matter of finding new symbols, rites, words, and concepts that actualize the gospel in the new circumstances.[243] However, if other cultures embody other modes of living life, conceptualizing reality and the world, including different cosmogonies,

---

240   Concerning this point, Rahner conceded that notions such as revelation maybe construed specifically from a European horizon, responding to what European theology finds to be vital. But such an approach does "not exactly propagate a concept of revelation that is easily accessible for African and Asian cultures, especially since hundreds of thousands of years between primordial revelation ... remain unfilled" (Rahner, "Fundamental Theological Interpretation," 720).

241   Magesa writes, for example, that the Christian concept of love is too abstract for most Africans as well as the imposed narrow views of marriage and family. He points out that often, they have brought cultural deterioration instead of cultural enrichment.

    We believed in love that is expressed in symbolic exchange of gifts, ritual visits and exchange of vows or agreements between the clan members of the betrothed before marriage. In this regard, marriage was a matter between relatives of the bride and the groom. After marriage the two groups were held responsible for the outcome [of the relationship] of the newly wedded couples. This has been watered down by the Christian concept of marriage, which is highly influenced by western, Euro-American values (Magesa, *Anatomy of Inculturation*, 11).

242   Magesa, *Anatomy of Inculturation*, 11.

243   Tornos, "La nueva teología de la cultura," 24. See also Dulles, "The Emerging World Church," 3–4, 11.

then the unresolvable and inevitable clash between the gospel and cultures will be the result.[244] These issues, I would argue, need further elaboration in official Roman Catholic documents.

As I stated above, *Gaudium et spes* affirmed that people are protagonists in creating their own cultures as part of an affirmation of the emergence of a new culture of human solidarity. Since the Council took place, the Catholic Church has emphasized the intrinsic connection between faith and humanity, equating being human with being cultural. Gallagher makes this point in reference to Pope John Paul II. For him, the pope's comment that humans are the subjects and architects of cultures points to something in the "very constitution of humanity."[245] The council has also confirmed that divine disclosure was/is (necessarily) mediated through the cultural, and that the gospel message and the human responses are expressed through concrete cultural forms. Although left undeveloped, the most common biblical example used to speak of these two dynamics coming together is the incarnation event in Jesus Christ.[246] The incarnation is seen as analogous to the relationship between the gospel and cultures. Inculturation is seen as following the steps toward incarnation. Just as Jesus entered humanity and healed it and transformed it from within, so also the Gospel enters other cultures and transforms, uplifts, corrects, and confirms them from within.

The analogy of the incarnation goes deeper since the incarnation also exemplifies the pinnacle at which the divine enters created-human existence and is necessarily bound to the cultural.[247] Seen this way, the cultural takes on a prominent role in unveiling for us a different understanding of humanity that counters and goes beyond abstract universalizing notions. In the incarnation humanity is revealed as fundamentally cultural and contextually specific. We can say that the cultural determines "how a human group understands itself, understands life, and understands the world in which they live and express this understanding through social practice and symbolic activity."[248] This insight is commonly used in discussions of the cultural, but it is only one side of the more complete argument. Drawing on

---

244   Tornos, "La nueva teología de la cultura," 24.

245   Gallagher, *Clashing Symbols*, 50. For Gallagher, this is the way by which Pope John Paul II goes deeper than Vatican II in establishing a connection between the nature of culture and human nature as self-transcending.

246   It is not difficult to see why the analogy of incarnation was often used to explain the encounter between culture and faith/gospel. See Schreiter, "Faith and Cultures," 746.

247   Azevedo, *Inculturation and the Challenges of Modernity*, 25.

248   Presmanes, "Inculturation as Evangelization," 66.

Azevedo's analysis of Geertz we can additionally affirm that the cultural is the "deepest code to reveal a human, social group and make it understandable."[249] The two sides must be held together in tension. The cultural gives a concrete human group the meaning of life, claims Azevedo, but if we do not know what *life* is for a group, how they live it and express it, then we simply have no insight into the group at all.[250] We can appreciate, then, that humanity—in its rich diversity—is unveiled as people live out their lives in their particular cultural milieux. There is no "universal human;" we are all socially located and culturally bound human individuals and communities. Therefore, it is as people live the faith within their cultures that their own humanity is perfected and unveiled to the world. In the words of *Gaudium et spes* "It is one of the properties of the human person that he [or she] can achieve true and full humanity only by means of [a] culture."[251] It remains to be debated if the differences between cultures imply ontological differences. When speaking of other cultures are we also talking about other humanities? This aspect, I propose needs further elaboration as well.

The implication of this discussion on humanity is that by encouraging inculturation and by sincerely being open to the richness of the various cultures through inculturation, the Church can potentially cooperate in ushering in a new integrated understanding of humanity that takes lived and living cultures as crucial theological sites. Instead of focusing primarily on the unity of the church, the challenge will be to celebrate its diversity as a constitutive element both of its *catholicity* as well as its unity.[252]

Conclusion

The complexity of the various theological strands within Catholicism is enormous and cannot be addressed properly with such focused discussion. My intention here has not been to exhaustively analyze the complex series of changes that the Catholic Church has been undergoing, nor to provide an exhaustive sample of the many players involved in these discussions. Rather,

---

249   Azevedo, *Inculturation and the Challenges of Modernity*, 10.

250   Ibid.

251   Vatican Council II, "*Gaudium et spes*," 53.

252   Here I resist the tendency to prematurely surrender to fears of division by emphasizing unity. This tendency is found in all official documents and among theologians for example (Presmanes, Tornos, and Azevedo). My point is that by celebrating diversity the Church is already creating the conditions for unity.

I have illustrated—in broad strokes—the complex set of issues that have contributed to internal changes regarding debates on faith and the cultural within the Catholic Church since the turn of the twentieth century. I have documented how some early incipient shifts received a fuller articulation at Vatican II. Subsequently, these changes in approach were solidified, built upon and developed by several popes and key thinkers after Vatican II contributing to a radical shift within Catholicism. It is worth noting, however, that inherited ideas of cultural superiority from the colonial period have influenced Catholic thought much longer than Vatican II and continue to haunt some expressions of inculturaltion.

As I have argued, the theological implications of the changes proposed by inculturation are enormous, and if taken seriously can potentially transform the Catholic Church into a truly universal community of local communities, each distinctly cultural. Certainly, the notion of inculturation promises to enrich our theological understandings of the relationship between the phenomena of cultures and the Christian faith, humanity, and divine disclosure. Based on a broader understanding of the cultural, inculturation offers refreshing ways to understand God's activity among cultural groups and even in other religions.

The full implications of these insights, as well as their reception and adaptation in the Global South have yet to be explored more fully, but the prospects are very positive. There is still a need to more fully engage inculturation in terms of theological production and faith expressions. As has become evident, many of the concerns and issues debated feed into my proposals about the cultural. In my view, a theology of the cultural can help us to further articulate our understanding of the relationship between the gospel and the cultural. Until now the key concern of the Catholic Church in engaging other cultures has been the task of evangelization. This is the prism through which the other cultures of the world are viewed. The official documents here explored do not address how humans can possibly understand the gospel or perceive the divine disclosure when it is entirely mediated through their own cultural traditions. The idea that the gospel transcends cultures is haunted by the fact that in its present configuration, the pervasive expressions in Catholic Christianity are intimately woven with Western European cultures. To de-Europeanize the gospel will necessarily mean that other cultural expressions of Christianity will have to arise, many of which will be radically different from the pervasive European expressions.

In fact, as other cultures have appropriated and inculturated the Gospel message overtime, they have also engaged in theological reflection. These reflections differ greatly from prevailing Eurocentric theologies and theological

methods.[253] Looking to the future, one asks how will the Catholic Church welcome those perspectives and theologians who until now have been absent
from "mainstream" Catholic theology? Similarly, considering questions about
the cultural more intentionally, the Church also needs to address issues related
to the degree to which the gospel can be considered culturally conditioned and
whether it changes as it interacts with the cultures of the world. I do not take
this question lightly. A careful glance at popular expressions of Catholicism in
many parts of the world demonstrates that inculturation also includes a reorientation of what we have traditionally understood as the gospel, so much so
that the expressions of the peoples sometimes become entirely unrecognizable in relation to inherited Eurocentric practices. To me, these reframings of
the Gospel from below promise to help us reclaim the divine commitment to
life, while at the same time excising our understanding of the gospel from its
colonizing content. They also signal a deeper relationship between the gos-
pel/faith and the cultural that needs further theological elaboration. These are
some of the concerns that a theology of the cultural needs to highlight and
upon which it ought to reflect.

---

253   See for example, Espín, *Grace and Humanness*; Agbonkhianmeghe E. Orobator, *Theology
       Brewed in an African Pot*; James Cone, *The Cross and the Lynching Tree* (Maryknoll,
       NY: Orbis Books, 2011); Mercy Amba Oduyoye, "Gospel and Culture in Africa" Irarrázaval,
       Inculturation; Diana Hayes, *Standing in the Shoes My Mother Made: A Womanist Theology*
       (Nashville, TN: Fortress Press, 1999); Orevillo-Montenegro Muriel, *The Jesus of Asian
       Women* (Maryknoll, NY: Orbis Books, 2007).

CHAPTER 8

Understanding the Cultural Pneumatologically

The idea that "culture is the fact of man [*sic*] while the gospel is
God's intervention," for all its easy, acceptable clarity, oversimplifies
things…Equally insufficient, I think, is the idea that culture forms a
creation from below while the gospel comes from on high. Culture,
as an act and attainment of humankind created in the likeness of
God, is not outside the rays of the divine energies; it is not unrelated
to the breathing of the Spirit who controls all things, "the visible
and the invisible." The creative work of people upon nature is a gift,
a commandment and a possibility given to the first created couple,
a consequence of being "in the likeness of God" (Gen. 5:1). The
Orthodox tradition holds that this "likeness" was not lost, nor made
useless following the Fall. Thus, humankind remains the recipient
of the messages of God's will and of the energies of his Spirit.[1]

ANASTASIOS YANNOULATOS

Introduction

Throughout this book my intention has been to reclaim the intimate interwoven character of "culture" and Christianity. As I showed in chapters 4 through
6, scholars tend to create a wedge between the cultural and the Christian faith /
the gospel. Furthermore, their theologies—which are by definition cultural
theologies—presuppose that they have access to the "right" version of the gospel designating any expression that does not resemble theirs as a corrupted
version. In this chapter, I shift gears in order to propose my own theological
approach to the cultural, which, I have suggested, refers to the complex processes of culturalization which, for me, is a dynamic and changing network of
socially and historically inherited codes and segments of codes that regulate
and make possible inter-human interaction in a given society; that provide the
frame and lenses for interpreting reality; and that constitute the set of guiding principles by which humans and societies interact with their surrounding
environment and the divine.

---

1 Anastasios Yannoulatos, "Culture and Gospel: Some Observations from the Orthodox
   Tradition and Experience," *International Review of Mission* 74, no. 294 (April 1985): 187.

Most scholars (with the clear exceptions of Tanner, Gorringe and Rieger) continue to uphold the gospel as transcultural, as some-thing that can easily be distinguished and separated from cultural traditions, though they generally admit that it can never find expression outside of the cultural.[2] Christianity and the gospel are imagined as inhabiting the world of ideas; central tenets are therefore understood to be transferable without any (substantive) impact on content between cultures.[3] This assumed abstract version of the Christian message or the Gospel is understood as transcending any and all cultures. As I have argued, such proposals ensure that the dominant (Western European and Euro North American) *cultural* theologies and expressions of the gospel remain unchallenged. Also, among Catholics, Pope Francis shows a significant shift within the Catholic Church's understanding and approach toward other cultural traditions with profound implications for the development of a theology of the cultural. It is this theology of the cultural that will be the concern of this last chapter.

In order to bypass pervasive dualistic views of the cultural, in this chapter I offer my theological approach to the cultural. I propose that cultures be understood as the ubiquitous phenomena that impact all aspects of human existence even religious traditions and faith.[4] I insist that, what is at stake is a serious examination of the cultural dimension of the complex network of cultural processes at work as humans live life, relate to each other and the environment, and make sense of reality. I suggest that the cultural plays a central role in mediating the human-divine encounter and should be considered constitutive part of the original divine creative intent. Even further, instead of simply affirming that the cultural mediates religious faith (Christian faith), I also pay special attention to what enables cultural elements to mediate religious faith as well as its connection to human-divine interaction. Instead, while focusing on the conditioning effect of the cultural, and while highlighting the intimate relationship between the cultural and the Christian faith, I propose to redirect our attention toward the divine activity in the cultural dimension. The theological articulation of the cultural I offer revolves around four key axes: 1) The cultural and its relation to Creation; 2) the cultural and its destructive power; 3) the cultural in relation to the divine kenotic act of salvation i.e., Christology and Pneumatology; and 4) the

---

2 P. Mario L. Peresson, "Inculturación del Evangelio en un mundo pluricultural."

3 A similar critique of notions of Tradition can be found in Orlando O. Espín, "Traditioning."

4 Although throughout the book I focus on Christianity, I contend that the relationship between religious faith and culture is intimate and interwoven. As we have seen, Christian theologians, in varying degrees, have frequently argued that Christ (and Christianity) can transcend culture. This is the argument I dispute.

cultural as the place-*locus* of divine revelation. These four axes, I insist, will provide us with a better theological appreciation of the cultural in relation to faith.

I want to point out that I draw great inspiration from Latina/o theology, the Pentecostal impetus to reclaim the activity of the Spirit in the world, and decolonial, postcolonial, and liberationist theological currents. Although I do not explicitly discuss each of these rich currents, I draw on them to articulate my theological proposal.

Culture as Starting Point and Base for Our Reflection

To reiterate, I locate my reflections within the Christian tradition. In light of that, let me repeat (along with Tanner) that I do not view Christianity as culturally independent from the larger society. Instead, I see Christians as engaged in dynamic processes of crossfertilization, deeply dependent on the larger cultural context. In other words, I do not ascribe to the belief that there is such thing as a "Christian culture" but rather culturally particular ways in which Christians behave and express their faith in God. My operating assumption is that (together with Van Til) all collectives of peoples are also cultural collectives; the development of the cultural is most emphatically not an achievement of the Western European Euro North American world alone.[5] As a result, I do not ascribe to the view that there can be a radical separation between the gospel, Christ, and our understanding of the Christian God, and the cultural because our notions of God, angels, Christ, etc. are also deeply cultural insofar as they are embedded within specific cultural milieus. There are no "pure" unmediated experiences[6] but only culturally mediated and culturally conditioned experiences of the divine.[7]

---

5   Henry R. Van Til, *The Calvinistic Concept of Culture*, 26–27.
6   Peter D. Neumann, *Pentecostal Experience: An Ecumenical Encounter*, Princeton Theological Monograph Series (Eugene, OR: Pickwick Publications, 2012), 29. According to Neumann, even mystical experiences are mediated. They are organized through extremely complex epistemological processes. Thus, he concludes that "the notion of unmediated experience seems, if not self-contradictory, at best empty." (Ibid.).
7   Indeed, many theologians have rejected experience as criteria for divine disclosure in their attempt to maintaining the "objective" radical separation between the divine uncreated and the human created world. They want to preserve (guard) the divine from being "co-opted" but in doing so disallow the actual close interaction of God with creation. But as Neumann adds, experiences of the divine are "mediated through the horizons of specific linguistic, cultural, and historical situations in which humans find themselves" (Neumann, *Pentecostal Experience*, 30). It is for this reason that Gallagher emphasizes the need to go beyond notions of a "pure" gospel that remains untainted by the cultural. See Michael Paul Gallagher, *Clashing Symbols*, 62.

The implication of these affirmations is that the interaction between humans and the divine can only ever be filtered and mediated through the cultural. The result is a bidirectional cultural mediation and conditioning: not only is the divine self-disclosure mediated and conditioned through the cultural but the human response to the divine invitation is also culturally mediated and conditioned.[8] In other words, just as the call from God cannot be heard or understood outside of the concreteness of the cultural milieu of people, so also the human response to the divine invitation, what we call conversion and expressions of faith, is not "some abstract philosophical construct" but a concrete act made within the confines of human particularity within a cultural community.[9] Thus, the cultural demarcates the meeting point and constitutes the meeting "place" of the divine and the human in an historical concrete sociocultural context.

Orlando Espín asserts this necessary role of the cultural in mediating the intimate relationship between the mystery of the divine and the mystery of the human experience of the divine.[10] He argues that the cultural provides the social, cultural, and spiritual platform and grammar for engaging with and responding to the divine. Because the cultural is the ubiquitous aspect that permeates all of human reality, our understanding of the divine is limited by the very concreteness of our sociocultural context and location.[11] The degree to which the cultural conditions human experience of the divine is such, claims Espín, that "when human beings believe themselves to be encountering the divine" they are in fact encountering that which their own cultural context and tradition "allows them to understand precisely as 'divine.'"[12] So he concludes that no experience of God occurs in a vacuum; there is no "pure," a-cultural encounter with the divine.[13]

---

8   See Jorge Presmanes, "Inculturation as Evangelization, 67. See also Yves Congar, "Christianity as Faith and Culture," *East Asian Pastoral Review* 18, no. 4 (1981): 304–10.

9   Presmanes, "Inculturation as Evangelization," 67.

10   As he asserts, "the role of culture also means for Christianity that the way a people or a person experientially perceives the love of God, and the way they respond to it, will always be cultural. In other words, there is no acultural Christianity, just as there is no acultural option for God, love, and salvation" (Orlando O. Espín, "Grace and Humanness: A Hispanic Perspective," in *We Are a People! Initiatives in Hispanic American Theology*, ed. Roberto S. Goizueta [Minneapolis, MN: Fortress Press, 1992], 145).

11   Orlando O. Espín, "Popular Catholicism: Alienation or Hope?" in *Hispanic / Latino Theology: Challenge and Promise*, ed. Ada María Isasi-Díaz and Fernando F. Segovia (Minneapolis, MN: Fortress Press, 1996), 310.

12   Ibid.

13   Drawing on Gonzalez's play on culto (cult) and cultivo (cultivate) as two aspects of the cultural, we can say that cult is the mode in which cultures respond to the challenge and promise of the *mysterium tremendum*. See Justo L. González, *Culto, cultura y cultivo*, 46.

But the effects of the cultural go beyond simply understanding the divine. For Espín the cultural also conditions the human response. Situating himself within the Latina/o cultural tradition, he claims that his Latina/o culture is the necessary prism through which he perceives God's grace and love, and through which he responds to it. To be Latino/a is not for him a superficial peripheral aspect determined by an accident of birth, but rather is the "very condition within and through which [he hears] the gospel and respond[s] to it in faith."[14] The Latina/o cultural background/ universe—as with any other ethnocultural tradition—provides a unique web of culturally interconnected elements (epistemology, identity, understanding of reality, values, symbols) that shape the *encounter* with the divine. Latinas/os can only perceive, understand, and respond to the divine in Latina/o cultural ways.[15] More precisely, the "God" experienced by Latinos/as in the U.S.A. "is (necessarily) culturally and socially contextualized in ways possible only to them, and expressive of the language, symbols, understandings, and image(s) of the divine shaped by their culture, by their 'social place'," and by the larger range of social issues reflected in society.[16]

I further propose that affirming the necessary mediating and conditioning nature of the cultural, also dismantles the false dichotomies perpetuated by Niebuhr and his followers, that is, "Christ" and "culture," "Christianity" and "culture," and the "gospel" and "culture." Christ, Christianity and the gospel on one hand and the cultural, on the other, cannot be easily separated and do not occupy entirely different spaces. As I illustrate later on, to see them as encased within their own silos actually runs the risk of denying what took place in the incarnation. It further undermines divine activity in this world and ignores the interconnection between the work of the Spirit and the cultural sphere as made manifest in the event of Pentecost. Stated succinctly, neither our understanding of God, Christ, or the gospel stand outside the cultural. The cultural is not a peripheral aspect of human existence, but is part of the very fabric of being created as human beings by God.

The Cultural and Creation

I begin with a reconfiguration of our understanding of the cultural and creation. God's creative force and energy of life created humanity and continues to create even today. God also creates humans and instills in them the capacity

---

14   Orlando O. Espín, *Grace and Humanness*, 134.

15   Ibid.

16   Orlando O. Espín, *The Faith of the People*, 94–95.

to create cultures; there is a connection between the human capacity for the construction of cultures and original divine creative intent. As humans are born and interact with other humans and their immediate environment, they enter the complex processes of socialization and culturalization. Since infancy children begin to be shaped and their humanity begins to develop as a result of the myriad culturally conditioned interactions of which they are part. Collectively and as individuals, we all traverse the path of socialization and culturalization in our particular cultural communities and as we grow in our culturally conditioned humanity. It is in this way that we also collectively and individually participate as co-creators with God, as we create cultures that are life-giving and which foster growth in our humanity.

The cultural plays another crucial role, it is the necessary and only space within which humans can respond to and interact with God. Van Til's narrow view on the meaning of human existence, for example, led him to think of humanity as having a single task: the service of God. For this reason, he concluded that the cultural was but a means to express one's religious faith in God.[17] Schilder also followed a similar train of thought; he saw the cultural as having a single task, that of cultivating humanity for the service of God.[18] Both theologians placed the motivation and origins of the cultural in Godself. The difference is that Van Til places the divine intent in the divine imaging of humanity while Schilder places it in the cultural mandate of Genesis 1:28. I will return to these differences later on but for now my point is that the author of Genesis implies that there is an intimate connection between the creation event, human activity, and the emergence of the cultural. We can infer, then, that God's creation of humanity included the capacity to create and construct cultures, the cultural is by extension an inherent aspect of the creation of humanity, therefore, a gift from God.

Admittedly, cultures are imperfect human constructs! As Van Til would say, humans precede the cultural (he uses culture) and are the creators of the cultural.[19] However, such a view limits the depth of what I am trying to say here. As the Genesis narratives shows, the interaction between the divine and humanity is already marked by cultural elements on two key points: God gives humans a cultural mandate to multiply and populate the earth (1) and humans are made in the image and likeness of God (2). Let us consider these two aspects

---

17   Van Til, *The Calvinistic Concept of Culture*, 28.

18   Klaas Schilder, *Christ and Culture*.

19   Van Til, *The Calvinistic Concept of Culture*, 28.

The Cultural Mandate

As we saw from Schilder and Van Til in chapter 4, the obvious implication of the Genesis 1:28 passage is that humanity is charged with the task of engaging in cultural activities. This cultural engagement can be interpreted as the way through which humans fulfill God's cultural mandate. Schilder was correct in saying that humanity's ability to fulfill this mandate was not revoked, despite the destructive effects of sin. The mandate is part of the original divine creative intent. However—and contrary to Schilder, Van Til and Frame—the intention behind the mandate is not limited to pleasing or approaching God. John Frame, for example, considers that human engagement in cultural activity is a divine command that cannot be ignored; "Adam must develop culture because that is God's desire. Culture is for God's sake. So it is subject to God's commands, God's desires, God's norms, God's values."[20] However, such a position represents only one side of the debate.

Frame ignores human agency and capacity, which is my primary concern here. Certainly, the cultural mandate must be understood as having as basic premise God's "paternal" care for humanity.[21] The Genesis theologian conceives God as "father" and his activity for Adam and Eve as expression of God's care. It is in this way that one must interpret the description of God engaging in the cultural activity of tailoring clothes for them (Gen 3:21). In the same way though, the cultural mandate is oriented to push humanity towards developing technologies and skills that will enable them to survive, transform, and interact with their immediate environment and with each other.[22] We can infer then that cultural capacity is both constitutive of being human *and* a divine gift provided for humans to live and grow in their humanity. The origin of this cultural capacity, I would argue, is directly connected to being made in the image and likeness of God.

The Cultural and Divine Imaging

The affirmation that humans are made in the image and likeness of God (Gen 1:27) is deeply suggestive. According to the author of Genesis, humanity is the closest physical expression of the divine,[23] notion which, according to Ravasi, is

---

20   John M. Frame, "Christianity and Culture."
21   Gianfranco Ravasi, *Guía espiritual del Antiguo Testamento*, 115.
22   Ravasi tells us that the collaboration between God and the man as described by the author of Genesis celebrates the function of the sciences. He adds, "Muy lejos de ser "oscurantista" y de temer el progreso científico, la Biblia lo considera como una misión confiada al hombre por el mismo Creador." (Ravasi, *Guía espiritual del Antiguo Testamento*, 76).
23   Ravasi, *Guía espiritual del Antiguo Testamento*, 51.

directly linked to Israel's rejection of images and idolatry (Ex. 20:4). The close connection between humanity and divinity expressed by the Genesis theologian allows us to unlock three key theological insights which elucidate the cultural nature of humanity, humanity's capacity for cultural activity, and the divine connection to the cultural. First, the divine imaging means that humans are able to engage in cultural activities because they were created to be cultural. To be human is also to create culture. We can say together with Konrad Raiser that the cultural is humanity's "second nature" in terms of social relations.[24]

Second, the construction of cultures and the engagement of the complex and messy processes of culturalization constitute the distinctly human ways in which people live out their humanity. In view of the great plurality of cultural traditions in the world, we can conclude that each cultural tradition is a different realization of what it means to be human.[25] Humans engage the cultural because they are human and furthermore, as they engage the cultural they grow in their humanity.[26]

The Divine imaging places all human being in the same cultural playing field; because of our shared humanity we all are able to engage in cultural activities and construct cultures.[27] (We can say the same thing about religious activities). In other words, all cultural traditions embody the divine care for humanity as well as display the unique ways in which human collectives live out and grow in their humanity. The status of a cultural tradition and its development and "advancement" cannot therefore be determined by the criteria of only one tradition, as was the case with European colonialism in relation to the other cultures of the world. Rather, it is determined by the way in which each tradition ensures that all of its members participate in multiple processes of culturalization and cultural construction in order to ensure their own humanity is safeguarded. Here I want to bring to bear the idea of the image of God as one of the most important Christian foundations

---

24   Cited in Gallagher, *Clashing Symbols*, 57.

25   Another way to put it is to say that the plurality of cultures corresponds with different ways of facing the question of the meaning of human existence. See Gallagher, *Clashing Symbols*, 48.

26   As Pope Francis writes, "The human person grows more, matures more and is sanctified more to the extent that he or she enters into relationships, going out from themselves to live in communion with God, with others and with all creatures" (Francis, *Laudato Si*).

27   In the words of Van Til, "Culture, then does not belong exclusively to the so-called *civilized* nations, but is the activity of man [*sic*] as image bearer of his Creator in forming nature to his purposes. Man is a cultural creature, and civilization is merely the external side of culture" (Van Til, *The Calvinistic Concept of Culture*, 27).

for equality. It is not an abstract concept but is always concretely situated and culturally instantiated.[28]

Third, the divine imaging does not only say something about humanity and humanity's capacity for cultural activity. Being image bearers also gives us a glimpse into the inner workings of the divine. If indeed cultural activity is an expression of being created in the image of God, does it not follow that humans in their cultural contexts reflect (by way of analogy) the plurality of God whose inner interrelationship is governed by a kind of cultural perichoresis? Because humans are shaped by social relationships which in turn are permeated and conditioned by culture, we can surmise that humans as image bearers mirror the divine in the cultural sense. In other words, being image bearers extends even to the cultural dimension of the divine. As a result, we can view the internal dynamics of the Trinity as being shaped by social relations, permeated and conditioned by specific processes of "culturalization" along with "cultural dynamics and interactions" proper to the divine. It is for this reason that I am arguing that the cultural plays such a central role in mediating the divine's self-disclosure to humanity and humanity's response to the divine.

The question of divine cultural activities and the understanding of God as a cultural being become clearer when we see it through the Jesus event. Christologically speaking, the Jesus event is the point at which God binds Godself to the cultural dimension of humanity in order to enact our salvation and be self-disclosed as the *God for us*. It for this very reason that when we participate in culture-making processes we encounter, engage, and imitate the divine. The cultural becomes a site/position/place, a locus of divine activity and theological reflection, as Latina/o theologians would argue. The cultural however is also deeply impacted and shaped by the human (sinful) condition.

Grace and the Destructive Power of the Cultural

Traditional Christian theological expressions consider creation as an act of divine gracious-self-giving. In a related move, I want to also suggest that creation should be understood as a kind of kenotic act of grace on the part of God making room for creation, the non-God. But traditional theological approaches also draw a wedge between God and the cultural, or between grace and the experience of grace via the cultural. As I have emphasized already, humans are created by God with the capacity to create and construct cultures, which allows us to think of

28   Timothy J. Gorringe, *Furthering Humanity*, 237.

the cultural as an inherent aspect of the creation of humanity. Thus, to speak of grace in cultures is no abstract matter. Understanding grace in human experience theologically can only really be accomplished when is seen as part of the inter-connected web of culturalization processes within specific cultural traditions. In other words, when we speak of cultures, grace is implied insofar as grace enables humans to approach the divine, just as it enables humans to perceive and under-stand the divine invitation which is always dressed in cultural garments.

Orlando Espín balances the tension between God's grace and the experi-ence/expression of it in the cultural: he considers "grace-in-itself" as outside the scope of created reality and as such transcending history and cultures. He proposes, however, that such an imperceptible expression of grace is only made manifest to humanity in culturally conditioned ways as "grace-for-us-and-within-us." Had it not been because the divine entered the realm of the cultural, humanity would not have been able to see, touch, hear the actions of the "God-who-is-for-us." The divine self-giving, Espín notes, occurs "in real history and culture and not in some imagined, generic world."[29]

Contrary to Western European and Euro North American theological artic-ulations of grace which have tended to deny the cultural, and in so doing failed to see the colonizing character of their own theologies, here I emphasize the close connection between grace and the cultural. We could say with Karl Barth that "Grace is the majesty, the freedom, the undeservedness, the unexpect-edness, the newness, the arbitrariness, in which the relationship to God and therefore the possibility of knowing" God is opened to humanity by Godself.[30] But such an eloquent articulation remains an empty gesture without acknowl-edging the fact that humans can only have access or perceive grace through culturally conditioned signs and symbols. It is because of the cultural that the divine invitation, the human perception of the divine invitation, and the human response to God are effectively mediated.

But how is grace operating in the cultural? Divine common grace is the other side of the human (sinful) condition. It enables humanity to act in and struggle for culturally just and humanizing ways and in careful respectful interaction with the rest of creation. It is also grace that allows us to explain the capacity of the cultural to mediate the human-divine relationship. This is the paradox with which we are wrestling: how can cultures, as imperfect constructs, enable humans to express their faith, engage the divine, and translate the divine self-disclosure in ways that make it possible for humans to communicate the divine mystery in comprehensible ways?

---

29   Orlando O. Espín, "An Exploration Into the Theology of Grace and Sin," 124.
30   Gorringe, *Furthering Humanity*, 125.

Such questions helpfully prevent us from romanticizing the cultural. I argue that the primary goal of culturalization processes is to build up humanity, to affirm life in the rest of creation, and to respond to the divine invitation of love. However, it is also important not to idealize or romanticize processes of culturalization. Because cultures are human constructions, they have within them the powers of destruction and dehumanization, just as humans do.[31] It is within cultural parameters and using the available cultural tools that people are either humanized or dehumanized.

These destructive elements in each cultural tradition signal to the disruption of God's gracious pneumatic activity in the cultural. They can be better understood as symptoms of a deeper-level corruption of cultural traditions that can be identified as the marks of "human sin." The Genesis creation accounts point to an idyllic original world in which all things were deemed to be *good* by God. But the story does not end there; the events narrated put on display the disruption and distortion of the relationship between Adam and Eve, humans and God, and humanity with the rest of creation.[32] Drawing on Paul's notion of the "absolute inclusiveness" of sin (Rom. 1:18–31), Nicholls (along with many other scholars) claims that the totality of a cultural tradition is "tainted with sin and some of it is demonic."[33] In line with this understanding of the far reaching impact of sin, it can be said that sin does not merely/ only corrupt cultures but it also corrupts the human ability to measure, understand and perceive such corruption.[34]

However one resolves the extent of the impact of sin in humanity and by extension in cultural traditions, my point is that sin can also only be expressed in culturally conditioned ways. I reassert that humanity's "sinful" inclinations are most heinously found expressed in cultural processes and modes of social organization, in the ways in which humans justify oppression and injustice and especially in how the imposition of one cultural tradition upon others is justified.[35]

---

31   Orlando O. Espín, "An Exploration Into the Theology of Grace and Sin," 123.

32   Gallagher tells us that if "God created all that is good, human culture at its best seeks to start from that gift and to build our world with the same freedom and love. Biblically, this is the ideal image, but even within the early chapters of Genesis shadows come, culture turns sour and the results are exile, violence and Babel" (Gallagher, *Clashing Symbols*, 106).

33   Bruce J. Nicholls, *Contextualization*, 18.

34   González, *Culto, cultura y cultivo*, 73.

35   Ibid., 68–69.

My intention here is not to engage complex debates on sin. Rather, I merely seek to point to the type of cultural dynamics that can be ascribed to human sin. The destructive power of sin in cultures is evident in the way relationships with people and the rest of creation have been distorted. Such destructive power is abundantly clear in societal structures which culturally construct and en-trench relationships of subalternity and oppression. In relation to the rest of creation, the destructive tendencies of cultures are epitomized in the way humans exploit the environment; deplete non-renewable natural resources; and reduce every form of life, including human life, to the interests of profit making and consumption.[36]

More specifically, the human tendency to conquer and colonize must be understood as concrete expression of sin. Sin at the level of the cultural means the domination of one culture over another, affirms Marilyn Legge.[37] It finds expression in the outright demonization and destruction of the cultures and religious traditions of the Indigenous peoples of the world, for example. Native American scholar George Tinker illustrates this point when he describes the cultural complicity of Christianity with colonization. He wonders why Christians are led to believe that until the birth of Jesus, God cared only for one small people on the face of the earth, "leaving all others to ignorance, 'sin,' idolatry, self-destruction, and eternal damnation."[38] Tinker posits that the gospel message only gets complicated for Indigenous peoples because it came with the clear inference that "'God's' love (in the Jesus event) was denied Indian peoples until God, in God's graciousness, sent White people to kill us, lie to us, steal our land, and proclaim the saving gospel to us."[39]

"Modern" conquests, invasions, and colonization did not take place out of an altruistic sense of sharing cultural advances with those who shared the same humanity. Rather, they took place because of greed, ambition, and an unfettered desire for the lands and riches of the originary peoples of the world. It was accompanied by a profoundly distorted self-perception of human and cultural superiority—expressed in the form of military might and self-perceived

---

36   González writes: "... por razón del pecado el ser humano ve ahora al otro ser humano como objeto de explotación, y por el mismo motivo ve la tierra como enemiga renuente de la cual hay que extraer el sostén, así también, por razón del pecado, cada cultura ve a las demás como parte de un ambiente hostil y, por tanto, contrincante que se debe eliminar o absorber" González, *Culto, cultura y cultivo*, 69.

37   Marilyn J. Legge, *The Grace of Difference*, 117.

38   George E. "Tink" Tinker, *American Indian Liberation: A Theology of Sovereignty* (Maryknoll, NY: Orbis Books, 2008), 132.

39   Ibid.

technological advance—that saw no moral conflict between religious traditions, especially including Christianity, and the dehumanization (killing, enslaving, exploiting) of the ("other") peoples of the world. In the words of González,

> Because of sin all cultures have imperialist ambitions. Because of its own nature, any culture imagines itself to be the best mode of responding to the realities of life and of interpreting those realities. But when confronted with another culture with an alternate way of responding to reality and of interpreting it, that alternate mode threatens its very being and, therefore, that other culture is perceived as an enemy that must be defeated … In a certain way, that is the base of imperialism. Through history, empires have self-justified as the carriers of a superior culture, whose benefits they want to share with their neighbours.[40]

As I have insisted, every human collective has its processes of culturalization which establish cultural parameters that regulate the behavior of those who compose each group. Here it is worth recalling the role of ideology in the formation of cultural and moral hegemonic control of the masses along the lines of Antonio Gramsci (see chapter 1). Every human collective creates its own system of codification of reality through the cultural. Gramsci helps us see how the ideology of the dominant classes plays a fundamental role in determining the processes of culturalization, even though his analysis is limited to the sociopolitical level.[41] However, I insist that all members of society participate in these processes. As Azevedo states, when we account for all the actors, we see clearly the levels of confrontation, resistance, oppression, domination, and the exclusions and marginalizations that a given system creates. All these expressions within the processes of culturalization cannot be hidden from the concrete character of quotidian activities as documented by lived life.[42] In relation to Christianity, Tanner's proposal (see chapter 6) of the relational aspect of cultures is helpful as a way to understand how Christianity finds expression by borrowing elements from other cultural universes. Because cultures are developed through processes of struggle and social contestation with push and pull, the dynamics between the various sectors of society, the church, and the Christian faith also reflect those societal processes, tensions and struggles.

---

40   González, *Culto, cultura y cultivo*, 69.
41   Hughes Portelli, *Gramsci y el Bloque Histórico*.
42   Marcello de Carvalho Azevedo, "Comunidades eclesiales de base en Brasil," 255.

I agree with Tanner in her reclaiming of the relational aspect between Christianity and the culture of a specific society. But a critical aspect of cultural processes is the potential for exclusion, marginalization, oppression and the exploitation of peoples, which she does not engage. It is this aspect to which Espín points when he affirms that popular religious traditions display the sins and wounds of a specific cultural tradition, "promoting or justifying behaviors or attitudes that might be judged unacceptable."[43]

Part of the purpose of this analysis of the destructive (sinful) nature of the cultural is to resist inherited tendencies which focus on individual sin often in isolation from grace. In line with liberation theologies, I emphasize that systemic sin can include specific cultural manifestations of racialized and gendered social structures designed to privilege a few people while excluding large portions of humanity. Some of the most obvious examples of this kind of sin include Nazism, Fascism, Apartheid, segregation laws, cast cultures, and capitalism. But any societal structure designed to stifle the advance of a sector of society on the basis of their gender, physical ability, "racial" and ethnic background, socioeconomic status, cultural tradition, religious affiliation or any other social marker of exclusion, can be considered inherently sinful.

From this vantage point the widespread exploitation of entire peoples; racialized discrimination; the impoverishment of whole sectors of people; the present pervasive focus on consumption and profit; all forms of environmental exploitation and degradation; and the commodification of life itself pervasive in the present systems of globalizing neoliberal expressions of capitalism, are clear indications of the profound social impact of cultural sin. As part of this cultural corruption, I decry, along with Pope Francis cultural imperialism, lamenting the loss, destruction and disappearance of other cultures.[44]

---

43   Orlando O. Espín, "Traditioning," 7. Elsewhere speaking of Latina/o popular religious traditions he elaborates:

> "The courage and the fear, the hope and the fatalism, the faith in God and the temptation to magical manipulation, the strength of the family and the machismo of our patriarchal society, the deep respect for motherhood and the stereotyping of women—all this and much more are to be found in Hispanic popular religiosity. To admit these strengths and wounds is to acknowledge that Hispanic popular religiosity is a reflection of our reality and of our culture" (Orlando O. Espín, "Grace and Humanness," 150).

44   Francis, *Laudato Si*, 145.

At the same time, and as I have argued, the cultural also embodies divine grace. While we can appropriately say that cultures are carriers of sin, we equally can say that they are also simultaneously carriers of grace. While sin contributes to the corruption of human cultures, grace acts as a restraining force in the cultural sphere, making it possible for humans to engage in cultural activities which realize their God-given potential and enable cultural traditions to mediate the human-divine interaction. Stated differently, the providential act of grace upon creation enables humans to engage in life-giving and life-protecting cultural activities.

In other words, just as sin—especially structural sin—is expressed culturally, so too is God's grace made manifest through human action (which is culturally conditioned). Latina/o theologians have effectively emphasized this tension by noting that popular expressions of Christianity are bearers of culture and identity. As such, writes José David Rodríguez, Latina/o popular Christian expressions are "an instrument to hear and testify to the divine revelation in authentic and culturally specific [Latina/o] ways, which ... carry the impact as much of grace as of sin."[45]

The intersection between nature (the human condition), nurture (the cultural) and the divine outworking through/in humanity becomes obvious here. Grace embodied in the work of the Spirit is the generating force that moves humans to respond to the cultural mandate and to struggle against injustice and evil. Liberation presupposes the act of grace in and through the cultural. Since humans are always situated in a given cultural tradition, it should come as no surprise that cultural traditions can be sites of the divine outworking and therefore a *locus* of theological reflection. This insight is one of the great contributions of Latina/o theologies.[46] It is for this reason that Pope Francis sees that "nature and culture are intimately linked." He goes further by affirming that "grace supposes culture and God's gift becomes flesh in the culture of those who receive it."[47]

I reclaim here Van Til's (and Schilder's) notion that since the cultural (they use culture) is part of the divine imaging, sin did not invalidate the

---

45   José David Rodríguez, *Justicia en Nombre de Dios: Confesando la fe desde la perspectiva hispano/latina* (México D.F.: Publicaciones El Faro, 2002), 121.

46   Orlando Espín, ed., *The Wiley Blackwell Companion to Latino/a Theology* (West Sussex, UK; Mjalden, MA: Wiley Blackwell, 2015); Néstor Medina, *Mestizaje*; Arturo J. Bañuelas, ed., *Mestizo Christianity: Theology from the Latino Perspective* (Maryknoll, NY: Orbis Books, 1995); Orlando O. Espín and Miguel H. Díaz, eds., *From the Heart of Our People: Latino/a Explorations in Catholic Systematic Theology* (Maryknoll, NY: Orbis Books, 1999).

47   Francis, *Evangelii Gaudium.*

divine mandate nor our human responsibility and ability to fulfill the cultural task. This task is understood to prepare humans for, and mediate the relationship with, the divine.[48] As I have insisted, the primary purpose of culturalization processes is to build humanity and celebrate life as sacred. The move toward this commitment to life becomes therefore a posture of resistance against the facile equating of any given cultural tradition with the gospel message.[49] Such a posture also has inherent in it an ethical imperative to stand against, resist and confront structural sin and evil, in order to instead create the conditions for participating in building the reign of God.[50] In other words, the relationship between gospel and the cultural must lead to liberation from captivity, or to say it another way, from that which is godless in a cultural tradition. It must lead to dismantling inherited cultural theologies from their colonizing and dehumanizing tendencies as well as from any pretension to have a monopoly on the gospel message.[51]

Admittedly, it is not easy or possible to separate or distinguish the negative and positive aspects of human existence. Even though one can conceptually sanitize reality wishing for a better eschatological reality to come, cultural processes and cultures are profoundly affected by the sinful condition of humanity. As a human construct, the cultural displays the ugly side of the human condition in its power to destroy life. This means that cultures, as part of human reality need redemption.[52] For this reason, the Jesus event of incarnation plays a central role in furthering our understanding of the divine outworking in the cultural. In fact, the relationship between "gospel" and "culture," "Christianity" and "culture," and humanity and the divine find a particular expression and clarity in the event of incarnation.

---

48   Van Til, *The Calvinistic Concept of Culture*, 57, 141.

49   Diego Irarrázaval warns against romantic tendencies to harmonize culture and the gospel in ways that ignore the destructive dehumanizing effects some expressions of inculturation have left. The focus on *liberation* as a necessary prerequisite for evaluating inculturation opens the door to understanding some versions of inculturation as oppressive, monocultural, colonizing, imperialistic, male-centred, and ethnocentric. See Diego Irarrázaval, *Inculturation*.

50   As Gallagher puts it, "culturally entrenched structures of sin are always in need of recognition and of liberation" (Gallagher, *Clashing Symbols*, 107).

51   The presence of sin in all cultures is yet another aspect for which no culture can claim to be "better suited to incarnate the Christian message, or better suited to theologically understand it" (Orlando O. Espín, "An Exploration Into the Theology of Grace and Sin," 123).

52   González, *Culto, cultura y cultivo*, 65.

The Cultural and the Jesus Event

The incarnation is the greatest point of contention when it comes to considering the relationship between the cultural and Gospel/Christianity, the cultural and humanity, and the cultural and the divine.[53] In earlier chapters I mentioned how the incarnation figures prominently as a metaphor and model for imagining the relationship between the Gospel and culture, particularly for the Catholic proposal of inculturation.[54] However, since the construction of cultures and cultural processes are fundamental aspects of human existence, and if we take seriously the implications of the divine taking on full humanity, by necessity we then have to conceive of the cultural as a necessary element in the incarnation. It follows that the divine act of redemption/salvation also includes the cultural.[55]

If we see the necessity of the cultural in the incarnation, redemption and salvation, it is possible then to redraw the parameters of the divine kenosis, reimagining what the divine took-on in the incarnation. If indeed the incarnation involved God limiting Godself by taking on everything that is part of being human, then we can reconsider our understanding of the kenosis to include the cultural as "part and parcel of what the divine took-on in the incarnation."[56] Carlos Enrique Morales Sut claims that God in Jesus also redeemed cultures and transformed them to the service of the reign of God.[57]

---

53 Gallagher reminds us that the incarnation has a long-standing role in Catholic theology, for example. He recalls that as Pope John Paul II was wrestling with the notion of inculturation, he expressed that the neologism (inculturation) "expresses well aspects of the 'great mystery of the incarnation.' Therefore, inculturation imitates so to speak, that embracing of humanity by God in Christ, in order to give flesh to the gospel again in different cultures" (Gallagher, *Clashing Symbols*, 106).

54 For example, Robert Screiter reminds us that the Incarnation was another term used during and prior to Vatican II. Much in line with the notion of inculturation, he writes that the analogy of the incarnation of Jesus—who emptied himself and took flesh as one of us—was the operating idea and pattern to imitate, in order to become truly a part of the human culture. See his Robert Screiter, "Faith and Cultures," 746.

55 Néstor Medina, "The Pneumatological Dimension of Orlando Espín's Theological Work and Its Implications for Engagement with Pentecostal Communities," *Journal of Hispanic/Latino Theology*, Thursday September 16 2010, Http://www.latinotheology.org/node/96 (accessed October 12, 2010).

56 Ibid.

57 Carlos Enrique Morales Sut, "El resurgimiento de la espiritualidad maya a la luz del avance del Camino según Hechos (segunda de dos partes)," *Kairos* 48 (Enero—Junio 2011): 117.

Yet surprisingly, the incarnation, or more specifically the Jesus event, becomes "a stumbling block" for all those who engage the cultural in theological terms. Difficulties arise as scholars reflect on the relation between humanity (the created) and the divine (the uncreated). Many scholars engage in a kind of cultural theodicy by which they want to preserve the transcendent character of the divine in relation to cultural issues and processes. "Western" traditional theology especially has insisted on the divine nature of Jesus, setting the cultural aside. This approach continues to predominate theological debates in mainstream theological circles.

In fact, many scholars abandon the Jesus of history and the implications of his humanness for theology (in this case a theology of "culture") and opt for celebrating the transcendent nature of the divine and the Christ of faith instead. Paul Metzger, for example, preserves the divine-human separation by stating that during the act of "entering the human sphere," the Word (for him basically the divine) was not fused with a particular culture, "not even the [Jewish] culture in which the Word entered time and space as a human being."[58] Metzger wants to protect divine sovereignty, so he insists that the "Word"—by which he means the gospel—even as it is passed on to other cultural groups, cannot be overwhelmed by any one particular culture. He concludes that, "the Word transcends culture even in its enculturation."[59]

For Metzger, the interaction between the divine and the cultural only takes place at the level of witnessing to the divine, "the word of culture." As he sees it, God's Word stands in, with, and *over* (the word of) "culture;" but the latter is not parallel to the former. The Word of God does not become one with or descend to the word of culture.[60] When God's Word becomes present to culture's word, the Word of God elevates culture's word to participate in the life of the Word. The word of culture does not become the Word of God except in a "mystical" sense.[61] Yet Metzger does concede that the Word is not amorphous, "... Jesus Christ exist[ed] as a man of flesh and blood in our sphere, a [human] like us, as an historical phenomenon."[62] He argues that Jesus, as incarnate, was

---

58   Paul Louis Metzger, *The Word of Christ and the World of Culture*, 154.

59   Ibid.

60   He adds, "Because the Word is not exhausted by or reduced to his incarnate existence. The Word as Jesus Christ can enable other words to bear witness to himself and take form in other cultures, again without being overwhelmed by those cultural forms" (Metzger, *The Word of Christ and the World of Culture*, 154).

61   Metzger, *The Word of Christ and the World of Culture*, 141.

62   Ibid., 151.

not generic humanity but Jewish flesh.[63] As such, the Word was also not simply incarnate but also enculturated.

Because Metzger is well aware of the historical dangers of domesticating the gospel, he embraces cultural particularities as ways to ensure that Christ is not subsumed by any given cultural tradition or "other Christian sub-cultural construals of Christ, under a particular form."[64] Unfortunately, by attempting to safeguard the separation between the human and the divine, Metzger truncates the human out of the equation. His paradigm leaves no possibility for any sense of human agency or participation in the divine redemptive saga. Humans are simply passive recipients of divine activity, and the cultural is but a tool which plays an insignificant role in the divine disclosure. His sensibilities to the risks and dangers behind claims to universality ought to be applauded. However, the problem of his proposal remains; his view of the redemptive and self-communicative acts of God entail placing everything human aside.

J. Kameron Carter challenges us to interrogate the present theological problem of race by examining the racialized problematic of articulating a theology that does not baptize the accomplishments of the "white" "race" as Christian.[65] But he, like Metzger, highlights the dialectic gap (*diàstema*) between God and the creature (humanity) and Christ and the *cultural*, which he argues is bridged or traversed in the very person of the Logos and through the Trinitatian unity of the Logos with the Father and the Holy Spirit.[66]

---

63   For Metzger, the gospel takes root in cultures. Yet the divine nature transcends the function of the cultural as well as Jesus's Jewishness instead of working through it. In this way, he preserves the separation between God and the cultural, in their respective dimensions, in order to argue against the domestication of the gospel message in any culture. Lucien Legrand arrives at similar conclusions concerning Jesus' *Jewish* flesh. As he puts it, "The Word found human expression in a Jewish culture." "This Jewish culture of Jesus is both a bridge to his historical identity and constitutive element of the Christian confession of the incarnated Word" (Lucien Legrand, *The Bible on Culture*, 75).

64   Metzger, *The Word of Christ and the World of Culture*, 156.

65   J. Kameron Carter, *Race: A Theological Account* (Oxford, UK: Oxford University Press, 2008). Appropriately, Carter's proposal intends to dismantle any theological, ideological, or cultural apparatus that results in the endorsement of inherited ("white") Eurocentric theologies as the highest expressions of the Gospel. For a fuller discussion on and critique of the cultural implications of Carter's theological proposal (along with the proposals by Willie Jennings and Brian Banthum) see Néstor Medina, "Transgressing Theological Shibboleths: Culture as Locus of Divine (Pneumatological) Activity," *PNEUMA* 36, no. 3 (2014): 1–15.

66   J. Kameron Carter, *Race*, 166.

Carter argues that human self-articulation problematically leaves out that which cannot be articulated; cultures, as appropriate identity spaces, fall short of showing the proper identity of people, the full meaning of what it means to be a creature.[67] For this reason he distances himself from "cultural" theologies, including liberation theologies, because he is convinced that in Jesus people's cultural identities are disarticulated and rearticulated within the Jewish covenantal relationship epitomized in the Jewish Christ.[68] For him, the central problem with current theological articulations is that they fall outside—or attempt to distance themselves from—inherent Jewish covenantal connection and roots. The future theological direction must therefore be one that locates itself within a Christological perspective that does not seek to separate Jesus from his Jewish roots and Christianity from its Jewish heritage.[69]

For Carter, this theological shift and reconfiguration, which situates Jesus within the covenantal relation of YHWH with the people of Israel, becomes the trope by which and in which all people find and enter into a relationship with God through the Holy Spirit.[70] Carter, however, gives little recognition

---

67   Carter makes it clear that "To be in Christ...is to be drawn out of tyrannical narratives of identity (and the social orders they uphold), such as modernity's narrative of racial identity generally and the pseudotheological narrative of whiteness particularly, and into the identity of Israel as performed in Christ's Jewish flesh" (J. Kameron Carter, *Race*, 355). He draws on Charles Long's notion of opacity to make his point, claiming that human self-articulation is always opaque: "creatures present themselves or are visible in such a way that their visibility cannot be captured or enslaved without a massive and violent distortion of their existence as creatures ..." (Ibid., 154).

68   For Carter, Jesus's life embodies, therefore, a kind of linguistic *kenosis* by which the impoverishment, dispossession and powerlessness of human languages and cultures in properly or fully articulating humanity are replaced-overcome by a new Pentecostal tongue of the Logos. By implication he is basically saying that to focus on one's culture or group betrays the original intent of a divine disruption of culture as represented in the divine covenantal relationship between Israel and YHWH. See J. Kameron Carter, *Race*, 309–10.

69   Carter wants to preserve Jesus' covenantal Jewishness as a fundamental aspect of his Christology. He argues that the Christological vision of love is unintelligible apart from the story of Abraham and his covenant with YHWH. See J. Kameron Carter, *Race*, 358 J. Kameron Carter, *Race*, 358.

70   Carter completes his reasoning by bringing together Christ, Pentecost and the Spirit. The flesh of Jesus is a social reality or a space into which people enter through the action of the Spirit. As the quintessential cultural marker, language is set aside by the new covenantal mode of life of the *ecclesia* enabled through the Holy Spirit at Pentecost. J. Kameron Carter, *Race*, 338.

to the fact that human understanding and engagement of the divine can only be done by means of the cultural. He seems to operate with an idea of a Jesus that stands above any cultural tradition even including his own Jewishness. As a result, his picture of the covenantal Jesus comes across as ahistorical and overly mystical, with no real engagement of the culturally conditioned human experience. In his schema, the union between God and humanity is actualized through a cosmic Jesus, leaving the historical Jesus with little. By trying to preserve the transcendent character of God, Carter sacrifices the divine imminence made manifest in the Jewish Jesus and continually actualized by the Holy Spirit among the specific diverse cultures of the world. Ultimately, Carter fails to see that our perceptions and understanding of the divine pass through the cultural filters that we have inherited and which condition our theological reflections, and, as I have argued, are gifted to us by God.

Similarly, Luis Enrique Benavides is yet another scholar who privileges the Christ of faith and the evangelical claim of a divine universal promise of salvation over the historical Jesus.[71] He rejects cultural and contextual theologies in general and Latina/o theologies specifically. Particularly concerned with the universal promise of salvation in Christ, Benavides understands God and Christ as transcending history, including the cultural. In Benavides' theological framing the Christ of faith ought to be the principal focus of salvation. Any emphasis on the historical Jesus, as is the case with Latina/o theologies, is depicted by him as an act of politicizing theology and Jesus.[72] His point is that Latina/o theologians should cease to emphasize the particular nature of Jesus along with their own contexts, and instead recognize that Christ represents the essential unity of God and humans.[73] Instead of

---

71   Luis Enrique Benavides, "North American Hispanic Theologies: A Tillichian Revisioning,"
        Ph.D. dissertation (Boston, MA: Boston University, School of Theology, 2000).

72   According to Benavides, Latina/o theologies (and other cultural and contextual the-
        ologies) should strive toward the creation of universal principles. He is so enamored
        with abstract and ahistorical Western theological traditions that he sees Latina/o the-
        ology (and by extension other cultural theologies) as missing the sophistication of
        Western theologies because they attempt to arrive at universal principles. Since in his
        opinion Latina/o theologians lack theological language and sophistication, he sug-
        gests to them the work of Paul Tillich as resource. He is so convinced that by adopting
        Tillich's universal theological language Latinas/os will quickly realize that cultures
        are not as important as they appear to be. See Benavides, "North American Hispanic
        Theologies," 6, 26.

73   Benavides, "North American Hispanic Theologies," 128.

drawing their identity from colonization[74] and politicizing Jesus, Benavides argues that Latinas/os should look for their identity in the Christ of faith, who brings people to God to find their external (and spiritual) fulfillment.[75] This, he argues, is true liberation.[76]

Benavides basically builds an arguments for salvation as an event realized in a spiritualized, ahistorical, and acultural space; by focusing on the Christ of faith, he dehistorizes Jesus and salvation.[77] In contradistinction, I contend that for Latinas/os to abandon their historical identity and anchor it in the Christ of faith as suggested by Benavides would require them to replace their theological categories with those which are abstract and ahistorical and come out of the Western European, Euro North American traditions. Benavides captivation with Western traditional categories and theologies prevents him from understanding the fundamental points of Latina/o, contextual, and liberation theologies: theology is not a mere exercise of intellectual gymnastics, but a critical reflection on the peoples' experience

---

74   Benavides argues that the fundamental problem with Latina/o theologies (and liberation theologies) is their exclusive focus on a metaphysics of history without including a "metaphysics of being (ontology and transcendence)." He feels that Latina/o theologians are too preoccupied with being recognized and accepted in U.S.A society; they seek authenticity at the expense of ignoring the divine presence. As a result, he criticizes Latinas/os who affirm their identity as a result of a double colonization, noting that colonization is not a fact to be used as a source of identity. Not taking into consideration the enormous negative cultural impacts of colonization, he still insists that colonization is "a social and religious mistake" to be forgiven and forgotten. See Benavides, "North American Hispanic Theologies," 130, 137, 152.

75   Benavides, "North American Hispanic Theologies," 151.

76   Benavides, "North American Hispanic Theologies," 128. Benavides undermines Latina/o theology because of what he considers their "this-worldly" character. For him, Latina/o religious symbols are not transcendental. Symbols such as *La Morenita* (the Brown Lady), *La Raza Cósmica* (the Cosmic Race), and others designed for resistance and survival do not fit well into the north American context and therefore must be reinterpreted, replaced, or left aside. His argument is that present Hispanic religious symbols do not provide them with a true sense a liberation.

77   Leonardo Boff is clear in this regard. According to him, God's love can only be expressed in concrete ways; it cannot remain a universal or abstract concept. It reaches people where they are using the elements of the person's life, culture and context as a mediation for such love. In other words, the universal salvific will and love of God is historized and incarnated in the rites, doctrines, and traditions of a religion, as well as in the ethical codes of a society. See Leonardo Boff, *Church: Charism and Power: Liberation Theology and the Institutional Church*, trans. John W. Diercksmeier (New York, NY: Crossroads, 1985), 93.

of faith in God. As Latina/o theologians insist, all theological affirmations emerge and respond to a specific contextual reality.

There are many other examples which show how most scholars, when confronted with the question of the cultural and Christ, the gospel and the cultural, and Christianity and the cultural opt to emphasize the Christ of faith and his transcendent, even transcultural character. I want to propose that such a proclivity is in part the result of not taking seriously the historical character of the Jesus event. These scholars engage in a cultural theodicy argument because of a "quasi-platonist" dualistic understanding of creation and creator which operates in their theological schemas. It is premised on the idea that it is possible to distinguish and separate the gospel from the culture in which it is expressed. While it is possible to argue such a point conceptually, in actuality it is impossible to separate the gospel from the cultural. Furthermore, because the full range of experiences of human existence are filtered through the cultural, it is therefore impossible to stand outside the cultural sphere even to grasp the gospel message.

Let me restate that Jesus Christ came as a human being and therefore was necessarily bound to a culture.[78] As we have seen through this volume, many have tried to foreclose the discussion by affirming that the gospel message is not exclusively tied to any particular cultural tradition. But as I have insisted, such a move undermines the cultural mediation of the divine disclosure in the Jesus event. The Johannine idea that "The Word became flesh" is the basis of my claim here; the divine became human flesh *in* the cultural.[79] The fact that

---

78   In the words of Timothy Gorringe, "The doctrine of the incarnation claims that God took flesh at a particular time and place, taught in a particular language, and was tortured to death under particular laws. The purpose of this, however, was the redemption of history, which is to say, the offering of a clue to the meaning of the whole historical process, what we have called the long revolution" (Gorringe, *Furthering Humanity*, 100).

79   Gorringe takes seriously Jesus' enfleshment: Taking on flesh, for him, is central for embodiment. That Jesus became flesh means he was not an avatar, a brief encounter. Instead, he provides us with an account of how it might be possible to talk about God in a world where the powerful hide their inconvenient decisions and the poor are crucified; "where there is nothing whatsoever, no knowledge and no revelation, which is not mediated by the body." He asserts that "Flesh," as John spells out in some detail in the course of his mediation, means culture—food, world symbols, the way in which we cherish bodies. See Gorringe, *Furthering Humanity*, 18. Along the same line, Orlando Espín also celebrates the historical specificity of Jesus: "...Christ lived in a specific time period, in a specific land, within a concrete history, and within a single culture. Jesus of Nazareth was a first-century, Palestinian Jew, and there is no way to responsibly understand him by disregarding these historical, geographical, and cultural facts" (Orlando O. Espín, "Grace and Humanness," 144).

Jesus embodied full humanity in history means that he worked with human hands, thought with a human mind, acted with a human will, and loved and hurt with a human heart and emotions. At the same time, all aspects of his humanity were shaped, conditioned, and framed by his first century Jewish cultural tradition. If we accept the logic of the incarnation, Timothy Gorringe suggests, we can say that the fact that the Word took-on flesh means that it also took on the cultural.[80] Jesus' cultural particularity cannot be overlooked or overstated.

The incarnation must be understood as God's act of translation of the meaning of God into the culture-specific terms of a first century Palestinian Jew.[81] The specificity of Jesus' Jewish culture transformed the cultural into a central feature without which the divine self-disclosure in the incarnation could not have taken place and without which it could not have been conceived or understood. I reemphasize that the divine communication and self-disclosure took place and continues to take place within the realm of the cultural. The divine, claims Enrique Dussel, is disclosed right where people are and people are precisely within the sphere of the cultural.[82] The Jesus event is God's *cultural* response to humanity using the available cultural means to communicate the divine intent. The Christology that stems from this series of affirmations is oriented toward a conviction that the incarnation is the quintessential celebration of God's cultural act for humanity. God's message, through this one cultural event, is that God is for us in ways that can only be perceived and discerned culturally.

The incarnation provides for us the grammar to understand the cultural nature of the divine kenotic act in all the breadth of what God took on in the event of Jesus. The incarnation is not "a philosophical first principle" but a "way of reading a particular historical event, the life and death of a first century Jew."[83] The theological implication is that the incarnation appropriately reveals the humanity of God and affirms unequivocally the value and goodness of creation, including the cultural. As a result, we can also say that Christianity does not reject the world (that is creation, humanity, and the cultural), but can

---

80   Gorringe, *Furthering Humanity*, 257.

81   Andrew F. Walls, "Eusebius Tries Again: The Task of Reconceiving and Re-Visioning the Study of Christian History," in *Enlarging the Story: Perspectives on Writing World Christian History*, ed. Wilbert Shenk (Maryknoll, NY: Orbis Books, 2002), 19. See also Gallagher, *Clashing Symbols*, 106.

82   Enrique Dussel, *Ethics and the Theology of Liberation*, trans. Bernard F. McWilliams (Maryknoll, NY: Orbis Books, 1978), 53.

83   Gorringe, *Furthering Humanity*, 126.

only comprehend its God and the incarnation event through human ways of being in the world, through the cultural.[84]

As I see it, the tendency to disconnect the cultural and the divine is a form of Docetism for its inability to appreciate the full humanity of Jesus, or even Nestorianism for its inability to see the activity of the divine operative together with Jesus' humanity. The connection between the cultural and the historical Jesus is not accidental to the divine redemptive act. Since the cultural is all-encompassing, as I suggest here, it includes all aspects of human existence. Moreover, it is a gift to humanity and part of the divine creative act. The gospel does not transcend the cultural insofar as it finds resonance in elements from every culture. And Christ does not transcend cultures in the sense that cultural specificities are unimportant or irrelevant. Instead, the incarnation represents a celebration of historical cultural specificities as the sites of the divine disclosure and invitation, and the medium through which humans can approach God. A rejection of a universal, amorphous, acultural version of Christianity is in order at this stage. In fact, a Christianity that "stresses the logos *asarkos*, may ultimately be the most adulterated in cultural form, the most syncretistic in shape, and, in turn, the most imperialistic in its missionary enterprise."[85]

The work of incarnation cannot be understood properly outside of the work of the Spirit just as the cultures's work of building up humanity cannot be understood away from the work of the Spirit. José Comblin reminds us that the ongoing renewal of creation by the Spirit includes the regeneration of human beings, which starts with a new humanity made in the image of Christ.[86] As indicated earlier, grace plays a central role in enabling the cultural to mediate the divine-human interaction. Yet grace is made manifest and actualized only through the energizing activity of the Holy Spirit. In the same way, the relationship between the human and the divine as well as the mediating role of cultures must be situated within the scope of the activity of the Spirit. To that we now turn.

---

84   The humanity of Christ gives us the confidence to appreciate particular cultural traditions as potential languages in which the gospel can be articulated. Michael Gallagher expands this idea stating that "if cultures need Christ for their fullness, in another sense Christ needs cultures in order to continue and complete the gift of the Incarnation in different contexts of history" (Gallagher, *Clashing Symbols*, 107).

85   As Metzger comments, "The only truly international gospel is one that accounts for the incarnation of the Word in the plethora of cultures. By denying such enculturation of the Word, one fails to guard against the absolutizing of one's own culture's particular appropriation of the Word" (Metzger, *The Word of Christ and the World of Culture*, 155).

86   José Comblin, *The Holy Spirit and Liberation*, trans. Paul Burns (Maryknoll, NY: Orbis Books, 1989), 46–47.

An Attempt at a Cultural Pneumatology

The Spirit in Culture

The energizing activity of the Spirit animates the cultural mediation of the divine disclosure to humanity as well as the human response to the divine.[87] In other words, the Spirit works in the cultures of the world and empowers inculturation, as Michael Sievernich would say.[88] The unmediated Spirit has a mediating role when she brings humans together with the rest of creation, places people in a relationship with one another, and establishes and sustains the relationship between the divine and humanity. While God expresses Godself in and through cultures, the divine agency is universal in scope and is evidenced in signs of the transforming activity of the Spirit in all ages and all around us.

Comblín advances that the activity of the Spirit—the Spirit who filled the whole earth—was also "present in all that was good in pre-colombian cultures."[89] Vitalino Similox Salazar and George Tinker challenge us—from their particular Indigenous traditions—to take seriously the divine activity among the Indigenous peoples of the Americas before the invasion and conquest of the Americas. Similox Salazar asserts that the "first manifestation of the God of the Bible and Creator of the Universe among the Maya peoples did not take place at the arrival of the Spanish priests." In fact, he avers,

> every culture finds meaning in life, develops ethical systems and expresses its spirituality as an echo of the divine voice that speaks to all human beings, both personally and in their social relations. These are conduits of divine revelation to humankind, in particular time, space, and cultural modalities.[90]

---

87   This is the main concern of Oscar García Johnson as he considers the need to discern how culture is perceived as a category able to embrace both the transcendence of God's Spirit and the inextricable diversity of today's people's identities. See Oscar García-Johnson, "The Mestizo/a Community of Mañana: A Latino/a Theology of the Spirit," Ph.D. dissertation (Pasadena California: Fuller Theological Seminary, 2005), 50.

88   Michael Sievernich, "Jesuit Theologies of Mission," 50.

89   Comblin, *The Holy Spirit and Liberation*, 49.

90   Vitalino Similox Salazar, "The Invasion of Christianity Into the World of the Mayas," in *Crosscurrents in Indigenous Spirituality: Interface of Maya Catholic and Protestant Worldviews*, ed. Guillermo Cook (Leiden, NL: Brill, 1997), 37–38. Once this point is recognized, he insists, we can understand the second theological reference point: the possibility that the Bible can be read and interpreted in light of different cultures, as is the case with the oral or written "Bible" of the Indigenous peoples of the Americas. See Ibid.

Similarly, Tinker affirms that we cannot be trapped into thinking that "God has only spoken this good news through Jesus, or that the only way to salvation is through a Euro or Amer-European message brought by the colonizer to the conquered."[91]

Jeff Gros joins these voices when he states that the Spirit has been present and active not only in the Christian Church but also in human history and in various cultures.[92] As he views it, the Spirit brings humans closer to the divine creator. It is through the Spirit that the divine comes near and that the work of redemption is brought to completion. Such divine activity through the Spirit can only be perceived and understood through the lenses of cultural traditions. Thus, it would seem strange for the Spirit not to be active in the very arena of the cultural where people search for meaning.[93]

As I have been proposing throughout this book, cultural processes and cultural traditions, at their best, enable us to live out our humanity, in the process of maturing and building a more humane world. At the same time, there are no cultures which are finished products because humans are still in the process of becoming. It is in this human context, in humanity that the divine creative process continues to be actualized just as the divine redemptive work also continues through the activity of the Spirit.[94] These two

---

91   "Tink" Tinker, *American Indian Liberation*, 106. For Tinker,

> "American Indians represent cultures and communities that predate by thousands of generations the euro-western invasion of the Americas. We were people who knew the spiritual side of all life, who had firm experiential connections with the Creator, who had well-developed ceremonies to help us maintain harmony and balance in the life of our communities and the world around us. We were communities of peace, most of whom did not even have words for war. Thus any Indian liberation theology must take these ceremonies and spiritual traditions seriously. It must begin with the specifics of Indian cultures and cultural values" (Ibid. 128).

92   Jeffrey Gros, "Word and Spirit, Church and World. The Final Report of the International Dialogue Between Representatives of the World Alliance of Reformed Churches and Some Classical Pentecostal Churches and Leaders 1996–2000," *Pneuma* 22, no. 1 (Spring 2001): 16.

93   Amos Yong, *Beyond the Impasse: Toward a Pneumatological Theology of Religions* (Grand Rapids, MI: Baker's Academic; Paternoster Press, 2003), 46.

94   Echoes of the continuous redemptive work and its relation to cultural processes and cultural traditions can be found also among Catholics: "Christ now is at work in the hearts of men through the energy of his Spirit. He arouses not only a desire for the age to come, but, by that very fact, he animates, purifies and strengthens those noble longings too by which the human family strives to make its life more human and to render the whole earth submissive to its goal" (Vatican Council II, "*Gaudium et spes*," 3.38).

aspects find concrete expression in concrete cultures. In other words, the
cultural is a central feature of the creative scheme as well as of the redemptive process marking the point of intersection between the activity of the
Spirit and cultural processes.

It is through the concrete phenomena of cultures that the Spirit empowers
humanity to imagine the future and to trace the paths it will take to get there;
the cultural plays an essential role leading us toward that coveted reality of
the fullness of humanity as defined by Christ. In order to capacitate humanity to accomplish this vision, the Spirit also energizes the cultural. While the
incarnation event elevates the cultural in its capacity and role to reveal divine
self-disclosure, it is the activity of the Spirit which animates the cultural in
its capacity to mediate, however imperfectly and limitedly, the human-divine
relationship. The Spirit's energizing of the cultural further encourages humans
to respond to the divine in culturally conditioned ways both because it is the
medium available for engaging the divine and because the cultural is part of
the divine imaging in humans.

Simply put, the cultural plays a crucial role as point of contact between the
divine and the human. While we can agree with Amos Yong that the point
of contact is pneumatological, between the divine *pneuma* and the human
pneuma,[95] such a reality would remain elusive to us if it were not because of
the fact that the cultural provides us with the tools and mechanisms for perceiving, understanding, and responding to it in adequate, albeit culturally conditioned ways. In the words of Pope Francis, "The presence of the Spirit gives
Christians a certain connaturality with divine realities, and a wisdom which
enables them to grasp those realities intuitively, [and in culturally conditioned
ways] even when they lack the wherewithal to give them precise expression."[96]
The "impossibility" for cultures to access and communicate the divine mystery is turned into a "possibility" because of the activity of the Spirit. As Espín
puts it,

> "All expression of the "faith-full" intuitions of the Christian" people are,
> of necessity, not equal to the intuitions they communicate. The [cul-
> turally conditioned] expressions are *human* means through which the
> Spirit leads the whole Church to a deeper and clearer understanding
> of revelation. As human means these vehicles of understanding are

---

95   Amos Yong, *Spirit-Word-Community: Theological Hermeneutics in Trinitarian Perspective*
        (Aldershot, England: Ashgate, 2005), 41.

96   Francis, *Evangelii Gaudium*, 119.

subject to the same conditioning limitations of all human things.[97]
(emphasis original)

In a way, the Spirit makes use of the cultural network of symbols, signs
and codes available to humans so that they can appreciate the divine self-
communication. The Spirit does not set the human or the cultural aside
but enlivens it as means to make the divine self-disclosure and experience
possible. Drawing on the related concepts of cultivation and cultus, the
Spirit aids in the cultivation of human beings. It is the force which animates
the cultural and makes it possible for humans to live their humanity to the
fullest. It also creates the possibilities for humans to respond the divine
through cult.

The same divine commitment to life that we see in Jesus is also embodied in the Spirit. It is the Spirit that empowers and animates cultural groups
to resist colonizing forces that seek to eradicate them. It is the Spirit that
inspires cultural-social movements against the exploitation of people and
the despoliation and contamination of the earth. We can say, together with
Gorringe, that all that is life affirming in cultures and other religions is therefore a response to the Spirit of God.[98] By animating the cultural, the Spirit
enables people to find in their cultural traditions the resources to resist
and continue to confront oppression. By energizing the cultural, the Spirit
provides—through cultural traditions—the avenues for people to resist
what opposes God's original intent for them to achieve full humanity. In a
way, we can say that the Spirit is the biogenetic force in all cultures. It is the
force that engenders and defends life as well as passionately seeks the full
realization of all of humanity's (and creation's) virtues and potentialities.

The Incarnation, the Spirit, and the Cultural

Our premise for understanding the activity of the Spirit is the event of incarnation. In the gospel narrative Christ and the Spirit operate together. But the
gospel story does not end there. The Spirit was also present since conception.[99]
Jürgen Moltmann helpfully underscores the significance of the relationship between the incarnation and the Holy Spirit. In his pneumatological-
Christological framework he points out that the classical Christological

---

97   Orlando O. Espín, *The Faith of the People*, 79.

98   Gorringe, *Furthering Humanity*, 258.

99   Néstor Medina, "Unlikely Siblings? Pentecostal Insights from the Catholic Teachings on
      Mary," in *Third Receptive Ecumenism Conference Proceedings*, ed. Paul Murray and Paul
      Lakeland (Oxford, England: Oxford University Press, Forthcoming).

doctrine of the incarnation cannot be understood apart from the Son's conception by the Spirit; neither can the messianic tradition be interpreted apart from
the Spirit's anointing of the Son.[100] In this respect, Moltmann sees a dynamic,
ontological relationality between the Son and Spirit. He wants to avoid any
suggestion of "exclusive christomonism" in the human-divine encounter and
instead portrays Jesus Christ in relationship to the Spirit and in so doing opens
humanity to the full relationality of the Trinity.[101]

However, even Moltmann's discussion of the incarnation event is too
sanitized. If indeed we cannot understand the Son's conception apart from
the activity of the Spirit, we also cannot understand the incarnation apart
from embodied human agency and cultural activity in Mary. As I have discussed elsewhere, the activity of the Spirit in the incarnation encompasses
the work of conception.[102] Mary's womb is the place where the Spirit—
oozing with life-giving force—initiates the divine enfleshment. Her womb
is the site of the divine taking-on humanity through the energizing power
of the Holy Spirit. It is at the moment of conception that the "Divine Word"
gains concrete, bodily/fleshly/physical and relational character. The incarnation is not an abstract concept nor an event that took place in the realm
of the metaphysical. Rather, it is very much part of the realm of the physical, embodied reality of human-created existence. It is also at the moment
of conception that the incarnation gains cultural significance and culturally concrete expression. Mary's Magnificat exemplifies this culturally conditioned (human) woman assent and response to the Spirit's invitation to
inhabit her.

I am arguing that the human relational aspect of Jesus did not develop
outside of the cultural. The Spirit was responsible for energizing Jesus'
Jewish culture to be able to proclaim and articulate the gospel message in
cultural ways perceptible by his contemporaries. Furthermore, the book of
Acts tells us that the Spirit was also responsible for founding the church
on the day of Pentecost and is responsible for sustaining the Church today.
We can confidently say that the Spirit operates by helping believers live the
Christian life as they mature into full humanity. And it is the Spirit that
ensures that we comprehend and respond to the divine invitation through
the available cultural material.

100   Jürgen Moltmann, *The Way of Jesus Christ: Christology in Messianic Dimensions*
       (Minneapolis, MN: Fortress Press, 1993).
101   Ibid., 74.
102   Medina, "Unlikely Siblings?"

A Pneumatological Kenosis?

A focus on the relational emphasizes the moment at which the work of incarnation and the work of the Spirit meet in order to work out salvation. At the same time, the uninterrupted thread of divine activity is embodied in the Holy Spirit. Again, it follows that we reconsider the kenosis event.[103] While the Jesus event created the conditions for humanity to approach the divine, it is only through the ongoing work of the Spirit that actualization is possible.[104] We could speak of a kenosis of the Son and a kenosis of the Spirit. But the act of divine incarnation—by which I mean the extent to which the divine enters the created dimension and inhabits the created order including by way of drawing on the available cultural elements to make the divine visitation perceptible— is not something that can be fragmented. It is rather a kenosis of the triune God. If indeed the external works of the Trinity cannot be divided (*Opera trinitatis ad extra indivisa sunt*), it follows that the present divine interaction with humanity facilitated by the work of the Spirit and mediated through cultural symbols, signs, patterns of imagination, etc.[105] is the extension of an original divine kenosis which began at creation.

However, Kenosis must not be seen as the final phase of the divine activity through the Spirit. Rather than understanding it as placing limits, it is instead opening a new space for divine activity in human cultures. Just as the incarnation opened humanity as locus of divine activity, the engagement of the cultural by the Spirit is not a limitation but an opening out to the divine-human interaction. In the divine kenosis, the Spirit's activity in humanity extends to taking on the cultural in order to make possible such interaction.

---

103 According to Teresa Okure, "This is the rationale for Jesus' self-emptying: to make room in himself for humanity, thereby uniting persons with God" (Teresa Okure, "Jesus and the Samaritan Woman," 413). It is this understanding that is behind the notion of kenosis found in Philippians 2:6–11.

104 Moltmann describes the dynamic relationship between Jesus and the Spirit. For him, "the self-emptying of God, expressed through the Son in the Incarnation," was expressed through the Spirit at Jesus' baptism. When the Spirit condescended on Jesus, He emptied himself of the "eternity of God," taking up abode in the "vulnerable and mortal human being Jesus" (Moltmann, *The Way of Jesus Christ*, 93).

105 According to Espín, if the human partner in the experience did not have the means of understanding and interpreting it, he/she would not have had it. The culture within which the experience happens offers the human subjects the hermeneutical tools needed: symbols, language, patterns of imagination, etc. See Orlando O. Espín, *The Faith of the People*, 94.

This kenotic model I call elsewhere *pneumatological cultural kenosis*,[106] draws from the relationality characteristic of the social Trinity. As I suggested earlier, the intimate perichoretic dance of eternal mutual interrelationship and interdependence internal to the Trinity can be understood in socio-cultural terms. The inherent human proclivity to build cultures can also be understood as an aspect of the human imaging of the divine. It is for this reason that I understand the cultural as a divine gift. In other words, at the moment of creation humans are imprinted with the capacity to construct cultures; they need to engage in cultural activities and processes in order to interact with the rest of creation, with each other, with the divine, and to understand all of it in coherent and meaningful ways.

The Cultural and the Building of Ecclesia

For Christians, the church is the context in which the questions of the encounter between the divine and human, and their relation to the cultural receive concrete expression. Since the church comprises the immediate social context in which the corporate body of believers gathers to interact with the divine, the church becomes the sociocultural environment where believers are socialized to respond to God in the available cultural forms. Of course, these cultural forms are not independent or unrelated to the larger cultural contexts outside the church. Tanner is correct in stating that believers draw from the larger reservoir of cultural symbols, although I would also argue these are reconfigured to serve the purposes ascribed to them by each contextual group of believers. In other words, two cultural symbols may serve different functions and have different meanings in two different congregations.

My point is simply to state the obvious. When believers gather to express their faith to God in multiple ways, they do so by drawing on the cultural material available to them. It is by drawing on cultural forms which in turn are energized by the Spirit that believers can effectively respond to the divine invitation. Drawn by the Spirit, the religious service becomes the sacramental space of engagement in which interaction between believers and the divine transpires and the church is built up.

---

106   Néstor Medina, "Discerning the Spirit in Culture: Toward Pentecostal Interculturality," *Canadian Journal of Pentecostal-Charismatic Christianity* 2 (2011): 150. See also, Néstor Medina, "Jürgen Moltmann and Pentecostalism(s): Toward a Cultural Theology of the Spirit," *Toronto Journal of Theology: Love and Freedom: Essay in Honour of Harold G. Wells* 24, no. 1 (2008): 99–111, ed. Rob Fennell; Medina, "The Pneumatological Dimension of Orlando Espín's Theological Work."

Oscar García-Johnson furthers this discussion by proposing both the church and the Spirit as cultural agents.[107] In his postmodern approach, he critiques Latina/o theology for focusing on the immediate cultural realm and for leaving little room for the transcendent.[108] As a corrective, he proposes a pneumato-logical ecclesiology that reinterprets the church as the culture-making com-munity of the Spirit. He thinks that "Humanity is a sign of God's involvement with creation … [and] Culture is what we make of creation."[109] When humans participate in the culture-making process they encounter or engage with God. Although it is unclear whether he would include all of humanity in the culture creation venture as a meeting place with God, there is no doubt that he under-stands this dynamic at play in the context of the church.

García-Johnson uses a triadic sign approach to articulate his position: the uncreated invisible (the Spirit), the created invisible (the experience of the Spirit, the church) and the created visible (humanity).[110] For him, the cre-ated invisible points to the intersection of the Spirit of God with human-ity: "A space that is spiritually fecund." He says that since creating culture is the way by which the Christian community responds to God's involve-ment in creation, then the church (the created invisible) becomes the cre-ated visible-culture of the Spirit within the *created* visible creation.[111] The church is the created visible culture because it is the geographical place at which the Spirit of God intersects with humanity. For him, since the Spirit

---

107   Oscar García-Johnson, *The Mestizo/a Community of the Spirit*.

108   As he observes, the absence of the "transcendent and somehow *structural-mechanical* perception of culture" undermines much of Latina/o theology. See García-Johnson, *The Mestizo/a Community of the Spirit*, 48. Here García-Johnson's own inability to see the radical methodological shift proposed by Latina/o theology becomes evident. He stum-bles on Latina/o theologies insistence that one cannot access the divine but through the culturally conditioned experiences of faith of Latina/o communities. Thus, whereas García-Johnson takes the divine as his theological starting point, Latina/o theology starts from the faith of the people. The former can run dangerously into universalizing affirma-tions, which is one of the aspects that Latina/o theological proposals counter. The Latter, remains within the contextual, culturally conditioned and concrete experiences of faith of the people.

109   García-Johnson, *The Mestizo/a Community of the Spirit*, 66.

110   Ibid., 65.

111   García-Johnson, *The Mestizo/a Community of the Spirit*, 67. I must point out that there is a little vagueness in García-Johnson's use of the category culture and how it gets confused with the notion Church. On one hand, he uses it to mean the ways in which Christians respond to God. On the other hand, he also uses it to mean the Church as the visible cul-ture of the Spirit. He runs the risk of almost equating-confusing church with culture.

created the church, it follows that the church is the community of the Spirit. The church, that is the community of believers inspired by the Spirit, create culture as they approach the divine. In turn, the Spirit becomes a cultural agent because it operates within culture, that is, within the church. Thus, the Spirit is the cultural authoring agent of Christian experience. It is by working within the church that the Spirit brings transformation to the larger society.[112]

Unlike García-Johnson, I do not see the Spirit as almost exclusively working in the church, with the Spirit's work in society as an afterthought. Rather, I view the Spirit's work in cultures and in societies as part of the same kenotic act we have been discussing. Taking a cue from Leonardo Boff who invites us to see in the Trinity a model for constructing societies,[113] I want to propose the kenosis as a social-cultural pattern-model which challenges the way cultural groups relate to each other. Joerg Rieger suggests that the paradigm of kenosis means that dominant cultures must consciously divest themselves of status and privilege and place themselves in solidarity with the marginalized.[114] But instead of seeing it as "divesting" of something, pneumatological cultural kenosis moves us towards enrichment—the "taking-on" of (an opening out to) the cultures of others. In other words, the Spirit's work in culture pushes us toward inclusion, toward the daring act of recognizing the activity of the divine in the complex interchange of cultural traditions as all infused by the Spirit. In no other moment of the church of the New Testament does this divine move toward cultural inclusion become more manifest than in the event of Pentecost, to which we now turn.

The Cultural and the Spirit of Pentecost

As often talked about, the event of Pentecost marks the crowning moment at which the Spirit becomes more fully the protagonist in the story of salvation, the founder of the community of believers we now call the church, and the force and energy that revitalizes cultures in their ability—however limited—to comprehend and speak about the mystery of the divine. The event signifies a reorientation in the understanding of the relations between divine revelation and the cultural.

Crucial during the event of Pentecost is that the intervention of the Spirit caused those present to speak of the wonders of God in their own

---

112   García-Johnson, *The Mestizo/a Community of the Spirit*, 61.

113   Leonardo Boff, *Trinity and Society*, trans. Paul Burns, Theology and Liberation Series (Maryknoll, NY: Orbis Books, 1988).

114   Joerg Rieger, *Christ & Empire*, 42–44.

language; language being the quintessential cultural identifier. Speaking from the vantage point of the First Nations of Canada, Stan McKay and Janet Silman identify language as a carrier of the cultural. For them, it is not possible to separate the cultural from the rest of life; there is no room for compartmentalization.[115] As they put it, language embodies the logic of the cultural. Language also goes beyond words and signs; it includes emotions, nonverbal gestures, and intuitions, all of which are socially constructed and culturally conditioned, and contribute to making human activity intelligible. In sum, language "is culturally bound and no human can get around that."[116]

Developing the notion of language as culture-bearer, Stephen Long proposes what he calls a "metaphor" of culture: he uses "metaphor" because of its multiple uses and meanings, which cannot be determined but by paying attention to their use.[117] He suggests that language is the most appropriate indicator for the cultural because of its character making "sense only within the context of everyday activities that we do not so much invent as inherit."[118] In terms of theology, he calls the focus on language the "linguistic turn" as shorthand to highlight the inseparability of language from knowledge.

Drawing on Long's idea of the linguistic turn and applying it to the event of Pentecost, we can say that the event of Pentecost does not bracket out the cultural, rather, it serves to illuminate that the cultural is the aspect of the human existence which is the site of divine pneumatic activity. As McKay and Silman showed, the shift toward language is not a capitulation to logocentrism (as described by Derrida). Rather, the linguistic turn can also emphasize the reclaiming of the oral character of the cultural. According to them, our language continues to carry the cultural, and that is the key.[119]

The Jerusalem Council in the book of Acts 15 is the second critical moment in the welcoming of diverse cultural traditions as carriers-venues of the gospel message I wish to highlight here. The Church was born in the context of

---

115   Stan McKay and Janet Silman, *The First Nations: A Canadian Experience of the Gospel-Culture Encounter* (Geneva: World Council of Churches, 1995), 43.

116   Ibid., 49.

117   Stephen Long, *Theology and Culture*, 8–9.

118   Ibid., 9.

119   McKay and Silman emphasize the holistic approach to religion among Cree and among First Nations, Inuit and Métis people generally. For them, it is not possible, if the culture is healthy, to separate religion from the rest of life, these two cannot be compartamentalized. See McKay and Silman, *The First Nations*, 43.

a cultural-religious conflict, says Dagoberto Ramírez,[120] but according to him, the passages of Jeremiah 12:15; Amos 9:11 and Isaiah 45:21 demonstrate that the conversions of peoples from different cultural traditions were seen as an eschatological fulfillment of the divine creative intent to bring all of humanity to fullness. Acts 15 represents an opening up of the divine covenantal relationship once reserved only to Israel now extended to all the world;[121] the requirements of observing or adopting the Jewish cultural religious traditions and rituals are withdrawn.[122]

Both the event of Pentecost and the council at Jerusalem trace a new theological path for understanding the role of the cultural. They represent the establishment of a cultural-linguistic polyglossa (polyglossolalia), plurivocity and multiculturality as constitutive concrete signs of the divine kenotic pneumatological activity. Instead of being disarticulated by the Jesus event interpreted within the Jewish covenantal relationship as we saw in Carter, I propose that cultures are rearticulated at Pentecost as the mediums through which

---

120   Dagoberto Ramírez, "Exégetico-hermenéutico de los Hechos de los Apostóles, Capítulo 15," *Ribla* 12 (1992): 149. Ramírez notes that in the story leading up to the Jerusalem council there is a tension that finds resolution in the historical meeting. Starting with Antioch identified as a place of conflict then going to Jerusalem which represents the place of discussion and solution and then back to Antioch as the place where a new era, the Christian era of mission begins. See Ibid., 140.

121   Ramírez, "Exegético-hermenéutico de los Hechos," 143. Gorringe adds that "If we read the story of Pentecostal from the standpoint of Herder's claim that language is the heart of culture, then the point of the story is that the gospel comes to all cultures in their own terms." He further states that no policy informed by incarnation can be universalizing if this means the elimination of difference. "Equally, no cultural policy informed by incarnation can be chauvinist" (Gorringe, *Furthering Humanity*, 101).

122   The example is also seen in Paul, writes Comblín, as he breaks with his own people and religion, Judaism in order to emphasize that "all nations become part of Christ with equal rights" (Comblin, *The Holy Spirit and Liberation*, 47). Here is one aspect in which I depart from Carter, particularly his insistence in emphasizing the divine covenantal relationship of God with Israel and by extension with the rest of humanity. Even when he clarifies that "Israel's destiny is not solipsistic; its election is to be itself precisely by being more than itself: that is, by being for the world. It is to be a nonnationalistic nation, a different kind of people—the people of YHWH" (Craig A. Carter, *Rethinking Christ and Culture*, 309). Carter seems to have in mind some ideal that he calls Israel, which is probably the equivalent of the notion of the Church, but in doing so he places critical strictures on the historical specificity of other cultural groups. Indeed, he focuses on the theological-spiritual identity of people as the people of God, but their historical and cultural identities are rendered inconsequential.

humans engage the divine—even as imperfect human constructions—and the site upon which the divine is at work.

At the same time, Pentecost and the Jerusalem council also embody a call to human cultural kenosis. Here the Pentecostal reclaiming of the events of Pentecost as a pivotal moment of divine pneumatic activity impacts my reflections. The Pentecostal miracle through which those present hear each other speak the wonders of God in their own language is highly subversive. Those in the position of privilege, the Jewish-Hebraic tradition, make room for— kenotically open out to—the myriad other groups, languages, and peoples of the known world by speaking the greatness of God in those languages.[123] Both events represent the Spirit's move against ethnocentrism and toward celebration of particularities. As Yong comments:

> Herein lies another miracle of Pentecost: the spirit empowers people to be agents of liberation; the Spirit breaks down the prejudice and ethnocentrism of those in power to include those who have been left out … The cultural glossolalia modeled on the day of Pentecost called people to place their own cultural particularities within the liberating circle of the global village. Pentecostals speak of the affirmation of all people and cultures, each having their place and contributions.[124]

We see in those two events the emergence of a universal community of many nations, tribes, peoples and languages; in other words, many cultures.[125] They mark a time for the creation of unity but not uniformity. What takes place there at the moment of Pentecost, writes González, is that the "gospel is preached and incarnated in a multitude of languages and cultures."[126] On Pentecost the event of the tower of Babel gets reinterpreted.

---

123   Prior to Pentecost and the Jerusalem council, Judaism represented the monopoly of the mystery of God. It was thought that the Hebrew language was the language of God. See González, *Culto, cultura y cultivo*, 79.

124   Yong, *Spirit-Word-Community*, 118.

125   It is important to remember, says González, that the centers of missionary vitality are not in the Global North, "that the majority of Christians are not white and that the gospel is preached to hundreds of languages, few of them of European origin … So much so that we can say that what we are witnessing is a kind of global Pentecost, in which each person listens and lives the gospel in their tongue and within their own culture" (González, *Culto, cultura y cultivo*, 88).

126   González, *Culto, cultura y cultivo*, 11.

Pentecost, Babel and Rejection of Cultural Imperialism

Discussions on Pentecost are often associated with the events at Babel, especially since both incidents have to do with etnocultural diversity. Many scholars speak of Pentecost as overcoming Babel, because Babel is interpreted as
a symbol of confusion and divisiveness. Ethnocultural diversity is therefore
thought of as resulting from God's *punishment* against human arrogance and
sin. One good example of such view was expressed by Eusebius the bishop of
Caesaera who thought—according to Swedish Theologians Gustaf Wingren—
that "the tower of Babel and the evil division of languages represented the
small states which the Roman Empire had defeated. The peace that God had
promised meant one kingdom, one emperor, one language, and one religious
faith."[127] In the same way, Andrew Greeley assesses that "the great Scholastic
theologians of the Middle Ages concluded—largely from the tower-of-Babel—
that if it were not for sin there would be no diversity in the human condition.
In other words, the fantastic pluralism of cultures in the world is at best an
evil caused by human sinfulness..."[128] As a result, many theologians even today
view Babel as a tragic failure marking the "loss of the unity that God intended
for ... creation ..."[129]

I want to suggest, however, that there is no basis for viewing ethnic and cultural plurality as the result of God's judgment against sinfulness. In fact, those
interpretations which perceive diversity as divisive are the products of colonizing hermeneutics at work; they are part of a residual hermeneutical coloniality
which wrongly seeks to promote a monocultural understanding of the divine
creative intent.

Countering these negative interpretation of Babel, Mark R. Kreitzer proposes that the events at Babel mark the fulfillment of God's original blessing which commands humanity to "fill the earth" (Gn. 1:28) and the similar
divine mandate to Noah and his family to do the same, as part of the post-
flood covenant as recorded in Genesis 9:1.[130] He argues that the building

---

127   Cited in Mark R. Kreitzer, *The Concept of Ethnicity in the Bible: A Theological Analysis*
      (Wales, UK: The Edwin Mellen Press, 2008), 135, note 165.

128   Cited in Kreitzer, *The Concept of Ethnicity in the Bible*, 123. To the contrary, Bernhard
      Anderson thought that ethnocultural diversity was God's way of keeping sin in check;
      "By means of ethnolinguistic and resulting cultural diversities, God keeps checking sin's
      spread to the whole race" (Cited in Ibid., 129–130).

129   Kreitzer, *The Concept of Ethnicity in the Bible*, 123.

130   Kreitzer points out that according to Genesis 10: 5, 20, 31, and 32, all the lands, lan-
      guages, clans-families, and peoples of the earth came from the three sons of Noah. This
      affirmation explains how, for him, the scattering at Babel was crucial for the population

of the tower shows the human hubris and refusal to fulfill the divine man-date.[131] The divine judgment upon human hubris was to stop the building of the tower, which inevitably resulted in the scattering of the people. He con-cludes that, the scattering of the people must be understood as an "unmit-igated good" because it forced humanity–now diversified, to fulfill "God's creational commission."[132] In other words, for Kreitzer, God takes it upon God's self to scatter the people; dispersion "over the earth is the method by which" God puts this blessing into practice. The implication, of course, is that geographical, political, and linguistic diversity is not sinful but is rather the expression of the divine will from the beginning (Gn. 1:28).[133] Rather than homogeneity and monoculturalism, ethnocultural plurality and diver-sity is to be welcome as a divine blessing.

Meanwhile, Sandro Luckmann argues that the construction of towers in the period served as military fortifications of cities.[134] Instead of interpreting Genesis 11:1–9 as a divine curse aimed at all of humanity (and against cul-tural diversity) because of the pride inherent in wanting to reach heaven, he proposes that the Babel story is instead an account of rural resistance against the city and military world.[135] In this reading, the tower-building project

---

(filling) of the earth. Moreover, he notes that for the author of Genesis it seems that the sons of Adam and Noah can only receive a "name" by going (scattering) anywhere upon the whole face of the earth where God leads and excercise dominion there as his Vice-regents. See Kreitzer, *The Concept of Ethnicity in the Bible*, 110, 118.

131   In line with Kreitzer's position, Walter Brueggemann proposes that the monoculturality of the city is a rebellion against the cultural mandate. While, for him, scattering over the earth should be understood as punishment, true unity was "expressed by dispersion all over the earth" in loyal obedience to God. See Kreitzer, *The Concept of Ethnicity in the Bible*, 130.

132   Kreitzer, *The Concept of Ethnicity in the Bible*, 116. He adds,

Since the ethnic diversity is not a curse, a more contextual read would be to say that "God dispersed mankind at Babel after the worldwide Flood." This language creation and the dispersion seem clearly to be a direct divine response to man's [*sic*]obstinate rebellion against Yahweh's command, repeated at the creation and at the new begin-ning after the flood. He directed the sons of Adam to multiply, spread out, and fill the earth, thus scattering them throughout its every section (Gn 1:28; 9:7) (Ibid., 136).

133   Kreitzer, *The Concept of Ethnicity in the Bible*, 127, 137.

134   Sandro Luckmann, "Babel e Pentecostes: Testemunhos a favor da diversidade e da dis-persão," *Vida Cotidiana*, May 2010, 270.

135   Luckmann, "Babel e Pentecostes," 270. "O relato de Babel é um como de resistência cam-ponesa em relação ao mundo citadino e militar."

epitomizes the cultural imperialistic impetus and objective of bringing about the homogenization of peoples and cultures in the speaking of only one language and gathered in one place (Gen. 11:1, 4). Divine intervention occurs "in the sense of eliminating the possibility of a single language and the possibility of all the peoples living in one place under the power of the oppressor.[136] That is, God denounces and fights an oppressive system, of forming a people, and a single language."[137] What happens at Babel is actually an embodiment of the divine move to counter imperial aspirations for ethnocultural and linguistic homogeneity, and to guarantee cultural diversity in the dispersing of the people groups. Read in this way the action of God is understood not as punitive but as positive; "God perceives that the project is anchored on the oppression and exploitation of peoples, symbolized by the military tower. God sided with the small clan groups in their cultural diversity and their territorial expansion ..."[138]

Since the account was written during the Babylonian exile, we can infer that it is a condemnation of those empires who sought to consolidate their imperial powers by uprooting the Israelites and deporting them, all the while enculturating/assimilating them into the culture and language of the empire (Babylon and Persia). Enacted in the context of yet another empire (Rome) and having just survived the previous empire (Greek), the event of Pentecost can be understood as well as a divine intervention against cultural homogeneity and empire. Seen this way, Pentecost not so much inverts Babel as it continues the

---

136   Miroslav Volf is another scholar who supports this position arguing that at Babel "God broke up the collective project, interrupting" "the totalitarian project to centralize, homogenize, and control," leaving "political, economic, and cultural ... difference, ... [and] multicentrality" (Cited in Kreitzer, *The Concept of Ethnicity in the Bible*, 137). The imperial implications of Babel are obvious for Volf. As he sees it, At Babel, God breaks the collective hubris and the emergence of a one-world imperial power, which "strive[s] to make their own name great by erasing the names of simple people and small nations" (cited in Ibid., 136).

137   Luckmann, "Babel e Pentecostes," 270. "A construção da torre de Babel representa o prejeto citadino-militar-imperial que objetiva homogeneizar os povos, falando uma só lingua, reunidos num só lugar (Gn 11:1, 4). No versos 5–9 Deus interfere no sentido de eliminar a possibilidade de uma lngua única e a possibilidade de viver todos os povos num mesmo local so bum poder oppressor. Ou seja, Deus denuncia e combate o sistema opresor, de formar um povo, uma única lingua."

138   Luckmann, "Babel e Pentecostes," 270. "Deus age em Babel na garantia da divesidade cultural e a dispersão dos povos. Assim, a ação de Deus não for punitiva, mas positiva. Deus precebeu que o projeto de Babel estaba ancorado na opressão e exploração dos povos, fato simbolizado pela torre militar. Deus se pôs ao lado dos pequenos grupos clânicos em sua diversidade cultural e na sua dispersão territorial ..."

divine action for cultural diversity that began at Babel.[139] At Pentecost God speaks "to each ethnie in their own, beautiful, and unique, God created" language ... (Acts 2:4–11...).[140] Both events represent the divine created design for cultural diversity in opposition to homogeneity.[141] There is also a divine liberative move implied here because God's actions break the illusion that hegemonic cultures are absolute. The critique is not against the unity of human beings but against projects that seek to create artificial cultural uniformity and a homogenization of humanity.

The event of Pentecost can also be understood as the divine Spirit's response to colonizing projects which see the erasure of cultural traditions as a requisite for the construction of a global reality.[142] In the words of Kreitzer,

> Christ's redemption [did] not restore a condition in the church like that before Babel or like that of Israel. Neither the mono-ethnic proto humanity nor a Hebrew monolingual, mono-cultural ideal serves as the model for a unified church in a "new humanity" in Christ. The new humanity is rather to be pan-cultural, pan-lingual, and pan-geographical.[143]

As the continuation of the kenotic act of Christ in his act of "taking on the cultural," Pentecost unveils the activity of the Spirit empowering the church to fulfill the divine command by scattering the people throughout the face of the earth. Pentecost marks the historical move of the Spirit to fill the world with the rich cacophony of ethnocultural diversity that is the church, and in so doing counter colonizing attitudes of ethnocultural homogeneity.

For Christians today, the present-day impetus toward globalization— shorthand for the global market economic network with its accompanying commodification of life and destruction of the environment—should also be included as the kind of homogenizing-colonizing cultural network opposed by the events of Babel and Pentecost. Babel and Pentecost reveal the divine disposition in favor of cultural diversity and offer the possibility of resistance

139 As Luckmann puts it, "Pentecostes é a reafirmação de Babel.... em Pentecostes Deus faz uso da diversidade cultural no anúncio de Suas maravilhas" (Luckmann, "Babel e Pentecostes," 271).

140 Kreitzer, *The Concept of Ethnicity in the Bible*, 345.

141 Luckmann, "Babel e Pentecostes," 271.

142 See Daniela Augustine, *Pentecost, Hospitality, and Transfiguration: Toward a Spirit-Filled Vision of Social Transformation* (Cleveland, TN: Center for Pentecostal Theology Press, 2012), 15–42.

143 Kreitzer, *The Concept of Ethnicity in the Bible*, 345.

to proposals predicated on the propagation of globalization.[144] In the end, the cultural activity of the Spirit on the day of Pentecost denies that any group could have a monopoly on the Gospel message, or on the divine, by mediating the encounter through only one ethnocultural community. It also denies the pretension of dominant cultural theologies in their claims to universality.[145] The activity of the Spirit on Pentecost embodies resistance to cultural imperialism.

Pentecostal and Cultural Identity as a Pneumatic Gift

Having gone now almost full circle, I want to reiterate my theological perspective that cultures and the human capacity to construct cultures are divine gifts and part of the divine imaging. I have argued that cultures play a central role in the human-divine interaction. We have also seen that the events of Babel and Pentecost demonstrate that cultural difference is in fact a divine gift. When the disciples received the Holy Spirit, it resulted not in their amassing more power but in their openness to share that power with foreigners.[146]

In fact, Pentecost is not a denial of cultural traditions but the actual divine spreading of grace and love to the whole world;[147] "Pentecost represents this calling. The nations do not lose their identity: each speaks in

---

144   In the words of Luckmann: "Babel and Petnecostes revelam a disposição divina em favor da diversidad cultural e da dispersão geográfica dos povos, também se concebe que estas são as possibilidades de resistência às propostas oriundas da implantação da *globalização*" (Luckmann, "Babel e Pentecostes," 274–275). Elsewhere he adds that "Deus se posiciona contra aqueles projetos que visan centralizar o poder, explorar os meios de produção e uniformizar a humanidade" (Ibid., 270).

145   The cultural character of these theologies is evident, writes Orlando Costas. As he pointed out, "it does not take much effort to show how theology—from the patristic writings to the present—has been situational through and through. Indeed it has been generally bound to the experiences in categories of western culture.... And Biblical Contextualization is rooted in the fact that the God of revelation can only be known in history. Such a revelation comes to a specific people in concrete situations by means a particular cultural symbols and categories" (Orlando Costas, *Christ Outside the Gates: Mission Beyond Christendom* [Maryknoll, NY: Orbis Books, 1982], 5).

146   González, *Culto, cultura y cultivo*, 83.

147   The gospel of Luke points to the dissemination of the gospel message without boundaries and borders where there had been there before. Moreover, the transgression of ethnocultural boundaries can be found in the exchange between Jesus and the Syrophoenician woman in Mark 7:20–30. According to Julien Smith the passage goes against ideas that the gospel obliterates ethnic identity. In fact, she claims, the passage shows that it is only as member

its own language; the new humanity does not lose its diversity through being unified in Christ. The Spirit does not oblige the nations all to wear the same clothing."[148] Stated differently, Pentecost reveals that the traditional interpretation of the Babel narrative is not viable. Pentecost represents the unity of humanity as created by God, but it is a humanity that does not seek the suppression of cultural differences. In the end, "the Holy Spirit creates unity without destroying differences."[149] Diversity is part of the divine creation, part of the work of God. In the final analysis, Pentecost marks an in-breaking of the Holy Spirit in which God places cultures at the centre of the creation account and in the order of salvation. Instead of being a "suspension" of cultural differences as many have claimed, Pentecost is in fact the divine, public act of a free and liberating radical inclusion of differences mediated by the Holy Spirit. Here and elsewhere cultural differences play a crucial role in the act of divine self-disclosure. In particular, the Incarnation and Pentecost show that culture is a site of divine disclosure as well as a *locus* of theological reflection

The (Inter)Cultural and Divine Revelation

To this point, I have been insisting that the cultural plays a central role in mediating the interaction between human beings and the divine, by enabling and providing the means to comprehend and respond to the divine invitation, and through communicating the gospel message. As far as I am concerned, this move helps articulate how the gospel and the cultural are closer than most scholars have been willing to concede. I have argued that the root of the reluctance to admit to an intermingling of the gospel and the cultural entails an intrinsic aversion to mixing the divine and the human because of an operative neo-platonist framing by which creation, the material realm, and humanity are conceived of as being incompatible with the uncreated, the divine, and the

---

of a specific ethnic and cultural group that anyone receives the gospel. What is even more important is the fact that Jesus is not constrained by the established social boundaries and his actions actually show that "Jesus has now abolished all social and ethnic boundaries" (Julien C. H Smith, "The Construction of Identity in Mark 7:24–30, 477). Smith argues that the point of the gospel writer was to show that the social, ethnic, cultural and gender boundaries no longer had the power to limit the coming of the reign of God into areas and among the cultures and ethnic groups that were previously presumed to be absent.

148   Comblin, *The Holy Spirit and Liberation*, 47.

149   Luckmann, "Babel e Pentecostes," 273.

spiritual. Furthermore, this framing has been intensified and entrenched, as we have seen, by the Euro North American colonial/imperial projects which attempted to universalized one (Eurocentric) culture (or family of cultures) and one (Christian-in its European expressions) religion above all others. Contrary to these approaches, I have been arguing instead that the cultural must be understood as intrinsic to what it means to be human, but human as created in the image of God. I have also suggested that the internal intra-Trinitarian relationship can be articulated in cultural terms; human cultural activities can be understood to mirror the divine internal cultural relations of love, mutuality, and interdependence, when these are oriented to the preservation of life, engaged in the struggle for justice, and standing against all that undermines and destroys life in all its forms.

I have also been arguing that neither humanity nor the gospel, nor the event of incarnation, nor the divine self-disclosure can be understood or conceived of outside of the space of the cultural. The gospel, the Jesus event, the Church, and humanity do not exist in a pure, ahistorical, a-cultural state that can be transferred and communicated facilely from cultural tradition to cultural tradition. Rather, each of these is deeply impacted and conditioned by the cultural context. It follows that to speak of the "transcendent" character of the gospel is only possible (if that is possible at all) when it is passed on from one cultural tradition, as a culturally conditioned experience of the gospel, to another cultural tradition, which takes then the gospel and re-shapes it according to its own internal cultural processes and codes.[150]

I have proposed an alternative to the abstract idea of the gospel as being supracultural, transcendent, international, and universal. In light of the narratives of the Tower of Babel and the event of Pentecost, we can instead affirm that the richness of the gospel lies in its myriad concrete cultural expressions. These events demonstrate that no cultural tradition holds a monopoly on the divine disclosure, can domesticate the gospel, or can claim itself to be the highest expression of the gospel. Rather, divine disclosure has been given to humanity, embodied in the entire range of cultural traditions of the world. Moreover, each cultural tradition has glimpses of the divine self-disclosure

---

150 We can agree with Peter Neumann that "Experience is that which is communicable within the context of a cultural-linguistic community—meaningful to others and to the experiencing subject, based on the pre-existent horizon of meaning through which experience is interpreted. To reiterate, there is no uninterpreted, raw, or innocent experience that can be appealed to as a neutral, unbiased authority—experience, in this sense, only occurs mediated within a defined community or tradition" (Neumann, *Pentecostal Experience*, 37).

which then become clearer and richer as we engage in intercultural[151] discussions with the other cultures of the world.[152] In other words, our views of the divine are incomplete without engaging other cultures' perspectives of the divine. One could say, in fact, that it is only in this way that revelation could be considered to be transcultural, or better still, intercultural, since it inhabits multiple cultural traditions. It is for this reason that Mercy Amba Oduyoye challenges us to seek a "Gospel culture," by which she means the mutual fertilization between local cultures and the gospel message. She also suggests the mutual interpellation between dominant cultural versions of the gospel and local cultures. In both instances, she insists that a Gospel culture "will evolve when we are rid of all that negates fullness of life and blasphemes against the image of God in humanity."[153]

To sum up, we arrive to the truth of the gospel collectively and in dialogue. Such an assertion rejects the notion that there is one universal humanity which exists at the level of the abstract as criterion to judge all other expression of humanity. Rather, there are many human cultural universes which need to enter into conversation with each other in order to discern a larger picture of the divine. Likewise, interculturality affirms the fundamental importance

---

151   Here I deploy the category of interculturality not to mean: A theoretical position nor
        the dialogue of or between cultures … in which cultures become closed spiritualized
        entities; rather, interculturality points more accurately to that posture or disposition by
        which human beings prepare themselves to live … or habituate themselves to live "their"
        identity self-references in relation to those called "others." That is to say, sharing them-
        selves and co-living with them. It is about an attitude that opens human beings and pro-
        pels them toward a process of cultural and contextual re-learning and relocation (Raúl
        Fornet-Betancourt, *Crítica intercultural de la filosofía latinoamericana actual*, Raúl Fornet-
        Betancourt, Colección Estructoras y Procesos: Serie Filosofía [Madrid. España: Editorial
        Trotta, 2004], 14–15). "En este contexto conviene señalar un breve paréntesis que por
        interculturalidad no se comprende aquí una posición teórica ni tampoco un diálogo de
        y/o entre culturas (o, en este caso concreto, un diálogo entre tradiciones filosóficas dis-
        tintas) en el que las culturas se toman como entidades espiritualizadas y cerradas; sino
        que interculturalidad quiere designar más bien aquella *postura* o *disposición* por la que
        el ser humano se capacita para … y se habitúa a vivir "sus" referencias identitarias *en rel-
        ación* con los llamados "otros," es decir, compartiéndose en convivencia con ellos. De ahí
        que se trate de una actitud que abre al ser humano y lo impulsa a un proceso de reapren-
        dizaje y reubicación cultural y contextual."
152   Orlando O. Espín, "Toward the Construction of an Intercultural Theology of Tradition,"
        47–48. In the words of Gorringe, "A theology of culture … is a theology which understands
        the full implications of the gospel claim that I meet God in my neighbour" (Gorringe,
        Furthering Humanity, 28).
153   Mercy Amba Oduyoye, "Gospel and Culture in Africa, 47.

of many cultural universes over and against one universal culture. It refutes monochromatic, univocal and monocultural expressions. In intercultural debates, then, there is no room for the sacralization of any one culture as the closer or most perfect expression of the Gospel.

Our portrait of the divine is enhanced and our cultural traditions enriched as other cultural groups help us see how they view the divine:

> In the diversity of peoples who experience the Gift of God, each in accordance with its own culture, the Church expresses her genuine catholicity and shows forth the "beauty of her varied face." In the Christian customs of an evangelized people, the Holy Spirit adorns the Church, showing her new aspects of revelation and giving her a new face. (Redemptoris Mission says) Through inculturation, the Church "introduces peoples, together with their cultures, into her own community," for "every culture offers positive values and forms which can enrich the way the Gospel is preached, understood and lived." In this way, the Church takes up the values of different "cultures and becomes *sponsa ornata monilibus suis*, "the bride bedecked with her jewels" (cf. *Is* 61:10)"[154]

Let us not belabor the point! The central implication of this discussion is that the divine self-disclosure is always culturally bound, mediated, and conditioned. The affirmation that the cultural and cultural traditions are therefore appropriately *loci* of divine self-disclosure and theological reflection and articulation is in my view the single most important contribution of Latina/o theologies.

From their own ethnocultural vantage point, Latina/o theologies have demonstrated how the central feature of the cultural can be a fruitful *locus* for theological reflection. With categories such as *mestizaje, en y de conjunto, lo cotidiano*, and *acompañamiento*, to name a few, these scholars have demonstrated the theological richness inherent in their own cultural traditions.[155]

---

154 Francis, *Evangelii Gaudium*, 116.
155 Some small samples of the voluminous wealth of theological works from Latina/o theological perspective are: Medina, *Mestizaje*; Orlando O. Espín, *The Faith of the People*; Espín and Díaz, *From the Heart of Our People*; Ada María Isasi-Díaz, *En la Lucha / In the Struggle: Elaborating A Mujerista Theology* (Minneapolis, MN: Fortress Press, 1993); Justo L. González, *Mañana: Christian Theology from a Hispanic Perspective* (Nashville: Abingdon Press, 1990); Roberto S. Goizueta, *Caminemos con Jesús: Toward a Hispanic/Latino Theology of Accompaniment* (Maryknoll, NY: Orbis Books, 1999); María Pilar Aquino, *Our Cry for Life: Feminist Theology from Latin America*, trans. Dina Livingstone (Eugene, OR: Wipf and Stock Publishers, 2000).

Because their theological proposals claim to emerge from an unabashedly Latina/o cultural position, they also exemplify the culturally conditioned character of theological articulations. Their writings affirm that the people's culturally conditioned lived experiences of faith in God embody the theological reservoir from which they draw.

For this reason, I insist that the cultural is the unavoidable means, filter and prism through which God is encountered and responded to by humans in whichever cultural context. Moreover, the cultural tradition within which the encounter occurs offers people the hermeneutical tools needed to make sense of such an encounter.[156] Luis Pedraja considers that even if it were possible for humans to receive an unadulterated direct revelation from God, the recipients of such a revelation "would still need to conceptualize and articulate it within the context of their own language and culture."[157] Relatedly, Samuel Silva Gotay problematizes Tillich's maxim that *culture is the form of religion*, by asserting instead that we must say that *humans are culture* "somos cultura." In his opinion, it is from the vantage point of who we are that we understand, live, and express our religious experiences in all dimensions.[158] Espín takes it further by declaring that while we can say that the source of revelation (God) is not necessarily bound to the cultural dimension, when the revelation is discerned, it is the cultural that plays a central role "because the human partner is intrinsically shaped and bound by culture."[159]

Espín brings the cultural and revelation even closer together by articulating the dynamic between Christian revelation, divine initiative, and the cultural. If indeed we can claim that the cultural is "the necessary means, condition, and possibility of revelation, it is plausible to consider revelation as 'intrinsically and necessarily cultural'."[160] Stated differently, within cultural traditions we also find hidden kernels of the divine disclosure available only to those who are members of a given cultural tradition. Indeed, if the cultural is a fundamental aspect of being human, and if the central

---

156 According to Espín, one's culture becomes the interpretive backdrop that provides the symbols, language, patterns of imagination, and so one with which to decipher the human-divine encounter. See Orlando O. Espín, "Popular Catholicism," 310. See also Orlando O. Espín, *The Faith of the People*, 95.

157 Luis G. Pedraja, *Teología: An Introduction to Hispanic Theology* (Nashville: Abingdon Press, 2003), 22.

158 Samuel Silva Gotay, "Impacto cultural del Protestantismo en Puerto Rico, 36.

159 Orlando O. Espín, "Traditioning," 4.

160 Ibid.

role of cultural traditions is to enable humans to live their humanity, does it not follow that cultural traditions are reservoirs of divine disclosure, sites of theological reflection within which the divine self-disclosure finds concrete expression?

The cultural is not simply a necessary condition for revelation which points to a *real* revelation outside of the cultural. Rather, the divine self-disclosure enters into a more intimate incarnational relation with the cultural. I am insisting that it is fundamentally and inherently cultural. The divine draws from available cultural resources to find concrete expression for revelation and in so doing turns the cultural into a deposit of and site for divine disclosure.[161] For these reasons, cultural traditions must be understood as epistemological sources from which to think theologically. Insofar as cultural traditions constitute entire universes that value life, respect the environment, and celebrate the dignity of humanity, they can become sacraments of the divine disclosure. In light of Pentecost and the Jerusalem council, we can assert that it is not necessary to adopt/adapt another cultural tradition in order to have an encounter with God; it is from the vantage point of and within one's own cultural tradition that one finds stored glimpses of the mystery of the divine.[162] Many of those glimpses only get unlocked when cultural communities engage each other in mutually enriching and interpellating intercultural conversations.

According to Espín, one source where God's self-revelation is located is in the religious imagination of cultures. Reflecting on Latina/o popular piety, he holds that popular religions reveal the "'faith-filled intuitions' of a community of faith and culture through patterns of meaning embodied in metaphorical and symbolic activity."[163] These faith-filled intuitions, holds Espín, are the backbone of what the Catholic tradition has termed the *sensus fidelium*.[164] He concludes that if "religion is the socialization of the experience of the

---

161 Jorge Presmanes identifies this reorientation in the Apostle Paul's encounter with Gentile cultures, which for him (Paul) become a locus of revelation. This encounter leads Paul to a break with the "Old Testament salvation history as Paul himself had previously understood it" (Presmanes, "Inculturation as Evangelization," 71). For the Church, adds Presmanes, it also meant a break from salvation history as it was understood by Jewish Christians and from their own understanding of revelation.

162 I call them glimpses because I consider that each cultural tradition only contains a partial view of divine revelation. In many ways, then, the relationship between revelation and culture both reveals and conceals God.

163 Cited in Presmanes, "Inculturation as Evangelization," 71.

164 Orlando O. Espín, *The Faith of the People*, 66–77.

divine, and if in Latino Catholicism the divine is identified with the Christian divine, then this religion of the subalterns claims that the *Christian* God is to be found in and through the culture and experiences of those considered insignificant ..."[165]

Final Remarks

By bringing the cultural and the reality of the divine into a closer relationship, I have argued that we can insist that the cultural plays a central role in the divine-human relationship. Along with this affirmation and since the cultural also plays a crucial role as a basic tenet of being human, I have established four key implications: one, the cultural is a divine gift; two, the cultural is part of the divine creative intent; three, the cultural is a basic aspect in humanity's imaging of the divine; and fourth, one of the purposes of the cultural, as a divine gift, is to aid us in reaching full humanity. I have also suggested that our understanding of the connection between human divine imaging and the role of the cultural could help us understand, by way of analogy, the internal perichoretic relationship of mutual love in the Trinity.

Consistent with a liberationist perspective and a Latina/o theological framing, I have opted to reinterpret the Jewishness of the historical Jesus, the cultural concreteness of the incarnation, in order to propose the central role of the cultural in divine disclosure and to highlight culture as *locus theologicus*. Drawing on Pentecostalism, I also reclaimed the activity of the Spirit in the incarnation and the irruption of the Spirit in the Church on the day of Pentecost. The activity of the Spirit is thus extended into the cultural as an intrinsic aspect of human existence. I furthermore argued for the extension of our understanding of the divine kenotic act so as to include the activity of the Spirit in the cultural.

This Liberationist/Latina/o-Pentecostal perspective helps us to celebrate the human cultural dimension and challenges us to view cultural diversity as a fundamental aspect of creation. It also unmasks all theological perspectives as decidedly cultural, as emerging from specific cultural traditions; all theologies are cultural theologies. In other words, there are no theologies that bypass or are not conditioned by the cultural context out of which theologians write. My proposal refutes theological currents which seek to undermine the centrality and crucial role of the cultural by claiming for themselves a superior, universal

---

165   Orlando O. Espín, "Popular Catholicism," 323.

and acultural position. Scholars who have built complex intellectual edifices in order to attenuate the role of the cultural have presented descriptions of the divine disclosure as both ahistorical and acultural. I posit that the tendency to undermine the role of the cultural in the human-divine interaction stems from an operative binary docetist-quasi platonist frame that sees the uncreated, spiritual, God as incompatible with the created, material, human reality. As I have argued, such proposals betray themselves because of the very culturally-conditioned character of their own theological reflections. In contrast, in the present changing landscape of Christianity, we see new and exciting emerging theologies that are beginning to offer us alternative ways to conceive the theological. These currents are taking their concrete cultural contexts as starting points for doing theology and in doing so are reconfiguring theology in deeply fundamental ways.

Conclusion

> It is our wish that we have not the world that we want or that the powers want, but that it be a world where there is room for everyone; as many worlds as necessary, so that each man and woman have a life with dignity and that everyone be satisfied with what their concept of dignity signifies.[1]
>
> ZAPATISTA MOVEMENT

We have come full circle in considering how the cultural has played and continues to play a crucial role in the multiple ways in which people experience, perceive, and express the Christian faith. As I have argued, the complex networks of signs and symbols by which people codify life, existence and relationships, what I call processes of culturalization, and the multiple concrete expressions of the phenomena of the cultural, in the form of particular cultural traditions, must be understood as constitutive of our humanity and therefore a divine gift. In other words, the cultural is not an aspect that can be bracketed out as if it has no direct impact in the way we consider human agency and reflect theologically upon divine activity in this world.

Contrary to "modernist" perspectives I have insisted on the interwoven relationship between Christianity and the cultural sphere. Not only do we find signs of this interrelationship in the creation account and the rest of the biblical text, but we also see it in the ways in which Christianity was profoundly altered by imperial culture and ethos, and ultimately corrupted when it was wedded to multiple Western European and Euro North American imperial projects. These deeply cultural—and "Christian"—colonizing projects caused a profound distortion among Western Europeans and Euro North Americans in the way they saw the relationship between the cultural and their version of Christianity. Their cultural theologies and sense of cultural and religious superiority blinded them to seeing and respecting the humanity, cultures, and religious traditions of the peoples of the world.

In many ways, those same cultural blinders are responsible for the ways in which the cultural expressions of Christianity in other parts of the world are dismissed as "syncretic" while the Western European and Euro North American

---

1 María Alejandra Giuponni, "La voz de 'los del color de la tierra': Notas sobre la teoría zapatista," in *Libertad, Solidaridad, Liberación: Homenaje a Juan Carlos Scannone*, VII Jornadas Internacionales Interdisciplinarias Río Cuarto, 5 al 7 de noviembre de 2003, ed. Dorando J. Michelini, et al. (Buenos Aires, Argentina: Ediciones del ICALA, 2003), 388.

© KONINKLIJKE BRILL NV, LEIDEN, 2018 | DOI 10.1163/9789004363090_011

cultural expressions are thought to reflect the "real," "uncorrupted" versions of Christianity. As I have showed, these attitudes are also found in the ways theologians seek to "safeguard" an assumed acultural version of Christianity and its gospel message from being "domesticated" or "adulterated" by other cultural traditions. The concern stems from the belief in the radical incompatibility between the divine and creation-humanity. But as I have argued, such an incompatibility is a false dichotomy; it does not make sense when one considers the role of the cultural in the creation event, the biblical narrative, the Jesus event, and the event of Pentecost. These moments in the divine-human interaction demonstrate that even the divine self-disclosure cannot be understood to be outside of and in intimate connection with the cultural.

The scholars from many disciplines and various Christian and ethnocultural traditions which I draw on to bolster my arguments are but a sampling of some of the voices that until now have remained absent from mainstream debates on the cultural. As I have shown, they exemplify the rich intellectual and theological reservoir that can enrich and reconfigure mainstream theological debates on the cultural and its multiple connections to the Christian faith.

Drawing from Latina/o theology's insistence on culture as a *locus* of theological reflection, I demonstrated how, instead of "corrupting" the faith, these theological currents (and other cultural and liberationist theological currents such as Black theology, Minjung theology, Native American theology, etc.) offer new avenues for rethinking the reality of the divine, God's activity in this world. They also provide us with new avenues for appreciating the profound impact of the cultural in the ways people understand the divine and express their faith.

This book is an invitation to engage theological conversations on the cultural. The caveat is that we can no longer ignore the long-standing legacy of cultural colonization still operative in debates on the cultural. For us to engage in truly intercultural discussions about the cultural and how the cultural in its multiple concrete expressions relates to Christianity, we will have to ensure a profound de-Europeanization of the very premises of the debates. The clear implication is that the challenging of the "normative" character of "modernist" intellectual categories provincializes/decentre them as one family of cultural expressions among multiple other cultural traditions. The enormous possibilities, as yet untapped, promise new understandings of our humanity in multiple concrete expressions and new understandings of the reality of the divine and the Spirit's activity in this world.

The inevitable implication in terms of appreciating the culturality of human existence involves a fundamental rethinking of the theological task in the way it is carried out and taught. It leads to a radical rethinking of the scope of our assumed theological premises and intellectual structures, and (re)locates them within their proper cultural tradition and as responding to that specific cultural context. In this sense all theological articulations are, in the end, culturally specific and culturally conditioned. If we take this point seriously, theological education must also be fundamentally transformed both in challenging the present (Western European and Euro North American) theological canon and in creating space for the other theological voices of Christianity. The adoption of the fundamental cultural character of reflections also leads to a "Babel effect." It implies the dismantling of any one theological current's pretension to normativity and truth. It also results in a better understanding of our humanity as made in the image of God and helps us reposition the cultural's centrality in our experiences of faith in God.

Index

Printed in the United States
By Bookmasters